Practicing Transcendence

"The greatest merit of Christopher Peet's book is that it introduces a new, academically-grounded concept of the Axial Age and its place in world history in a way that is accessible to a wider audience. The general reader and professionals in the humanities and social sciences will equally find this book a really exciting read, a true intellectual journey."

—Dmitri M. Bondarenko, *Director of the International Center of Anthropology, National Research University, Russia*

"Christopher Peet has done a remarkable job of bringing together this complex history in lucid prose. He presents a new perspective on the key idea of transcendence that emerged in the axial age, which marks 'the Axial road not taken,' undervalued by 'Big religion' as well as scholars thus far. Most notably, he reveals how transcendence needs to be understood not simply as an idea, but as living spiritual practices bodied forth by visionaries in small communities then, and just as available as vital resources now. The self-transcending self, as the practical aim of a variety of axial spiritual practices, remains a viable and potent path to offset our power-centered civilization today."

—Eugene Halton, *Professor of Sociology, University of Notre Dame, USA*

"The Axial Age—the period from 800 B.C.E. to 200 B.C.E., when the religio-philoso-phic foundations of the world religions were created—has over the past several decades been the subject of a burgeoning literature in history, civilization studies, sociology, and political science. In *Practicing Transcendence: Axial Age Spiritualities for a World in Crisis*, Christopher Peet provides a masterful synthesis of the now vast literature relating to the Axial Age. His interpretation emphasizes the visionary ways in which figures of the Axial Age in China, India, Israel, and Greece responded to crises in the civilizations of their times. The esteem previously accorded to the famous works of S.N. Eisenstadt and Robert N. Bellah must now be shared with Peet's contribution; his work is truly indispensable to future scholarship on the Axial Age. Peet bookends his analysis with an introduction and conclusion highlighting the pertinence of Axial Age visions and practices to the crisis of civilization that we, citizens of global society, experience today with the growing assaults on our shared environment."

—Victor Lidz, *Professor Emeritus of Sociology, Drexel University College of Medicine, USA*

Christopher Peet

Practicing Transcendence

Axial Age Spiritualities for a World in Crisis

Christopher Peet
The King's University
Edmonton, AB, Canada

ISBN 978-3-030-14431-9   ISBN 978-3-030-14432-6   (eBook)
https://doi.org/10.1007/978-3-030-14432-6

Library of Congress Control Number: 2019932957

Cover art 'Axis Time' by Alicja Warszynski
Cover design by Tom Howey

This Palgrave Macmillan imprint is published by the registered company Springer Nature Switzerland AG
The registered company address is: Gewerbestrasse 11, 6330 Cham, Switzerland

to children and wild things -

by your innocence
we measure our worth

ACKNOWLEDGEMENTS

Protagoras is credited with saying there are two sides to every story. That has certainly been true for the writing of this book. On the one side, it has been a solitary effort, a despairing meditation, and a long and lonely work. The other side, equally true, is that I could not have done it without friends, family, community, spiritual communities, and professional networks that have supported me throughout.

My scholarly community at The King's University has been one of constant support and quiet encouragement, and my thanks to my many colleagues there for their generosity and wisdom and for numerous conversations both disciplinary and interdisciplinary. The Western Canadian Theoretical Psychology group has offered context for informal dialogue and regularly recurring conviviality for two decades now for which I am grateful. An unexpected invitation from the Karl Jaspers Society of North America provided me a rare opportunity for collegiality with Axial Age scholars at a conference of the American Philosophical Association that assisted in completing the work; thank you.

Thanks to my community of faith at St. Paul's United for community and communion, and for the same but in a different, more interior way, from the centering prayer group. Thank you for your companionship and hours of good conversation—and countless more hours of shared silence. Thanks especially Lynnda, Susan, and Charles for your kindness and guidance on the journey.

Friends and family I mention last because they are not least: my father, who left in the middle, and my mother, who left at the end; Leo, you leave a deep and lasting mark; Sheena and Oliver, your presence has been a blessing; Susan and Dave, always with me in spirit. And above all others, my gratitude to Hannah, Logan, and Tatiana, for bearing with me, and for your love.

My gratitude to all of you. All shortcomings and errors in the book, of course, are mine alone.

CONTENTS

LIST OF FIGURES

CHAPTER 1

The Relevance of the Axial Age for a World in Crisis

This book is about the Axial Age. While some version of the idea has been put forward by scholars for over two centuries now, in recent decades scholarly interest has increased and intensified. However, its interest is not only for scholars; as two of those scholars—American sociologist Robert Bellah and German sociologist Hans Joas—claim, "The question of the Axial Age is not just academic: the deep self-understanding of educated people of all the world's cultures is at stake. How we think about the Axial Age is to some extent how we think about ourselves and the human project at this perilous moment in history" (2012, p. 6). I concur. That the world is in crisis is why I've written this book, and why I think the scholarly interest in the Axial Age should extend more broadly, too.

THE WORLD IN CRISIS: OLIVIA'S STORY

A group of about a dozen of us were camping together last summer—friends and family, grandparents and kids, sharing a few campsites. At one point as we were gathered around the campfire—some of us cooking, others playing guitars, others talking—Olivia, a four-year-old girl, became overwrought and began sobbing, on the verge of a panic attack. "I don't want that to happen! I don't want that to happen!" she cried over and over again, her anxiety palpable. Something had reminded her of a video segment from the opening ceremonies of the 2016 Olympics that had provoked a panic attack when she first saw it. The scene shows what the potential flooding of coastal cities across the world due to a rise

© The Author(s) 2019
C. Peet, *Practicing Transcendence*,
https://doi.org/10.1007/978-3-030-14432-6_1

1

in sea level might look like. We tried to stem her anxiety by reassuring her, holding her, trying to calm her. Someone tried reasoning (at a far too adult level). None of it worked; predictably, the reasoning least of all. I tried distracting her through stories of my family that come from the Netherlands: a whole country that should be under water because it is below sea level but which is dry and safe because of their dikes. This worked. Olivia calmed: she became intrigued by stories of dikes and windmills and wooden shoes; she started to engage the stories, started smiling, and laughed at the funny parts. Success! Panic attack averted.

It is a strange "success story." Not because adults shouldn't try to shield children from suffering anxiety. But because Olivia is, without any doubt, right. Her anxious response, verging on panic, seems to me to be the most rational, truthful, appropriate, and properly human response to a scenario as horrifying as rising sea levels flooding cities. It is the response that any human being should feel if he or she truly tries to imagine the consequences of global climate change. The scale of change, destruction, and suffering that can be plausibly conjectured, for this century and into the next, is overwhelming. And of course, rising sea levels causing coastal cities to be flooded is only one of many such apocalyptic scenarios for the near future that are each and all as frightening to imagine as they are plausible. We don't want that to happen! We don't want that to happen!

Psychologically, the moral of this story is that in most cases the human psyche cannot deal with the anxiety that ensues if it genuinely tries to face "the end of the world." We can't be reassured, or calmed. Nor does reason help because, given our current world situation, some kind of an end-of-the-world scenario, in some sense of that phrase, is the most reasonable prospect for the near future. It is because reason can connect the dots between the facts of our world in the present and their most plausible consequences in the near future that we are anxious. I emphasize the near future here. Unlike a child panicking upon learning that the sun will go supernova in five billion years, an irrational anxiety that misunderstands the time scale, we cannot say this about Olivia. The consequences of climate change are happening now and will continue to happen within her lifetime. Olivia's anxiety is rational. The best we could do was distract her.

If the anxiety is too much, as it was for Olivia, the human psyche does not have many choices. The two I consider most basic and commonplace: denial and distraction. Denial is the more simple and basic option; we deny the evidence and deny our reason and put our heads in the sand. Distraction is somewhat more sophisticated and involves doing something else, getting caught up in some focus that is more manageable and less overwhelming. For one example, work: Yes, the world is ending, but we're too busy to help out. Distracting ourselves means we avoid looking at the evidence, we look somewhere else and apply our reason and effort there—perhaps, with even more determination and intensity. I suspect the most widespread and understandable psychological responses to our present global situation involve varying degrees of denial or distraction; there is a great diversity of forms of flight into far more restricted foci that absorb attention, whether hedonistic, compulsive, addictive, self-destructive, masochistic, or narcissistic (cf. Hamilton, 2010).

Cognitively, there is a different moral to be drawn from Olivia's story: That global events and processes, despite being, well, global in scale and arguably far removed from ordinary, everyday life, can and do manifest in individual awareness. That things happen on a global scale means they are "big," but not big in an abstract or far-removed sense. Global scale as big means events otherwise disparate and unconnected are not; everything becomes thoroughly interconnected to each other and effects from 'somewhere' that would otherwise be far-removed show up 'here' in some form. Global scale means there are no far-removed events or effects, but an interconnectedness that is pervasive and manifests at multiple levels—including the individual. One such example of the linked-up chain of interconnections: The potential flooding of coastal cities of the world in the near future is due to the projected rise in sea levels due to the melting of the polar ice caps due to global warming due to increased carbon emissions due to human activity. Another such example: Brazil, a country with one of the highest levels of climate change awareness among its population, hosts the global sporting event the Olympics, puts on a many hours long opening ceremony that includes a video segment on climate change focused on the flooding of major coastal cities (like Rio de Janeiro, where the ceremonies are being held), which is viewed by a four-year-old girl in Canada, who suffers a panic attack as she grasps the meaning of the flooding images. The first chain of interconnected processes was ecological and causal; the second, cultural and technological. These two chains in turn are themselves connected: The facts of the first meet the consciousness animating the second and this meeting manifests in a particular meaning, experientially, for an individual person. For Olivia, it manifested in acute anxiety.

I'm arguing that someone like Olivia, who finds the anxiety of contemplating such a potential disaster overwhelming and breaks down into a panic attack, presents a rational, healthy response that in effect represents quite clearly the basic psychological dynamics for any of us who try to face end-of-the-world scenarios. In part, Olivia's response represents the psychology so clearly because she is a child and thus lacks the sophisticated defensiveness and elaborate dishonesty of the adult. In part, it is because the threat to the ego by a crisis manifests reactions that are infantile, in the sense of psychologically basic, cognitively undeveloped and emotionally powerful. What is not represented in this example, nor in the discussion above which I qualified by adding the phrase "for the most part," are those of us with greater psychological resiliency who can face our contemporary world in crisis without denial or distraction. Of course, the same psychological dynamics apply to the more resilient adult ego, too, and thus trying to deal with world crisis risks depression, despair, hopelessness, rage, cynicism, nihilism, breakdown. We need courage, we need resolve, commitment, and hope; in a word, we need resilience to be able to face our world in crisis. We need to listen to the crying of a child.

In sum, Olivia's story provides us with two crucial takeaways. The first is psychological: Inseparable from our current world in crisis is the end-of-the-world anxiety that accompanies it. The second is cognitive: That our current world, as a globalizing world, is profoundly and pervasively interconnected across all its many levels, including the level at which it comes into conscious awareness, the individual level. Both of these points, taken together, are a key part to how the contemporary world is unprecedented. We face a global crisis, which is unprecedented in human history, and "we" are not a particular nation or ethnic group, or particular class, or particular elite, but we are truly all humanity, globally interconnected into a universality—at least, factually—that is also unprecedented. End-of-the-world anxiety works in tandem with global interconnectedness against our ability to proactively do anything about the global crisis; they impair our response-ability to face the crisis of our times. Psychologically, our fragile egos are confronted with a crisis of overwhelming proportions; cognitively our limited conscious awareness fails to grasp our inextricable embeddedness in a world of overwhelming complexity. For you or I to face "the end of the world" is so difficult because it is overwhelming: Psychologically, we feel too much anxiety, while cognitively we feel lost. There is ample cause today for denial, distraction, despair, and hopelessness.

We cannot afford these. The world is in a crisis of global proportions. It is unprecedented in all of human history. We are the cause of this crisis. The history that has led to this crisis is our history. We must take responsibility for it. We must face this crisis—for ourselves, for Olivia, for the earth itself.

Against overwhelming anxiety, we need to develop our resilience; against an overwhelming complexity of information, perspectives, and possibilities, we need to gain our bearings and find some perspective on ourselves and our present moment. We need resilience to face our world in crisis; we need perspective on the present so that we are facing in the right direction and perceiving on the right scale.

The Axial Age

This book is about the Axial Age, a period of several centuries around 2500 years ago when, according to scholars, a series of events happened that prove utterly decisive for the history of the world and relevant to our current world. Since learning about the Axial Age and studying the scholarship, I too am convinced of its importance. This importance is not restricted to scholars and historians only; as the quote that opened this chapter from Bellah and Joas (2012) claims, it is important for "educated people of all the world's cultures" at this present "perilous moment in history," too (p. 6). Following their lead, this book is written not only for scholars, but also for a broader educated audience. And it is also motivated by the perception that our present, globalizing, world-historical moment, is "perilous"—a perception clearly shared by Olivia and many others, with anxious consequences for all.

What is "the Axial Age"? How is it relevant to today's world? If you consider some of our contemporary world's most pressing problems that would justify evaluating our moment as "perilous," the relevance of historical events that happened more than two thousand years ago might appear remote. Today, we face refugee and immigrant crises caused by war and famine; global climate change and the effort to prevent the global mean temperature from rising; peak oil and the energy crisis around fossil fuel-based economies and the need to move to renewable energy sources; terrorist attacks; the increasing disparity between rich and poor; ecological "tipping points" and the mass extinction of species... As one critic responded to the relevance question upon hearing my argument regarding the Axial Age: "No, it's too long ago."

This book presents my argument for the Axial Age and its relevance. I hope to convince you of the Axial Age's relevance for understanding today's world and for responding to its problems. Understanding the Axial Age provides perspective on the present; more so than this, it provides a way to put the present into perspective that is also a proposal for how to develop and deepen one's psychological resilience. In this chapter, I will present a brief summary of what the Axial Age is, before expanding in some more detail on how the Axial Age is relevant.

What Is "The Axial Age"?

German philosopher Karl Jaspers in the wake of World War II proposed a span of several centuries, from 800 to 200 BCE, as constituting a dividing line or "axis" between a long prehistory of human beings before and the emergence of a world history after. Therefore, Jaspers called it "the Axial Age." Jaspers was not the first to remark this time period as historically significant, nor was he the first to elaborate this remark into a full-fledged thesis. He was, however, the first to do so in a way that proves very influential. In the last few decades, scholarship examining the Axial Age has exploded—a big part of my motivation for writing this book. What is it about this time period that has caught the attention of scholars?

Over these centuries, a small number of visionaries, sages, and prophets in a handful of ancient civilizations delivered sophisticated critiques of their civilizations while developing equally sophisticated, and radically original, alternatives. Scholarship has settled on four ancient civilizations in particular: Greece, Israel, India, and China. Greek philosophers like Pythagoras and Socrates, the Hebrew prophets of the Old Testament like Isaiah and Jeremiah, in India the Buddha, the writers of the Upanisadic texts (crucially foundational for Hinduism) and Mahavira (crucially foundational for Jainism), and numerous Chinese sages like Confucius, Mo Tzu, and Lao Tzu, all live within the span of several centuries in the middle of the first millennium BCE. Each proposes critiques-and-alternatives, several of which go on to become basic and foundational for the major world religions and/or major world civilizations. As a friend of mine wisecracked: you mean a bunch of "wise guys" show up, at around the same time, in a few different places, and go on to change the world? Although expressed jokingly and not too scholarly or profoundly, that is indeed the gist of it.

The appellation "wise guys" is a wisecrack, but also a fairly useful shorthand. Many descriptors are too limited to capture the full range of diversity of the Axial Age "wise guys"; calling them "thinkers" or "philosophers" is too intellectually biased, whereas "holy men" or "prophets" is too religiously weighted. One solution is to always present lists—philosophers, prophets, holy men, and sages. Another is to choose from the few overarching terms, like visionaries, luminaries, teachers, or spiritual masters, or Max Weber's apt term, "spiritual *virtuosi*" (there are many to choose from; Eric Voegelin [1974], will suggest "sensitive and active minds," Runciman [2012] "righteous rebels," Robert Bellah [2011] uses the phrase "moral upstarts" [p. 264] but later prefers "renouncers" [pp. 574–575]). Not too scholarly nor profound, and certainly irreverent, wise guys works pretty well as an overarching term. As well, in terms of gender awareness, the bias in calling them "guys" is accurate: the Axial Age visionaries were overwhelmingly male, although in working out the implications of their spiritually revolutionary visions there is a clear potential for gender equity and gender inclusivity. But that gets us ahead of ourselves in terms of an introduction to the Axial Age and its luminaries. The question we need to look at: What is it these wise guys accomplished?

Probably, the best shorthand phrase to describe the center of gravity to the Axial Age is that it was a "breakthrough to transcendence" (Schwartz, 1975). The truth claimed by the Axial Age visionaries is critical of the local, ethnic, political, historically bound self-understandings, or worldviews, of their particular civilizations. In retrospect, to apply a modern term not used then but applicable, the sages of the Axial Age exposed these perspectives as ideologies. That is, the religious, mythological, cultural self-understandings in ancient Greece, ancient Israel, ancient India, and ancient China were elaborate systems of thought that justified and legitimated cultural practices of law, morality, ethics, ritual, and so on. This included justifying and legitimating the injustices, sufferings, violence, lies, and evils that were built into those cultural practices and self-understandings. Over against this ideological defense of the status quo (to anachronistically use another modern word) which served the existing hierarchies of power and protected those who profited from it, philosophers, prophets, holy men, and sages presented powerful and courageous criticisms on moral, ethical, and spiritual grounds. In fact, one apt characterization offered of the Axial Age is that it was "the age of criticism" (Momigliano, 1975), as the human capacity to criticize thought and action greatly expanded.

The visionaries of the Axial Age did not only criticize. They also proposed a positive alternative vision, key to which was the claim that this alternative applied to, and was accessible to, everyone: the truth they proclaimed was presented as universal. The alternative vision of reality they advocated was argued to transcend the limits of geography, of kinship, of ethnicity and culture, of power, and of history. In claiming universal spiritual truths that transcended particular limits, and from which transcendent viewpoint existing mythologies and cultural self-understandings were exposed as limited and ideological, the Axial Age spiritual *virtuosi* "broke through" the existing horizons of thought of their time to a whole new "level" for thinking above and beyond, and claimed to be morally, ethically, and spiritually, higher than and better than, the understandings then in place. One of the first systematic attempts to understand the Axial Age, preceding Jaspers by almost a century, describes it not in terms of "transcendence" but as "a moral revolution" (Stuart-Glennie, 1873; see also Halton, 2014). The Axial Age isn't just a change in thinking that can be characterized as "different," but it is a change in morality and ethics that proposes new, higher ideals for goodness, truth, and justice. The gods of the old religions are exposed and taken to task, or ridiculed even, for their capricious and immoral behavior, while divinity and the sacred on the new Axial Age conception necessarily included a moral dimension; the god ceases to operate exclusively as a more powerful being, but also embodies a higher moral level of goodness. In raising the bar on truth and goodness and justice, this should not be misunderstood as claiming people become more truthful, better, and more just in their thoughts and actions. This isn't true factually in terms of what happens in history, and it isn't true because it oversimplifies how the Axial Age's impact should be understood. What the Axial Age's "breakthrough to transcendence" or "moral revolution" accomplishes is that thoughts and actions become judged and evaluated according to higher moral and ethical standards. By this account, the Axial Age as "the age of criticism" was not merely an increase in intellectual ability, but above all an increased moral and ethical demand placed on thought and action. This increased capacity is a dramatic change, but one that translates indirectly and complexly, not straightforwardly, into thought and action.

These breakthroughs to transcendence, like small seeds that grow into giant trees, begin small but grow into the world religions of major civilizations that compose much of the world history of the last two millennia. Judaism has existed on the fringes and in the interstices of Europe and "the West," rooted in the Israelite Axial Age; Buddhism, Hinduism, and Jainism are rooted in the Indian Axial Age; and Confucianism and Taoism are rooted in the Chinese Axial Age. In terms of adherents, these major world religions account for close to thirty percent of the world population. Of course, this leaves out the two largest world religions, which account for more than half of the world population: Christianity and Islam. Many scholars coming after Jaspers expand the definition of the Axial Age to recognize this and include the founding of the world religions of Christianity and Islam as part of the Age. This greatly extends the time frame from 800 BCE to 700 CE, too, with the disadvantage that fifteen centuries instead of six is not so much a "dividing line," but a sloppy smear. Christianity (both western and eastern) and Islam are each rooted to differing extents in the Greek and Israelite Axial Ages, both in terms of their deep indebtedness to Greek thinking, rationality, and philosophy, as well as to the Israelite conception of monotheism, prophecy, and the importance of scripture. Christianity and Judaism share a significant amount of scripture of the Old Testament. Islam quite accurately characterizes both along with itself as "Religions of the Book." All three share certain founding figures as well, like Abraham. In these respects, Christianity and Islam are indebted to the Axial Age for much of their founding inspiration. Today, the civilizations/religions based on what these spiritual teachers and masters accomplished compose the bulk of the population of the world. Their life stories, their writings, or writings about them by their disciples (not all of these visionaries wrote), and sayings ascribed to them, become the canonical foundational texts for the worldviews of the great world religions. Adherents of Christianity, Islam, Judaism, Hinduism, Buddhism, Confucianism, and Taoism compose the great majority of the contemporary global population of seven billion.

Let me briefly illustrate this claim with a table (Fig. 1.1), as it is basic to Axial Age scholarship, whether Karl Jaspers' thesis, Robert Bellah and Hans Joas' claim that began this chapter, or my argument in this book. Taking an "Introduction to World Religions" textbook off my shelf, and finding the world population breakdown provided there (Partridge, 2005, p. 354), helps us with illustrating this claim. Partridge (2005) provides world population figures, which I have adapted in terms of whether they are clearly Axial world religions (like Christianity, Islam, Hinduism, Buddhism) over against those that are clearly not (like "animism"). This leaves us with a third group that I've called "mixed," because the

Religion	Population (in millions)	Axial	Mixed	Not Axial
Christianity	2246	2246		
Islam	1427	1427		
Hinduism	901	901		
Chinese folk-religion	409		409	
Buddhism	381	381		
Judaism	15	15		
Animists	246			246
Sikhism	26		26	
Other religions	153		153	
Non-religious/atheists	944		944	
Total	6748	4970	1532	246
Percentage of total		73.7 %	22.7 %	3.6 %

Fig. 1.1   World religions by population (Adapted from Partridge, 2005)

categories provided would "mix," to an unknown degree, movements that are clearly Axial with those that are not. "Chinese folk-religion" includes significant numbers of adherents of Confucianism and Taoism. "Sikhism" is its own religion, of course, but with significant reliance on and "borrowings" from Hinduism and Islam or, in different terms, significant amounts of Axial content. The category "non-religious/atheists" would include much of Greek Axial thinking, for example, as informing Western secular humanism; it could include many Confucianist followers, too, as "non-religious." The category "other religions" would include Zoroastrianism or Jainism.

Viewing Fig. 1.1 in terms of percentages of world population, and acknowledging that we have no idea what percentage of the 22.7% of the "Mixed" category should count as Axial (let's use a range of 1–99%), gives us an idea—admittedly rough, admittedly simplistic—of what percentage range of world population could be called "Axial": somewhere between 75 and 95% (using a range from 1 to 99% of the "Mixed" category added onto the 73.7% that are "clearly Axial"). Admittedly rough, admittedly simplistic, nevertheless this number does capture a truth about how people subjectively self-identify in terms of belonging to particular religious groups or belief systems. Much of the roughness and oversimplifying is because we are dealing with the fuzzy indeterminate realities of subjective self-identification and sense of belonging. These are not clearly definable objects. Despite these problems, there is a reality and truth behind the fuzziness. Saying "We were raised orthodox Jews but I converted to Christianity while my brother became a dyed-in-the-wool atheist," or claiming that Confucianism has been a crucial constituent of Chinese civilization for over two thousand years, or statistics that show Islam to be the fastest-growing religion in the world today, all do have reality and truth to them.

If we accept the claims of Axial Age scholarship, then in a similarly rough-simplistic-fuzzy way we can say that 75–95% of the world population today thinks in terms that were created during the Axial Age. This statistic gives us an easy handle to make sense of the Bellah and Joas (2012) claim at the opening of the chapter to the "not just academic" importance of the Axial Age for "all the world's cultures" (p. 6). It helps makes sense, for example, of Jaspers' (1953) perhaps otherwise puzzling claims that in the Axial Age "Man, as we know him today, came into being" (p. 1) or "Our present-day historical consciousness, as well as our consciousness of our present situation, is determined... by the conception of the Axial Period" (p. 21). The notion that 75–95% of the world today "thinks" in Axial Age terms also helps explain Eric Voegelin's (1974, p. 331) astonishing and otherwise seemingly absurd claim that "Nothing much has happened during the last 2500 years"!

I've framed the above discussion in terms of the world religions. I could have done so in terms of major civilizations and their worldviews instead. Western civilization, Chinese civilization, Indian civilization, and Arabic civilization trace their thinking back to pivotal understandings that are largely inseparable from the religious history. What exactly is the relation between a religion and a civilization? I don't have an answer but it is clear that for most of history since the Axial Age, including the present, they can't be clearly distinguished. Is there such a thing as "Western civilization" separable from Christianity, or "Europe" without Greek thought? Can we understand Islam apart from Arabian civilization, or Indian civilization apart from Hinduism, Buddhism, and Jainism (or, vice versa in both cases)? Confucianism and Chinese civilization? I take it as obvious that you can't, and this is a key part to Jaspers' claim about the significance of the Axial Age for world history: It has contributed to how "we"—meaning here the great majority of the world's population—think today. To take as an example, imagine a contemporary Western "secular humanist" who rejects religion and is thus dubious about the importance of the Axial Age. If deeper inquiry proves that the secular humanist thinks about the world in terms developed by Greek Axial Age thinkers—or to say the same thing differently, within the horizon of thought articulated by classical Greek philosophy—then the Axial Age thesis applies to him or her.

The reversed version of this inseparability—that religion and civilization are identical—is also not true. There are some pretty clear differences, aren't there? For example, that religion is more concerned with spiritual matters, civilization with political matters; religion has priests and believers and belief systems, civilization has kings and citizens and thought-systems... Of course, these face-value distinctions are very loose indeed. They won't hold up as definitive under closer scrutiny. Part of the problem is that the concept of "religion" is itself a peculiarly modern Western "invention" (cf. Masuzawa, 2005). Nevertheless, I take it as obvious that religion and civilization are not exactly the same thing, either, even if it is difficult or impossible to determine where one ends and the other begins. So, the civilization/religion bathwater is dirty, but doesn't justify throwing out the baby: Civilization and religion are neither entirely identical (we need both terms), nor are they entirely separable (their histories intertwine).

Acknowledging we don't want to be bogged down by the complexity of this definitional problem, I do want to point out one crucial characteristic of the ambiguity of the "world religion or world civilization?" relation: Both stake a claim of identity. This characteristic explains some of the ambiguity and confusion around their relation and is ultimately tied to the common roots of both in the Axial Age. The claim to transcendence made by Axial Age visionaries becomes an utterly crucial and defining orientation for those who think or believe in it. Transcendence becomes utterly crucial and defining for peoples' identity. Insofar as both world religions and world civilizations incorporate transcendence into their own self-definitions, the identities of their members are implicated in these claims to transcendence, too. Much of this book explores and hopefully explicates how a claim to universal transcendence creates a powerful and complex possibility for identity that has historically proven compelling, problematic, dynamic, and seemingly irreversible for how we think about ourselves.

There is a lot more to the Axial Age than this brief description, just as there are many more aspects to what its visionaries propose than transcendence. For introductory purposes, this brief summary will suffice. The detail will come in Chapter 3 especially and in general throughout the whole of this book. Now that we have a sense of what the Axial Age is, let's turn to our second introductory question: What is its relevance to today?

THE RELEVANCE OF THE AXIAL AGE

Describing what the Axial Age is ought to have immediately conveyed one very significant claim as to its relevance for today: its historical relevance. In short, the Axial Age is of decisive importance historically because it lays out the contours for what I call the shape of the present. The impact of the Axial Age breakthroughs in thought has contributed decisively to world history over the past two millennia. We think in the terms and categories laid out during the Axial Age by the particular Axial Age tradition to which we belong. Jaspers, a philosopher, uses the apt philosophical turn of phrase of "horizon"; other words we could use are a worldview, or a paradigm. Broader than the notions of terms and categories that name meanings explicitly, the notion of horizon is meant more pervasively and is meant to encompass a whole space of meaning in which thinking occurs, including the unspoken implicit background against which explicit terms and categories gain their meaning. Emphasizing the historical relevance of the Axial Age is in line with what scholarship presents, too: to deal with our contemporary world and address its problems, it is crucial for us to get our bearings and gain some perspective on our present moment.

A second way the Axial Age is relevant to us today, which we could call its comparative relevance: We are in the midst of a decisive historical moment which might perhaps be a "second Axial Age." Just as the first proved decisive in historical retrospect, so too might our own moment. What can we learn by comparing our time to the first Axial Age? Again, this is in line with what scholars have explored. There is no consensus on whether we are indeed in a second Axial Age; some argue in favor of this view, others against. Regardless, it is worth exploring. My own view on this is that the two ages are very comparable in terms of their social and political conditions. I discuss these in more detail in Chapter 4; the comparability between then and now can be summarized in terms of an unprecedented growth in civilizational power, or "axial times of power". The middle centuries of the first millennium BCE see an extraordinary increase in the size of ancient civilizations and empires, with a whole host of corresponding changes socially, economically, technologically, and politically. This dramatic change in living conditions is not a wholesale good change. If anything, it is the opposite for the majority of people: There is also an extraordinary increase in social inequality and injustice and oppression, in slavery, in warfare and military conquest and conscripted labor. In short, these changes cause widespread despair and anxiety. These centuries witness an unprecedented increase in human suffering. They also motivate among those living on the margins of civilizational power—this is the focus of Chapter 5—the first Axial Age's breakthroughs to transcendence.

I argue much of our present moment to be similar due to globalization and massive technological advancement ushering in a time of rapid and unprecedented change. Combined with the effect on the environment, globally, as we see in global climate change and a mass extinction of species, I perceive similar widespread despair and anxiety. Whether these circumstances will motivate a "second Axial Age" in terms of visionary breakthroughs to guide us into the future remains to be seen. A significant difference between the two ages lies in precisely the fact of historical relevance of the Axial Age for our world today: We have a precedent to which to compare ourselves. Depending where you stand on the accomplishments of the first Axial Age will affect how the comparison goes. If you consider the Axial Age as where we went wrong, for example, now is our chance to right things. Or if you think the Axial Age was right, but its full potential has not yet been reached, now is our opportunity to bring out its full potential. There are further, more nuanced interpretations of the Axial Age possible.

The third way the Axial Age is relevant that I explore in this book is more my own interpretation rather than anyone else's, which I hope will garner some serious consideration. In contrast to the philosophical, historical, or sociological interpretations that dominate the Axial Age literature, I interpret the Axial Age psychologically. One consequence of my psychological interpretation was already evident above: I interpret the key notion of transcendence not primarily as an idea that redefines how a collective tradition thinks and theorizes, believes and dogmatizes, but primarily as a transformation and extension of identity. After the Axial Age, people's identity is reformed toward a broader, putatively universal, group; the breakthrough to transcendence provides a transcendent locus of identification. A second consequence based on my psychological interpretation: I see the relevance of the Axial Age in terms of its practical spirituality. In my view, scholars have not appreciated sufficiently Jaspers' claim that "the Axial Period too ended in failure. History went on" (1953, p. 20). That the Axial Age could both "end in failure" and decisively contribute to world history, should strike anyone as puzzling, if not astonishing! This divergence between what it failed to accomplish and what it did contribute structures much of this book and is the overt focus of Chapter 6. Unraveling a little bit of this puzzle helps introduce, too, how to understand the Axial Age and its relevance, as well as my own particular interpretive take on it.

The Axial Age was a kind of revolution: an effort at a revolution in spirit, above all. While it "succeeded"—if you can describe spiritual efforts in terms of success and failure—in small groups of disciples gathered around individual teachers and was carried on by small communities that gathered around these disciples, it did not succeed in overturning the established socio-religio-political order or dissolving the formation of ever bigger empires. Ironically, in "failing," it proves to contribute to the very thing—"big power"—against which it was revolting. Powerful civilizations and huge empires domesticate the revolutionary potency of Axial Age thought and put it to work for them to extend their size and power yet further, enabling the development of "great world civilizations." Religious reformers took the revolutionary and inspirational new understandings from the Axial Age visionaries, selectively using these understandings to criticize existing religion and mythology even as they go on (in decidedly unrevolutionary fashion) to found new "great world religions." Contributing ideas or beliefs or a new way of thinking or believing, however, was not the primary goal of the Axial Age visionaries. Yes, this is what history in the form of world civilizations or world religions took from them. Relative to what the Axial Age spiritual *virtuosi* practiced and embodied, however, this amounts to a mis-taking. What I call the Axial road not taken was their practical response: first, to reject the too large scale of power of civilizations; second, to form small communities centered, not on power, but on spiritual practices; third, to perform spiritual practices centered, not on the ego, but on overcoming the ego and thus, transforming oneself. This practical, spiritual response aimed at personal transformation was what the Axial Age *virtuosi* considered foundational for the good life. On this interpretation, the Axial Age response to the world and its problems could be summarized in these two questions: What is your small community? What is your spiritual practice?

Interpreting the Axial Age in this way opens up a whole series of questions relative to the dominant scholarly interpretations: These could be grouped into political, religious, ecological, and psychological questions.

The first of these is the question of the relation of Axial Age responses to the issue of civilizational power. If the Axial Age responses can be called spiritual, idealistic, and small-scale, the contrast is drastic to civilization at the time, which was "this-worldly," tough-minded, and large-scale. Certainly, a series of questions could be raised about how a spiritual response can be not directly political but can prove to have, indirectly, potent political consequences. Within this series of questions, it is the moral and ethical emphasis on the Golden Rule, on nonviolence, love, and compassion, wherein we can see some of the most potent consequences, including hope, for contemporary politics.

A second series of questions involves the relation of the Axial Age visions to the world religions founded on these. To establish a world religion requires large-scale organization, at the center of which are questions, again, of power. If the fundamental premise to the Axial Age responses is a rejection of power, especially large-scale power, then the founding of large powerful world religions is a betrayal of their very founders' intentions. A whole train of consequences follow from drawing a sharp distinction between the Axial Age and world religions. What Axial Age holy men meant by "this world" (of sin, ignorance, illusion, suffering, that has lost the *Tao*) vs. the transcendent "other world" (of redemption, knowledge, enlightenment, release, congruence with the *Tao*), was meant in a small-scale, practical spirituality, personal transformation sense, not in a big metaphysics, elaborate doctrine, supernatural ontology sense. Similarly, what they mean by transcendence is either not so much a metaphysical question or it is not even a metaphysical claim at all! What transcendence means is both a deep mystery and an unmysterious practical question that turns on the degree of "self-work" someone has done (in the sense of quantity and quality of spiritual practice undertaken and degree of overcoming the ego achieved). Similarly, the distinction between Axial Age meanings and world religion appropriations of these applies to the notions of universality and salvation: For world religions, these are tied into criteria of identity for group membership (and thus, ironically, a powerful means of exclusion of others). For Axial Age practitioners, universality asserts a radically inclusive ethics that imposes severe standards of self-responsibility and self-discipline upon the individual. Salvation becomes something tied to the mystery of transcendence and thus more personal and practical, and more mysterious.

A third interesting set of questions raised by my interpretation of the Axial Age: What are the ecological consequences of a widespread adoption of Axial Age small communities centered on spiritual practices aimed at overcoming the ego? Could the cumulative consequences of such small-scale, but widespread, actions be the "salvation" of "this world"? A lot of scholarly attention has rightfully been focused on the intimate tie-in between world religions and that these are "salvation" religions. This was the great sociologist Max Weber's interest, and he saw salvation as the distinctive innovation that marked the great world religions by comparison with other religious understandings. This focus and interest emphasizes salvation in a world religion sense of supernatural intervention by an "other world" and raises all sorts of theological, philosophical, and metaphysical questions and puzzles. On my interpretation, salvation was meant by Axial Age visionaries in a practical spirituality sense, dependent upon a person's degree of personal transformation. If we engage the problem of "this world," that is our present world's ecological crisis, from this personal-practical emphasis on salvation rather than a world religion metaphysical one, what difference will this make? I'm not claiming that the Axial Age visionaries were ecologically preoccupied. But, just as their spiritual response to the crisis of their time had, indirectly, potent political consequences for how people should live, so too I understand their response as having, indirectly, potent ecological consequences. Above all, this is evident in their advocacy of ascetic self-control and disciplined self-denial, which have immediate and far-reaching consequences ecologically in terms of what this means for people's consumption practices and values as built into their way of life. Within the spiritual resources of the world religions is ample room for collaboration with environmentalists around consumption and sustainability (Gardner, 2002).

And finally, the fourth interesting question concerns the psychological consequences of the practical spirituality the Axial Age spiritual *virtuosi* advocated. If we recall Olivia, whose story opened this chapter, and my claim that faced with our world in crisis we deny and distract ourselves if it is too much, or court despair and despondence if we try to be resolute and responsible, the personal transformation effected through spiritual practice has immediate and far-reaching relevance, especially for developing and deepening resilience in troubled times. It should be self-evident why we need to develop and deepen our resilience in order to face the challenges confronting us in the twenty-first century. In addition, and not so immediate nor self-evident, are some of the subtler psychological consequences of Axial Age practical spirituality. Decentering from our habitual default egocentrism not only has the good consequence of increasing our psychological resilience, it also surprisingly reframes and, most importantly, re-scales our concerns. The counterintuitive insight I am advancing here, based on the Axial Age advocacy of spirituality, is that our ordinary investment in the world and power (which is obviously egocentric) and our supposedly non-egocentric anxieties about the end-of-the-world are both different expressions of the same egocentrism. They only appear as being different because in being concerned, anxious, fearful, despairing, about the plausibility of an end-of-the-world scenario, we don't see how our egotism is at work. In the very experiencing of that anxiety, the ego has subtly reinserted its centrality, by playing off the sensational scale invoked and surreptitiously reintroducing itself into the drama and frisson created in considering something so truly terrifying and terrible as the end of the world. But, and here is where the counterintuitive psychology is at work, the ego is performing a defensive, self-deceptive maneuver that preserves it in self-centered sensation—even as that sensation is based on an imminent, real threat that would destroy the ego, among other things. No, the reasoning is not quite logical; it is, however, quite psychological.

If this psycho-logic strikes you as perverse, well, it should, because it is. If it also strikes you as unlikely, all I can ask is that you consider it. We shouldn't need Star Wars movies to know that we all have a dark side; ordinary experience should be enough to convince us of that. Only the most narcissistic ego could really believe it is nothing but light and deny its shadow. Spiritual practice aims to expose and recognize the ego and its deep investment in power in how it perceives the world—as well as its deep, perverse investment to survive at any cost, and the long shadow this casts. The psychological consequences of such practice are to retract the ego's investment, in both worldly power and its shadow, leading counterintuitively to far smaller and more immediate concerns and more proportionate anxieties relative to the self. Seemingly, leading to less care about the world, and less anxiety about the end of the world... but in actuality it is a deep re-scaling of concern outside an egocentric frame, and hence is smaller, more immediate, more proportionate; and more authentic, more real, and—at least when viewed spiritually—more truly effective.

AIMS OF THIS BOOK: A SYNTHESIS AND SUMMARY OF SCHOLARSHIP, AND THE AXIAL ROAD NOT TAKEN

This book is trying to accomplish two related, although different, aims regarding the Axial Age. First it presents, in accessible simplified summary, what scholarship has to say about the Axial Age, including therefore its relevance for today. This means a great deal of simplifying, especially due to the explosion in scholarship in the last few decades. It also means synthesizing in that most of the scholarship is written by specialists and experts in their fields addressing their peers or Axial Age scholars, and thus not very accessible to a broader, more general audience. About the only books available that do this at present are Karen Armstrong's *The Great Transformation: The Beginning of Our Religious Traditions* (2006) and Ken Baskin and Dmitri Bondarenko's *The Axial Ages of World History: Lessons for the 21st Century* (2014).

Second, this book presents my own interpretation of what the Axial Age was really about and my interpretation of what its relevance is for us today. In summarizing and simplifying what positions the Axial Age scholars take, the generalization I've noticed is that most focus on the idea of transcendence, in some form or other. Hans Joas (2012) provides perhaps the most concise summary of scholarship's interpretation of the Axial Age: "it would perhaps be even more precise, although maybe a bit pedantic, to speak of the age of the emergence of the idea of transcendence" (p. 11). Transcendent ideas become crucial for orienting new, expanded civilizational worldviews, for example, the centerpiece for new cultural and political ideologies. Or, these ideas are examined for how they ground and orient a philosophy—some systematic theory, metaphysics, ontology, or epistemology. These ideas have also been interpreted less cognitively or intellectually, and more attitudinally and affectively as basic to belief systems, as is the case with the interpretations of their Axial Age founders by the world religions themselves. This is also the case with many of the scholars of religion who study the world religions, explaining how these ideas can be built up to whole canons, scriptures, doctrines, and theologies or cosmologies as the framework on which to hang an entire institutional organization of religious life. Karen Armstrong who I mentioned in the previous paragraph, for example, argues that the central Axial contribution is compassion, which is not so much an idea as a relational attitude, character virtue or moral value. Contrary to some contemporary views that equate religion with violence, Armstrong argues strongly against this perception by pointing out the roots of the world religions in the Axial Age and the latter's emphasis on compassion as being more truly what world religions teach. Sociologists, who especially in recent decades have come to the fore as a major force in Axial Age scholarship, tend to be more empirical in looking at which social group(s), i.e., intellectual elites, carried these ideas, and how these ideas become institutionalized. A psychologist might look at all of these aspects and point out that what is psychologically crucial is how it impacts how and with what people identify; it transforms identity. Whether ideas, worldviews, ideologies, philosophies, beliefs, doctrines, theologies, virtues, institutions, or identities, the emphasis is on the "mental," or the cognitive or intellectual, side. Even scholars who reject the term "transcendence" as being too loaded with religious or ideological baggage, emphasizing, for example, greater reflection, or greater creativity, or increased reflexivity, increased sense of agency, or a new-found sense of history, are still emphasizing cognitive-intellectual capacities. Above all, the emphasis on how the Axial Age is a "breakthrough" is in terms of a new idea, a new way of thinking, or a new cognitive capacity.

My interpretation is not completely contrary to this, but it does involve a shift in emphasis that I consider pretty significant. For example, I concur with Karen Armstrong that compassion is perhaps the central value for all the world religions and that it stems from the Axial Age. But emphasizing compassion as a value begs the question of how people can come to be compassionate at all. It is not something that automatically happens by being a member of a world religion, for example. Similarly, I concur with the notion of a "breakthrough to transcendence," and the worldview-transforming importance of the very idea of transcendence, and the ways of thinking that inform whole new civilizational self-understandings. Nevertheless, what I understand the Axial Age to have been about, the real breakthrough that we should credit to the philosophers, prophets, holy men, and sages which underlies, or in my preferred term stabilizes, the breakthrough in terms of new ideas, new beliefs, new consciousness, new values, new cognitive, moral, and ethical, capacity, new ways of thinking, is their emphasis on spiritual practice. The shift in emphasis is to understand compassion, and ideas, indeed to understand the spirit, as something that must be practiced, cultivated, and trained. The shift is to the notion of transcendence as a reality that can be experienced, but to "realize" this—to come to understand, and to "make real"—depends on a radical transformation of one's own person. This transformation involves overcoming one's ego, one's egocentrism and egotism, through sustained, systematic, spiritual practice. To express the point crudely, transcendence is not an idea and not something you think, it is something you practice. The Axial Age breakthrough is to the practice of transcendence. The practice is what is behind, is what grounds, or informs, the meaning of the idea. You cannot bypass the practice and go straight to the meaning. You can of course try this, but the result will necessarily be that you misunderstand the idea and distort its meaning. As Chapter 6 aims to demonstrate, sustained spiritual practice "systematically deconstructs" the structures of ordinary consciousness and stabilizes the emergent levels of transcendent consciousness that "ground" the idea of transcendence, universal ethics, the values of compassion and love. What the Axial Age discovers, or innovates, is sustained, systematic, disciplined practice, on the self, that transforms it away from ego-centeredness toward a higher center of consciousness beyond the ego—invoking "transforming," "higher," and "beyond," to describe what the practice is about, I've basically given a definition, although in experiential terms according to what the spiritual practitioner is undergoing, for "transcendence."

An analogy to make the point about the difference between idea and practice: Trying to teach what transcendence is to the unpracticed person is like trying to teach what adult sexuality is to a prepubescent child. The child will certainly form an idea of adult sexuality based on the teachings, but without the development and maturation that transforms the child into an adolescent, the idea will be a strange distortion that mis-takes the true meaning. The teaching will necessarily fail and the idea formed will necessarily be distorted. From an Axial Age viewpoint, a person cannot gain access to ultimacy, cannot know the true meaning of transcendence or universality, cannot say what is ultimately meaningful, without a corresponding development and maturation that transforms the personality through spiritual practice. Without training in *askesis* (the ancient Greek word for "spiritual exercises"), without having pursued some form of asceticism—I'm using the phrase "spiritual practice" as I think it is probably the best general description, while a word like asceticism connotes overly sensational versions of what I mean (see Fraade, 1986, pp. 253–260, for an excellent discussion of this point; also Wimbush & Valantasis, 1998)—people will form immature and irresponsible ideas about the ultimate reality of spirit.

Not only that: If engaging in serious spiritual practice toward personal transformation has the consequence that one's understanding of spirit and ultimacy transforms too, then the Axial road not taken leads to a different destination than that of gaining a mature and responsible idea about ultimate reality. The analogy to the prepubescent child holds here too: After puberty, adolescents tend to become interested in practicing and experiencing the reality of sexuality, not in thinking about it as an idea. In retrospect, they realize that part of the distortion in their prepubescent thinking was in trying to understand the mysterious reality of sexuality as an idea at all! So too with the mysterious reality of transcendence that the Axial Age *virtuosi* discover: The immature, undeveloped thinker mistakes the problem to be that of having the wrong idea. The deeper mistakenness here is considering the primary significance of transcendence to consist in being an idea at all.

Contrary to the emphasis on the idea(s) of transcendence that civilizations and religions took from the Axial Age, the emphasis of the Axial Age visionaries was on spiritual practice(s) to transform the personality toward transcendence. The emphasis of scholarship on the Axial Age has been on the ideas it contributed to world history and the revolutionary differences those ideas have made to human consciousness and how we think. My perspective is that the distinctive contribution of the Axial Age is its developing an extraordinary and revolutionary understanding of spirit and therefore of spirituality (more precisely, different spiritualities in the plural) based on practice. While this too has an effect on consciousness and thought—indeed, arguably a much greater effect on consciousness and thought, as the Axial Age's revolution in spiritual practice was directly concerned with transforming these—this effect is secondary in significance to what the spiritual practice is primarily about. What scholarly attention to this shift in emphasis might begin to unravel is just how these Axial Age ideas of transcendence form; there is a significant gap between the social conditions that motivated them and the presentation of these ideas by an Axial Age visionary (both sides of which gap scholarship has said a lot about). If, as I argue, it is spiritual practice which fills this gap, a new focus for scholarly interest in the Axial Age presents itself. It was okay for an earlier scholarship on the Axial Age to describe it in terms of "multiple and parallel leaps in being" (this is the phrasing of Eric Voegelin, a contemporary of Jaspers; Voegelin, 1957, pp. 1–24), but it is to be preferred if we could say with more precision in what these "leaps" consist.

One immediate objection: Sustained, systematic, disciplined practice was not invented or discovered during the Axial Age. It's far older. Shamans were already doing this; arguably, even earlier, the very performance of the hunt by hunter-gatherers was like this in the form Paul Shepard calls "the sacred game" (see Halton, 2014, pp. 65–69); Native Americans would pursue a vision-quest; and isn't Indian yoga many thousands of years old? With the exception of yoga, the point is valid. All of these are sustained, systematic, disciplined practices, and the outcome of practicing them is indeed some degree of transformation of the self. But there is one significant difference, which is the "Axial" difference. The object of the practice was not one's own consciousness; the focus of the discipline was not inward upon one's own self in order to expose and overcome one's own ego, that is the Axial "discovery" or "innovation." The significant difference between pre-Axial practices that have some contemplative or meditative or ascetic component (as the just cited practices all do) and Axial practices of contemplation or meditation or asceticism is the latter's inward focus on the transformation of the self. In all the pre-Axial examples, the goal is "external," whether to gain contact with the spirit-world for healing, or the hunt, or the vision; "inward" changes were side effects or at best preparatory, but they were not focal. As for yoga: I don't know for sure, but based on the scholarship I've been researching for this book, yoga originates in the Axial Age and not earlier (this argument and the evidence for it is presented in Chapters 5 and 6). Yoga, like Buddhist meditation, Confucian self-cultivation, Taoist inner cultivation, or Greek contemplation, emerges from the Axial Age and exemplifies the kind of sustained, systematic, disciplined "practice of transcendence" that I argue is the Axial Age's distinctive contribution to world history.

What was of primary significance was transcendent, ultimate reality: *Yahweh* for the Old Testament prophets, *Tao* for the Chinese sages, *Logos* for the Greek philosophers, *Brahman* for Hindus, *nirvana* for Buddhists. The self, consciousness, thought, and the spiritual practices themselves were important because they were what someone encountered as obstacle, what had to be gone through, in order to achieve the higher goal of a reality and truth that transcend the means of achieving it. As any performer knows, whether athlete or artist, practice is indispensable, but it is so not for its own sake but ultimately in the service of the real game or the true art. Because ultimate truth is transcendent, we must transcend our limited selves in order to know this truth, and transcending one's self takes a lot of practice! For the Axial Age visionaries, spiritual practice was indispensable in developing the right relationship to (or participation in, or unity with, or surrender to, or loss of self in, or obedience to, or...) transcendent, ultimate reality and truth. A common metaphor is "waking up": noting that the point of waking up is not to go back to sleep, nor to spend the rest of the day in bed marveling that one is awake! The claim of the Axial Age spiritual revolutionaries based on their own training and personal transformation was that the "ideas" (or values, or ideals, etc.) one realizes as transcendent universals are things like love, compassion, selflessness, and that these were ultimately meaningful not because they were good ideas but because they were higher spiritual realities.

What history took from the Axial Age was not the whole story presented by those visionaries. Also, what history did take away from the Axial Age, it largely mis-took. The Axial Age *virtuosi* propose a new, transcendent locus of identification for ultimate reality. The nature or identity of the gods, of sacredness, or for nontheistic understandings like Buddhism or Taoism the nature or identity of truth is dramatically shifted. However, in (mis)taking the true meaning of transcendence and universality as articulated by Axial Age thinkers—proposing an even bigger locus of identification than that provided by existing civilizations and religions—the door is opened for a new form of collective identification at an unprecedented scale. And therefore too the door is opened for civilizational or religious power to expand further, to a yet greater, further unprecedented, scale. (And, too, for new forms of ethics and metaphysics and morality and all kinds of good; but also for pathology and megalomania and all kinds of evil.) Like the proverbial scientist whose high-minded intention to do good through a scientific invention—nuclear energy? Great!—is then mis-used by the government in collusion with the military to create a terrible weapon that does evil—nuclear bombs! The horror!—the breakthroughs of Axial Age visionaries enabled (mis)use by the very civilizations and religions those visionaries criticized. Empires expand and religions proselytize, and transcendence as a spiritual ultimate critical of unspiritual power becomes instead instrumentalized into a means to exercise power beyond current limits (and in principle, *qua* transcendent, beyond *any* limits). Transcendence and universality were taken up by the state to deepen and extend political power; transcendence and universality were taken up by the new institutions of religion to found a deeper and more extensive religious power than had ever before existed.

This means that, on my reading, what has been of decisive importance for history since the Axial Age and for the shape of the present has been a partial and distorted interpretation of the original visions of reality and ultimacy proposed by Axial Age visionaries. So we need to look at what history mistook from the Axial Age, as well as the Axial road not taken. To do the latter we will need to examine the Axial Age visions on their own terms. The visions of ultimacy articulated during the Axial Age were revolutionary in their time and continue to be revolutionary even 2500 years later. How Axial Age sages, holy men, and philosophers understood ultimacy, for example, depended on personal transformation as the fundamental prerequisite to responsible thought and action. Big civilizations took the ideas of transcendence and universality, translated these into metaphysics and ideology, and extended the reach of their power. Big religion took the ideas of transcendence and universality, translated these into doctrine and institution, and extended the reach of their power. The sages and *virtuosi* of the Axial Age would have rejected both developments as dangerously and irresponsibly mis-taking the true meaning and significance of transcendence: Transcendence is a reality to be lived (not 'thought about' as an idea), and to be able to do so one needs to transform one's self through spiritual practices of meditation, prayer, contemplation, fasting, exercises of the mind and the body, isolation, the training of attention, techniques of breathing, techniques of visualization, the giving up of worldly attachments and possessions, and so on. In short: Transcendence is a reality to be realized through practice.

The Axial road not taken as a possible contribution to world history was not taken up into the mainstream of historical developments afterward. It did survive, however, as fringe possibilities on the margins of the great world civilizations and great world religions: monastic groups, hermits, mystics, heretics, contemplatives, unorthodox practitioners, heterodox movements, and alternative communities. I claim the world needs to recall these spiritualities, in the sense of remember, recollect, and retrieve. In this sense of recall, much of this book is historical. Humanity is being put to the ultimate test in our contemporary moment and remembering, recollecting, and retrieving Axial Age spiritualities—more precisely, their spiritual practices—can assist us.

Will they assist us enough? Is it realistic or plausible to believe that we can "save" our world in crisis? Is it possible? Can we find any grounds for hope that human being can achieve sustainable, nonviolent ways of living on the Earth together? Or is this hoping against hope?

HOPE

Above all, according to the visionaries of the Axial Age, to begin to answer these questions we need to put them, and our world in crisis, into the proper perspective: We need to get the scale right. The very phrase "hoping against hope" points toward this: Derived from Romans 4:18, "Who against hope believed in hope," I interpret as meaning there are two different scales to hope. Viewed on the scale of "this world," we put our hope in technology, in governments, in political processes, in economic organizations, in big business and corporations, and so on, to innovate, make policy, fund and police us into sustainability and nonviolence. In short, we put our hope in power, as the only effective approach, as the bottom line, as the only really effectual way to get things done. The scale of "the other world," of spirit, takes a very different view on reality and hence on what is "really real." As one example, the spiritual bottom line is moral and ethical, the "Golden Rule" of not doing to another what you would not want another to do to you (Wattles, 1996). A different example: I'm not sure a spiritual approach would endorse a bottom line at all. What is at issue is the spiritual *quality of meaning* of action, of effectiveness, and of reality, and this quality suffuses, holistically, the whole; as such it is indivisible to this or that level, irreducible to a bottom line. The key difference in scale between this-worldly power and other-worldly spirit: the role of the ego in the perception of the world. To view this world egocentrically is to see it only in terms of power; to view this same world, spiritually, refuses this reduction to power and means the world as other than only this; as other than what the ego knows and controls, desires and fears; as other than what human power can make of the world.

Let me try to make this point in two ways. The first is by a quote that demonstrates, in a somewhat humorous fashion, the difference between an egocentric view and one that transcends the ego. The quote is taken from Sudhir Kakar's *The Ascetic of Desire*:

> In spite of a life devoted to meditation, prayer and books, Brahmagupta was like many other monks I have come to know and admire who are perpetually cheerful, who laugh easily and loudly, the laughter not springing from a sense of humour but from an evolved spirit of mischief and playfulness. Sometimes, watching the frequent and obvious merriment of these monks, I have wondered whether the Buddha's message is indeed about

the world being full of pain and sorrow; or perhaps, the Enlightened One has left a secret message for his monks, a cosmic joke which never palls with any number of re-tellings, which makes them laugh so much. (2000, p. 157)

The Buddha's message is, of course, that the world is indeed "full of pain and sorrow," and he left no "secret message." The monks are not in on some "cosmic joke," or avoiding the darkness, evil, and imperfections of the world; indeed, a common Buddhist theme upon which to meditate is some fact of suffering, like one's own death. Monks are perhaps "perpetually cheerful" and "laugh so much" not "in spite of a life devoted to meditation, prayer and books," but because of it. The logic of this, however, necessarily transcends that of the ego.

Let me make the point a second way, trying a little thought experiment using history. Imagine it is 2000 years ago, putting us around the year 18 CE. The Roman Emperor is Tiberius, recently ascended to the throne after the death of Caesar Augustus a few years earlier. Tiberius, well aware that the Roman Empire has been an empire for less than 50 years and the Pax Romana around for even less than that, convenes a gathering of the best minds. He aims to solicit their best guesses on how long the peace and the Empire will last, as well as gather proposals on what will be the most decisive factors for both the near and far future of world history. We can imagine the debates and discussion, on the role of the emperor, of the Roman political, legal, and administrative system; we can surmise emphasis on the military might of the Roman army, its navy, its superior technology and tactics, the potential threat posed by neighboring empires, some discussion of barbarians and slaves. At a stretch, we can even imagine the Romans being willing to examine outrageous proposals that strained credibility about the role of the slaves in world history, or the barbarians, or the various conquered provinces. One such outrageous proposal is presented by the Third Prefect of Judaea Valerius Gratus (he will be succeeded by Pontius Pilate), discussing the belief of some of the Jews in the coming of a messiah who would overthrow the Romans. Valerius finishes his presentation describing some genuine would-be messiahs he has witnessed wandering around the land preaching wildly about "the kingdom of heaven," "turning the other cheek," "loving one's enemies," and other such wild and ludicrous claims.

Admit that, in this little thought experiment, even if you've stretched with me this far, we cannot stretch any further and realistically imagine the Romans taking this outrageous proposal seriously. Is there any possible chance that one of these so-called messiahs, a young, poor, carpenter's son, who has gathered a small group of fishermen-cum-disciples around him, will play a decisive role in history? A role intertwined with, but eventually proving even more decisive than, the role the Roman Empire, its army, or its Caesar will play? Any chance that he would found a religion that would transform the Empire and outgrow and outlast it? From the rational point of view of the ego, which views the world through the lenses of power, no. (And admit further that, in the present, when you hear news of ecological catastrophes, or of international wars, or of rumors of wars, you place a considerable amount of your hope, in the "powers that be." Surely, it is the USA, or the European Union, or the United Nations, our technology or our military or our governments, or perhaps cutting-edge research, big corporations, and transnational organizations like the IMF or World Bank, wherein our only realistic, effective hope lies?)

The aim of this little thought experiment is to show up the difference between the scale of power and the scale of spirit. There is simply no way the Romans could have predicted that in only a few centuries, the Empire itself would convert to Christianity, or that Christianity would go on two millennia later to have over two billion adherents. Our imagined Roman thinkers would not be entirely wrong, of course: The Roman Empire does play a potent role in history, and that it was as powerful as it was for as long as it was is key to understanding Christianity, as well as Europe, the West, and world history. That they would not even have known of Jesus, or in the cases in which they did, would not have considered him important, is entirely understandable and rational. We are no different in these respects from the Romans. Therefore, we should take note: They would be proven by history to be spectacularly wrong. That Paul's advocating of hoping against hope (in his letter to, ahem, the Romans) proves vindicated by history is not something anyone could have known or predicted.

My point is not some argument for God or divine intervention or miracles or a supernatural interpretation of history or anything like that. Neither am I arguing, as David Nicol (2015) does in his book *Subtle Activism*, who also appeals to the importance of spiritual practices to address our contemporary problems, that there is a mystical efficaciousness of spiritual consciousness to subtly effect change and positive transformation. I am proceeding on far more empirical and historical assumptions about the place, role, and effectiveness of spiritual practices. The point I am trying to make is that history unfolds unpredictably, mysteriously, and surprisingly and involves many more empirical factors in addition to power. In this existential fact resides, I think, considerable grounds for hope—grounds different than those of "big power" to which we, just like the Romans, "naturally" (i.e., egocentrically) turn. An eloquent and compelling argument illustrating this point, using numerous examples of the recent social movements, global activism, and populist and grassroots successes, is made by Rebecca Solnit (2016) in her *Hope in the Dark: Untold Histories, Wild Possibilities*. "Ideas at first considered outrageous or ridiculous or extreme gradually become what people think they've always believed. How the transformation happened is rarely remembered… our hope is in the dark around the edges, not the limelight of center stage" (p. xvi). History does not turn out the way a view too focused on what is currently powerful can predict. What happens in history is often unexpected and surprising, and ideas, individuals, or movements that seemed marginal and anomalous can become dominant and central. This fact of history is utterly indispensable to remember and to inform our own perceptions of the meaning of our contemporary world in crisis, for hoping against hope that all is not lost and that we are not too late. Analogously, the influence of the Axial Age spiritual *virtuosi* on world history was also unexpected, surprising, and could not have been predicted. It seems to me that history amply bears out Kallistos Ware's (1998) observation: "Often it is precisely the men and women of inner stillness – not the activists but the contemplatives, fired by a consuming passion for solitude – who in practice bring about the most far-reaching alterations in the society around them" (p. 6). It was not only Jesus who accomplished such a marvel: A similar story could be told of figures like Socrates or Isaiah or Confucius or the Buddha in terms of their historical influence, and how incongruous that influence appears relative to the incredible power of their surrounding empires.

On my reading, the Axial Age was a time period in history when human power scaled up in an unprecedented and disturbing manner. The advent of this new scale of power has since proved decisive for the unfolding of world history. It also motivated responses from Axial Age visionaries at that time, responses that also became woven into the fabric of that world history. Their responses were spiritual ones that focused on the moral and ethical crises the new scale of power had created, and which proclaimed a way of salvation for the spirit that would redeem and overcome the evils of the world. Today, human power has scaled up again to a new unprecedented and disturbing level, globally altering the climate, simmering with the threat of global conflict, and provoking end-of-the-world scenarios that are as rationally and empirically plausible as they are anxiety-inciting and despair-provoking. Are the responses of the Axial Age "wise guys" relevant to today and for our world in crisis? Do they provide a potential way to help save us from ourselves? Can they help us to achieve sustainable, nonviolent ways of living on the Earth together? I believe they do, although I confess that in believing this I am not offering a prediction, but hoping against hope, sharing it with you, and leaving you to decide on where you stand for yourself.

References

Armstrong, K. (2006). *The great transformation: The beginning of our religious traditions*. New York and Toronto: Alfred A. Knopf.

Baskin, K., & Bondarenko, D. (2014). *The Axial Ages of world history: Lessons for the 21st century*. Litchfield Park, AZ: Emergent Publishing.

Bellah, R. (2011). *Religion in human evolution: From the Paleolithic to the Axial Age*. Harvard, MA: Belknap.

Bellah, R., & Joas, H. (2012). Introduction. In R. Bellah & H. Joas (Eds.), *The Axial Age and its consequences* (pp. 1–6). Belknap: Cambridge and London.

Fraade, S. (1986). Ascetical aspects of ancient Judaism. In A. Green (Ed.), *Jewish spirituality: From the Bible through the Middle Ages* (pp. 253–288). New York: Crossroad.

Gardner, G. (2002). *Invoking the spirit: Religion and spirituality in the quest for a sustainable world*. Washington, DC: Worldwatch Institute.

Halton, E. (2014). *From the Axial Age to the moral revolution*. Basingstoke: Palgrave Macmillan.

Hamilton, C. (2010). *Requiem for a species: Why we resist the truth about climate change*. London and Washington, DC: Earthscan.

Jaspers, K. (1953). *The origin and goal of history*. New Haven and London: Yale University Press (originally published in 1949).

Joas, H. (2012). The Axial Age debate as religious discourse. In R. Bellah & H. Joas (Eds.), *The Axial Age and its consequences* (pp. 9–29). Cambridge and London: Belknap.

Kakar, S. (2000). *The ascetic of desire: A novel of the Kama Sutra*. New York: Harry Abrams.

Masuzawa, T. (2005). *The invention of world religions*. Chicago: University of Chicago.

Momigliano, A. (1975). *Alien wisdom: The limits of hellenization*. Cambridge: Cambridge University Press.

Nicol, D. (2015). *Subtle activism: The inner dimension of social and planetary transformation*. Albany: State University of New York Press.

Partridge, C. (2005). *Introduction to world religions*. Minneapolis: Fortress Press.

Runciman, W. (2012). Righteous rebels: When, where, and why? In R. Bellah & H. Joas (Eds.), *The Axial Age and its consequences* (pp. 317–334). Belknap: Cambridge and London.

Schwartz, B. (Ed.). (1975). Wisdom, revelation, and doubt: Perspectives on the first millennium B.C. *Special Issue of Daedalus, 104*(2), 1–7.

Solnit, R. (2016). *Hope in the dark: Untold histories, wild possibilities*. Chicago, IL: Haymarket Books.

Stuart-Glennie, J. (1873). *In the Morningland or the law of the origin and transformation of Christianity, Volume 1: The new philosophy of history, and the origin of the doctrines of Christianity*. London: Longmans.

Voegelin, E. (1957). *Order and History, Vol. II: The world of the polis*. Baton Rouge: Louisiana State University Press.

Voegelin, E. (1974). *Order and History, Vol. IV: The ecumenic age*. Baton Rouge: Louisiana State University Press.

Ware, K. (1998). The way of the ascetics: Negative or affirmative? In V. Wimbush & R. Valantasis (Eds.), *Asceticism* (pp. 3–15). New York: Oxford University Press.

Wattles, J. (1996). *The golden rule*. New York: Oxford University Press.

Wimbush, V., & Valantasis, R. (1998). Introduction. In V. Wimbush & R. Valantasis (Eds.), *Asceticism* (pp. xix–xxxiii). New York: Oxford University Press.

CHAPTER 2

World in Crisis

Before we engage in detail the thesis of the Axial Age as proposed by Karl Jaspers, look at its world-historical context, its particular sociological manifestations, and its distinctive contributions, as we will do in the remaining chapters, we need to get some grip on our present moment, and the unprecedented fact of how our world is in crisis, in this chapter. While I lay a lot of emphasis on it being historically unprecedented, and the shape of the present being due to history, this should not be understood as some kind of "unnatural" human deviation. Indeed, the opposite: The present as a historical outcome proves predicated upon deeper natural, evolutionary process. We human beings, and our history, are an outgrowth of evolution and processes like natural selection. Here is an excerpt from Charles Darwin's (2001) description of the latter in *On the Origin of Species*:

> ...the struggle for the production of new and modified descendants, will mainly lie between the larger groups, which are all trying to increase in number. One large group will slowly conquer another large group, reduce its numbers, and thus lessen its chance of further variation and improvement. Within the same large group, the later and more highly perfected sub-groups, from branching out and seizing on many new places in the polity of Nature, will constantly tend to supplant and destroy the earlier and less improved sub-groups. Small and broken groups and sub-groups will finally tend to disappear. Looking to the future, we can predict that the groups of organic beings which are now large and triumphant, and

which are least broken up, that is, which as yet have suffered least extinction, will for a long period continue to increase. (pp. 118–119)

Most obviously, human beings have become "one large group," if not the largest, on the earth. Within that large group, the increasing, conquering, and reducing of sub-groups, is an indisputable, and violent, fact of our history, while simultaneously the "branching out and seizing on many new places" means the earth has become filled with humans into every nook and cranny. It is due to the global scale attained by these two facets and thus their corresponding potential scale for destruction that has led to our world being in crisis.

WORLD IN CRISIS

Let us briefly return to Olivia's story and her tears. I concluded the story emphasizing that we need to face our world in crisis; we need to take responsibility for how the world is and where it appears to be heading. But who are the "we" who must take responsibility? Initially, one could say, as I did in the previous chapter: "we" means all human beings or universal humanity. Within that characterization, of course, are many who cannot take the kind of responsibility needed, nor should we expect it of them, children like Olivia, for example. Different, but analogous, would be those deprived of power by their circumstances, for whom immediate needs, whether food, shelter, or safety, rightly loom foremost. Before those with power, security, affluence, and leisure can demand any responsibility from the poor, the disenfranchised, the oppressed, or the refugee, at the very least they have to demonstrate it themselves. My arguments in this book are aimed at those who are trying to consciously confront the plausibility of the end of the world happening in our lifetimes. Those who are able and willing to face that the world is in crisis, and this will be a fact for the duration of our lives that needs to be faced honestly and courageously, know that this will demand the utmost of our rational and empirical abilities (that is, our science, technology, and philosophy) as well as the utmost of our spiritual, moral, and ethical abilities (that is, our courage and our capacity to believe and to hope; much of which is tied into the powerful resources embodied within world religions, and historically behind those, within Axial spiritualities). This demand is further complicated, as it has been our science, technology, philosophy, religion, and spirituality that have also been central contributors to our world's being in crisis. Let's not underestimate how difficult this demand is, for any of us. Humanity is facing its ultimate test in the twenty-first century. Many articulate and educated persons are bearing passionate witness to this perception. World-renowned naturalist David Attenborough, addressing the United Nations Conference on Climate Change in December 2018, put it this way: "The collapse of our civilizations and the extinction of much of the natural world is on the horizon."

A key piece to what makes this test so "ultimate" is that our contemporary world situation, when taken as a whole, is unprecedented. It is unprecedented in evolutionary terms and in historical terms. That the world within the last century has become thoroughly interconnected into a single world-system through technology is unprecedented. A human population of seven billion alongside the rate of population growth are both unprecedented. The visible outcome of our collective human impact upon the earth in terms of effecting global climate change and a mass extinction of species is unprecedented. That we *homo sapiens* have a sufficient degree of sapience that we are consciously aware that "the collapse of our civilizations is on the horizon" is unprecedented. That we are consciously aware that our world is in crisis, and that it is unprecedented, is unprecedented! All of these together, taken as parts of a single whole, add up to the historical and evolutionary fact that the present moment of our world in crisis has no precedent.

I'd advise you to please, let yourself sit with these claims. For at least a moment.

…

Acknowledging that our contemporary world situation when taken *as a whole* is unprecedented should not mislead us into overlooking the precedents for *parts* of our current situation. These are indispensable for helping us to understand the present. There are precedents for the emergence of world-systems through advancements in technology. There are precedents for explosive population growth, for the human extinction of species en masse, and for global mass extinction events. There are precedents for societies collapsing, for societies facing ecological crises, for people perceiving that "this is the end of the world," and for the anxieties evoked by such an end-of-the-world perception. And of course I'm arguing the Axial Age is the precedent for our contemporary world in crisis.

Acknowledging such precedents is strategic, for helping us to gain perspective on the present moment. Another stratagem is to identify some of the key aspects of our unprecedented present moment which illuminate its shape, and a third is to simplify the many components of our world in crisis by identifying which are overarching and that take priority. The aim of this chapter is to gain some clarity about what we mean by "the world" and how it is unprecedented by sketching out the shape of the present in terms of key aspects and priorities.

THE SHAPE OF THE PRESENT: KEY ASPECTS

One key aspect to the world in the present has already been named: It is a world in crisis. It is not a world in decline, or at ease, neither nostalgically looking back at greatness nor looking optimistically forward to a golden future.

A second key aspect of what gives the present its shape in contemporary terms, also already named, is its interconnectedness. This is both the long slow outcome of historical process and in the last century the rapid outcome of technology. The interconnection of the different worlds of peoples mean we cannot consider them in isolation from each other, nor the particular crisis of any particular world in isolation from the whole: They have all come together, not into a singular homogeneous mass, but into one, complex, global, world-system. I do not agree with those who argue that contemporary end-of-the-world scenarios reflect a specifically Western concern due to the perceived demise of Western power and dominance. This view underestimates the fact and significance of global interconnectedness.

The third key aspect that follows from the fact of interconnectedness is globalization. While the interconnecting of the globe into a single world-system is above all through technology, globalizing is its cultural correlate. Different peoples and cultures have been brought—forced?—closer together. Whether war, genocide, and "ethnic cleansing," or trade and tourism; whether refugee crises, illegal immigrants, and trafficking, or the Olympics, the World Cup, and world music, as our world is globalizing, what different peoples (ethnicities, religions, nation-states, subcultures, and civilizations; and cutting edge scientists, technologists, and futurists) consider ultimately meaningful come into contact with each other. Cultures have different worldviews its members think with and live by. That these worldviews differ and include within themselves conceptions involving what people consider ultimate, this meeting of different cultures and worldviews is best described, initially at least, as a clash. As this chapter will expand, there are different meanings to what a culture considers "the world," depending on what we consider ultimately meaningful. Globalization means that many different worlds, formerly somewhat autonomous or "far apart," are now thrown together. They clash. In fact, I consider this manifestation of globalization its most significant meaning, and in this respect, globalization or a clash of ultimates are interchangeable ways of describing this key aspect of the present.

The focus on globalization as a clash of ultimates also asserts something about the shape of the present that is historically new and different from the nineteenth and twentieth centuries and from "modernization": The world is not dominated by a specific power, or particular process, or central conflict. This is not the story of "the West," of Europe, or of America; not the story of a singular process of modernization that leaves all traditions behind or of a singular process of secularization that leaves all religions behind; not the story of the Cold War, or the New Age, or the "new world order": The current world is a story of multiple actors, multiple voices, multiple traditions, multiple viewpoints, and multiple civilizations. This extends beyond the present. If the world does not come to an end, the future is up for grabs, from a plurality of potential centers of power and from multiple civilizational perspectives, and thus, the clash of ultimates in the present will crucially shape our future. Eisenstadt's (2000) phrase "multiple modernities" captures this key aspect of the present: Modernization is the historical process that becomes globalization, with the post-Cold War difference that we are realizing the radically distributed and decentralized multiplicity of this "process" (rather than it being a distinctively and singularly Western development exported to the rest of the world).

These four key aspects that help to roughly sketch some of the shape of the present, then, are: first, that the world is in crisis; second, that it is an interconnected world and interconnection dominates over isolation and autonomy; third, that globalization means that different conceptions of what is ultimately meaningful clash, and thus, we must attend to the fact of this clash of ultimates; and fourth, that there is no singular, central power driving the current historical processes of interconnection, globalization, and crisis, but that there are multiple processes of modernization, that is, multiple modernities. We could add a fifth key aspect, also already named, but which summarizes the shape of the present taken as a whole: Our present moment is unprecedented.

THE SHAPE OF THE PRESENT: PRIORITIZING CRISIS

In addition to identifying precedents for and key aspects of the present, identifying priorities within our world in crisis is another part of my discursive strategy in this chapter. Since the world in crisis has many different levels, dimensions, and aspects (or is a "global megacrisis" [Halal & Marien, 2011] of all the various crises of the world combined), prioritizing those that are most important, for example, as overarching or encompassing, or as most basic or causal, is a way to fruitfully understand it. The prioritizing strategy I'm following in this book: The numerous possible types of crisis—economic, political, societal, ethical, ecological, the energy crisis, etc.—are reducible to two overarching categories: ecological and political. By overarching, I mean all the other crises can be subsumed under and understood as subsets of the ecological and political crises. Ethnic conflicts and the threat of assimilation of a smaller society by a larger society can be subsumed under the political. Societal collapse scenarios, for example, depend fundamentally on political choices. Or for example economics can to a great extent be subsumed under the political, until at a certain point it gives way and can be understood as subsumed under the ecological. The political and ecological are separable insofar as they have different foci, although they are also pervasively intertwined.

The ecological crisis has as its central focus the relation of humans to the natural world; more specifically, the facts of collective human impact on the globe; our collective "ecological footprint" (Rees, 1992). Global climate change, the extinction rates of species, carbon production, habitat destruction, ecosystem collapse, resource depletion, pollution levels, ocean acidification, and more are all evidence of this impact. At the heart of the problem, and therefore too the solution, are our practices of consumption. Levels of resource depletion, habitat destruction, waste production, and so on all depend on consumption practices. Note this means human population in itself is not the problem. North America has a disproportionately high impact on the environment not because of its population but because of its high levels of consumption (as does Europe and the "rich parts" of Asia). A common illustration used to make this point is that if everyone followed North American consumption practices, we would need four (or five?) Earths to support the human population. Addressing the ecological crisis will require moving from our current destructively high levels of consumption that have become normal for affluent society toward lower and more sustainable levels of consumption, levels that are closer to the more ascetic side of the spectrum.

Key to understanding the ecological crisis is appreciating the interconnectedness of the ecological systems of the Earth. While myths and later philosophies and metaphysics around the world and throughout history have often expressed metaphorically and poetically, this theme of interconnection, the dynamic power of modern society, whether in its science, its technology, or its industry, has been at odds with such holistic treatment. It is only in the last decades of the twentieth century with the growing awareness of global climate change and widespread environmental destruction that ecological interconnectedness has demanded serious scientific attention. Perhaps, in part, we have also come to realize the importance of this because through technology we have culturally, economically, and politically become interconnected ourselves within a single world-system of human making.

Above, I redescribed globalization as a clash of ultimates instead, as the latter phrase better captures the significance of how we are experiencing globalization. This redescription can be applied ecologically, too, which translates our ecological crisis into different terms: the fact of very different, and ultimately clashing, values being assigned to the environment than those built into a people's way of life. A people's way of life unavoidably assumes a certain level of consumption, a certain distribution of resources, and some size of ecological footprint. This distribution is managed, that is, that way of life has an economy. The economic model will stipulate what are the minimum standards for the quality of that way of life. Particular economic values define "quality of life," set the "standards," and establish what level counts as "minimum." Running throughout all of this description are values considered ultimate.

The way of life lived by a minority and aspired to by a majority of peoples today assumes a specific economic model usually dependent on industrial production in turn dependent on nonrenewable resources, which is proving to constitute an unsustainably high level of consumption. Due to this unsustainably high level, particular ecological limits are reached, thresholds are passed, and capacities are exceeded. For example, Rockström et al. (2009) describe "planetary boundaries" in terms of a "safe operating space" for humanity and note that the thresholds of three of the proposed nine categories have been exceeded. But the language of ecological limits, thresholds, and capacities, which could be extended to include critical masses, tipping points, ecosystem collapses, and species extinctions, is a terminology of ultimates: ecological ultimates. Human economic systems, because of the ultimate values implicitly built into them as to what constitutes quality of life by humans culturally, clash with earthly ecosystems, because of the ultimates naturally built into the latter ecologically. The "ultimacy" built into a particular economics in terms of what is considered the "bottom line," or "basic," or "non-negotiable" plays out in the form of a people's way of life, that is, now meeting the ultimate limits of a finite planet with finite resources. The ecological crisis is a clash of ultimates. This extends yet further, as how the ecological crisis is interpreted depends on one's ultimate beliefs. Perhaps most well known here is the clash between climate scientists and a significant percentage of evangelical Christians in the USA who deny the reality of climate change.

The second overarching category for world crisis is political. While in the broadest possible terms the focus of politics is the relations of people to people—which distinguishes it from the ecological focus on the relations of people to nature—it is more specifically about the exercise of power. In terms of trying to "prioritize" among the many aspects of the world in crisis, I understand all the social crises in the world as ultimately reducible to the political category. Societal collapse scenarios, for example, depend fundamentally on political choices. In terms of the exercises of power, the state as a political unit is definable in terms of the monopolies on power it assumes for itself: a monopoly on violence, or a monopoly on taxation, or a monopoly on particular resources, sovereign control over a territory, autonomy within its borders, and so on. But the new reality of interconnection erodes and undermines monopoly, sovereignty, and autonomy and exposes these understandings as issuing from older political realities that perhaps no longer obtain. In this political respect, the interconnectedness of all the peoples of the globe—the ancient understanding that the Earth is one—is indeed unprecedented and demands to be understood.

The political implications of this interconnectedness and its undermining of traditional politics we have seen manifest in all kinds of peaceful ways over the last couple centuries, but we have also seen, and continue to see, the dangers of conflict. World War II was a truly global war; the Cold War threat of "mutually assured destruction" presented the possibility of nuclear destruction on a global scale. The potential for either of these remains. Indeed, military technology has developed beyond what was available in the 1940s; nuclear capacity, the efficacy of and availability of weapons of mass destruction, and biological and chemical weapon capacity have all increased. Far beyond World War II, destructive capacity is in the possession of more nations and states than ever before. Incomparable to World War II, destructive capacity is also in the possession of groups, both intra-national and also internationally networked, that are much smaller than nations (most obviously, I'm referring to terrorists and extremist groups). Add to all of the above: World population has approximately tripled (to seven billion plus) since the 1940s population of around two and a half billion. In short: The potential for conflict, violence, and destruction, manifesting at a global scale, is unprecedented.

These political potentials considered in the context of ecological crisis and population growth—conflicts over energy, conflicts over resources, and conflicts over international responses to shared crisis—will only be exacerbated, as the ecological crisis means, among other things, a dwindling supply of (conventional) resources, while population growth means, among other things, increased demand for resources. The key aspects to the shape of the present, of interconnection, a globalization that manifests as a clash of ultimates, and multiple modernities all complexly interrelate within contribute to world crisis. The latter can be reduced to a political crisis and an ecological crisis. These are analytically separable but empirically inseparable. The political crisis is something we are "in," in the sense of potential: if a spark sets off a global conflict... The ecological crisis, we are "in," as it is happening in the present. But we are also in it in the sense of potential, too. The demand confronting us ecologically is concerted action, now, to minimize our impacts, to minimize the extent of global climate change and global temperature increase, to conserve species and to protect habitat and resources, and to prevent the full scale destructive potentials of global climate change and mass extinction of species that we are observing and near-future scenarios that we can plausibly predict. Thus, we need to examine both of these in turn in some more detail.

GLOBAL POLITICAL CRISIS: CLASH OF ULTIMATES OR CLASH OF CIVILIZATIONS?

The precedent for the clash of ultimates as potential violent conflict between peoples can be found anytime in our evolution or history: whenever there has been conflict or war between different groups. More specifically, however, the precedent for violent conflict on a global level is World War II, the first truly global war. That it was followed by the Cold War, and others like the Gulf War (1990–1991), 9/11 (in 2001), the Iraq war (2003–2011), and the Syrian crisis (2011–present) show that political tensions show no signs of abating, and World War III is, indeed, a highly plausible prediction.

Perhaps the most well-known theorist who has speculated on this potential for future international conflict in the wake of the Cold War—notably, *not* to abate this potential but to guide American policy on how to navigate it—is Samuel Huntington. His thesis was formulated in terms of a "clash of civilizations" (1993, 1996), a phrasing that frequently recurs in media coverage and which has occasionally found its way into the speeches of American Presidents. (Notably, utilized quite differently; President Bush used the phrase post 9/11 to garner support for the "war on terror," while President Obama cited the phrase as being divisive, simplistic, and inflammatory rhetoric vis-à-vis US-Islam relations.) In short, Huntington's thesis is a well-known reference point to use for the contemporary political situation of our world. Huntington's phrasing foregrounds an obvious analogy to my notion of a clash of ultimates. There are indeed a few significant similarities between Huntington's view and my own. A more thorough comparison will show that there are more differences between our views than there are similarities and that the differences are more significant; in short, Huntington's thesis of a clash of civilizations presents an ideal foil to my own argument.

Huntington proposed in the 1990s that we were entering a new, i.e., post-Cold War, world order defined by a clash of civilizations. By direct analogy to the Cold War between the USA and the USSR as the two global superpowers, Huntington envisioned a more pronounced version of conflict writ much larger than nation-states or superpowers, instead as larger nation-state coalitions or blocs. In post-Cold War times, the unit of identity for these blocs becomes civilizations. Huntington proposes "seven or eight," namely Western; Latin American; Orthodox (referring to Eastern Orthodox Christianity); Islamic; Hindu; Sinic (referring to Chinese); Japanese; and "maybe" an eighth African. Huntington leaves out Judaism: "in terms of numbers of people Judaism clearly is not a major civilization" (1996, p. 48, note). He also leaves out Buddhism arguing that "although a major religion, [it] has not been the basis of major civilization" (1996, p. 48), but includes it on his "World of civilizations: Post-1990" map. (Note that if we utilize his map which includes Buddhism as a mapping of "civilizational identity," seven of the nine civilizations Huntington proposes are products of the Axial Age, a proposal similar to Chapter 1's rough approximation of 75–95% of the world thinking or believing in Axial terms.) These civilizational blocs have correspondingly larger populations and territories than nation-states. He argued that while in the Cold War political identity was ideologically attached to the nation-state, post-Cold War political identity would be culturally attached to one's civilization:

> A civilization is thus the highest cultural grouping of people and the broadest level of cultural identity people have short of that which distinguishes humans from other species. It is defined both by common objective elements, such as language, history, religion, customs, institutions, and by the subjective self-identification of people. (1996, p. 43)

In distinction from a lot of other political theory, which might emphasize economic, geographic, or ideological factors, Huntington laudably pays attention to the importance of cultural factors. In characterizing culture, Huntington listed its "objective elements" like language, religion, customs, and institutions, after which he added "subjective self-identification." Again, Huntington's attention to identity is laudable, because like culture it has been underemphasized by political theorists. Identity is important culturally, for sure, in terms of ethnicity; there is also religious identity, gender identity, citizenship, and so on. As Huntington says, "People have levels of identity" (1996, p. 43). In fact, his entire civilizational argument turns on the importance of identity: "The civilization to which he belongs is the broadest level of identification with which he strongly identifies" (1996, p. 43). In turn, his entire historical argument rests on the importance of civilizations. Huntington claims "Human history is the history of civilizations. It is impossible to think of the development of humanity in any other terms" (1996, p. 40). In advancing this latter claim, Huntington relies on perhaps the pre-eminent historian of the twentieth century, Fernand Braudel, who says in his *On History* (1980):

> …as far as anyone interested in the contemporary world is concerned, and even more so with regard to anyone wishing to act within it, it 'pays' to know how to make out, on a map of the world, which civilizations exist

today, to be able to define their borders, their centers and peripheries, their provinces and the air one breathes there, the general and particular 'forms' existing and associating within them. Otherwise, what catastrophic blunders of perspective could ensue! (pp. 210–211)

Braudel's work as a historian has substantially elaborated this claim in the work cited and in others like his *A History of Civilizations* (1994). (Braudel's work in this respect, encapsulated in the quote just cited, was one of two substantial inspirations for my own choice of the map metaphor for the Axial Age. The second was David Christian's [2005] "big history" masterpiece, *Maps of Time.*) This Braudel quote is an inspiration shared with Huntington (he too cites this quotation [1996, p. 36]), for he also relies on the importance of having a map. In fact for Huntington, the map did most of the heavy lifting for his thesis. In terms of the picture Huntington had sketched about civilizational identity, the emphasis on a map would seem to make good sense. Huntington provides a map comparing the post-Cold War civilizational distribution to that of the Cold War and pre-World Wars globe and lays out his rationale for the "clash of civilizations" thesis as being precisely to provide a new map of the globe to understand international politics. A map simplifies and hence distorts to some extent, but in selecting out particular features from the complexity, it can be an invaluable shorthand.

All of these aspects of Huntington's thesis—his emphasis on culture and identity, on the importance of civilizations for understanding world history, and the helpfulness of a map—should be evident in my argument, too. A signal contribution of the Axial Age was to propose a transcendent locus of identification, with the consequence the founding of civilizational traditions whose boundaries for cultural identity transcended those previously identified with kinship, with ethnicity, with region, or with the state, and became the new broadest level of identity possible. To the extent that Huntington's map of the contemporary world works to define human cultural identities at the civilizational level, "it is impossible to think of the development" of this map without reference to the Axial Age.

So far, so similar. Further comparison, however, shows greater and greater differences and disagreements between our two approaches. The most significant difference involves how we understand the political level as relating to the cultural-civilizational-identity level and thus too how we understand the different importance of a map. The vice "civilization" as a category has, which Huntington seemed to consider a virtue, is that it provides sweeping generalizations like "the West" over against, say, "Islam." (Note that good criticism of Huntington's thesis has pointed out that its primary purpose is to provide a rationalization of "the West vs. Islam" thinking [Said, 1997].) It's not that sweeping generalizations are necessarily wrong or bad; like a good map, they can be very helpful for getting a handle on complex territory. If looking at lengthy swaths of history, some sweeping generalizations are probably necessary. But, in every case it is only a starting point that precedes more particulate, detailed description; it is not a basis for prediction, for planning, for understanding, and for distinguishing what is important from what is unimportant. It is certainly not a basis for action, nor is it accurate for specifying.

Civilizations in the sense Huntington, Braudel, and I are using the word are historically derived psychological identifications with a type of cultural level. They are *not* geographic *or* political realities. It is at precisely this very general level that I am discussing the great world religions/civilizations and their roots in the Axial Age. But I don't think you can, or should, draw any political implications from this, as the strength of the identification is not political, but historical and cultural and psychological. These aspects of civilizations in defining broad macro-cultural identities could be argued to be an indispensable preface before conducting detailed, particulate analysis at an appropriate level of political specificity. Huntington however seems to take what I'd call the prefatory description as doing the work of political analysis. It doesn't, just as the civilizational map should not be interpreted as a political map. It isn't! In doing so, Huntington's argument moves from very debatable to downright wrong and dangerously misleading. If we look at his clash of civilizations thesis in his own words, I think it becomes clear:

> It is my hypothesis that the fundamental source of conflict in this new world will not be primarily ideological or primarily economic. The great divisions among humankind and the dominating source of conflict will be cultural. Nation states will remain the most powerful actors in world affairs, but the principal conflicts of global politics will occur between nations and groups of different civilizations. The clash of civilizations will dominate global politics. The fault lines between civilizations will be the battle lines of the future. (1993, p. 22)

The invocation of "fault lines" by Huntington is as suggestive an image as it is downright wrong. Accepting this image entails thinking of civilizations as fated to clash when they meet, like tectonic plates that cause earthquakes and terrible destruction when they grind up against each other. And this fits Huntington's map of the globalizing post-Cold War World, as his entire hypothesis is presented here in stark terms of unavoidable conflict. Huntington's entire thesis could be boiled down to this one predictive claim that "The local conflicts *most likely to escalate* into broader wars are those between groups and states from different civilizations" (1996, p. 29, emphasis added). In paying attention to local conflict (which will certainly happen) and especially to their potential for escalation as allies and enemies and neutrals attend fearfully or opportunistically around these (which potential is, in our globalizing interconnected world, the great danger), Huntington is surely correct. In claiming that these conflicts will "most likely" escalate into civilizations clashing, he is not. This dangerously misleading attempt to simplify the historical-cultural heritage of civilizations (along with all the complex psychology evoked in person's identifications with and belonging to those heritages), into overgeneralized categories so as to do the political work of rationalizing and justifying divisive ideologies and particular interests, is exactly how the "clash of ultimates" description in this book is *not* to be interpreted. Huntington assumes, endorses, and furthers the issue that I call tribalism. With the only difference from the past is that today tribalism is writ globally large. And the tribes are equipped with weapons of mass destruction. What is, in evolutionary psychology terms, one of our most basic and primitive and hence emotionally powerful needs, for the ego to identify with the group or tribe, is joined to one of humanity's most cognitively advanced and scientifically sophisticated achievements: modern technology. The combination is lethal, to the point of endangering the world.

In this latter respect of reinscribing tribalism within modern politics, the "clash of civilizations" thesis presents an interpretation of how our world in crisis might go into international violent conflict on a large scale, with the potential to become a World War III divided along "civilizational" lines. Unfortunately, I cannot deny this potential as possible, nor therefore that this interpretation is plausible. It is. But it is precisely because of this possibility and its plausibility that we should feel an imperative force to face it, prevent it, identify and overcome the tribalist thinking that motivates it, and seek alternatives. In this respect,

Huntington's argument is an ideal foil for my own, as the fact of a clash of ultimates between different cultures and civilizations raises into consciousness just what is at stake beyond the survival of my culture, my civilization, and my worldview: the survival of something of intrinsic value beyond my egocentric valuations, and this is the survival of human, historical ethnodiversity.

I am arguing for this alternative in the following terms: A spiritual interpretation of the cultural potential of civilizations based on the historical importance of the Axial Age assists in steering our tribalist potential for violence through escalation of conflict into a very different direction. Like the visionaries of the Axial Age, I am opposed to tribalism in favor of universal humanity. And like those luminaries, I am not advancing a political argument, but a spiritual one—one that has, however, momentous political consequences. On this spiritual reading of tribal difference, the ultimate meaning of the multi-ethnic, multi-national, and multi-civilizational configuration of human cultures that have evolved across the globe is that of a nonviolent ideal of a deep and rich ethnodiversity that we ought to preserve, celebrate, and enhance. (In the chapters ahead, we will see how the Axial Age interpretation provides an alternative to Huntington's tribalist thinking. Jaspers in Chapter 3 will propose a new kind of universal ideal that understands the fact of difference positively, as promoting an "ideal of boundless communication." Shmuel Eisenstadt in Chapter 5 will suggest a different way of understanding our multi-civilizational heritage as rooted in the Axial Age, as instead the unfolding of "multiple modernities" drawing upon deep historical resources articulated within their traditions that provide civilizationally specific dynamisms for meeting the challenges of the contemporary world.)

PRECEDENT FOR THE GLOBAL ECOLOGICAL CRISIS: MASS EXTINCTION EVENTS

When we turn to the global ecological crisis, we adopt a very different time scale than that of recent history. In evolutionary perspective, what the world is currently undergoing ecologically is *not* unprecedented. This fact is hugely significant! If our ecological crisis was utterly unprecedented, we could indeed postulate some abominable mutation in human being that runs entirely contrary to nature, we should feel crippling guilt, and perhaps we should join the "Voluntary Human Extinction Movement" (which endorses the voluntary self-extinction of the human race for the sake of nature [!]). But global climate change and a mass extinction of species are not an unprecedented case if we look at the record from natural history. Nature is no providential order aiming at harmonious equilibria, but capable of cruel destruction many degrees of order greater than what humans have ever achieved. The significance of this claim is potent, I think, in particular for all those who romanticize or wish to see in nature some divine, loving, or healing presence (cf. Taylor, 2010). This romanticizing is evident for example in images like Mother Nature as caring, or Mother Earth holding us in her loving embrace, or Gaia as our womb-sweet-home. Yes, we can be blessed with sweetness and light in the course of our lives, and yes, the Earth is a beautiful and extraordinary jewel to be treasured, and yes, it is our home. But this is cherry-picking our evidence from only one half of the story. We need to consider and take seriously the other half of the story, too.

Periodically recurring drastic changes in global climate appear to cause "mass extinction events": High rate of species extinction and massive biodiversity loss across a geographically wide range of the globe in a short time period (short by evolutionary and geological timescales, which are measured in the tens to hundreds of millions of years). Mass extinction events have occurred regularly throughout Earth's evolutionary history. To be precise: With some exceptions, approximately every 26 million years there is a mass extinction event (Raup & Sepkoski, 1982, 1984). The cause of this periodical mass extinction pattern is unknown. Or, to say this somewhat differently, although global climate change seems to be the common causal factor behind mass extinctions, it's not known what causes the climate change. (Eldredge [1991] emphasizes habitat loss in tandem with climate changes.) The one exception to the causal uncertainty question is also the most well-known extinction event: The dinosaur extinction is due to a massive asteroid impact that caused the climate change.

After the extinction event has happened, and the earth re-establishes some new climate equilibrium, life reasserts itself and, interestingly, gains new degrees of adaptation (i.e., there is creative new emergence of species that didn't exist before, evolving from the survivors into new, rapidly forming ecosystems). One metaphor used to describe this pattern of mass extinction followed by creativity and emergence: Nature reshuffles the deck. Or, in Leakey and Lewin's (1995) metaphor: "Mass extinctions do not merely reset the clock of evolution, jolting it back for a while; they change the face of the clock" (p. 67). In terms of diversity, the many potential habitats of the world are relatively empty (relative homogeneity and low diversity); there is a profusion of adaptive possibilities available and proliferation of adaptations that fills these habitats, relatively rapidly, prior to the pruning back through processes of natural selection, the establishing of a new ecosystem (a new biodiversity equilibrium), and the re-assertion of "normal" Darwinian processes which had been "suspended" during the extinction event.

Within this long-term pattern of periodic mass extinctions, five mass extinctions in particular stand out, in terms of exceeding a very high percentage, for example, the first, which ends the pre-Cambrian 500 million years ago, 83% species loss. The asteroid impact around 65 million years ago triggered a massive climate shift causing 76% species extinction, including the dinosaurs. The most dramatic of these extinctions is marked in geologic terms as the end of the Permian era, about 250 million years ago. In this event, 96% of species biodiversity was wiped out. From the 4% that survived, all of the remaining enormous biodiversity of life forms into the present has evolved. (To be more precise, the issue from a macroevolutionary perspective of biodiversity loss isn't really at the level of species, but loss of phyla or genera or families, as these are more consequential losses in the long term. Our contemporary extinction event likely includes these, too, but our attention is certainly caught, and rightfully so, by species mass extinction.)

Mass extinctions are natural events. Viewed morally, ethically, and compassionately, they are terrifying and appalling: The loss of life is unimaginable, the degree and extent of extinction across species extensive. The last years of species are surely lived out in terrible pain, fear, and anxiety, likely with illness, disease, starvation, and loneliness, all of which would be to some extent mitigated, to some extent compounded, at whatever level of conscious understanding and comprehension they would experience such death and suffering. If animals could symbolize and story, I suspect their view of "Mother Nature" or "Mother Earth" during a period of mass extinction would tend toward the spouse-killing eater-of-her-own-offspring Kali version of the maternal! Viewed in a microevolutionary framework, that is assuming a particular established equilibrium with a particular biodiversity profile within a particular climate regime, a mass extinction event is "the end of the world" for the majority of those species. Viewed in a longer-term macroevolutionary perspective, these mass extinctions are also extraordinarily creative and generative: from the mass destruction of many species, emerges a small percentage of survivors from whom, as the Earth recovers and repopulates its surfaces and depths with life again, a new and more extensive biodiversity emerges. The end of the old world; the beginning of a new world. On the one hand, belying our self-interested interest in the anomalous outcomes of survivals, the statistically most significant lesson of evolution is extinction: 99% of all species that have ever existed are extinct. On the other hand, the qualitatively significant lesson is a raising of the ceiling on biodiversity and complexity as the outcome of periodic mass extinctions. From which greater biodiversity and complexity at the ceiling emerges, too, higher levels of consciousness. For example, while it is true that the last great extinction wiped out dinosaurs, it is also true that the dominance of dinosaurs in the previous era prevented the emergence of our current biodiversity of flora and fauna, including mammals like us. (Just as in our current era of the Anthropocene, human dominance is reducing biodiversity and preventing the emergence of whatever could come after us.)

Viewed graphically, there is on the one hand, overall, a gradual increase in biodiversity of species across massive evolutionary time. Darwin was right: Natural selection gradually modifies descent which brings about slow increase of biodiversity in the long term (see Fig. 2.1a). However, viewing the mass extinction events as crucial in that process shows a violent interruption within the process that breaks up the otherwise gradualness in the slow time frame. The increase in biodiversity after such an event also seems to break through the "ceiling" that held relative to the "phase" before the event (terms like eons, eras, and such are already taken and don't apply here). "While these mass extinctions each led to substantial loss of taxa, all were followed by increased rates of species formation that led to levels not only equaling but in each case exceeding the original diversity prior to the extinction event" (Ward & Kirschvink, 2015, p. 157). Darwin was wrong: Generalizing from microevolutionary scale of natural selection of increased biodiversity as a gradual, long-term process up to a macroevolutionary scale overlooks that there are cataclysmic events that break up the long-term processes, with rapid jumps in diversity through adaptive radiation happening quickly in the aftermath of such events. The overall pattern is not, however, gradual; rather plateaus, cataclysms (mass extinction, followed by rapid re-population and "re-diversification"), plateaus at a higher level (see Fig. 2.1b).

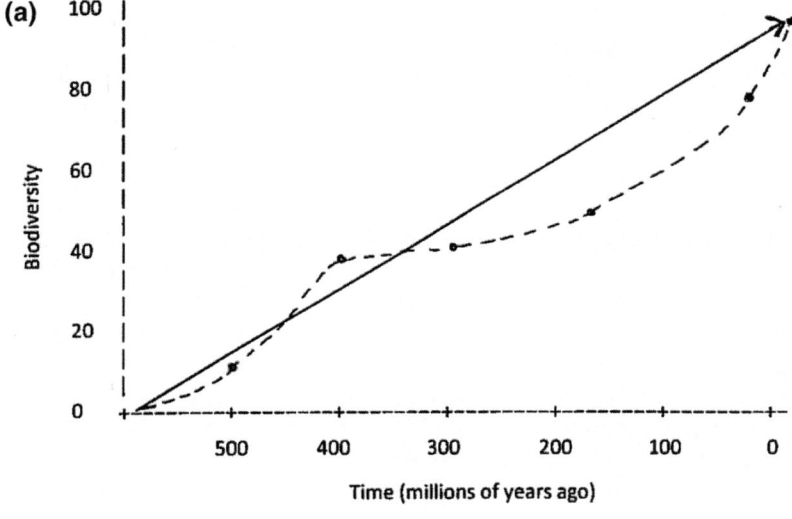

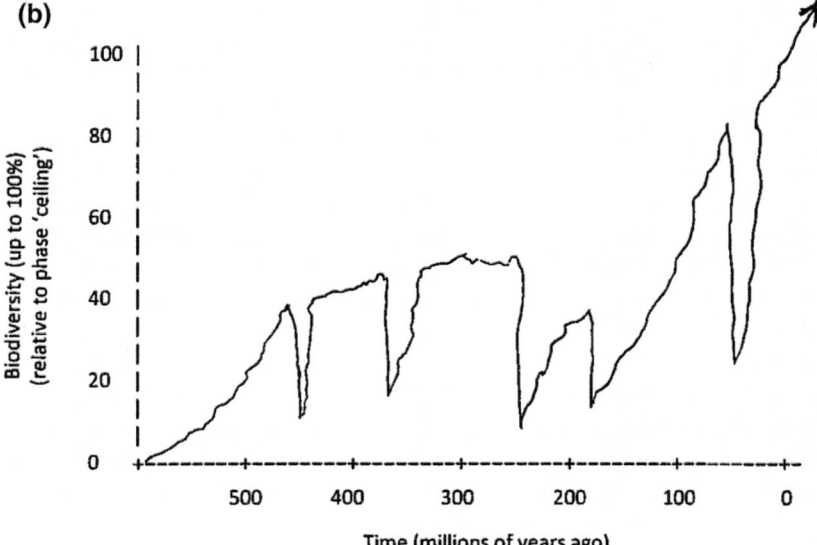

Fig. 2.1 **a** "Gradualist" evolution. **b** Evolution via mass extinction (Adapted from Raup & Sepkoski, 1982, 1984)

So mass extinction events are nothing new: paroxysms, or seizures, or fever crises that are terrible for life on Earth to undergo but at the end of each, a new world has been born and new life emerges. We are currently in one now, the Sixth Extinction. In this case, there are a couple of features that *are* new and unprecedented: *We* are undergoing it, and part of our evolutionary distinctiveness is our level of self-conscious awareness. We are animals aware of mortality, including our own; we have developed morality and ethics and compassion as part of our highly evolved consciousness and evaluate pain, suffering, destruction, and evil as unwanted, often as unnecessary, often as evil. Our current highest ever degree of biodiversity would not exist, nor would we, nor would our highly evolved consciousness, without all the prior mass extinctions, that continuously "raised the ceiling" of evolutionary possibility.

The second aspect of this Sixth Extinction that is new is that *we* are its cause. Global climate change is not being brought about by physical or biotic causes like a massive asteroid impact, Ice Age, widespread volcanic activity, or solar storms. It is being brought on by collective human impact due to industrially enabled, unsustainably high levels of consumption and pollution. Mass extinction events in the past, brought on by natural causes, had the consequence of breaking the species dominance that ruled a particular global equilibrium. This was followed by a relatively rapid post-extinction jump in biodiversity. Our present extinction event is being caused by our species dominance. Thus, a significant difference between this Sixth Extinction and all others is that there will not be an "emptying" of the niches for the small percentage of surviving species to re-inhabit, proliferate, diversify, and evolve. Assuming our survival, our species dominance across the globe will prevent such an aftermath.

However, just as the threat to "my" survival—my culture, my tribe, my civilization, and my way of life—brought on by the potential for a clash of civilizations as the outcome of our political crisis prompted a spiritual interpretation of the *ultimate meaning* threatened by that outcome to be the human ethnodiversity of cultures, the threat to survival of a mass number of species brought on by the Sixth Extinction event prompts a parallel spiritual interpretation: *biodiversity* as a natural universal ideal. If, spiritually, biodiversity is an ultimate value that we are able to read into the evolutionary story of Earth, then it crucially figures into being part of our taking responsibility and facing our world in crisis. If there is a "natural ideal," or ultimate meaning, to draw from this evolutionary story which includes the evolutionary emergence of human being as well as our moral, ethical, and compassionate consciousness, then the ideal or meaning is this: *that we are here to care for and love biodiversity*, of which we are a part, and which macroevolution reveals to always be, ultimately, a fragile achievement. That the consequence of past mass extinction events is the highest species biodiversity in evolutionary history and that we, with our high-level consciousness—a product of that increased degree of biodiversity—now threaten that biodiversity dramatically underscores this imperative of care.

TRIBALISM AND EXPANSIONISM: THE EVOLUTIONARY ROOTS TO CONTEMPORARY CRISIS

Near the beginning of this chapter I reminded us of Olivia and her crying, emphasizing that "we" need to face and take responsibility for our world in crisis. "We" is presumably universal humanity; more precisely, those of us within that category with power and affluence are those of us who need to take responsibility. We can imagine other divisions within "universal humanity," of course, that are *not* helpful: that divide us in such a way that we are set against each other and prevent the sort of concerted, co-ordinated, unity of response that we presumably need to muster "to save the world." In the long history of human being, the truth is that "universal humanity" is an idea that has entered our minds only recently—one of the signal contributions of the Axial Age, in fact. Prior to this time, humans thought of themselves *exclusively* in terms of whatever particular group(s) to which they belonged. This form of thinking—"tribalism" for short—is something we need to overcome. Not doing so places us squarely into the global political crisis of potential for escalation of a local conflict into a global one, a potential World War III or a potential "clash of civilizations." Notice that I am claiming that both tribalism and its overcoming in the form of an ideal of universal humanity are both evolved: The latter, however, has evolved much more recently, and insofar as it has not taken universal hold on human thinking to overcome our tribalist thinking, it is an example of evolution still in process.

As Darwin's description of natural selection at the opening of this chapter makes explicit, thinking of ourselves in terms of groups is not exclusively a human characteristic, nor does belonging need to be primarily in terms of thought. It is basic to evolutionary process and to natural selection; it is, to some extent, in our genes and neurons. Presumably, so too are the processes of "conquering," "supplanting," and "destroying" of other groups, the "triumph" of the larger group, the eventual disappearance of the "smaller," the "broken," the "less improved" groups. I am not proposing some version of social Darwinism. In calling in Axial fashion on the most privileged and enfranchised to take on the greatest responsibility and to bear that responsibility also for the sake of the weak, the powerless, and the suffering, the argument basically runs contrary to any survival-of-the-fittest rationale. It also runs counter to current global patterns of wealth distribution (see Fig. 2.2). Less than 9% of the world have more than 85% of its wealth, whereas more than 90% of the world have less than 15% of its wealth. These discrepancies have spiraled even further out of scale with the wealth of the new "global super-rich" (the 0.1% at the very top within the top 1%) reaching unprecedented levels in recent years (Freeland, 2012). Using wealth as a proxy for power, it is clear that inequalities of power are another key aspect of the shape of the present, and I would claim an equally clear contributor to our world in crisis. But it would be a mistake to think this an entirely unprecedented aspect of history or contribution to our present. It isn't; the only thing new in this case, as with so much else about our contemporary moment, is the *scale* at which it is enacted.

Just as belonging to a species is evolved, not distinctively human, and not necessarily a cognition, all of which ramps up into tribalism for human beings as we bring that evolved capacity into consciousness and think in those terms, so too is it entirely natural for organisms to expand into whatever space is available to them. For human beings, the difference of human cognitive ability—"sapience"—greatly scales up our capacity for "expansion," not least because we "make space available"

% of total world population	% of total world wealth
0.7	45.9
7.9	39.7
21.3	11.8
70.1	2.7

Fig. 2.2 World wealth distribution (Adapted from Credit Suisse Global Wealth Report, 2017)

beyond what is environmentally given. Bringing that evolved capacity into consciousness and thinking in those terms is what I call *expansionism*. Historically, the emergence of civilization itself, and its subsequent trajectory, is ultimately explicable in terms of *the expansion of power*. Hand in hand with that expansion has been that the power has been unequally distributed. These historical facts, building on our natural evolutionary capacities, lead to our present moment (we will look at this whole story in detail in Chapter 4). Expansionism, like tribalism, is an entirely natural, evolutionary outcome. Today, however, our expansionism is threatening to overturn planetary boundaries, ignore ecological limits, change the global climate, and cause a mass extinction of biodiversity. Like tribalism as an evolved capacity that we now need to evolve beyond, so too we must evolve beyond expansionism.

Combined, the powerful effects tribalism and expansionism are having on the environment and on ourselves as a species are clear: They have run their course and lead to an evolutionary dead end. Our ways of thinking and living in tribalist, expansionist terms have led to crisis. We need to overcome these, and we need to draw on other ways of thinking and living, other possibilities for thought and life, and take responsibility for our world in crisis.

Viewed politically, our global discord, division, and seeming incapacity to co-operate fits the Darwinian description of natural selection quite well. Viewed ecologically, Darwin's prediction "that the groups of organic beings which are now large and triumphant, and which are least broken up, that is, which as yet have suffered least extinction, will for a long period continue to increase," accurately summarizes our current world population figures (seven billion and rising) as well as the fact of the Sixth Extinction as a global mass extinction of species caused by our species dominance. In short, much of our current world in crisis is an entirely natural evolutionary outcome of our "human nature." Fortunately, the latter is not something ultimately fixed or unchangeable, it is something evolved *and* evolving. Unfortunately, however, insofar as human nature is something *evolved* over the long term, it is structured in deep, basic, primitive, and powerful patterns that we understandably but mistakenly perceive as fixed and unchangeable. Tribalism is one such structuring of human nature: humans thinking of themselves exclusively in terms of whatever particular group(s) to which they belonged and *not* in universal terms. Unchecked, it manifests as our political crisis. Expansionism is another: Humans expand into whatever available space, and further alter space to make more available, and spread further and expand further and consume the resources within that space. We do so not in accord with ecosystem constraints or environmental limits, however, but relative to what is within our power to do: and that power oversteps natural constraints and limits. Unchecked, it manifests as our ecological crisis. To check these, we need to raise them into critical conscious awareness, as premise to thinking, acting, and living differently. This is a tall order! It means raising an evolved structuring of human nature, which we mistakenly perceive as fixed and unchangeable because it is structured in deep, basic, primitive, and powerful patterns, into critical, reflexive, conscious awareness, in order to choose to think, act, and live, differently. Can we do this? We can, and we already have; the precedent for doing so has already been laid out for us by the wise teachers and spiritual masters of the Axial Age—and what the rest of this book is about.

Taking Responsibility for Our World in Crisis: Evolving Spirit Overcoming Evolved Nature

To conclude this chapter, and gain a better sense about just what the Axial Age visionaries achieve that is relevant for us to take responsibility for our world in crisis, we need to be more precise about this evolutionary "structuring of human nature" in terms of tribalism and expansionism. In a description to which we will return often, in our evolutionary origins as *homo sapiens* the individual human ego learned to identify itself with the collective group. In terms of evolutionary psychology, this ego-identification with the group is part and parcel of survival. Note that in identifying beyond its individual locus, the ego is in effect "expanding" itself, an act that forms the basis not just for tribalism, but for expansionism, too. Whether the family (or "kinship system"), the tribe, the ethnicity, the village, the city, the state, the nation, the civilization, the "race," the so-called universal world religion, for deep, basic, primitive, and powerful evolutionary reasons, humans have formed and developed their identities *not* in universal terms, but in terms of their particular group. Tribalism has dominated the human mind from our origins in Africa two hundred thousand years ago until our globalizing world of today.

There are a lot of consequences to tribalism. Viewed positively, from the inside of the tribe, there are support and nurture and protection, a feeling of security and sense of belonging, strong bonds of affection, a clarity of identity, and shared values. These can be, and often are, experienced by the individual as deep, basic, primitive, and powerful. Tribalism can also be viewed negatively, especially in terms of the relations between tribes: suspicion, distrust, stereotyping, discrimination, prejudice, fear, scapegoating, and hostility, to the point of violent conflict and war. Entire branches of psychology—social psychology and cognitive psychology, in particular—show the deep, basic, and primitive power of these processes in biases in our thinking, categorizing, relating, and so on. Modern science and technological advance have put a veneer of progress over this evolutionary background, but as the twentieth century demonstrated such "progress" also contributed to more advanced ways of committing violence and war, more efficient efforts at genocide. (Pinker [2012] shows clearly that genocide, though a modern word, is an ancient practice.) Whether archaeology, anthropology, or history, evidence shows that differences and disagreements between tribes have rarely been dispassionate or mild: The difference of the other tribe from our own is experienced as a deep, basic, primitive, and powerful threat to "us." Thus, violence to the point of war *seems* to be basic to our tribalist "human nature."

One aspect to tribalism and violence that is of relevance for facing our world in crisis, and which impairs our capacity to take responsibility, is the aspect of *ultimacy*: The human being, unlike the animal, is not born into an unquestioned natural world of natural beings, natural processes, and natural things. Presumably, for the animal, survival of the species, or of the gene, is what is ultimate—although the animal is not consciously aware, in a *sapient* sense, of this ultimacy as driving their action. The human being is born, questioning, into a world both natural and cultural, made up of natural beings, processes, and things, but also and inextricably, of cultural beings, processes, and things, which includes ideas, values, beliefs, and meanings too. It is the tribe to which the person belongs that provides him or her with a cultural world. And just as the natural world, which as spatial, temporal, and physical, situates the animal within a context that has certain ultimate limits, i.e., a horizon for action and perception in which the animal moves and acts and perceives, the cultural world does something analogous.

Culture provides the context of ideas, values, beliefs, and meanings in which the person thinks and speaks and evaluates, situating the person's *identity* in a particular space of meaning that reaches its limit, its horizon, in terms of *ultimate meanings*. In distinction from animals in the natural world, humans have the ability to inhabit cultural worlds that set particular horizons of meaning in which we reason, value, belief, and identify. This ability is due above all to *our capacity for symbolic reference* (Deacon, 1997). Ideas, values, beliefs, identity, and how we therefore understand "ultimacy" are all rendered meaningfully real to us through our evolved capacity for symbolic reference. That all of these, including the capacity for symbolic reference, are evolved should not mislead us into thinking they are innate, instinctive, or hereditary. A huge part of the evolutionary distinctiveness of human adaptation is that our horizons of meaning, our social context, and our cultural world are not internalized in any of these senses and thus not at any direct cost to the genetic or the neurological. Rather the distinctiveness is that these are "external" to the individual, i.e., they are social, cultural, and historical artifacts, on which the individual depends and with which she or he interacts. Our genetics and neurology have adapted themselves to work "prosthetically" with "external" information systems, semiotic systems, and symbolic systems.

Put simply, the distinctive adaptation is *learning*. In a sense, this learning, which is always necessarily within a social context of culture, or a collective process before it becomes an individual property, and even then never fully, is the empirical key to all human distinctiveness. As "big historian" David Christian (2005) puts it, "collective learning is the most important distinguishing feature of human history" (p. 284). As evolved capacity, to symbolize is both an entirely natural capacity, and the distinctiveness of "sapience" that sets us apart from other animals as it is also a cultural capacity that is learned. For human beings qua *homo sapiens*, cultural evolution takes over from natural evolution. Through the fusion of natural and cultural realities afforded by our capacity to symbolize humans live oriented to what is meaningful in life. By ultimate I mean what one considers as the ultimates of that meaningfulness; what grounds it, limits it, and renders it sensible constitutes its significance. What is ultimate sets a hierarchy of values ranging from insignificant to what is ultimately significant; ultimacy names what is worth living for, which includes what one is willing to kill others for, and what one is willing to die for, too; what we are willing to sacrifice, and what we are not. Thus, that a key aspect of the shape of the present is a clash of ultimates is an entirely natural consequence of our evolutionary history, of our evolved capacities of tribalism and expansionism. But equally natural, is our evolved *and evolving* capacity to symbolize what this state of affairs means to us and to critically evaluate this meaning against a whole hierarchy of values leading up to what is ultimately meaningful. Our world in crisis throws all these ultimate questions, together, into an interconnected, unprecedented clash of meaning. Within this complexity, however, we can prioritize what, above all, needs to be overcome.

Whereas the ecological crisis can be narrowed down to devolve on human *practices of consumption* as utterly crucial, the political crisis of our times can be narrowed down to devolve on the *potential for violence* as crucial. Placing that potential for violence alongside the fact of inter-connection, the issue at the basis of the world's crisis viewed politically is that of *escalation*. As World War II made evident and our discussion of the clash of civilizations thesis emphasized, a local conflict introduces a possibility for escalation that can grow to include the entire world. In terms of precedents, that *the* precedent politically for interconnectedness was a global war of incredible destruction cannot be overemphasized. This in itself is *the* key political aspect of our world in crisis. Conjoined with the ecological crisis, the issue shifts to that of communication and co-ordinating collective action across different political actors—and again, conflict between peoples and its potential for escalation would act as the greatest obstacle for such co-ordination of effort.

Comparing these two overarching categories, the ecological and the political, in terms of what they can most fundamentally be reduced to—ecologically, our *practices of consumption* as issuing from *expansionism*; politically, the potential for *escalation of violence* as issuing from *tribal-ism*—there immediately emerges a common denominator: the *problem of scale*. Expansionism scaled up leads to the current scale of human impact on the globe due to our consumption practices that is at the root of our ecological crisis. We have to make our levels of consumption, its scale, ecologically *sustainable*. Tribalism scaled up leads to the current scale of potential violence due to escalation from a local conflict to global pro-portions—the meaning of "escalate" is to scale up—that is at the root of our political crisis. We have to find ways of living together *nonviolently*. In both cases, the solution is to scale down; for the sake of the Earth that we are destroying (an Earth that includes us, and the destruction of which is destroying us, too), we must scale back our levels of con-sumption, while for the sake of human being and to prevent destroying each other, we must scale back our levels of violence, acknowledging the potential for escalation of violence to a global level.

At the root of the increase in scale is technology. I have not added technology itself as an aspect or a precedent or a priority in the same way as I've focused on the ecological and the political, but there is no doubt that it is our technology that brings all of these precedents, aspects, and priorities together, as well as bringing the whole world together, into its present shape. As we will see in the next chapter, Jaspers understood, in the immediate aftermath of World War II, the problems of world history in precisely these terms: Technology presents humanity with a deep spiritual challenge, as technology manifests culturally a clash of ultimates. As this chapter has tried to spell out, the latter is a key aspect to our world in crisis, with potent political and ecological ramifications. Understanding the Axial Age's place in evolution and history—the substance of Chapters 4 and 5—as well as engaging the response made by its visionaries and wise men as addressing the problems of our time, too— the substance of Chapter 6—promises to assist us today in understanding, and addressing, our world in crisis.

<h1 style="text-align:center">REFERENCES</h1>

Braudel, F. (1980). *On history* (S. Matthews, Trans.). Chicago: University of Chicago.

Braudel, F. (1994). *A history of civilizations* (R. Mayne, Trans.). New York: A. Lane.

Christian, D. (2005). *Maps of time: An introduction to big history*. Oakland: University of California.

Credit Suisse Research Institute. (2017). *Credit Suisse Global Wealth Report*. https://www.credit-suisse.com/corporate/en/research/research-institute/global-wealth-report.html.

Darwin, C. (2001). *On the origin of species*. University Park: Pennsylvania State University.

Deacon, T. (1997). *The symbolic species*. London and New York: W. W. Norton.

Eisenstadt, S. (2000). Multiple modernities. *Daedalus, 129*(1), 1–29.

Eldredge, N. (1991). *The Miner's Canary: Unraveling the mysteries of extinction*. New York: Prentice Hall.

Freeland, C. (2012). *Plutocrats: The rise of the new global super-rich and the fall of everyone else*. Toronto: Doubleday.

Halal, W., & Marien, M. (2011). Global megacrisis: Four scenarios, two perspectives. *The Futurist, 45*(3), 26–33.

Huntington, S. (1993). The clash of civilizations? *Foreign Affairs, 72*(3), 22–49.

Huntington, S. (1996). *The clash of civilizations and the remaking of world order*. New York: Simon & Schuster.

Leakey, R., & Lewin, R. (1995). *The sixth extinction: Patterns of life and the future of humankind*. New York: Anchor Books.

Pinker, S. (2012). *The better angels of our nature: Why violence has declined.* New York: Penguin.

Raup, D., & Sepkoski, J. (1982). Mass extinctions in the marine fossil record. *Science, New Series, 215*(4539), 1501–1503.

Raup, D., & Sepkoski, J. (1984). Periodicity of extinctions in the geologic past. *Proceedings of the National Academy of Science, USA, 81,* 801–805.

Rees, W. (1992). Ecological footprints and appropriated carrying capacity: What urban economics leaves out. *Environment and Urbanization, 4*(2), 121–130.

Rockström, J., Steffen, W., Noone, K., Persson, Å., Chapin, III, F. S., Lambin, E., … Foley, J. (2009). Planetary boundaries: Exploring the safe operating space for humanity. *Ecology and Society, 14*(2), 32. http://www.ecologyandsociety.org/vol14/iss2/art32/.

Said, E. (1997). *Covering Islam: How the media and the experts determine how we see the rest of the world* (Rev. ed.). New York: Vintage.

Taylor, B. (2010). *Dark green religion: Nature spirituality and the planetary future.* Berkeley: University of California.

Ward, P., & Kirschvink, J. (2015). *A new history of life: The radical new discoveries about the origins and evolution of life on earth.* New York and London: Bloomsbury.

CHAPTER 3

Karl Jaspers and the Axial Age

An Explosion of Scholarship

Scholars have been aware of the events and significance, in some form or other, of what we now call the Axial Age, for over two centuries now. With a few exceptions, most of the early scholarly awareness was not systematically developed into a full exploration, but consisted of drawing attention to the time period and remarking that it appeared to be of immense significance. The following lengthy quote by British scholar of Buddhism and translator of Pali texts Rhys-Davids (1903) is paradigmatic of this pattern:

> Then suddenly, and almost simultaneously, and almost certainly independently, there is evidence, about the sixth century BC in each of these widely separated centres of civilization [i.e., Rhys-Davids is referring to China, India, Persia, and Egypt], of a leap forward in speculative thought, of an new birth in ethics, of a religion of conscience threatening to take the place of the old religion of custom and magic. In each of these countries similar causes, the same laws regulating the evolution of ideas, had taken just about the same number of centuries to evolve, out of similar conditions, a similar result. Is there a more stupendous marvel in the whole history of mankind? Does any more suggestive problem await the solution of the historian of human thought? ...The intense interest, from the world-history point of view, in the sixth century BC – the best dividing line, if there was ever any, between ancient history and modern, between

© The Author(s) 2019
C. Peet, *Practicing Transcendence,*
https://doi.org/10.1007/978-3-030-14432-6_3

the old order and the new – would be sufficient excuse, if one were needed, for a somewhat detailed consideration of this particular point. (p. 239)

There are a number of features within this quote deserving attention, not least because it is paradigmatic of the earlier scholarly view on the Axial Age. We will engage these more closely below, and how they become expanded by Karl Jaspers throughout the remainder of this chapter. One in particular demands our immediate notice. Rhys-Davids proposes the image of a "dividing line" within world history, which if any such exists would be "in the sixth century BC," between "ancient history and modern." It is in precisely this sense of a world-historical dividing line that Karl Jaspers uses the concept of an "axis time" (*Achszenheit*) that becomes in English "Axial Age" or "Axial Period." It is Jaspers' coining of the notion of an "Axial Age" and developing a provocative thesis about it at the mid-twentieth century that seems to have made the difference within scholarship, as there is a veritable explosion in scholarship in recent decades by comparison with earlier sporadic interest. It is in part because scholarship on the Axial Age is growing at such an explosive rate in the last decades that I'm writing this book. To give you a simple quantitative sense and to illustrate the claim that scholarship has been "exploding" in recent decades, Fig. 3.1 shows numbers of publications on the Axial Age by decade from 1950 to 2009 (cf. "Secondary Literature" (Bellah & Joas, 2012b, pp. 471–537).

The post-Jaspers situation is a dramatic contrast to the pre-Jaspers situation. From 1771 until 1949, there were about 30 scholarly works on the Axial Age, of which most did not present any focused or extended treatment. The one that did, John Stuart Stuart-Glennie, in 1873, was largely unknown and passed almost immediately into obscurity—to such a degree that Jaspers falsely and unknowingly claims credit for being the

Fig. 3.1 Secondary literature on Axial Age, by decade

Dates of publications	Number of publications
1950–1959	27
1960–1969	40
1970–1979	46
1980–1989	123
1990–1999	239
2000–2009	440

first to outline the Axial Age thesis in systematic fashion (cf. Halton, 2014). After Jaspers' publication, this number is matched in the first decade alone; this in turn proves a modest quantity by comparison with the exponential growth in interest with each passing decade (see Boy & Torpey, 2013, for a more detailed look at this "explosive growth").

This explosive growth informs Hans Joas' claim that the Axial Age thesis "has become widely, but not universally, accepted," and that "the Axial Age debate of the last decades is… one of the most important developments in the area of the comparative-historical social sciences" (2012, p. 9). The growth in interest and increasing acceptance of the thesis among scholars is good news for "educated people of all the world's cultures" if the Axial Age is in fact relevant for their "deep self-understanding at this perilous moment in history" (Bellah & Joas, 2012a, p. 6).

The explosive growth also asserts an obvious and convenient layout for presenting what the Axial Age is: There is a first stage in scholarship, of sporadic and speculative efforts here and there across a couple of centuries, of which Jaspers marks the end. The second stage of scholarship after Jaspers' work has enough of a speculative skeleton to work with that it begins to slowly, systematically, and empirically, put meat onto the bones and flesh out the thesis on the Axial Age in far greater detail, and with far greater care. In this chapter, I will briefly discuss the early first stage of scholarship, before engaging Jaspers' work in detail.

First Speculations on the Axial Age

Scholars had noted the "stupendous marvel" that happened "around the sixth century BC" for a very long time, in terms analogous to those in Rhys-Davids' quote above. The earliest known example for this kind of "noting" was in 1771 in the work of a French Zoroastrian scholar who described a "revolution" in religions across the ancient world in the sixth century BCE. Almost a century later in 1856, the German scholar Ernst von Lasaulx argues for a comparative approach to understanding religious revelation as the basis for a philosophy of history. Key to the comparison was his noting of the "remarkable coincidence," around 600 BCE, of a number of programs of religious reform undertaken across a diversity of Old World civilizations. In short, although some of the descriptions vary, scholars describe the period in time around the sixth century BCE in similar ways to the Rhys-Davids' quote. There is a "sudden," "simultaneous," and "independent" set of happenings across several "widely separated centres of civilization"; in retrospect what seems to have happened was a "leap forward," a "new birth," a transformation of "the old" that draws a "dividing line" within world history.

The explanation for such a "stupendous marvel"? Well, scholars didn't know, and admitted so, all the time marveling... even as they confidently could conjecture the form such an explanation must take. Some of this confidence was due to nineteenth-century prejudices and certainties. Some of the confidence was because the explanatory form was purely abstract: There must be similar causes, similar conditions, a similar process of gestation within civilizations, and a similar effect—the same "laws of evolution of ideas" at work. Save for a few exceptions—Lasaulx being one of them; Stuart-Glennie another—there are no systematic attempts to provide even a "somewhat detailed description"; scholars by and large provide a perfunctory noting of this "suggestive problem" or "remarkable coincidence," albeit always drawing, in similar speculative terms, the same picture.

Thus, prior to Jaspers, the state of scholarly speculation on what has, post-Jaspers, become "the Axial Age" had developed a minimal description. Although it was minimal, it was a repetitively consistent description. The effect of the repetition was to help consolidate the perception that there was indeed a reliable, consistent object of study there—the events of this time, its mysteriousness, a brief listing of famous figures or names, its world-historical consequences—regardless of whether it was characterized as a "stupendous marvel." What versions of the Axial Age thesis prior to Jaspers all share is recognizing and emphasizing a before-after scenario that happens around the sixth century BCE in the Old World civilizations (China, India, Persia, Mesopotamia, Egypt, Greece, and some include Rome). Before, all ancient civilizations, religions, and their manner of thinking have a certain characterization evident in their myths, ethics, politics, social practices, and so on. After, a small, select number of those civilizations/religions had formed a new, qualitatively different mythology, ethics, politics, social practices, and so on. These civilizations are independent of each other, so there is no influence or communication between them to explain the synchrony. Within these select civilizations, particular individuals, either famous figures like Confucius or Socrates or the unknown authors of texts like the *Upanisads* or Deuteronomy, are the catalysts for these transformations. Finally, this new way of thinking and practicing proves to be of great historical importance and influence until the present day, above all, but not exclusively, in the sphere of religion.

Above all, what is qualitatively different are what one could call "high culture" or "high consciousness" features: There is a "revolution" in consciousness in the civilization/religion—the ambiguity is crucial—in the sense of a transformation in thinking, a leap in ethics, the birth of philosophy, the emergence of a new morality. Further, this qualitative difference in thinking and practicing is, in a variety of senses, understood to be higher or better or somehow more than what went on before (or, less limited than what went on before), that is, more civilized, or more humane, or more conscious (or, less primitive). There was philosophical reflection and metaphysical speculation in pre-Axial civilizations; after the Axial Age, there is much more. Ethics was practiced in societies before; after, the ethics is better articulated and more extensively applied. There was concern for suffering in pre-Axial religions; after, there is far more concern, for far more people, more elaborately described, more passionately pursued, more vehemently argued.

How potent was this transformation? The scholars interested in it perceived it in similarly breathless terms to Rhys-Davids. Eric Voegelin (1974), a contemporary of Karl Jaspers, makes the most brazen and provocative claim of anyone, hyperbolically emphasizing the significance of the Axial Age even beyond Rhys-Davids' dramatic claims; by comparison with then, "nothing much has happened during the last 2500 years" (p. 331).

By comparison with earlier scholarship, Karl Jaspers' (1949) book *Vom Ursprung und ziel der Geschichte*, translated into English in 1953 as *The Origin and Goal of History*, proves to become a dividing line of its own, in terms of the history and development of Axial Age scholarship. Before Jaspers, save for a few exceptions like Lasaulx or Stuart-Glennie there were no "detailed considerations." Scholarship was occasional, unsystematic, and uncoordinated. After Jaspers, scholars find a way to take seriously and critically the Axial Age as a viable thesis that is more than speculative, to increasingly specify the cluster of elements that compose its "stupendous marvelousness" and thus in which civilizations it occurs, as well as to increasingly detail its social and historical—and more recently, evolutionary—conditions and consequences. And as the numbers attest, scholarly interest explodes (see Fig. 3.1). In short, the Axial Age becomes a fertile, ongoing, multidisciplinary research focus.

Why does Jaspers' thesis make such a difference? I don't know. Like prior scholarship, his thesis is more speculative than empirical.

His is not the first formal, quasi-systematic effort; the thesis has been accurately described by a scholar as "a bold idea, briefly sketched" (Wittrock, 2005, p. 62), which does not distinguish it from earlier scholarship. The book overall has some deep flaws and shortcomings. Certainly, a significant difference is the sheer quantitative growth of scholarship and particularly specialized scholarship, between the mid-nineteenth century and the mid-twentieth century: There is simply far more detailed material and methods available from archeology, linguistics, anthropology, history, and so forth, to draw on. Beyond that significant, but obvious, difference, my speculation is that the difference does not have so much to do with the scholars themselves, but with their audience. The pre-twentieth-century European context for scholarship is dramatically different in numerous respects from the mid-twentieth-century Western scholarly context. Whatever these differences, after the World Wars and the breakdown of European empires, the globalizing world proves receptive to the empirical investigations of a two-centuries-old scholarly speculation. I also suspect that a further reason for the receptivity has to do with the increasing plausibility of the analogy between the crisis in civilizations that provokes the Axial Age and our own world crisis.

KARL JASPERS: THE MOTIVATION FOR THE AXIAL AGE THESIS DUE TO THE AGE OF TECHNOLOGY

Karl Jaspers (1883–1969) was a German scholar who began his career in psychology before moving into philosophy. Jaspers first proposes the Axial Age thesis as such in the wake of World War II. The war, which begins as a European conflict but escalates into a world war, is a prime example of the potential for escalation from regional into international violent conflict that globalization makes possible, as discussed in the previous chapter. For Jaspers, the significance of the war is that it marks the beginning of world history. "What is historically new and, for the first time in history, decisive about our situation is the real unity of mankind on the earth. The planet has become for man a single whole dominated by the technology of communications" (1953, p. 126). The emphasis on the "real unity of mankind" and the "planet as a single whole" is an emphasis on the oneness of universality. Universality is key for Jaspers' conception of the Axial Age.

Jaspers was acutely aware that the accomplishing of global interconnectedness through technology held out enormous potential for destruction. On the one hand, the destruction could be literal, as evident in
World War II. The destructiveness need not only be understood externally in terms of violence between peoples, but also internally in terms
of dehumanizing hatred, racism, xenophobia, and so on. (Jaspers experienced firsthand some of the evils of Nazi Germany; his wife was Jewish
while he was restricted from work and banned from publishing.) On the
other hand, what we could call the "existential" hand rather than the
literal one, contemporary technology can be perceived to threaten the
destruction of many cultural forms and values. This is certainly Jaspers'
perception, and it is shared by many others of his generation—Martin
Heidegger, Hannah Arendt, Hans Jonas, to name some fellow Germans;
Jacques Ellul, or Lewis Mumford are French and American contem-
poraries who also share this concern. To try to find a suitable umbrella
word, it threatens humanity spiritually. Jaspers is deeply concerned with
the destructive impacts of "the Age of Technology" on the human spirit:

> Technology has wrought a radical transformation in the day-to-day exist-
> ence of man in his environment; it has forced his modes of work and his
> society into entirely new channels: the channels of mass-production, the
> metamorphosis of his whole existence into a technically perfect piece of
> machinery and of the planet into a single great factory. In the process man
> has been and is being deprived of all roots. He is becoming a dweller on the
> earth with no home. He is losing the continuity of tradition. The spirit is
> being reduced to the learning of facts and training for utilitarian functions.
> In its first effects this age of metamorphosis is disastrous. We are living today
> in the impossibility of finding a legitimate form of life. Little that is true and
> trustworthy and that could sustain the individual in his self-consciousness
> comes to us out of the contemporary world. (1953, p. 98)

This grim existential assessment of how the Age of Technology defines
"the contemporary world" is Jaspers' overriding motivation for his philosophy. (Although the Axial Age thesis is crucial for Jaspers' argument,
it is only so as a supporting piece in the overall design of the book.
Readers might be surprised to know, for example, that in Jaspers' [1974]
own "philosophical autobiography" the Axial Age doesn't even receive
a single mention!) Of utmost importance for Jaspers was how to proactively engage and overcome the dangerous challenges technology poses

to contemporary civilization. He sees this as a universal challenge—mankind is a real unity, the planet is a single whole—and he sees it as a spiritual challenge: Technology threatens the human spirit, as per the quotation just cited. These challenges are what motivate and frame his interest in the Axial Age.

The Age of Technology has effected a universality in the sense of a material unity (or empirical, or factual, or instrumental unity) of humanity in creating an interconnected globe, but it is not the case that we realize, in the sense of understand or comprehend, what this fact means. This development contrasts strongly to the Axial Age. Spiritually speaking, Jaspers perceives the two Ages as utterly contrasted: "Then the plenitude, now the emptiness" (1953, p. 140). An empirical contrast between the two Ages is clear in terms of their global situation: During the Axial Age, the globe was not interconnected, but greatly broken up geographically and culturally into hundreds of thousands of noncommunicating peoples, tribes, foragers, states, civilizations, etc. No one knew the true extent of the world in a global sense, nor did they know the true extent of humanity across the globe. However, within that globe-spanning diversity, in several specific civilizations, there emerges for the first time the effort to consciously think of humanity as a meaningful unity, i.e., as universal. This happens despite the very real limitations technologically, practically, and cognitively for any real unity. These several diverse ways of "thinking universally" endure and remain active and dynamic within the self-understanding of world-historical civilizations that themselves endure to the present day (recalling Chapter 1, that compose 75–95% of the world population today). The different Axial Age civilizations produce different conceptions of what universality looks like, according to their own particular cultural origins and reflected in their greatly differing civilizational religions, ethics, philosophies, and worldviews. For Jaspers, these differences are crucially important, but these differences should not be understood as absolute such that they are incommensurable; they are still comparable because of their shared universalist orientation. How they understand universality differs; what they understand it to be differs; but that they are understanding what they are doing as oriented to a universal reference point is shared.

What happens in the Axial Age are the first imaginings of "mankind as a spiritual unity." These imaginings are speculative to be sure, but importantly they are rigorous speculations. This rigorous speculation on universal humanity happens millennia before universal humanity becomes an actual fact through technology in the twentieth century. Jaspers wants to bring these two "facts" together: the historical fact of the Axial Age which first thinks universality in the form of humanity as a spiritual unity, together with the contemporary fact of a technologically enabled material unity of human being on a single globe. The latter fact hides how the human beings technologically connected across the globe are spiritually divided and with a plurality of differing universals—and since universals are about what is considered ultimate, these conceptions don't just differ, they clash.

There are two important points of clarification here, which need to be appreciated if Jaspers' project is to be understood. Jaspers is an existential philosopher. He understands by history not the raw facts of what happened. What is needed for a fact or event to count as history is that it has to include some degree of conscious awareness, some sense of realized meaning in the minds of people. This more restrictive way of understanding history should not be confused with broader or looser uses of the word history that lack the emphasis on consciousness as definitive. Material history in the sense of the raw facts of what happened, disregarding any active consciousness, is not what Jaspers calls history. Therefore, that the possibility of a "real unity" of mankind had first been articulated and thought during the Axial Age is of utter historical significance. It means for Jaspers that the "world history of humanity derives its structure from this period" (1953, p. 262). In contrast to earlier speculations that the Axial Age was a stupendous marvel, a remarkable coincidence of world-historical significance, Jaspers is presenting here a more specific, more refined articulation of that claim: The Axial Age has world-historical significance because it is the first time in history when individuals began to think in world-historical terms of humanity as a spiritual, universal, whole; when "the spiritual foundations of humanity were laid" (Jaspers, 1951, p. 98). When we appeal today, for example, to universal human rights, and raise an outcry when these are violated by some particular group or in the name of some particular self-interest, we are thinking in precisely those terms. Thus, Jaspers, dramatizing the point in existential fashion, can claim that in the Axial Age "Man, as we know him today, came into being" (p. 1).

The second point is that the philosophical emphasis on world history ties the Axial Age speculations to a very different and influential trajectory of scholarship: the work in world history of scholars such as the German Oswald Spengler (1926–1928) and British Arnold Toynbee.

Spengler's *Decline of the West* (1926–1928; published in 1918) was enormously popular; Toynbee was widely read and influential throughout the 1940s and 1950s, best known for his twelve-volume *A Study of History* (1934–1961). To be sure there are significant differences between the two, but what they shared and why they were influential was their contemporary concern with understanding the rise and fall of civilizations, including Western civilization, put into a world-historical context. Jaspers also shares this concern, and by placing the Axial Age thesis onto center stage of this concern, he takes it out from the specialized work of civilizational area scholars, philologists, ethnologists, and religious specialists—think of Assyriologists, Egyptologists, Sinologists, Sanskrit scholars, classicists, and so on—and sets it instead into a broader comparative context of scholarship that in those decades had significant popular appeal beyond the academy.

To try to picture what Jaspers, motivated by the new stage in history that technology has initiated, wants to accomplish, a starting point is to juxtapose two images: the first of the world history of humanity, with the Axial Age as a "dividing line" that structures that world history, the second the contemporary world. For the first image of history let's imagine a time-lapse video. It again features the globe, but encapsulating all of human history: from the original *homo sapiens sapiens* appearing approximately two hundred thousand years ago in Africa, followed by their slow, uneven, and irregular population growth and territorial spread across the globe (a growth and spread that in retrospect might appear steady and inexorable). During this entire span, there is no conception of human beings in universal terms. Then, around twenty-five hundred years ago, the first such conceptions appear. These conceptions are ethical, philosophical, and religious articulations of human being in universal terms, which in slow, uneven, and irregular, fashion, grow and spread across the globe over the next twenty-five hundred years (a growth and spread that in retrospect might appear steady and inexorable). The growth and spread is carried by civilizations now self-defining themselves in those universalist terms which engulf, extinguish, or push out all the cultures with which they come in contact. Darwin's natural selection description that was quoted in Chapter 2 clearly obtains, first demographically, then ideologically: the "conquering," "supplanting," and "destroying" of other groups, the "triumph" of the larger group, the eventual disappearance of the "smaller," the "broken," the "less improved" groups… Their growth and spread from their geographic and historic points of origin continues until they span almost the entirety of the globe in demographic terms. (The spread of the idea, or "meme," of universal humanity until it spans the globe, loosely follows—recapitulates?—the earlier spread of humanity itself until we spanned the globe—not in exactly the same pattern, and far greatly accelerated.)

The second image: a snapshot of the globe, with its oceans and continents, on which is superimposed the whole uneven distribution of seven billion human beings, yes divided into countries and civilizations and so on, but simultaneously a single interconnected whole due to technology that crosses political and geographic and cultural boundaries. Within this snapshot, what Jaspers would draw attention to is conscious awareness in terms of thinking of humans in universal terms has spread to the entirety of humanity; well, to 75–95% of the entire global population, save for various indigenous cultures and tribes at their margins, in locations geographically isolated or environmentally extreme. To account for this snapshot, the time-lapse video made clear that something happened, "suddenly, simultaneously, and independently," about twenty-five hundred years ago, where the idea originates and then spreads.

I propose this, in crude and oversimplified visual form, is a key part of what Jaspers is hoping to accomplish. (His avowed aim in *The Origin and Goal of History* is, in his own simplest terms, "heightening our awareness of the present" [1953, p. v] through consideration of world history.) If we were able to picture the time-lapse video of the first image accurately, we would be able to truly comprehend the second snapshot image of a single interconnected globe and know the conscious meaning of the fact of a universal humanity. Or in other words, the conscious understanding put forward by the Axial Age in terms of a spiritual universality which develops and grows and spreads over the next 2500 years of world history, would flesh out the meaning of the contemporary situation of the Age of Technology, i.e., of our interconnected globe, our material universality. To picture this "structure of world history" accurately—I prefer to call it a map of world history, because although it is about what people think and consciously mean, that these people have particular geographies on the globe because of their belonging to particular civilizations that are geographically located, is crucial to the meaning too—we need to fill in the details of just what the Axial Age was about (its ideas), as well as the consequences that followed as these ideas endured and spread. This chapter will endeavor to do so, while our following chapter will put far more detail into our "time-lapse video" of world history.

Jaspers on the Axial Age Part 1:
A Spiritual Revolution in Consciousness

For Jaspers, the Axial Age was a revolution in consciousness: a revolt against thinking in exclusively particular terms (locally, ethnically, regionally defined, etc.) toward thinking that included universal terms. The special privileging of consciousness is key to Jaspers' understanding insofar as he belongs to that particular strand of German continental philosophy and its existential orientation. From this understanding, that an awareness enters into consciousness is a profound event. In the case of world history as an effort to think the history of humanity universally, if that something that entered conscious awareness is a universal conception of human being, it becomes the proper founding moment of world history. As we already know from the scholarly speculation in the two centuries prior to Jaspers' work, it will not be a single founding moment, but a select number of founding moments—"sudden, simultaneous, parallel"—that are "remarkably coincident" in time. These founding moments of consciousness of world history, if strung together like beads on a chain, form an axis that divides history into a before and after.

> If there is an axis in history, we must find it empirically in profane history... The spiritual process which took place between 800 and 200 BC seems to constitute such an axis. ...Let us designate this period as the "Axial Age." (Jaspers, 1951, p. 99)

Somehow, the difference, the Axial Age makes, is that this capacity to think in universal terms is developed. What does Jaspers mean in calling this development a "spiritual process"; elsewhere he says "This overall modification of humanity may be termed *spiritualisation*" (1953, p. 3)? Why does Jaspers choose the dates 800–200 BCE?

> The most extraordinary events are concentrated in this period. Confucius and Lao-tse were living in China, all the schools of Chinese philosophy came into being, including those of Mo-ti, Chuang-tse, Lieh-tsu and a host of others; India produced the Upanishads and Buddha and, like China, ran the whole gamut of philosophical possibilities down to skepticism, to materialism, sophism and nihilism; in Iran Zarathustra taught a challenging view of the world as a struggle between good and evil; in Palestine the prophets made their appearance, from Elijah, by way of Isaiah and Jeremiah to Deutero-Isaiah; Greece witnessed the appearance

of Homer, of the philosophers – Parmenides, Heraclitus and Plato – of the tragedians, Thucydides and Archimedes. (1953, p. 2)

We should feel familiar with this way of characterizing the Axial Age, as Jaspers here follows the format repeated by previous scholarship. With the exception of Iran and the single prophet Zarathustra, what is striking about the lists of named individuals in the four civilizational areas of China, India, Palestine, and Greece is the emphasis on an extraordinary proliferation of perspectives within each area. In no case are any singular nor can the numerous different approaches be reduced to some common essence. For China, Jaspers names Confucius, Lao-tse, Mo-Ti, Chuang-tse, Lieh-tsu, and a "host of others"; the point is the many individuals and schools present. For India, the Buddha is named as well as the *Upanisadic* texts (by unknown authors), but again Jaspers' point is that there is a great spectrum of different "isms" or schools that emerge. For Palestine, Jaspers names four Hebrew prophets, starting with Elijah, mentioning Isaiah and Jeremiah, and concluding with Deutero-Isaiah. Jaspers is sketching a chronology here, starting from Elijah as arguably the earliest or oldest prophet (discounting Moses as having prophet status), to Deutero-Isaiah, the title ascribed to an anonymous prophet(s) well known for his (their) particularly stringent version of monotheism. The point again is that within this time span was a profusion, this time of the great diversity of the prophets of ancient Israel and Judaea. For Greece Jaspers mentions Parmenides, Heraclitus, and Plato as examples of philosophers but in the same breath includes the epic poet Homer, the tragedians (i.e., Euripides, Sophocles, and Aristophanes), the "father of history" Thucydides, and the natural philosopher Archimedes. Again, an extraordinary flowering, inspired by exceptional individuals within one civilization, of movements, schools, communities, or sects, that are intellectual-ethical-religious... what I said above one could call either high culture or high consciousness features. In Jaspers' effort at a best umbrella term, the proliferations are spiritual.

These lists seem to be somewhat arbitrarily selected, because they are not meant to be exhaustive, but they are used in a more suggestive fashion as representative of a diversity and spectrum of views that proliferated in these four civilizations. Because Jaspers is proposing this breadth, he also expands and aims to render more precise the "around the sixth century BC" phrasing of earlier scholarship: He says "from 800 to 200 BC." In expanding the range earlier a few centuries, he can include, for example, Homer from Greece and the pre-Socratic philosophers; as well, the early Old Testament prophets who live in the eighth century BCE; similarly, the earliest *Upanisads* are (arguably) written around the ninth century BCE. In adding a few later centuries after 500 BCE, he can include the flowering of Greek philosophy after Socrates which continues until the death of Alexander in 323 BCE (often used to mark the end of the Greek classical era), post-exilic Israel when the Hebrew Old Testament is written; the numerous developments in China across many different schools prior to the Chin unification in 221 BCE, and similarly for India the Mauryan emperor Asoka's conversion to Buddhism (in third century BCE) could be used to mark the end of the Indian Axial Age. It is these proliferations as a whole across these several centuries that Jaspers argues is the axis of history due to their spiritualization of consciousness.

Reviewing these five civilizations to look for some simplifications of their diversity of expressions of this "spiritualization," two such simplifications immediately avail themselves. The first is cultural-geographic in terms of communication and influence between them: China and India, separated by the imposing Himalayan range, each constitute their own relatively independent geography and culture, with both in turn distant from Iran, Palestine, and Greece to the west (traversable, by lengthy journey, through a variety of routes that we later call the Silk Road, or by sea). The latter three Western civilizations—Western relative to India and China, and in its place on the Asian continent—are however near enough by geography and cultural connections over history that they constitute one connected geography; either "west Asia," the "near East" or, owing either to the dominant cultural styling or its geographic location, what Jaspers interchangeably calls "Hellas" or "the West."

A second simplification: If we define each revolutionary proliferation in terms of its own respective, distinctive "umbrella" term—smaller umbrellas than Jaspers' "spiritualization"—we can characterize Greece in terms of philosophical rationalism; despite significant differences in the near East between Iran and Palestine, both Zarathustra and the Hebrew prophets develop ethical monotheism; India, we could characterize as advancing a spiritual asceticism; and China, an ethical humanism. We will have to probe deeper to see if beneath the surface, there are indeed any further commonalties across these four "isms" or three geographical areas. Notice that some simplifications—it's a philosophical revolution! It's a religious revolution!—are problematic to apply; can we call the prophets of the Old Testament, or writers of the *Upanisads*, philosophers? Are Confucianism or Greek philosophy, religions? When Jaspers claims "Hermits and wandering thinkers in China, ascetics in India, philosophers in Greece and prophets in Israel all belong together" (1953, p. 3), the burden of proof is on him to describe how they "belong together."

JASPERS ON THE AXIAL AGE PART 2:
TRANSCENDENCE AND INWARDNESS

Along with universality that has already been emphasized as one element, is the notion that this overarching and singular universal reality is transcendent. For the most part, Axial Age movements in each civilization emphasized, to varying degrees, the transcendent character of ultimate reality vis-à-vis traditional conceptions of sacredness and vis-à-vis human capacities of language and thinking. Greek philosophical rationalism venerates, above all, the *Logos*—inadequately translated into modern English as "reason," *Logos* was understood in a far more holistic, deep, and sacred sense; the *Logos* as "divinely beautiful reason" might be a better translation here. The Hebrew prophets, of course, were radically focused on the one truth of YHWH, whose name could not even be written or uttered; in distinction to all their neighbors, the God of Israel was a transcendent God. The *Upanisads* articulate the mystery of *Brahman* as the transcendent One overarching all distinctions, with whom our individual soul (*atman*) needs to regain its true identity, while the Buddhists contend that transcending even that is the realization of all as oneness, that the interconnectedness of all (*pratitya-samutpada*) means the overcoming of any identity of any thing or any being, or emptiness (*sunyata*), the experiential realization of which is the "extinction" of the self (*nirvana*). In China, Confucians and Taoists, to name only the best-known, debate as to the transcendent nature of the *Tao*, Lao Tzu's *Tao Te Ching* famously stating "The *Tao* that can be named is not the true *Tao*." Relative to traditional religion and to traditional political thinking, transcendence was a revolutionary conception.

> The Mythical Age, with its tranquility and self-evidence, was at an end. The Greek, Indian and Chinese philosophers were unmythical in their decisive insights, as were the prophets in their ideas of God. Rationality and rationally clarified experience launched a struggle against the myth (*logos* against *mythos*); a further struggle developed for the transcendence

of the One God against non-existent demons, and finally an ethical rebellion took place against the unreal figures of the gods. Religion was rendered ethical, and the majesty of the deity thereby increased. The myth, on the other hand, became the material of a language which expressed by it something very different from what it had originally signified: it was turned into parable. Myths were remoulded, were understood at a new depth during this transition, which was myth-creating after a new fashion, at the very moment when the myth as a whole was destroyed. (1953, p. 3)

Based on this quote, the clear opposition to the "spiritualization" is myth; more precisely, unquestioned myth. Myth tells the stories of why and how the world is and came to be, how human beings came to be, the ultimate meanings of our sufferings and desires, how the tiger got its stripes, and so on. In being unquestioned, myth forms the unnoticed background for thought and practice; it explains, legitimates, honors, rationalizes, condemns, and praises—in a word, valorizes—a people's way of life. In putting myth into question, its status as unnoticed and as background can no longer remain the same. The very act of noticing what had been background is to make it foreground and focal to awareness. And in so doing not only the myths themselves and their claims are transformed, but also all the spheres of life that they had valorized become questionable too. So to question myth is to initiate a far-spreading ripple effect that reverberates throughout many of the spheres of society. Eric Voegelin, a contemporary of Jaspers who also develops extensive theorizing about the Axial Age, uses the description of myth as compact vs. differentiated. Myth was compact before the Axial Age and becomes differentiated afterward, due to the Axial Age and how it conceives transcendence as the ultimate ground for myth, initiating a dynamic of questioning until the present.

Rational thinking struggles against mythical thinking; monotheism struggles against polytheism; and a moral and ethical conception of religion (wherein, e.g., the unethical conduct of the gods themselves is questioned) struggles against a traditional conception of religion that suddenly, in comparison, appears much less rational, moral, and ethical than formerly. Myth itself as a category does not disappear, but is "remoulded." The stories of myth cease being direct expressions of truth told by gods to ancestors and passed on, and instead become "parables." They still tell the truth, perhaps, but now indirectly and symbolically and requiring an effort at interpretation. In emphasizing questioning and struggles and effort, Jaspers is arguing for a dramatic relocation of the truth of myth, from an unnoticed background inherited from tradition and collectively and compactly held together, to a far more psychological, far more individual, far more conscious, locus, that also has the consequence of differentiating, dividing up, and distributing the "truth of myth" into numerous new spheres—psychological, moral, ethical. The relocation of myth from unquestioned in the culture, to instead what a person believes, is a big part of why Jaspers calls the process "spiritualization"; and therefore, too, he lays stress on the existential uncertainties and anxieties that arose.

> What is new about this age, in all three areas of the world is that man becomes conscious of Being as a whole, of himself and his limitations. He experiences the terror of the world and his own powerlessness. He asks radical questions. Face to face with the void he strives for liberation and redemption. By consciously recognizing his limits he sets himself the highest goals. He experiences absoluteness in the depths of selfhood and in the lucidity of transcendence. (1953, pp. 2–3)

Just as myth in being opposed and questioned differentiates into a variety of spheres such as philosophy, ethics, religion, morality, and so on, so too does the locus of belief transform and differentiate through the activity of questioning. Gods cease to be facts and become instead questioned as to what they mean, or if indeed they exist at all. Established orders, whether natural or moral or political or social, cease from being "that's just the way it is" to become instead "why is it this way?", or more radically yet, "does it have to be this way?" In its unquestionedness, myth was embodied in collective practices, in ritual, in social organization, in temples and sacred places. Upon myth's being questioned, the locus of belief becomes "spiritualized," and suddenly the individual with his or her existential, questioning consciousness emerges as focal. Performing the ceremony, the ritual, or the sacrifice, in and of itself will no longer suffice. What is occurring internally in the individual, within his spirit or her mind, becomes crucial: The intention with which one performs the ritual, sacrifice, or ceremony is essential. Without an intending consciousness to animate the action as meaningful, those actions are empty.

With this change in understanding, ritual, sacrifice, ceremony, become characterize-able as external, as mere show or pantomime rather than the real thing; for ritual, etc., to count as real, it needs a corresponding inward dimension of the individual aligned with the outward appearance. Jaspers: "Man proved capable of contrasting himself inwardly with the entire universe" (1953, p. 3). The absolute is no longer out there in a physical spatiotemporal sense, where the hero must ascend the mountain to meet the god or descend into the depths of the earth to petition the goddess. Instead, the absolute is now sought after in the qualitatively different experiential sense of "in here," within the individual spirit of the person. As Voegelin (1956) puts it, "The personal soul as the sensorium of transcendence must develop parallel with the understanding of a transcendent God" (p. 235). Confucianism increases attention to ritual in terms of a rigorous program of self-cultivation. The emphasis on ritual sacrifice of the Brahmanic religion in India becomes a spiritual asceticism in the *Upanisads* through yoga, with Buddhism and Jainism arguing similarly for ascetic practices to discipline the self. God reveals to Jeremiah the new covenant wherein "I will put my law in their inward parts, and write it in their hearts" (Jer. 31:33), the contrast being, as Paul makes explicit in the New Testament, God's law "written not with ink but with the Spirit of the living God, not on tablets of stone but on tablets of human hearts" (2 Cor. 3:3). Jesus says: "The Kingdom of God is within you" (Luke 17:21). Greek philosophy finds its fulfillment in contemplation, whereby the self, or soul (i.e., the microcosm), harmonizes through disciplined effort to the cosmos (the macrocosm). The spirit, not physically or materially, nor in space-time, can descend into the inner "depths of selfhood" or ascend to the experiential heights where, in the "lucidity of transcendence," she encounters the absolute.

Jaspers on the Axial Age Part 3: Mystery and Identity

I've already mentioned how the Axial Age emphasis, to varying degrees, on the transcendent character of ultimate reality was revolutionary vis-à-vis traditional conceptions of sacredness; it was also a dramatic transformation in the understanding of human capacities of language and thinking, which ultimate reality transcends. Relative to human beings themselves, transcendence is a mystery. This is not an incidental or accidental fact, but ontologically necessary. Prior to the Axial Age, myth tells the stories of the sacred world of the gods and their powerful doings that is other to the profane world of mundane human activity. The Axial Age does not do away with this distinction, nor does it merely add some new dimensions like philosophy and ethics and inwardness. Myth, the sacred and the profane, gods and humans, and their distinction into the other world and this world remain, as does tradition, ritual, and sacrifice. What the Axial Age accomplishes in a handful of civilizations is a transformation in meaning of the whole ensemble of factors. The sacred and the gods become not superhuman, supernatural, magical beings who are larger than life and who live in cosmic extremes (among the stars, on mountaintops, beneath the ocean, and so on). Rather, in terms of how they are other and how their power manifests, the anthropocentrism within these conceptions becomes exposed and the otherness and power of the gods become instead far more mysterious. You will not find the god atop the mountain or below the ocean, because you've mistaken the nature of the god's otherness: not more powerful than human in a human way like being really strong or incredibly lusty or extremely long-living, not magical by analogy to human action, not other by living where humans would find it extreme or impossible. Deeper, or more transcendent, or more mysterious, than telling the seeker that they're looking in the wrong place, is telling the seeker that it's not a matter of looking at all. Instead, they have to see with "spiritual eyes"; the seeker must use that self-same spirit to be maximally aware that seeing with spiritual eyes is an inadequate metaphor. Myths do not, as the seeker used to believe, tell the straightforward facts of the reality out there; rather, they are parables that invoke a mystery into which the spirit has to find its own way, a reality that transcends the physical and also the human-conventional.

The phrasing just used of "transcends the physical," combined with the notion of the Axial Age accomplishing "a transformation in meaning of the whole ensemble" of inherited pre-Axial understandings, combined with the emphasis on critique and questioning, could also be understood as adding up not to mystery but to metaphysics. It could be argued, and a number of Axial Age scholars do argue this, that the breakthrough is to a higher form of rationality. To repeat, I don't want to pursue this particular avenue of "more" and "less" rational in comparing times (and peoples). However, what I would point out is that invoking transcendent mystery as key in a way that coherently questions and dynamically informs the inherited knowledge and thinking of tradition leads to a qualitative transformation in the "whole ensemble." It leads to a new kind of systematicity in reasoning and thought, in argument and logic. It is not that people were not systematic before, they were; but they were not systematic relative to a transcendent ground of meaning, or mysterious locus for reality, or a deeper inexpressible ideal, as the Axial Age visionaries and their followers were. The latter drives thought into new corners and beyond its inherited limits, forces argumentation to become more sustained and the intellect to sharpen and exercise itself in entirely new directions.

Crucially, transcendent mystery is not utterly inaccessible, nor understood to be accessible cognitively theoretically, but it is capable of being explored and in which we can participate. In doing so we transform, develop, and mature spiritually. That we can do this, means something about us and our inwardness is inherently mysterious, too; in fact, it means not just any "something," but means the most important spiritual identity within us is a mystery to us. The endpoint of this process is not that we solve the mystery. Although we gain more knowledge of, and become better able to experience, this mysterious ultimate reality, precisely because it is ultimate, its mystery simultaneously deepens. In the process of making these gains in knowledge or experience, any complete knowing or total experiencing becomes exposed as an immature understanding of the truth of the mystery, whose essential characteristic is to be unknown and beyond and to thus escape any attempt at capture or being grasped. (This characterization, in limiting the reach of cognitive ability both in principle and in practice, does so because I'm trying to present an account faithful to Jaspers' existential orientation wherein the "existential" denotes experiential modalities of will, affect, imagination, relational being, etc., irreducible to the "cognitive." This also accords, as I read it, with being in line with many of the mystical accounts of transcendent experience, and with scholarly accounts of mysticism, such as Otto's [1923] discussion of the "non-rational," or Hadot's [1995] arguments in favor of "spiritual" over against other adjectives to modify "exercise" [pp. 81–82, 127–128]. The same material could be presented with a more expansive role for the cognitive, or from a viewpoint more favorable to cognitive reduction. Many mystics themselves present mystical experience in such expanded cognition terms; for example, McGinn [1991] argues for "superknowledge" of transcendence, on the basis of particular mystical accounts. Bagger [2007] makes the following cognitive argument in regards to mystery: "The concept of mystery creates the expectation that some truths resist rational articulation. Because one expects not to understand these paradoxical truths, one's failure to understand them arouses less dissonance. ...Embracing a concept of mystery installs a second-order cognition that functions to reduce first-order dissonance" [p. 35]. One takeaway point from these differences, to which we will return from a sociological angle in Chapter 5: The Axial Age with its conception of transcendence, mystery, universality, etc., instates a volatile and unstable dynamism into human experience—in this case, cognitively.)

The Axial Age does not make gods and mythical reality even more superhuman than before, but it resituates the meaning of sacred otherness. Pre-Axially the god had a power greater than human, but the kind of power the god had was basically, a lot like human, i.e., superhuman. The Axial Age in articulating the power of the god as transcendent and mysterious means a power wherein "greater than" includes meaning being beyond, being other in the sense of radically different than, the human. Insofar as the otherness of the sacred, of the god—or acknowledging the Buddhists and materialists among the Axial Age movements, the otherness of true reality truly perceived—is like a human conception, we can be suspicious of it. In a word, the locus of otherness, or the new meaning ascribed to otherness, becomes transcendent. But even if we consider this transcendence as "wholly other" (a justly famous phrasing in religious studies literature), it is nonetheless a transcendent mystery that is not a blank unknown, but it has some accessible meaning to it, such that we can aspire to experience it, to know it in some necessarily limited, necessarily partial, sense, and in which we do participate. A spark, or hidden nature, or forgotten truth, or a submerged aspect of our soul, or unrealized potential of our mind, and so on, that is in us, is itself wholly other, is itself either transcendent or the means of access to transcendent reality. Thus, as the gods are transformed into an otherness that is neither superhuman nor supernatural but somehow a different kind of mysterious, so too in a lesser but still analogous way, human being is transformed too into the kinds of beings that, while we cannot become superhuman or supernatural beings, we can attain to being greater than what we were or are, but with the qualification added that the very process of self-transformation will itself change just what greatness means and what it consists in. For example, we might think, due to our issues with weakness and vulnerability, that greatness consists in becoming invulnerable, when it will turn out that accepting our weakness and admitting our vulnerability opens up dimensions of meaning—greater intimacy, care, and love—previously unknown that we recognize as a kind of greatness. In becoming "greater," we recognize that the invulnerable position is in fact the lower or lesser position. In becoming mysterious, both the nature of gods and the nature of human beings are changed and, as Jaspers puts it, their "majesty increased"; in being changed, part of what changes is the very register, or index, or most basically, the meaning, of what greatness is.

The meaning of performances of ritual and sacrifice changes accordingly too. Ritual and sacrifice has an inner dimension, and thus, mere observance of their demands will not suffice in being efficacious. Rituals become arduous spiritual exercises, disciplines, and practices that transform the inner life of the believer. It is no longer animals and children that are to be sacrificed on altars, but one's ego and its desires—lust, greed, pride, status—sacrificed through self-discipline, which is not an outward show but an inner struggle. "This world" becomes the egocentric will writ large into society and tradition. Further, that society and tradition are the lenses we wear to see others and the world, means this basic self-centeredness gets writ yet larger, as we interpret others and the world in such a way our attention becomes focused on greed-filled self-interest, fear-filled self-preservation, and pride-filled self-aggrandizement. Simultaneously, we become blinded to a deeper, selfless perception of the true meaning of others and of the world's spiritual possibilities. The hold of "this world" can be overcome through the rigor of prayer and meditation that transforms one's spirit such that the spiritual reality of the "other world" can begin to appear—not to the eyes, but to the heart and the soul.

A final transformation the Axial Age accomplishes, like a drawstring that ties the whole transcendent package together (and ties this presentation of Jaspers' thesis back to the opening points regarding the technologically effected real unity of humankind and which unity or universality requires a corresponding conscious realization), is that the new transcendent meaning of spirit, the new mystery of the sacred and the gods, and the new inwardness of the individual, is understood to be universal. It is not something unveiled, revealed, disclosed, remembered, attained, etc., as something exclusively for a particular ethnicity or for a particular people. (Judaism's claim to being "the chosen people" is complex in this regard; they are chosen in the sense of being the people to whom YHWH reveals Himself, but revealed as the one, true, universal God for all, to which the Jewish people must bear witness.) The meaning and truth of transcendence as universal, and the transformative consequences for the spirit that accompany an authentic orienting to its truth, is potentially accessible to any person or people regardless of ethnic membership, regardless of kinship relations, regardless of political citizenship or economic or social status. Subtly inserted within this transformed understanding of spirit is that any person is capable of accessing transcendence not automatically or mechanically or effortlessly, but the capacity depends on a transformation of that person. The capacity for self-transformation is available to anyone who makes that effort. And further, just as it transcends any particular membership group, so too it is not bound to any particular geography or place, nor is it bound to any particular history or time. As I tried to describe above in terms of how myth and the locus of belief is resituated and differentiated by the Axial Age, so too does transcendence transpose the meaning of spirit and reality relative to space and time. It is not bigger than all space, or older than all time, but introduces an other dimension of meaning into those terms and in so doing qualitatively transforms what they mean. The transcendent is certainly not bound to any human conventions, or to anything material (hence, the radical iconoclastic aspect of the Axial critique of idolatry). It is also not bound to any person; as we will see in the next chapter, the identification of the king with the god so crucial for pre-Axial mythologies of the state becomes untenable for an Axial believer. Rather, transcendence holds for anyone, including kings, and it holds anywhere (any place) and "anywhen" (any time).

Consequences of Transcendence: The Universal and the Individual

Transcendence provides a whole new plane of possibilities of identity for people. More precisely, as a universally available spiritual reality, it provides a whole new transcendent locus of identification, beyond those of ethnicity, kin, status, class, race, age, gender, the state, or even of history. This possibility for identification is so for groups or subcultures, for ethnicities, and for states; but what is truly momentous within the long arc of history is that this possibility is created for individuals, too. This pairing, of the universal to the individual, through a conceiving of a transcendence by definition beyond and irreducible to any existing category, is of enormous historic consequence and power. It creates a new degree and intensity to spiritual aspiration and releases an idealistic power that catalyzes all manner of psychological, cognitive, moral, emotional, and ideological dynamisms. Religions and civilizations that incorporate Axial thinking into their understanding tap into this power and dynamism. To cite one such consequence, for our understanding of freedom: The individual as a spiritual being is not, and cannot be, defined by any category less than the transcendent universal. I am not defined by my ethnicity, kinship relation, class, race, gender, and so on. As a physical being, I can be defined by my gender or skin color or my disability. As a political or economic being, I can be defined by my citizenship or my class or my income. However, it can be argued that none of these identify who "I really am." Ultimately, if who I am is defined by a universal spirit (Yahweh, or the *Logos*, or *Brahman*, or the *Tao*), my real, true identity transcends all those categories (or, with sufficient qualifications, the Buddhist conception of an interconnectedness so pervasive that identity itself is transcended in the experience of *nirvana*). This consequence manifests in a Martin Luther, supported only by God, who can defy the catholic, i.e., universal, church: "Here I stand!". It also manifests in modern Western individualism, for example, which appropriates and mis-takes the Axial Age conception of transcendence, and also manifests in the hugely important notion of human rights currently dominate in our globalizing world.

In part, the notion of transcendence can easily be raised to the status of universal as one key part of transcendence is that it is above and beyond the human. Transcendence breaks through the immanent ceiling inherent in all prior mythologizing, which even in its most vast and cosmologically inclusive, still snuck in some kind of anthropomorphism or human valuing and still held some criterion of human comprehensibility. The Axial Age in introducing the notion of transcendence creates a whole new criterion for spirit, a criterion as inescapable in its dissolving, disintegrating, criticizing effects on pre-Axial myth and traditions as it is seemingly impossible and unattainable on its own account of being essentially above and beyond the human. No human can become nothing but transcendence without leaving this world behind. Neither through a glimpse or experience of the transcendent, nor through prolonged exposure or repeated returns to it does the transcendent become internalized or a possession or in any way subordinate to the person or to this world. By definition, or as a spiritual fact, the reality of transcendence is beyond any individual and its meaning is beyond this world as defined by space and time.

Transcendence is also therefore beyond human comprehension and description and convention: Consequentially, it is described by the mystic as ineffable and indefinable, and this is meant as a positive attribute of reality (not merely, although it connotes this meaning too, a negative attribute of the limitations of description). Myth becomes parable. The *Tao* that can be defined is not the true *Tao*; the essence of transcendent truth in the *Upanisads* is "not this, not this!", while for Buddhism it is the self's realization that there is no self; Judaism (and Christianity and Islam, too) forbid the taking of God's name in vain and each elaborates a complex "negative theology"; the only thing, Socrates knows, is that he does not know anything. From the foundational Taoist text *Inward Training*: "The true state of that Way: How could it be conceived of and pronounced upon?" (Roth, 1999, p. 115). What will become described later as the *apophatic* dimension of mysticism is opened up within religiosity and spiritual experience. Silence, paradox, irony, ignorance, and every kind of indirection conceivable are employed as ways to negate the propositional and representative function of language while simultaneously affirming the non-propositional, expressive, and active functions of language which are capable of effecting, experientially through their performance, the conscious realization of meaning in the listener (Bagger, 2007; Katz, 1978a, 1978b, 1983, 1992; McGinn, 1991; Sells, 1994; Stace, 1960). Only through a heightened awareness of these differences can description in language truly be effective, not at capturing or even conveying the transcendent, but at signifying and symbolizing the proper human relation to the transcendent, the concern at the heart of "mysticism."

As an ideal reality above and beyond the merely human, transcendence is above all an orientation point or an orienting ideal in spiritual reality for we mere mortals to aspire to, for us to imitate or emulate, to unite with, before which to fear and tremble, to contemplate, to meditate on, to hope for, to love, etc. This is necessarily and inescapably so: and as such the transcendent is also beyond any monopoly, beyond any final word, beyond any exclusive access. Scholarship has registered this essential difference between transcendent reality and mundane reality by calling the Axial Age's distinctiveness a "breakthrough to" transcendence, as the "strain towards transcendence," trying to stress both the accessibility to transcendence as well as the impossibility of any comprehensive grasping or obtaining of transcendence. Hans Joas (2012) puts it the following way: "it would perhaps be even more precise, although maybe a bit pedantic, to speak of the age of the emergence of the idea of transcendence" (p. 11).

The Axial Age does not bring transcendent reality down into the world for everyone; it tries to awaken as many people as it can to look up to the idea of the transcendent as the ultimate meaning of reality to which we ought to orient our lives. In perhaps the most famous parable trying to explain this notion of the transcendent, Plato presents in Book VII of *The Republic* the allegory of the cave: The shackled residents of a cave who spend their life looking at shadows cast upon the wall from the fires burning behind them mistake these shadow images for reality. An escapee—from our point of view, the archetypal Axial Age wise guy; for Plato, he is modeled on Socrates—sees what is going on behind their backs and eventually leaves the cave and sees the sun, understands it as the true source of light and as indispensable for seeing, and gains a correct sense of reality. The truth of reality the escapee understands, embodied in the image of the sun as source of light, transcends—in multiple senses on multiple levels—the shadowplay the prisoners in the cave mistake for reality.

Of course, it is an allegory: The cave is society and the shadowplay the conventions of what society considers important and true. These conventions are none other than our egocentric desires and fears, writ large into society's values and way of life. These are a gross distortion and misunderstanding of truths and universals that, because they transcend the ego, require the person to transform—to leave the cave of the ego—such that he can begin to know the transcendent truth: The escapee looks up to the sun and realizes it is the source of light, which in turn is what is needed for shadows to be cast, too. Importantly, the escapee does not become the sun, ascend to its level, touch it, or in any way overcome the great distance between his person and the sun. As transcendent, the sun is above and beyond him; the escapee does not bring the sun down into the cave. As transcendent, it is meant to illuminate and orient mundane thought and action. Its transcendent distance is an essential part of what its reality is and how it is to be understood, even as the light that emanates from it is radically immanent as that which makes seeing—allegorically signifying thinking, knowing, understanding, and evaluating—possible. Despite this transcendent distance, the escapee's exposure to the sun's light is sufficient to effect a radical transformation in his knowing and being, exposing the egocentric ignorance in which he had been living.

COMPARING ACROSS AXIAL MOVEMENTS: AXIALITY AS A "FAMILY RESEMBLANCE"

I understand the commonalty between Jaspers' five Axial Age "spiritual revolutions" as being similar above all in the sense of a "family resemblance." The concept of family resemblance has been made well known by the philosopher Ludwig Wittgenstein as an alternative, or replacement, to "essentialism." In brief, the notion is that entities or phenomena may be similar enough that they can be considered belonging to the same class or type—even if they prove to have no single element or property in common—no identical essence—across all their different instantiations. Wittgenstein's own characterization, in trying to describe games, goes like this:

> What is common to them all? – Don't say: 'There must be something in common, or they would not be called "games"' – but look and see whether there is anything common to all. For if you look at them you will not see something that is common to all, but similarities, relationships, and a whole series of them at that. (*Philosophical Investigations*, § 66)

The argument applies to the Axial Age thesis insofar as "spiritual breakthroughs" are analogous to "games" in Wittgenstein's characterization. Rather than start with "religions" or "philosophies" or "civilizational worldviews" and say that because we're calling them that, they must be the same, instead we "look" at ancient Greece, Israel, Persia, India, and China, and we "see" not "something that is common to all," but a much broader and diffuse resemblance: "similarities, relationships, and a whole series of them at that."

For example, Zarathustra stands out immediately from Jaspers' list as the exception to the "efflorescence of isms" commonalty; but, perhaps there are other considerations for still considering this black sheep to indeed belong to the family, even if we accept him reluctantly and grudgingly—his "revolutionary prophetic" status by comparison with existing Persian religiosity, his insistence on the special nature of Ahura Mazda rather than the extant polytheism, his emphasis on the ethical consequences of piety, all bear resemblance to prophecy in ancient Israel, as well as to the internal critiques within India of ritual sacrifice and its inner meaning. For a different example, if transcendence is considered as the defining commonalty, China seems to present an exception as neither Confucianism nor Taoism are "transcendentally otherworldly" in their conceptions. Yet, in how they conceive of the Tao's "otherness" vis-à-vis cultural artifice, and the consequences for self-cultivation and self-development of a proper relation to the Tao, immediately bears comparative similarity to other Axial developments. Wittgenstein's family resemblance notion seems particularly applicable to Axial Age thesis in that no single element or combination of elements is common to all the different Axial Age movements or breakthroughs, yet they might still be considered as belonging together according to some other emergent qualities or collective features. In Wittgenstein's image, "the strength of the thread does not reside in the fact that some one fibre runs through its whole length, but in the overlapping of many fibres" (*Philosophical Investigations*, § 67).

If they lack some common essence, however, then on what grounds can one defend the similarity? Wittgenstein's argument was that if some sufficient amount of a cluster of elements overlap, across a number of examples, that marks them out as somehow similar, then they can be said to bear a "family resemblance" (Reference: The irony is that Wittgenstein derives the notion of "family resemblance" from Spengler's comparative approach to civilizational analysis, a key forerunner to Jaspers' in terms of world history and comparative civilizational analysis!). In Wittgenstein's words, "we see a complicated network of similarities overlapping and criss-crossing: sometimes overall similarities" (*Philosophical Investigations*, § 66). Key to this conception, too, is that the cluster of elements is not strictly definable and might differ in how it overlaps from case to case. A different way to phrase this: If how a number of parts are composed and patterned such that the overall Gestalt of otherwise different entities leads to the perception that they are comparable, then they have a family resemblance. Wittgenstein develops the notion in trying to explain games and applies it to how we understand numbers and, above all, languages (the notion of "language game" is probably Wittgenstein's most signature idea). Part of what is insightful about the family resemblance approach is that it gives credence to reasonable intuitions and perceptions about something in common even if that something can't be precisely articulated. Long before genetics research and DNA testing, people's intuitive ability detected resemblances among family members without being able to name what that resemblance was.

Comparing one "family" to another can show close relatives and more distant relatives, just as within a family there can be greater and lesser degrees of sameness across siblings, and beyond that, of cousins, etc. Although Jaspers doesn't mention Wittgenstein's notion of "family resemblances," nor does he make any methodological claims to support my ascription of this notion as applicable to him, I think it is the most accurate way to characterize Jaspers' comparative method. Given

Jaspers' overt indebtedness to Max Weber, I suspect Jaspers' approach if he made it explicit would most overtly be modeled on Weber's "ideal type" methodology. Weber, dealing with the same problem of comparative method, suggested the abstracting out from empirical particulars of an ideal type that, because abstract and idealized, would be a theoretical model to compare the empirical particulars against to be better able to describe them. Weber proposes this method not to enshrine ideal types as real or essential, but as a heuristic aide to improve the sociologist's ability to describe the empirical particulars of specific cases. Jaspers, a philosopher rather than a sociologist, is not attending to the empirical particulars in great detail. He could be said to be abstracting an ideal type of "Axiality" from the five civilizations, but he is doing this to delineate a dividing line within history of before and after, not so as to look more closely at Greek philosophers to see just how transcendental, mysterious, and universalizing their thought was or wasn't. I perceive Wittgenstein's notion of family resemblances to better capture both how Jaspers is actually working and the ideal consequences he hopes to achieve—a recognition of deep differences that stimulates an effort to communicate across them.

Yet a third way of trying to characterize Jaspers' way of working could be taken from the American philosopher and transpersonal psychologist Ken Wilber, who proposes a way of deriving what he calls "orienting generalizations" through comparative study of numerous theories. Different specialized theories, for example of developmental theories (Wilber's preferred example), don't easily translate from one into the other. They have different emphases, methods, questions that they bring to their study. On the other hand, all are studying development, so there ought to be some level of comparison despite these differences. Wilber deals with this by abstracting back from the specialized studies until he finds the sufficiently abstract level of generalization at which point the studies can be compared. Using this as the level from which to then orient his own theory, whose aim is not specialized like the theories he's examining but integral in that he wants to put the theories together, Wilber is able to propose "orienting generalizations" as the basis for his own integral theory. Jaspers, and Axial Age theorists more generally, could be interpreted as trying to derive "orienting generalizations" that characterize "the Axial Age" as an integral phenomenon, from the more specialized theories that are the different Axial Age movements in their respective Greek, Israelite, Indian, and Chinese contexts.

Jürgen Habermas, as a German philosopher closest to Jaspers in terms of intellectual heritage and context, considers Jaspers' to be endorsing a kind of historical version of Platonic idealism in his abstracting the core ideas of the Axial Age (Habermas, 1983, p. 49; see also Joas, 2012). Habermas is quite critical of Jaspers on this point. Interestingly, Habermas, who also shows significant interest in the Axial Age, shares Jaspers' "ideal of boundless communication." (At the time of this writing, he's been working on a manuscript, ostensibly still forthcoming, focused on its importance in terms of "cognitive breakthroughs" [cf. Mendieta, 2013, pp. 405–406].) Much of Habermas' career has been extensive exploration of this ideal and more broadly the notion of "communicative action." Presumably, he does not consider this ideal to be of the Platonic variety.

Of these possibilities—Wittgenstein's family resemblances, Weberian ideal types, Platonic idealism, Wilber's orienting generalizations, and Habermas' communicative ideal—it seems to me the different Axial Age movements are best described following Wittgenstein as bearing a "family resemblance": They are neither of a single essence internally to a particular civilization (as, e.g., Buddhism and Hinduism in India have significant differences in how they conceive of ultimate reality, as without or with a god; Confucianism and Taoism have a very different approach and understanding of the nature and meaning of the *Tao*, etc.), nor is there some such essence across different civilizations—the Chinese *Tao* is very different from the YHWH of Judaism, while the *Logos* of the Greeks is very different from Buddhism's *nirvana*. (The philosopher of religion John Hick [1989] advances the notion of family resemblance as core to his treatment of religion, too; he provides an articulation of how [pp. 3–5]. Just as basic and fundamental to his argument is also the distinction between pre-axial religions and axial religion [pp. 22–33].) But these differences are not absolute either. They each present "clusters of elements" that, well, resemble each other. Buddhism, Hinduism, and Jainism, could all be said to have a strong "sibling" relationship in their emphasis on meditation, their conception of ultimate reality as nondual, their rejection of this world as illusory and the cause of suffering, and the highest goal to escape from this world. This similarity signals belonging to the same Indian "family," which we could designate through some appropriate surname that captures the similarities; let's say, "spiritual asceticism." This is something Buddhism, Hinduism, and Jainism all share. Looking more closely at them, we'd see quickly that the degree of sibling rivalry is quite extreme: Each sibling defines itself polemically as the superior position and gives strong criticisms of the others. And so on, using this version of "family resemblance", Jaspers' list can be summarized as four families: in Greece, philosophical rationalism; in West Asia, Zoroastrianism and Judaism develop ethical monotheism (followed by Christianity and Islam, also in western Asia, centuries later); in India, spiritual asceticism; and in China, ethical humanism.

The real issue for the Axial Age thesis, however, is to show that these four "families" are in turn "related" and, at some level, share a family resemblance. Hopefully, at a brief glance at the four families just named, it is not clear how they could be said to be similar. It seems to me Jaspers argues that these four different families can be considered part of one "extended" family; not as close as siblings, but rather more like cousins spanning the range of first-, second-, and third-degree. They are related insofar as they share a broader kinship in conceiving of ultimate reality as universal, transcendent, mysterious, spiritual, and accessible inwardly; if my argument in this book bears up under scrutiny, they are also related in emphasizing a critical rejection of "big" power, advocating a countercultural turn toward small communities, organized around spiritual practices as the means for persons to access this ultimate reality. Through these practices that transform the person through overcoming the ego, the person is enabled to practice transcendence.

Concluding Remarks: Jaspers as a Significant Advance, and His Ideal of Boundless Communication

The Origin and Goal of History is a difficult, fascinating, uneven, and provocative piece of writing, in which Jaspers lays out his thesis for the Axial Age as on the one hand crucial, on the other subordinate in the sense that it is crucial relevant to our contemporary problems of the "Age of Technology." I've tried to summarize the main gist of his characterization of what the Axial Age is through describing a cluster of key elements: a spiritual revolution in consciousness, involving transcendence, inwardness, mystery, identity, the universal and the individual. Ideally, you have gained enough of a sense of the Axial Age that the ways in which Jaspers' "bold idea, briefly sketched" will be refined, rejected, clarified, and elaborated by later scholarship are understandable too. The scholarship on the Axial Age explodes after Jaspers and considerably improves the thesis in the process. But the scholarship does not entirely leave Jaspers behind in this process, and the advances they make are a credit to Jaspers' work and remain indebted to it.

Scholarship after Jaspers is enabled to extend his work in large part because compared to earlier scholarship Jaspers accomplishes a significant advance in understanding the Axial Age. First, in bounding the Axial Age in time (the six centuries 800–200 BCE), in number (five civilizations), and geographically (the three areas of China, India, and "Hellas" or "the West," i.e., west Asia and Greece, or perhaps best, "the ancient Near East") he focuses and greatly delimits the scope of inquiry. Second, in refining the notion of how to contextualize and compare developments in these centuries in these areas no longer in terms of lists of noteworthy individuals nor in terms of some mysterious singular essence they shared but instead as different clusters of a great diversity of movements that nevertheless display a "family resemblance" of common dynamisms and analogous elements, Jaspers articulates the idea of the Axial Age far beyond the mere noting of a "remarkable coincidence" or the "stupendous marvel" of a sudden, simultaneous, synchronous parallel development. Thirdly, Jaspers as an existential philosopher writing in a post-World War II context has two advantages in presenting the Axial Age thesis. One is the powerful and popular interest in exploring narratives of the fall or decline of Western civilization in the context of world history. Inserting the Axial Age onto center stage of this interest brings the thesis out of the somewhat enclosed domains of disciplinary specialists who had speculated about it, and into a comparative, generalist domain of much broader scope, of more contemporary interest, and in engagement with influential veins in scholarship at the time. The other advantage is Jaspers characterizing the Axial Age in terms of a revolution in consciousness; his existential, psychological, philosophical background affords him an extensive vocabulary to describe the perceived changes the Axial Age visionaries wrought in their respective civilizations. Together, these amount to a significant advance in the idea of an Axial Age. Like earlier scholarship, Jaspers' claims are still speculation; unlike earlier scholarship (with, as noted above, a few exceptions), it was a much more rigorous, interesting, and quasi-systematic speculation that afforded translation by later scholars into a viable research thesis that has been taken up by others and in which, decades later, interest continues to burgeon.

In concluding this chapter, I want us to look at one final contribution Jaspers' makes that is particularly insightful for how to think the clash of ultimates. This contribution is Jaspers' proposal for a universality that would resolve the issue of differences across the different Axial Age civilizations without reducing the differences to some singular essence. (To invoke the concept of family resemblance once again, the issue is how to recognize resemblances according to some similarity without ignoring or oversimplifying real differences between family members within the same family.) After all, while each Axial Age revolution might, in some abstract formal sense, have a similar or comparable conception of transcendence as characteristic of ultimate reality, in more concrete, particular senses, the different characterizations of transcendence are significantly different, in a way that cannot be reduced without terrible distortions.

Jaspers characterizes this fact of difference across the different Axial Age formations—and different within them as well (Hinduism and Buddhism, e.g., have profoundly diverging understandings of ultimate reality, despite both being developed within the same Indian civilization; the Greek philosophers are as irreducibly diverse as are the Chinese sages as are the Jewish prophets)—as crucially and fundamentally significant. This fact of difference refuses a monopoly of one particular formation as the universal truth and sets in its stead the "challenge to boundless communication" (1953, p. 19) across these differences. To try to consciously think the unity of humanity historically based on the Axial Age as pluralistic foundation means in practice to engage in deep and authentic communication with many others. This is what Jaspers is after. "Unity can be gained only from the depth of historicity, not as a common, knowable content but in boundless communication of the historically different in never-ending dialogue, rising to heights of noble emulation" (1951, p. 106). In contrast to global war as violent realization of the real unity of the world, it should be obvious why communication and dialogue are preferable. "A dialogue of this sort requires an area of freedom from violence" (1951, p. 106). These are desirable alternatives on ethical grounds: They present a nonviolent realization of unity, an ideal of universality that respects and preserves differences. True respect here neither reduces differences to one same cognitive content—hence Jaspers appeals to boundless communication, a never-ending dialogue—nor does it enshrine difference as some untouchable absolute—one's position can be communicated and dialogued. Nor is it a relativistic stalemate of incommensurably different positions; Jaspers sees the outcome of the dialogue process as a "rising to heights of noble emulation."

It now remains to connect the "challenge to boundless communication" as Jaspers' ideal of universality to the previous chapter's discussion of the problem of the clash of ultimates. The deep and perhaps intractable differences between people's conceptions of what is ultimately meaningful, means that if put together—more precisely, when the contemporary processes of globalization force these conceptions together—they will clash. But what form will this clash take? Is war and conflict unavoidable? Must a clash of differences take violent form? Jaspers offers a different, nonviolent way to conceive of clash: the apparent irreconcilability of different positions, their presumed intractability as each stakes claim to its own particular version of universality and ultimacy, could have the consequence of moving us into depth and boundless communication; as demanding freedom, respect, authenticity; as initiating a never-ending dialogue, argument, and debate, a demanding conversation that raises and ennobles us. This is, on the one hand, as ideals often are, an invitation to hope, a beautiful and inspiring notion. On the other hand, it also might appear, as ideals often do, as being, well, too idealistic, too impracticable and too unrealistic; Jaspers ought to change his name to Pollyanna, and so forth. Before rejecting Jaspers' beautiful ideal as impractical, however, we should examine what informs that ideal—the structure of world history, derived from the Axial Age—and above all, what the spiritual *virtuosi* of the Axial Age themselves put forward as being practicable.

REFERENCES

Bagger, M. (2007). *The uses of paradox (religion, self-transformation, and the absurd)*. New York: Columbia University Press.

Bellah, R., & Joas, H. (2012a). Introduction. In R. Bellah & H. Joas (Eds.), *The Axial Age and its consequences* (pp. 1–6). Cambridge and London: Belknap.

Bellah, R., & Joas, H. (Eds.). (2012b). *The Axial Age and its consequences*. Cambridge and London: Belknap.

Boy, J., & Torpey, J. (2013). Inventing the Axial Age: The origins and uses of a historical concept. *Theory and Society, 42*(3), 241–259.

Habermas, J. (1983). *Philosophical-political profiles* (F. G. Lawrence, Trans.). Cambridge: MIT Press (originally published in 1981).

Hadot, P. (1995). *Philosophy as a way of life: Spiritual exercises from Socrates to Foucault* (A. Davidson, Ed.). Oxford and Cambridge: Blackwell.

Halton, E. (2014). *From the Axial Age to the moral revolution*. Basingstoke: Palgrave Macmillan.

Hick, J. (1989). *An interpretation of religion: Human responses to the transcendent*. New Haven, CT: Yale University Press.

Jaspers, K. (1951). *Way to wisdom*. New Haven and London: Yale University Press.

Jaspers, K. (1953). *The origin and goal of history*. New Haven and London: Yale University Press (originally published in 1949).

Jaspers, K. (1974). Philosophical autobiography. In P. Schilpp (Ed.), *The philosophy of Karl Jaspers* (pp. 5–94). La Salle, IL: Open Court.

Joas, H. (2012). The Axial Age debate as religious discourse. In R. Bellah & H. Joas (Eds.), *The Axial Age and its consequences* (pp. 9–29). Cambridge and London: Belknap.

Katz, S. (Ed.). (1978a). *Mysticism and philosophical analysis*. New York: Oxford University Press.

Katz, S. (1978b). Language, epistemology, and mysticism. In S. Katz (Ed.), *Mysticism and philosophical analysis* (pp. 22–74). New York: Oxford University Press.

Katz, S. (Ed.). (1983). *Mysticism and religious traditions*. New York: Oxford University Press.

Katz, S. (Ed.). (1992). *Mysticism and language*. New York: Oxford University Press.

McGinn, B. (1991). *The foundations of mysticism: Origins to the fifth century*. New York: Crossroad.

Mendieta, E. (2013). Appendix: Religion in Habermas's work. In C. Calhoun, E. Mendieta, & J. VanAntwerpen (Eds.), *Habermas and religion* (pp. 391–407). Cambridge and Malden, MA: Polity Press.

Otto, R. (1923). *The idea of the holy: An inquiry into the non-rational factor in the idea of the divine and its relation to the rational* (J. W. Harvey, Trans.). London and New York: Oxford University Press.

Rhys-Davids, T. (1903). *Buddhist India*. New York: Putnam.

Roth, H. (1999). *Original Tao: Inward training (nei-yeh) and the foundations of Taoist mysticism*. New York: Columbia University.

Sells, M. (1994). *Mystical languages of unsaying*. Chicago and London: University of Chicago.

Spengler, O. (1926–1928). *The decline of the West* (2 Vols.) (C. Atkinson, Trans.). New York: Alfred A. Knopf (originally published 1918).

Stace, W. (1960). *Mysticism and philosophy*. Los Angeles: Tarcher.

Toynbee, A. (1934–1961). *A study of history* (12 Vols.). London: Oxford University Press.

Voegelin, E. (1956). *Order and history, Vol. I: Israel and revelation*. Baton Rouge: Louisiana State University Press.

Voegelin, E. (1974). *Order and history, Vol. IV: The ecumenic age*. Baton Rouge: Louisiana State University Press.

Wittrock, B. (2005). The meaning of the Axial Age. In J. Arnason, S. Eisenstadt, & B. Wittrock (Eds.), *Axial civilizations and world history* (pp. 51–86). Leiden: Brill.

CHAPTER 4

The Axial Age in Context: The Growth of Civilization and the Expansion of Power

INTRODUCTION

To get our bearings, to gain some perspective on our contemporary moment, and to be able to discern "the shape of the present," we need to take a long range, big picture perspective. The Axial Age as a world history thesis does that, even as world history as the human story itself belongs within the yet larger perspective of the evolutionary history of life on the planet. This chapter lays out the context for the Axial Age within the historical growth of civilizations during the first millennium BCE, above all their unprecedented expansion of power at that time. This "expansionism" is itself an extension of the natural and evolutionary tendency to expand. Webb (2015) puts it succinctly: "Now, everything we know about terrestrial life tells us that life has a natural tendency to expand into all available space" (p. 1). Darwin (2001) expressed the point most eloquently in one of his most well-known passages, using the now-famous image of a "great Tree of Life":

> The affinities of all the beings of the same class have sometimes been represented by a great tree. I believe this simile largely speaks the truth. ... At each period of growth all the growing twigs have tried to branch out on all sides, and to overtop and kill the surrounding twigs and branches, in the same manner as species and groups of species have tried to overmaster other species in the great battle for life. The limbs divided into great branches, and these into lesser and lesser branches, were themselves once, when the tree was small, budding twigs... Of the many twigs which

© The Author(s) 2019
C. Peet, *Practicing Transcendence*,
https://doi.org/10.1007/978-3-030-14432-6_4

flourished when the tree was a mere bush, only two or three, now grown into great branches, yet survive and bear all the other branches... As buds give rise by growth to fresh buds, and these, if vigorous, branch out and overtop on all sides many a feebler branch, so by generation I believe it has been with the great Tree of Life, which fills with its dead and broken branches the crust of the earth, and covers the surface with its ever branching and beautiful ramifications. (pp. 121–122)

This passage and image applies equally well to world history and the Axial Age, too, and we shall periodically return to it. Another advantage this image has: It develops the minimal geometric notion of a "dividing line" within world history into "branching and beautiful ramifications," a more adequate image of the complexities of the world-historical developments—the growth of civilization, the expansion of power—occurring in the first millennium BCE.

A BIG PICTURE PERSPECTIVE ON "CIVILIZATION"

Jaspers understood that "the simplest explanation of the phenomena of the Axial Period seems to lie in common sociological preconditions favourable to spiritual creativeness" (1953, p. 17). In this respect, Jaspers is repeating part of the formula developed over the centuries of speculating on the Axial Age, voiced for example by Rhys-Davids in the previous chapter: There must be similar causes, similar conditions, a similar process of gestation within civilizations.... However, in keeping with his existential philosophy, Jaspers is at pains to make sure that the achievements of the Axial Age as a spiritual high point in human consciousness would not be reduced to some material, evolutionary, or social scientific explanation. "No one can adequately comprehend what occurred here and became the axis of world history!" (1953, p. 18).

Be that as it may, it has not stopped a number of scholars from trying to discern, and a few offering, just such reductive explanations in terms of sociological factors; the Axial Age is explained by the rise in affluence, for example, or by the rise in literacy. The majority of scholars have not aimed at such reductive explanation but do study the social factors present. Both kinds of sociological work taken together have explored in earnest the "common sociological preconditions." Of most immediate and obvious significance: The Axial Age happens in the context of the Old World civilizations along the Eurasian east-west axis.

What is the relation of the Axial Age breakthroughs to "civilization"? We can ask this question both in a big picture way, i.e., the relation to civilization in general, as well as in terms of the relation of the break-throughs to their specific civilizations. The latter question involves look-ing at first millennium BCE Greece, Israel, India, and China. It also involves the further question as to what were the roles, status, positions, and so on, of the Axial Age visionaries within their respective civiliza-tions. In asking these questions, the accompanying question of common-alties and differences across the civilizations, and across the respective groupings of spiritual *virtuosi*, comes along too. This will be the focus of Chapter 5.

The fact of the exceptional or anomalous status of the breakthroughs needs to be kept in mind also. There are many more than four civili-zations during these centuries, and the rule or paradigm evident from these: no Axial breakthrough. (It is appropriate to further note, that "civilization" itself is the exception and not the rule in terms of human societies—less than 1% of all human societies have been "civiliza-tions"—a point to which we will return.) Since one of the aims of this book is to provide a sense of the shape of the present insofar as the Axial Age provides us with a map of world history, that this shape and map in turn depend on the shape of the civilizational past provided by a map of human prehistory is not surprising. What is perhaps surprising, is how insightful the big picture of civilization in the context of prehistory is for the Axial Age—and for our present, too—and is the focus of this chapter.

The Shape of the Past: Human Prehistory

Let's sketch this big picture, which returns us to our time-lapse video metaphor proposed in the previous chapter. I suggested we needed to reconcile two images: the first image a snapshot of our contempo-rary globalizing world, the second a time-lapse video of the globe from human prehistory to the present, with the Axial Age "breakthrough to transcendence" pictured on it occurring around 2500 years ago marking the key transition point. Up to that point, there was little to no con-ception at all, or at best an occasional mere inkling, of human being in universal terms: The identity of human being was always understood in particular terms (whether local, ethnic, tribal, or state terms). After that point, the inklings of universality articulated by the Axial Age visionar-ies, become inkblots that grow to the size of larger empires, and further outgrow and outlast such imperial boundaries until we have our contemporary world defined by half a dozen or so world civilizations/religions, with a smattering of isolated tribes of indigenous peoples at various geographically remote places. We'll return to this image, but for now will describe four details of the lengthy span of prehistory aspect of the timelapse, with a pause at appropriately significant time points of the video.

First detail: *homo sapiens sapiens*, or "anatomically and behaviorally modern human beings" (i.e., us!), appear in Africa. There are different evidences for the first *homo sapiens sapiens*, all in Africa. Pettitt (2018, p. 113) cites three groupings, the earliest predating 300,000 years ago, the transitional middle group dating between 350 and 125,000 years ago, and the latest, dating from between 125 and 70,000 years ago. McBrearty and Brooks (2000) argue for evidence sometime between 250,000 and 50,000 years ago (cf. also Stringer, 2002, 2016). For the sake of convenience, let's round off the origin date to 200,000 years ago, admittedly a rough, simplistic, and fuzzy estimate. For the first 130,000 or so years from this origin point, we see small groups mill about in Africa, and a very slow increase in human population. As this amounts to over half of the time-lapse video, even adjusting for the time-lapse speed, you might still feel like "fast forwarding" through this first half. One piece within this detail that you might miss, however, if you skimmed through it too rapidly: that the very slow increase in human population was not uniform, but uneven. Population size waxed and waned; reconstruction from mitochondrial DNA evidence suggests population dropped to as low as 10,000 at one point, with a maximum of about 1500 females, around 70,000 years ago, due to a particularly cold glacial snap at that time (Pettitt, 2018, p. 119).

Second detail: Long before *homo sapiens sapiens*, numerous different types of hominids evolve in Africa, and across Eurasia, for some millions of years. Modern human beings will replicate, albeit greatly accelerated, this migratory pattern. Owing to the cooling and warming patterns of the Earth's climate until 70–60,000 years ago, neither early hominids nor later types (like *homo sapiens Neanderthalensis*) prove able to range particularly far, nor settle with great longevity in any region (inclusive of Africa itself). Post 60,000 years, however, there is movement out from Africa, in the form of a continuing very slow increase in geographic spread for human groups into Asia, Australia, and Europe over the next tens of thousands of years. Fagan (2010) claims that "as far as we can tell, no modern humans lived outside Africa until around 59,000 years ago" (p. 89, cf. also p. 101). Corresponding to this spread is a continuing of the small tribe size, a continuing of the "milling about," or "roving." From 60,000 to 30,000 years ago, we see migration first into Western Asia ("the Levantine corridor," running from Red Sea to Black Sea) and into Southern and Southeast Asia; into Europe; and into and across the Southeast Asian land bridge of that time (present-day Malaysia and Indonesia) into Australia (~50,000–40,000 years ago) and into Far-Eastern Asia. By 20,000 years ago Northern Asia (Siberia) is reached.

The careful (or bored) observer will have noted, in addition to the geographic spread beyond Africa to three further continents, two further points of interest within this second detail: The first is the importance of a very long east-west Afroeurasian belt that becomes where the action is ("action" here meaning a very hyperbolic description for the really slow unfolding of human prehistory). The belt stretches along the southern edge of the Asian continent, touching at its western tip the eastern edge of the Mediterranean Sea (bounded to the north by southeastern Europe, to the south by northeast Africa), while its eastern tip extends to the Pacific Ocean along the east coast of Asia (bounded to the south by the island archipelagos of Indonesia and Oceania, and to the north by the great expanses of Mongolia). Thus, "Afroeurasian" is the technically correct term geographically, but effectively the bulk of it is Asian, with only a bit of Africa (i.e., Egypt and Mediterranean Africa) and of Europe (southeastern Europe, and the accessible parts of Mediterranean Europe). (The inhospitable Sahara in Africa and the geographical and climatic challenges of Europe's mountains and cold prove extreme challenges over these tens of thousands of years.) We might be further tempted to call this belt something like a "thoroughfare" due to the traffic-like movements and migrations of peoples west and east within it, if we let ourselves get caught up enough in the hyperbole of this description and were to forget the true timescale of the video. The point, to which we will return below, is that for reasons of geography and climate, this long, east-west, Afroeurasian belt, displaces the initial 130,000+ years of roving and milling about in Africa as being where the (human prehistoric) action is. Africa is the homeland, but it is the long, east-west, Afroeurasian belt that—to continue hyperbolically with the modern traffic metaphor—becomes "central station" for the dispersal of human beings to the rest of the world.

The second point of interest is, relative to the timescale and the extent of migration, the spread out of Africa is something of an "explosion" in the accelerated speed and more extensive reach of the *homo sapiens sapiens* dispersal, post-50,000 years ago. Pettitt (2018) calls this pattern a "first radiation" and offers an explanation for this (citing archaeologist Steven Mithen) in terms of a cognitive breakthrough based on "new connections between previously isolated mental domains [of] environmental, technical, and social intelligence," which gave a "cognitive fluidity" to human thought, combining natural and social symbolizing in a new unity that "gave *Homo sapiens sapiens...* a competitive edge over resident earlier human populations" (p. 100). Relatively speaking, post-50,000 years ago these humans spread beyond Africa throughout Europe, Asia, and Australasia, either assimilating through interbreeding or driving into extinction the other human populations there.

By 15,000 years ago the Americas are reached and humans begin to spread throughout both continents—what Pettitt (2018) calls the "second radiation" of human migration following the "first radiation" throughout the Old World. (A lot of sporadic evidence suggests far earlier entry into the Americas; but the sporadic, distributed, and uneven nature of the evidence implies that these early entries did not sustain themselves. However, these intrepid explorers crossed the Pacific and settled across sites in North and South America, we don't know, neither have we detected any continuity in identity between these early entries, and the far greater, sustained, and continuous to the present day, expansion of around 15,000 years ago.) After a mere couple of thousand years, this "second radiation" has spread throughout the extent of both Americas. This development also signals the completion of our second detail: the expansion of human populations across the inhabitable continents of the earth. Note that, depending on how one defines "globalization," above all on what timescale and significance scale one conjures in the background of the definition, it could plausibly be argued that globalization began at this point in time, about 12,000 years ago. (Some islands like Hawaii or Madagascar are not reached until about 500 AD; New Zealand by about 1000 AD. Antarctica is finally reached by 1820 AD. And yes, we get to the moon, too, in 1969—but since that "spread of humans" takes us off-planet, it's not really part of the story here.)

Third detail: While 12,000 years ago marks in terms of global spread the inhabiting of the Americas and thus expansion to all the major continents except Antarctica, it also marks the beginning of the next noteworthy development: Agriculture and animal domestication develop around 12,000 to 10,000 years ago. (Why the coincidence between reaching the Americas and agriculture and domestication? Global warming after the most recent "little ice age," both enables access to the Americas over the no longer ice-blocked land bridge from Asia and provides warm enough temperatures for agricultural production within particular fertile terrains that sustain grains, wheat, and rice, along the long, east-west, Afroeurasian belt. See Diamond [1997] for a wonderful summary of the latter.) This "Neolithic revolution" introduces major innovations that distinguish the new agrarian societies from all of the past of human pre-history as defined by hunter-gatherer or forager societies. (Of course, such a distinction between hunter-gatherer societies and agrarian is ter-ribly oversimplified and reduces the complexity of the sociological vari-ety of civilizational forms intermediate between the smaller-scale societies and larger civilizations. For a detailed overview of this complexity and variety, see Bellah, 2011, pp. 117–264; Johnson & Earle, 2000; Mann, 2012, pp. 34–129.) Our careful observer notes that these agrarian soci-eties mostly appear within that east-west Afroeurasian belt; that they all display much higher populations than all the previous human groups; and that they are sedentary, not roving or milling about, as all the previ-ous human groups were.

THE SHAPE OF THE PAST: FROM AGRICULTURE TO "CIVILIZATIONS" TO WORLD-SYSTEM

The advances accomplished by the Neolithic revolution have the conse-quence in the following millennia of an acceleration in the rate of overall world population increase, as well as an increase in tribe size (Carneiro [1978] estimates tribe size increases from about 40 to about 100), and in the cases of agrarian societies, much higher populations yet and the new possibility of amalgamation of smaller societies (rather than the fis-sioning of too-large societies or the fusing of too-small societies, and all the forms of differentiation and proliferation in between, as had been the rule). A careful scrutiny of this picture at this point would reveal that the agrarian societies, the majority of which are within that east-west Afroeurasian belt, show significantly higher populations than all other societies (i.e., higher populations than 99% of all other societies prior to, or extent with, these agrarian societies). The evidence also shows that over time these already higher populations of agrarian soci-eties demonstrate a steeper rate of population growth too; for example, after the introduction of agriculture to Britain about 6000 years ago, "this allowed the hunter-gatherers to settle, leading to a quadrupling of the population in just 400 years" (Goldin, Cameron, & Balarajan, 2011, p. 19). Within these agrarian societies: a small percentage—statistically anomalous, the exceptions rather than the rule—grow into cities, etymologically the root for the word "civilization," into states, into empires. Due to this development, the growth of human population and cultures ceases to be exclusively in terms of geographic spread (i.e., extensive growth) as intensive population growth of sedentary cultures emerges as an additional and alternative factor—"infill," if you like—within human prehistory. And recalling the earlier point that Asia geographically predominates the Afroeurasian belt, in cultural or civilizational or world-system terms, with the exception of Egypt the belt is Asian. Expansion of human being in terms of geographic spread and the differentiation and proliferation of human societies, which prohibited the expansion of human power relative to any particular society (expanding through extensive means), becomes the expansion of human being in terms of the increase of power: Powerful human societies now begin to expand into a larger size geographically by growing from a sedentary base, and they grow by amalgamating (and reducing the diversity of) societies with which they come into contact and which they assimilate (expansion through intensive means). This additional factor, of an expansion in power and an intensive growth in population, signals new evolutionary conditions for human cultures involving population pressures and densities, technological challenges of resource depletion, sociological and political challenges concerning social complexity and governance, and so on.

Focusing on these agrarian anomalies and the emergence of cities and civilizations also supplies us with our fourth and final detail for sketching this general picture of human prehistory leading to civilization. Beginning from around 3000 BC from within the few dozen agrarian sites within that east-west Afroeurasian belt emerge four river valley civilizations: in Sumer in the land between the Tigris & Euphrates rivers, i.e., Mesopotamia (beginning between 3900 and 3200 BC); around the Nile valley in Egypt (also around 3200 BC); around the Indus Valley in India (between 2300 and 2000 BC); and around the Yellow River and other rivers in China (around 1800 BC). Unlike the many other Neolithic-era settlements or centers, that pre-date or post-date the beginnings of these civilizations (e.g., Çatalhöyük in southern Turkey, around 5000 BC, or Minoan civilization in Crete, around 2500 BC), the four mentioned don't show the same collapsed-and-abandoned pattern at the end of their life span. (The Indus Valley is an arguable case: to what extent there is cultural continuity as Indian civilization relocates in the following centuries further east along the Ganges remains an unanswered question.) Instead, of collapse-and-abandonment, Mesopotamia, Egypt, the Indus Valley (arguably), and China show a far stronger degree of settled continuity in the same geographic area, in the sense that although there is change, dynamism, and collapses of specific civilizations, specific cities, or specific empires, there is also a rebuilding and resurgence of civilizations, cities, and empires. This continuity means we need to introduce a quite different criterion of significance to determine at what date to pause our time-lapse video. The east-west Afroeurasian belt which has cropped up several times during this description as a recurring feature of our general picture provides us with such a criterion.

Much of the significance of this belt has been explored in detail by Jared Diamond (1997) in his book *Guns, Germs, and Steel*. Diamond calls attention to shared geographic and climate features of the "E-W axis" (Diamond's phrase) of Afroeurasia which provide particular advantages to civilizations and cultures along the axis. Sharing the same latitudes despite great east-west distances enables significant technology transfer (cultivated strains of grain and wheat, domesticated animals, agricultural tools and techniques) across different, widely separated civilizations. A north–south orientation prevents this kind of transfer. By emphasizing, not individual civilizations in all of their glory and tragedy, but the broader network within which these civilizations are placed as parts of a larger interconnected system shines a revealing light on the anomaly of "civilization." The emergence, development, and longevity of a civilization do not depend exclusively on internal factors (although these are certainly important), but also on extra-civilizational factors (like climate, geography, diseases) and intercivilizational connections (like trade, warfare, travel, and information networks).

Interpreting the development of the four river valley civilizations in this light also provides us with a criterion for our fourth detail in our general picture: the degree of closure of the network or degree of consolidation of the interconnectedness of the intercivilizational system along the E-W axis of Afroeurasia (what Grinin & Korotayev, 2012, consider the "third phase" in the development of the Eurasian world-system). Interestingly, a scholar like Marshall Hodgson (1974) considers this consolidation the achievement of the Axial Age and that we should consider the age as historically decisive "because it resulted in an enduring geographical and cultural articulation of the citied zone of the Oikumene into regions" (p. 112). Beyond a particular civilization, however defined, its growth or decline, rise or fall, interactions with other civilizations, and interactions with its periphery societies or hinterland tribes (these are some of the commonplace terms used in world-systems theory to distinguish areas from civilizational centers or cores), has significant consequences and vice versa. "In 1000 BCE most of the Mediterranean was effectively prehistoric; by 500 BCE it formed a series of well differentiated zones within a world-system" (cited in Bellah, 2011, p. 656 n10). What effected this structuring of the Mediterranean from unconnected regions into a system with well-differentiated zones was primarily influence and pressure from the emerging civilizations in the Near East like Phoenicia, Assyria, and Persia, on the one hand, and the surprising "efflorescence" of the Greeks as a culturally shared, politically decentralized, sea-faring distribution of states, on the other (Ober, 2015). By extension, this transition is going on everywhere in and around the E-W axis of Afroeurasia through these centuries.

By about 200 BC, the relative autonomy (or if you prefer, "well differentiated zones") of the variety of civilizations along the east-west Afroeurasian belt, including that of our four river valley civilizations in China, India, Mesopotamia, and Egypt, has given way to a far greater degree of interconnection (Chase-Dunn & Hall, 1997). There are three main forms of interconnection. The first is probably the most significant: the development of the Silk Road (more precisely, silk roads in the plural; cf. Christian, 2000). In McNeill's (1963) words: "Shortly before the Christian era, contacts across Asia became institutionalized in the form of caravans that traversed the entire continent on a regular basis. Interaction among the civilizations of Eurasia intensified accordingly" (1963, p. 61). The second means of interconnection was sea-faring trade (Malay sailors reached China by 300 BC (Shaffer, 1994, p. 4); India and China began trade by the first century BC). The third means of interconnection was imperial conquest: The Achaemenid Empire at its height under Darius I reached from the Mediterranean to the Indus River (Waters, 2014). Greek and Indian scholars rubbed shoulders in the Persian court (McEvilley, 2002). Alexander the Great's Asian campaign ends two centuries of Achaemenid dominance, reinscribing and slightly extending its imperial reach, bringing him from Greece into what is now the Punjab in India (where the campaign ended, shortly before Alexander's life ends, in 323 BC). By the first century AD, the entire length of the E-W axis from Rome to China (i.e., from the Atlantic to the Pacific) can be described as "wall-to-wall empires" (Wright, 2000, p. 117; cf. also Korotayev, 2004). Thus, our fourth stage in our time-lapse video runs from the emergence of the first civilizations around 3000 BC until around the first century AD, when processes of growth in civilizational size and development of intercivilizational connections leads to the long east-west Afroeurasian belt becoming a world-system. Since this stage time-wise encompasses the centuries of the Axial Age, this fourth detail is also our final one and the most significant one in terms of the immediate context for the Axial Age. The significance is contained within the phrase "growth in civilizational size."

The phrase is deceptively simple. It hides an enormous complexity of growth factors including growth in population, in societal complexity, in technological ability, in political organization, in economic development, in amalgamation of other societies... above all, at the center of all of these, the effective factor is an expansion of power.

The phrase "growth in civilizational size," rooted in an expansion of power, also invites comparison to naturalistic evolutionary processes: As quoted at the opening of this chapter, "life has a natural tendency to expand into all available space"; it is like a "great Tree" which "covers the earth's surface with its ever branching and beautiful ramifications." The latter is one of Darwin's more celebrated images from *The origin of species*, and indeed, it does seem to encapsulate as a metaphor the history of expansion of humankind, too: We have grown and spread and set down roots and branched out, from African origins 200,000 years ago to seven billion of us inhabiting the globe today. I want to point out that this history of expansion of human being is continuous with the "natural tendency" to expansion evident in all evolutionary process. It is not some unnatural disease or mutation, as if humankind somehow stands outside evolution like an aberration. The emergence of agriculture, and civilizations, and their growth in size and expansion of power into the formation of the Eurasian world-system, is entirely in fitting with natural processes and leads (just as naturally) into world history. Acknowledging this natural fit, however, should not lead us to overlook what is also distinctive, and thus distinctively human, within this long-term process. Between the natural process of expanding into available space and our current unprecedented scale of technological domination of the planet, intercede a lot of mediating factors. From the basic evolutionary notion of adaptability to the distinctively human forms of power that manifest in our history, lies quite a spectrum of emergent properties.

I've mentioned some of these in Chapter 2: above all, our "sapience," as the capacity for symbolic reference, sets us apart from animals, in giving us distance from and power over our immediate environments. This capacity ratchets up into the complexities of cultures, such that humans inhabit a world of meaning that fuses both the physical horizon of action and perception with a cultural horizon of ideas, beliefs, and values. Thus, human prehistory evinces an extraordinary expansion of *homo sapiens sapiens* into all the continents of the earth, an extraordinary ethnodiversity, in a relatively short time. We are not bound by local or regional "niches," rather the tribe builds its own niche, which it is also capable of transforming, updating, revising, and changing, with far more malleability than an organism in a physical environment. The capacity for symbolic reference, the development of culture, the emergence of tribes and tribalism, our power over the environment, in turn ratchets up yet further when human being "breaks through" to agrarian society and later, to civilization and, as we will now explore, yet again during the first millennium BCE.

CONTEXTUALIZING THE AXIAL AGE: GROWTH IN CIVILIZATIONAL SIZE AND POWER

Robert Carneiro (1978) provides us with a particular angle on ethnic diversity that helps to sharpen our picture of the shape of the past yet further and begins to let us specify in greater detail the meaning of "growth in civilizational size." Between 10,000 and 8000 BCE, we know that world population was between 5 and 10 million people, while the size of a tribe was approximately 40, meaning therefore approximately 200,000 "autonomous polities" at that time around the world. Carneiro estimates that due to the innovations of the Neolithic revolution tribe size increases to about 100 over the next several millennia. Further, up till a certain point—sometime between 3000 BCE and 1000 CE—the pattern of societies differentiating and proliferating would exceed that of civilized societies amalgamating others. After that point, at least along the long east-west Afroeurasian belt, amalgamating—i.e., power—emerges as an increasingly crucial factor. Taking 1000 BCE as the mid-point within that time span as the hypothetical moment when that transition happens (an approximation that we will specify further below), Carneiro reasons there were about 600,000 autonomous polities present around the globe then.

Returning to our time-lapse video paused at 1000 BCE: We human beings had indeed been fruitful, we had multiplied, and we had "filled" (in some sense), the earth—several centuries before the book of *Genesis* was written. From human origins in Africa 200,000 years ago to 1000 BCE, what is above all evident is slow population growth, a corresponding global spread, and a corresponding steady increase in ethnic diversity. (The gradualness and steadiness of this evidence obtain from a suitably distant viewpoint; draw in closer, and the unevenness and nonlinearity of the ebbs and flows of these processes, takes on greater prominence.) In retrospect this point in time of 1000 BCE will prove to be the high point in human history for ethnic diversity, after which point amalgamation increasingly dominates over proliferation and we witness fewer and fewer "autonomous polities" that are also bigger and bigger. (If we used nation-state membership in the United Nations as our measure of autonomous polity, we're at around 200 in 2018; if we used Huntington's civilizations as our measure, we're at around 7 or 8 plus several dozen unamalgamated indigenous tribes; or depending on how we define "autonomous," we're now a global civilization of 1. Regardless of which, the striking feature diversity-wise is the precipitous drop: whether from 600,000 to 200, 600,000 to several dozen, or 600,000 to one. Amalgamation dominates indeed! Or, in the evolutionary terms of the Darwinian image of the great Tree of Life: "of the many twigs which flourished when the tree was a mere bush, only two or three, now grown into great branches, yet survive and bear all the other branches.")

Do we have any way to specify more clearly at what point amalgamation (regional expansion by power, by intensive means) overtakes proliferation (geographic expansion by spreading, by extensive means)? One way to do so is provided by world-systems theorist David Wilkinson (1993), who proposes that the current globalized world-system is singular and is the natural historical consequence of the amalgamation process that initiates and is then carried on by what he calls "Central civilization":

> The single global civilization is the lineal descendant of, or rather I should say the current manifestation of, a civilization that emerged about 1500 BC in the Near East when Egyptian and Mesopotamian civilizations collided and fused. This new fusional entity has since then expanded over the

entire planet and absorbed, on unequal terms, all other previously independent civilizations. (p. 226)

This claim is echoed by McNeill (1986), offering a retrospective corrective on his own earlier world-system work (McNeill, 1963), in which he states "It looks to me now as though the ancient history of Mesopotamia, Egypt, and the Indus civilizations, which subsequently merged into a cosmopolitan Middle Eastern civilization, was in effect recapitulated on an enlarged geographic scale after 500 BC, the principal actors having become China, India, and Europe, in addition to the Middle East" (p. 64). Wilkinson's proposing 1500 BCE as the starting point for an unending process of amalgamation matches well enough Carneiro's rough guestimate of 1000 BCE, as the time it takes from the first "fusion" of Egyptian and Mesopotamian civilizations—geographically at the Afroeurasian intersection point of the E-W axis or belt—into a network or world-system which comes to increasingly grow through amalgamations of other civilizations is some centuries.

In terms of giving us a highly simplified shape for human prehistory, from human origins in Africa until 1500 or 1000 BCE, whether one chooses demography (population growth), geography (global spread), or culture (ethnic diversity), from 200,000 years ago until about 3000 years ago, we're presented with a straightforward expanding growth shape for each of these three factors from a single origin point. At around 1000 BCE, however, the trajectories of the factors begin to diverge: Demographically, population continues to grow, with the difference that it grows faster. Driven by the anomalous agrarian societies that have become full-fledged sedentary civilizations, the rate of population growth increases. Geographically, global spreading comes to a near halt, as the majority of the arable surface of the earth has been filled (albeit sparsely). The pattern becomes no longer one of spread but one of infill within and between the sparsely filled areas of the earth. Again, this is above all evident within civilizations, thus above all evident along the long east-west Afroeurasian belt or Diamond's E-W axis.

The most dramatic divergence from the previous 197,000 years, however, is in terms of cultural identity: Ethnic diversity begins to drop. Again, this is driven by the rise in civilizations, again primarily along the E-W axis. It evidences above all the civilizational ability—Wilkinson would say "Central civilization's ability"—to amalgamate other societies (conquer, subjugate, annex, overwhelm, assimilate, and so on) which is to say, it indexes civilizational power.

Culture, ethnicity, and civilization, are all claims to identity. The developments of these mean the development of new loci of identification; with what group(s) does a person identify as a member? The decline in ethnic diversity from 3000 years ago until the present is one side of the coin; the flip side is the rise in group size or civilizational membership. The growth in size of civilizations through amalgamating other societies means ethnodiversity decreases while civilizational size increases. Thus, the shape of history from human origins until the present, in terms of cultural identification, would resemble a child's spinning top if time is represented as ascending vertically from an origin point and ethnodiversity represented horizontally. The tapering cone-shaped bottom of the spinning top represents growth from the origin point at the bottom (the handful of ethnicities of the first *homo sapiens sapiens* 200,000 years ago, milling about in Africa) up to the highest degree of ethnodiversity of 600,000 autonomous polities about 3000 years ago (the broadest diameter of the spinning top). The nearly flat top of the spinning top would represent the rapid diminishing from 600,000 to 200, or to a few dozen, or to one "Central civilizational" identity, over the last 3000 years. That is, without invoking an Axial Age within human consciousness as Jaspers does, we see the emergence of a dividing line within the whole history of the human race, around 1000 BCE, due to the rise in civilizational power—a factor that is not entirely conscious, and certainly not driven consciously, but rather a development that occurred due to natural, or largely unconscious, factors.

We can sharpen this detail yet further and specify the dividing line better, improving on Carneiro's decidedly rough 1000 BCE guess and Wilkinson's proposed date of 1500 BCE as the beginning of "Central civilization." Rein Taagepera undertook a series of studies in the 1970s to determine the historical patterns in growth of size of empires, measured in terms of amount of dry-land area considered under imperial control as recorded in historical atlases, using squared "Megameters" (Mm^2) as his unit of measurement (1 $Mm^2 = 10^6$ $km^2 = 386,000$ square miles). Beginning in 2850 BCE with the first recorded empire of any size (Egypt), Taagepera tracks the historical growth in overall size of empires until the present using the three largest empires' largest and smallest sizes, as well as difference between, as representative measures. He uses one hundred year intervals. Based on this approach, Taagepera discerns three phases within this five thousand year history in terms of size of empires. The phases are defined as follows: Phase 1, from 2850 BCE to 700 BCE, is defined by a total imperial size (i.e., size of 3 largest empires combined) ranging from 0 to 2 Mm^2 (the ceiling for largest individual empire size was 1.3 Mm^2); Phase 2, from 500 BCE to 1600 CE, defined by total imperial size ranging from 2.3 to 24 Mm^2, followed by Phase 3, from 1600 CE on, defined by total imperial sizes greater than 24 Mm^2. However, Taagepera notes that Phase 3 "has lasted for such a short time that one cannot be certain of its existence: Maybe it is just a continuation of Phase 2" (1978, p. 121). Put differently, in their first ~2200 years, from 2850 to 700 BCE, total imperial size showed a limit of a 2 Mm^2 ceiling, with the largest size for any one empire being 1.3 Mm^2; for the last ~2500 years post-500 BCE, empires show overall steady growth. That is, across a five thousand year history that shows a consistent growth in the size of empires, Taagepera discerns only one utterly distinctive transition period. This is the period between Phase 1 and Phase 2, wherein empires jump in size, breaking through the 1.3 Mm^2 ceiling evident in Phase 1, after which they regularly exceed this size. This one utterly distinctive transition period occurs during the centuries 700–500 BCE.

What happens during this period? Taagepera reasons as follows: The size of an empire is based on its "power delegation ability," which corresponds to the effectively enforce-able distance (of commands, punishments, taxation, etc.) from the imperial center. In Phase 1, the maximum size of 1.3 Mm^2 translates into distance from the center of around 650 km, corresponding to about one week travel by horse (assuming a horse travel distance of around 100 km a day). Phase 2 sees imperial size greatly increase (to a maximum size of 5 Mm^2), breaking through the Phase 1 ceiling. Taagepera speculates this is due to the development of bureaucratic systems. The key point is that a "breakthrough in power delegation ability" (Taagepera, 1979, p. 116) occurs in the transition period that enables empires to dramatically increase their size.

Yet another measure we can use to better specify the notion of a great increase in civilizational power is urbanization: the growth of cities, not in terms of land area like empires, but in terms of population. Sanderson (1995) says it "is clear that urbanization has been a striking feature of agrarian social growth over a period of nearly 4,000 years [from 2250 BCE to 1500 CE]" (p. 268). Keeping cities somewhat distinct from empires is relevant, particularly for civilizations like Mesopotamia or Greece which are more accurately a confederation of city-states rather than a singular territorial empire like Egypt. Sanderson (1995), in reviewing the patterns in population growth of cities, states: "A particularly large leap in urbanization occurs in the period between 650 and

430 BC" (p. 268). The number of large cities increases dramatically (from 28 to 41) while their overall population also increases dramatically, by a factor of three.

Putting all of these specifications together within our fourth, civilizational stage of our time-lapse scenario running from ~3000 BCE (first civilizations or empires) to 100 CE (the consolidation of the E-W axis of Afroeurasia in terms of the establishment of a "wall-to-wall empires" world-system stretching from Rome to China), focusing on agrarian societies, and recognizing that above all what we're trying to trace is an unprecedented growth in civilizational power, we have the following: (1) Somewhere in this time span the earth reaches its historically highest point of ethnodiversity, estimated by Carneiro at around 600,000 groups at around 1000 BCE, before amalgamation of societies as a historical pattern overcomes proliferation of societies as dominant, reducing ethnodiversity in favor of bigger and bigger civilizations. (2) Wilkinson's point is that around 1500 BCE Egyptian and Mesopotamian civilizations "collide" to a sufficient enough extent that they form a network or system that in retrospect proves to grow and amalgamate all other civilizations and civilizational systems with which it comes into contact until that "Central Civilization" becomes today's globalized world. (3) Taagepera shows convincingly that between 700 and 500 BCE is the most significant time period from 3000 BCE until the present in terms of a leap in growth in the size of empires. (4) Sanderson notes that between 650 and 430 BCE is the most noticeable period in growth in population size of cities within a 4000-year time span. Useful to keep in mind in reviewing these claims is that the latter two are working with specific measures and thus can specify dates with much more exactitude (700–500 BCE, or 650–430 BCE), whereas the former two are much more approximate guesses (around 1000 BCE; around 1500 BCE).

In terms of this big picture sketch of civilization—its emergence and growth—as context for the Axial Age, prior to looking at the specifics of each Axial Age civilization, what comes to the fore is the crucial importance of the E-W axis of Afroeurasia as setting. This axis is the geographic setting for the technological breakthrough(s) into agriculture. Within this axis is seeded (literally) the development of agriculture, agrarian societies, cities, civilizations, empires, and the eventually, emerging world-system that connects these aspects into networks of trade, war, disease, and diplomacy. There is some irony here, in that geographically the E-W axis is itself a dividing line of sorts, albeit a line of civilizational power slowly forming within an otherwise homogeneous spread of small, mobile, hunter-gatherer societies across the continents of the world. As the civilizations wax and wane along the long E-W axis of the Afroeuarasian belt, it is only at a high-altitude level of abstraction that its shape could be called anymore a "line." In keeping with the metaphors of visualizing, big pictures, and the "shape" of the past and the present, the Tree of Life metaphor described by Darwin, draws a more accurate image. There are a multitude of centers (bushes, perhaps?) networked together (think, twigs, and branches) across the length of Afroeurasian belt, that crisscross, grow, die off, sprout fresh buds, and are grown over, across many millennia. There is certainly no shortage of attempts to "overtop," "kill," and "overmaster," as well as no shortage of "great battles for life," undertaken. The outcome by the end of the first millennium BCE with the consolidation of the world-system of Eurasia is that the E-W axis has become a vigorous, thick growth, "a great branch" knotted with age, and source of "ever new branchings," increasingly covering the surface of Asia, and increasingly into Europe, "with its ever branching and beautiful ramifications." Indeed, as the remainder of this chapter will bear out, it would not be inaccurate to call the E-W axis of the Old World of Afroeurasia, the central trunk of the tree, not of Life in Darwin's evolutionary sense, but of world history in Jaspers' Axial Age sense. From this trunk, the visions of the Axial Age are "the fresh buds" that will grow and branch out into the major world religions and civilizations that now compose 75–95% of how the world thinks and what the world believes.

Viewed from the perspective of either evolutionary history (going back 200,000 years) or global geography (human beings having spread across the world by then), however, we need to remind ourselves that these developments of agriculture and later civilization are statistically the outliers; they are the exceptions, not the rule; strange anomalies. Viewed from the hindsight of today, of course, they are of crucial significance for world history. Further: Within this geographic axis, within the broad time frame of civilization between 3000 BCE and 100 CE, we find a particular historical axis or dividing line, a time period that divides history into before-and-after, above all in the centuries 700–430 BCE, wherein empires and cities show an unprecedented, explosive growth. This broad time frame is the historic setting for the sociopolitical breakthrough(s) in a few centuries into new forms of power. In these centuries, civilizational power as embodied in empires and cities broke through all prior constraints into a new configuration. The many great changes happening during these centuries, taken together, compose evolutionarily, geographically, technologically, historically, politically, and sociologically, a dividing line in history, an "axial time" in the general meaning of the phrase, in terms of the advent of a whole new scale to human power.

If this advent of a whole new scale to human power is accomplished through an intensification of the natural tendency to expand—an expansion of expansion, or "expansion squared," so to speak—then the explosive and unprecedented expansion of power in the first millennium BCE is, like the evolutionary emergence of culture that is both continuous with and creating distinctiveness from natural process, continuous with the earlier emergence of civilizations and the context for some innovative, discontinuous distinctiveness. Just as I dubbed the term "tribalism" in Chapter 2 to refer to the reflexive consequences of our ability to reflect on and think about the naturally evolved adaptation of tribal organization of human societies, such that not only is humanity divided up into a great diversity of tribes, but they in effect live in different worlds, so I will dub this self-referential ratcheting up of the natural process of expansion into "expansion squared" as "expansionism." Our world in crisis is a consequence of both: Tribalism combined with expansionism threatens us with the possibility of the World War III or a clash of civilizations, as our "tribes" have expanded to unprecedented size. Our inability to collaborate due to tribalism, together with the enormous power developed due to expansionism, is effecting global climate change and a sixth mass extinction event, the effects of these being to threaten many of our civilizations with plausible collapse scenarios. The roots of both tribalism and expansionism are natural and evolutionary. Their first clear manifestations of what happens when you put them together occur in the first millennium BCE as the advent of a whole new, unprecedented, scale to human power. Their clearly destructive consequences are manifesting in our own time as our world in crisis, accompanied by end-of-the-world anxieties provoked by the crisis. It also means that within our big picture of our civilizational past, we need to distinguish within that history between the growth in civilizational size as something continuous with natural processes of tribalism and expansion, and our exploration of the Axial Age visionary response which, as I understand it, articulates a distinctively different meaning that runs counter to both.

FROM AN AXIAL TIME OF POWER
TO THE AXIAL AGE OF SPIRIT

I want to be clear: These few centuries in mid-first millennium BCE as the significant time period within the three millennia as just described are not "the Axial Age." They aren't because the great changes—technological, sociopolitical, and economic—described were not consciously understood as such. For this axial time in the sense of a new scale to power to be considered an "Axial Age" in Jaspers' view, they would have to consciously understand it in those terms. They don't. (Note that none of the scholars mentioned in the previous section are "Axial Age scholars," nor do any of them mention or reference the Axial Age, with the exception of Sanderson, albeit not until 2018 [Sanderson, 2018].) No one in the first millennium BCE was consciously aware of the "civilizational moment" in the terms in which we've laid them out; no one knew evolutionary history, the precise shape of the globe or distribution of landmass on it (let alone knowing the global spread of humans), the importance of the E-W axis, the specifics of the origin, and the development of civilizations. It's unclear how much anyone at any one point on the E-W axis, say in Greece or in India or in China, would know of the other, before about the second century BCE. (Even within Western Asia or the Near East, the most culturally interconnected geographic area of the four Axial Age settings, it is unclear whether the Greek thinkers and Hebrew prophets were significantly cognizant, aware, or influenced by each other.) What I am intentionally dubbing an "axial time of power," intentionally not capitalized, is not "the Axial Age," precisely because none of these developments of power were consciously undertaken as such. In this regard, the axial time of power is a continuation of natural evolutionary process, in large part precisely because humans were not consciously aware of that time in those terms. For Jaspers, the Axial Age is a breakthrough in consciousness, awareness, morality, ethics, self-responsibility, and a spiritualization. The axial time of power is historical in a naturalistic, factual sense of having occurred; it is not historical in the sense of having occurred in people's consciousness and becoming an effective force in awareness. Rather, this axial time of power constitutes the full set of preconditions, both civilizational and world-systemic, that are the context within which and against which the Axial Age breakthroughs occur.

It is a mark of the sensitivity, or prescience, or genius perhaps, of the Axial Age visionaries that they show the degree of conscious awareness that they do of their civilizational moment as being one of an unprecedented, and terrible, new scale to power. They are deeply and radically critical of this power and denounce it in the strongest terms. Alongside these critical terms, which describe "this world," they articulate in positive terms an "other world" not defined by power but defined by a better, higher spirit. These terms, both critical and positive, are evidence for a high, or perhaps I should say expanded? level of consciousness and thus become the evidence for Jaspers' claim that this was the Axial Age. The spiritual *virtuosi* must have, at the most, only gained a fleeting glimpse of the tip of the iceberg of their civilizational moment as revealed to them locally and within a limited historical time frame, but it would seem to have sufficed for these sensitive souls to presciently intuit the implications far beyond (i.e., universally) that mere glimpse. They enjoin us to reject war, greed, cruelty, pride, lust, envy, all of which were visible manifestations at the tip of the iceberg of civilizational power. They bring into conscious awareness a conception of humanity as universal that extends far beyond local, regional, or civilizational power or affiliation; accompanying this conception is an injunction to love our neighbor or to be compassionate to all others or to recognize the innate humanity in "the other"; to practice peace, justice, mercy, humility, and to do so not only within one's existing "in-group" (defined by kin, or class, or region, or the state, etc.) but universally with all humanity. The "spiritualization" that Jaspers refers to in effect "capitalizes" the axial time of power into conscious meaning and thus, in retrospect, the Axial Age which structures world history. The difference the conscious awareness of the Axial Age spiritual masters makes with respect to the axial time of power in which they lived, is their critical evaluation of what this power means: If it means greed, exploitation, injustice, suffering, and evil, then, it is incumbent upon us to reject and deny such power and live instead humbly, justly, kindly, and mercifully (to paraphrase the Old Testament prophet Micah, Chapter 5:7).

In terms of these centuries marking the advent of a whole new scale to human power unlike anything ever witnessed before, and arguably never since (relatively speaking), this time is axial in the general sense of a dividing line or a turning point. And as such an axial time, it serves as the precedent for our own times: Globalization, world wars, the beginning of space exploration, global climate change, the Sixth Extinction, the new social media, nuclear power, and so many more possible examples are each and all manifestations of a whole new scale to human power. In the first millennium BCE, the new scale of power is due to the realization of potentials within civilization seeded by the possibilities for power implicit in agrarian society. In our twenty-first century CE, the new scale of power is due to the realization of potentials implicit in industrial society. The "civilizational moment" of these centuries BCE is the clear precedent to our contemporary "globalizing moment" in material, factual terms. Both are continuous with the natural tendency to "expand into all available space," as well as continuous with expansionism as that emergent human power to intensify and expand or "square" that natural tendency to expand, to distinctively human levels, degrees, and scales, far beyond any "natural limits."

Emerging from that axial time wherein a whole new scale of human power is developed unconsciously as part of the tidal flow of history, the Axial Age sages, prophets, holy men, and philosophers urge us to consciously resist that power and all the temptations it brings and instead to transcend all of the trappings of this world for a higher, spiritual, other world that was morally, ethically, socially, and politically better: far smaller in scale, far kinder, more just, more loving. What was "this world" to them? I think it's fair to respond: Human power enacted at an unprecedented new scale. On my reading, above all else the Axial Age spiritual revolutionaries are responding to the historically unprecedented increase in civilizational power, that they experienced in local, limited terms, but which they interpreted well beyond those limits. And which they interpreted morally, spiritually, and ethically; not an interpretive response like "what does it gain me?" but rather but "is it good? Will my gain be my neighbor's loss? Does the increase in my power mean the increase of my neighbour's suffering?" The premise for their spiritual revolution and the breakthrough to transcendence are their recognition, critique, and rejection of power; they attempt to raise into consciousness the true, spiritual meaning of civilization—as hubris, idolatry, illusion, suffering, vanity, sin, ignorance—and to offer an alternative spiritual vision that consciously turns away from "this world" for one of higher spiritual meaning, one of hope, nonviolence, and love. The prophets, philosophers, sages, and holy men point out the unprecedented new scale to human power did not manifest a new scale to peace, love, mercy, or justice, but manifested a new unprecedented scale of suffering and violence for the weak and unprecedented affluence and arrogance and pride for the strong, which meant unprecedented inequities, exploitation, violence, and injustices in their civilizations when taken as a whole. The clear and obvious parallels to our own times in these many respects do not, I presume, need any spelling out.

For our own "globalizing moment" to count as a second Axial Age (rather than an analogous "axial time of power"), we'd have to similarly "capitalize" the meaning of this time: We would have to raise our world in crisis into conscious awareness, critically evaluate its new scale of power and its unspiritual and antispiritual consequences—the evils, injustices, and suffering it foments, and on whom—and proceed to live radically differently according to spiritual values. On my reading, and in contrast to, say, Ewert Cousins' argument for this being a second Axial Age (1987), we aren't there. (Notice that we are prevented and in fact unable to evaluate these consequences as unnatural, because the axial time of power emerges through the natural process of expansion, ratcheted up exponentially through naturally evolved human distinctive abilities to symbolize, make culture, develop civilization, create world-systems, and so on, into expansionism.) Collectively speaking we likely have a greater conscious awareness of current events than they did during the first Axial Age due to the availability of information through technology and media, and due to our scientific level of knowledge. But by the very same token—that is, our technology, media, and science—our conscious awareness is of a different kind than during the Axial Age: Mediated through channels that make it abstract relative to our everyday lived experience, and make it present to us in the very terms of the self-same scale of power of which we need to be conscious. Other differences include the cognitive aspects of our consciousness being fragmented according to the disciplinary specializations of the sciences and our educational institutions, while existentially our awareness is "sequestered" into institutionally disparate domains of experience (this is sociologist Anthony Giddens' term [1991]). In short, we have in a sense greater conscious awareness than they could have had during the Axial Age. But in other senses, we are not further ahead. Our conscious awareness lacks the existential immediacy, moral urgency, and practical spirituality that appears as so characteristic of Axial Age consciousness. (I am not claiming that conscious awareness during the Axial Age is therefore better than ours or vice versa. I am highlighting what I consider some obvious differences; beyond those differences, they are not easily comparable, if at all.)

Nevertheless, despite some great differences in our conscious awareness, it seems reasonable to assume that just as they were then, we today are cognizant of the tip of the iceberg of contemporary power. Negative examples of this, as discussed in the second chapter, are evidenced in contemporary end-of-the-world anxieties manifesting in fear, denial, and a great diversity of forms of flight into far more restricted foci that absorb our attention, and preoccupy us with obsessive, or compulsive, or addictive, or self-destructive, or masochistic, or sadistic, or narcissistic, and so on, activities. They are negative in that their motivation stems from consciousness of our world in crisis but they manifest in self-centered, defensive ways. Positive examples manifest in ways of facing our world in crisis proactively, in individual acts of self-sacrifice, in broad-based movements aiming at altruistic reform, in ethical collaborations irreducible to self-interest. Our world in crisis is the visible tip of the iceberg, making itself into conscious awareness, unevenly, unsystematically, erratically, in fits and starts.

Another significant consideration in comparing our times to the Axial Age: I am talking in global, generalized terms about conscious awareness—to be found, I guess, primarily among the "educated people of all the world's cultures" (Bellah & Joas, 2012, p. 6), to recall the introductory chapter's opening quote—when in fact the Axial Age sages were an anomaly and were an elite. (Perhaps the analogy is quite direct: Statistically the "educated people of all the world's cultures" might well look anomalous and therefore "elite" statistically by comparison with the seven billion plus of today's world population.) The majority of hunter-gatherer societies did not become agrarian societies; the majority of agrarian societies do not become civilizations; the majority of civilizations along the E-W axis do not present Axial breakthroughs; within Axial Age civilizations themselves, the majority of people were not Axial Age visionaries. The Axial Age breakthroughs only occur in four civilizations, among a small group of persons, who in turn are not necessarily particularly influential at their time. Put differently, the conscious awareness evident in the breakthroughs is the statistical outlier, is the exception not the rule, and is a strange anomaly. But the development of civilization along the E-W axis, too, was the anomaly by comparison with the overwhelming majority of other societies. Viewed historically, this is even more dramatically so. Viewed in retrospect, it has been the anomaly of civilization, and then the anomaly of Axial Age visions, that have decisively influenced world history.

By analogy to today, that a coherent mass movement is not evident, nor any clear agreement en masse about the facts of a world in crisis, let alone how to go about addressing it, is to be expected. If a deep conscious awareness and a profound alternative vision is being, or has

been, developed, somewhere on the margins and peripheries of official, visible, or obvious power it is certain that we wouldn't know about
it. (That the "we" just emphasized is what is colloquially called "the
royal we" resounds with a deep historical irony in this context!) Such
an anomalous perspective will not be making the news—which absence,
fortunately, bears no relation to the real possibility that it might be
making history. And in this lesson from both evolution and world history—what we could, in a Christian idiom, call a "cornerstone" theory of evolution and history—I see a deep and radical source for hope
today. To recall Solnit's (2016) claim noted in the opening chapter:
"our hope is in the dark around the edges, not the limelight of center
stage" (p. xvi).

The Axial Age holy men, prophets, and philosophers were anomalies
or outliers in a few further senses, too. The most significant difference
on their own view is due to their conscious awareness being a trained,
disciplined one, in comparison with the untrained, undisciplined mind
of the layperson. The intensive sustained practice of meditation, prayer,
contemplation, mindfulness, or other spiritual exercises or ascetic disciplines, has well-documented significant effects on the mind.

The second sense of outlier is a sociological one due to the Axial Age
teachers, with their followers, not residing in the power centers of those
empires, but at their peripheries, in smaller, weaker, or threatened societies at the margins of the power centers. The Greeks develop much of
their "national" or "ethnic" self-consciousness due to their successful
defense against the Persian empire (the Greco-Persian war conventionally dated from 499 to 449 BC); the entire story of Israel and Judaea is
vis-à-vis neighboring empires, like Egypt from which they escape slavery,
or Assyria (conquering the northern kingdom of Israel in 722 BCE), or
Neo-Babylon (conquering the southern kingdom, destroying Jerusalem
and the temple, around 587 BCE, and overseeing the exile), or Persia,
which oversees the return from exile (538 BCE)and the building of the
Second Temple. Neither China nor India is unified empires or states
during the Axial Age: China is living in the wake of the dissolution of
the Zhou empire and eventually descends further into the period of the
"Warring States" (475–221 BCE) prior to a unification through the Qin
and then the Han empires, while Indian holy men live and travel betwixt
and between the many kingdoms and principalities along the Ganges in a
time of rapid urbanization and state-formation prior to the ascendancy of
the Magadha-Maurya empire (322–180 BCE).

The third sense in which the Axial Age *virtuosi* were outliers consists in the observation that they are not near the power centers of their smaller societies—some, famously, like Plato or Confucius, would seem to have had their "wise guy careers" kick-started due to failing in their political ambitions. Instead of being near the power centers of empires, or near the power centers of the smaller societies in which they lived, the Axial Age visionaries renounce such power and move further into the margins to become, if anything, doubly removed—quite literally through setting up small communities in remote areas, establishing schools on the outskirts of cities, relocating further afield into forests or caves or remote mountains, or, in many cases, being constantly on the move as itinerant travelers with their small group of disciples.

The New Scale of Power: Innovations in Ruling, Money, Literacy, and Ideology

Innovation in Ruling

In all these respects just noted the Axial Age visionaries are the exception, not the rule. There is a perfect appropriateness attaching to this phrase since "the rule" here refers to the power of civilization and empire which comes to be embodied in the ruler. Robert Bellah's (2011) last major work provides an evolutionary sociology that leads up to the great explosion in civilizational power that is the setting for the Axial Age breakthroughs. Prior to his sociological focus on the four specific Axial Age civilizations in which the breakthroughs occur, Bellah characterizes civilization more generally, describing the "archaic societies" of that time in terms of six crucial innovations. Probably the most important of these, like a drawstring threaded through the other five innovations that in being drawn gathers the elements together, is the great elevation in power and authority granted to the ruler—an elevation to, indeed, god-like status. In Bellah's words:

> Whereas tribal societies consist of small face-to-face groups, or of a few adjacent ones, archaic societies were territorially extensive and could include millions of people. It would seem that maintaining the coherence of such large and extensive societies required that the attention and energy that tribal ritual focused on the whole society now be concentrated on the ruler, elevated beyond normal human status, in relation to beings who were now not only powerful, but required worship. (2011, p. 265)

The breakthrough into a new scale of power "would seem to require" an accompanying innovation be granted to the ruler. In being "elevated" to the status of a god—the sacralizing of political authority and the domination of others through myths and rituals that establish the king, emperor, pharaoh, etc., as divinely ordained—the ruler is given a legitimation to his authority to match the elevated extent of civilizational power. Bellah argues that this "god-king-people complex" was of "central significance" for "*all* the archaic societies" (2011, p. 327, emphasis added).

Along with this crucial innovation, Bellah lists five further characteristics:

> The reality of archaic civilization was centralization of political power, class stratification, the magnification of military power, the economic exploitation of the weak, and the universal introduction of some form of forced labor for both productive and military purposes. (2011, p. 264)

These characteristics flesh out in more specific detail the form the new scale of power took. (1) Politically, it takes the form of centralization. The imperial center, or the royal capital, takes on a new and greater role than ever before. In this development, both the political elite (the royal family, the nobles, the aristocracy) and the religious elite (the priesthood) collaborated. Myth legitimated rule. The imperial center is as much about the temple as it is the palace. World-systems theorists will use different terminologies ("core, semi-periphery, periphery," or "core, periphery, hinterland," or "core, periphery, margins"), but all agree on characterizing these ancient civilizations in terms of a diminishing of power as one moves away from the center. (2) Socially, the emergence of hierarchy in the form of some type of class system is prevalent (with, of course, royalty and nobility and the priestly class at the top). Division of the people into ascribed roles or occupations occurs, with the hierarchy often considered to itself be divinely ordained like the role of ruler (the most well-known example of such being the Indian caste system). Division of labor greatly elaborates and becomes more complex. (3) Militarily, the size of armies increases, as does their organizational complexity; conscription by royal decree comes into use. Since a large army cannot sit idle for long, and the manifold increases in imperial power necessitate expansion, warfare increases. (4) Economically, wealth increases as does the "conspicuous consumption" among the ruling classes. This included the state religion, too: "Temples in antiquity were not just places of sacrifice and prayer but institutions, often very wealthy, with their own capital and work force" (Blenkinsopp, 1995, p. 152). Both the political apparatus of the state and the ritual apparatus of the religion—king and priest, palace and temple, and their accompanying cult and ritual, pomp and ceremony—expand dramatically. Conversely, the poor are exploited and become poorer; the widow, the orphan, the slave, and the disenfranchised in general, become increasingly visible victims of unjust and unequal systems embodying the new scale of power and the new inequities it introduces. (5) And finally, the ability of the government to demand labor to varying degrees—for example, to build pyramids, or temples—alongside conscription into the military, as just mentioned, becomes built into the normal, taken-for-granted functioning of civilization.

Innovation in Money

Alongside these several innovations Bellah notes as the forms the new scale to power took in how civilizations ruled their populace, crowned in the figure of the ruler-as-divine, are a few others of equal importance: the innovations of money, in literacy, and in ideology. The great increases in royal power, temple power, imperial size, military size, warfare, carry with them reorganizations of economic systems, too. The increase in size and complexity of civilizations and the accompanying elaboration and development of class hierarchies and increasing complexity in division of labor entailed the need for a standardized common currency, a universal measure that transcended the otherwise chaotic multiplicity of barter, informal trade, and informal credit as a system. Money becomes necessary. The appearance of money as a common currency works a cascade of changes on the old economy: the charging of interest on debt, for one, and thus too debt slavery, debt bondage, and indentured labor (forms of which were often intergenerational, too, meaning your children were born as indentured slaves). The confiscating of land for discharge of debt was also widespread, and thus, the ownership of private property is increasingly a key index for wealth and power. In short, the appearance of money sees the appearance of a "debt-interest-private property" complex. Duchrow and Hinkelammert (2012) date the emergence of this "new economy... back to the eighth century BCE" (p. 11).

The appearance of money also means the emergence of coinage and minting—literally, 'hard cash' in the form of coin appears—which increasingly displaces and replaces the older economy centered on both barter and credit. Where, when, and why does this appear?

> Coinage appears to have arisen independently in three different places, almost simultaneously: on the Great Plain of northern China, in the Ganges river valley of northeast India, and in the lands surrounding the Aegean Sea, in each case, between roughly 600 and 500 BC. (Graeber, 2011, p. 212)

Why in these three places, and why in those centuries? Graeber proposes the crucial importance of the increase in war, militarization, and conquest. A major innovation in these centuries was the use of mercenaries as warriors, which had the mixed consequences of, on the positive hand, increasing the likelihood of military success compared to a conscripted army but, on the negative hand, also the need for immediate payment—among other reasons, to forestall the even more negative possibility of the army turning on their employers. While looting during conquest accomplished the provision of immediate reward to the soldiers, in times of peace, during lengthy campaigns or in the instance of lengthy sieges, the loyalty of mercenaries could only be secured through paying them. The great increase in warfare, at this time, tied to the great increase in militarization, army size, and mercenaries used as warriors, leads to the need for hard cash, i.e., coins. Old systems of credit disappear while new systems of coinage appear. This means mints appear: For example, "by 480 BC there were at least one hundred mints operating in different Greek cities, even though at that time, none of the great trading nations of the Mediterranean had as yet showed the slightest interest in them" (Graeber, 2011, p. 227; for Greece in particular see also Seaford, 2004). Along with a proliferation of mints in these three areas, there is corresponding increase in the need for precious metals to supply the mints, hence mining, along with the need for labor to work the mines and extract the ore. While conquest meant loot for the mercenaries and tribute to the conquerors, it included tribute in the form of slaves who could in turn work the mines and produce the raw materials needed to fund the armies for further conquest—the development of what Graeber (2011) calls "a 'military-coinage-slavery complex'" (p. 229).

In short, the appearance of money—whether in the form of a debt-interest-private property complex, or of a military-coinage-slavery complex, most likely, both!—is one of the most visible tip-of-the-iceberg manifestations of the new power and is robustly correlated both in terms of centuries and in terms of geographic areas with the Axial Age. This is noted by a number of these scholars. For example, Graeber (2011) says:

> The attentive reader may have noticed that the core period of Jaspers' Axial Age… corresponds almost exactly to the period in which coinage was invented. What's more, the three parts of the world where coins were first invented were also the very parts of the world where those sages lived; in fact, they became the epicenters of Axial Age religious and philosophical creativity: the kingdoms and city-states around the Yellow River in China, the Ganges valley in northern India, and the shores of the Aegean Sea. (p. 224)

Other scholars have taken this robust correlation further, to causal and explanatory status: "Our thesis is that the new economy based on money and property was the main cause of the Axial Age religious and spiritual innovations" (Duchrow & Hinkelammert, 2012, p. 47). A social science study examining several variables such as energy capture, population density, political complexity, and economic development, led the authors to claim that "increased affluence" is the cause of the Axial Age breakthroughs: "economic development… explains the emergence of axial religions" (Baumard, Hyafil, Morris, & Boyer, 2015, p. 12). It is undoubtedly true that Axial Age critiques of civilization zero in on money as exemplary of the new economy and its accompanying suite of injustices. With the exception of Buddhism, all the Axial Age movements condemn usury. Confucians, Mohists, and Taoists alike rail against greed, usury, and violence; the Indian sages emphasize renunciation, foremost among what is renounced is involvement in the money economy, too. Solon in ancient Athens canceled all debt; Plato in the *Phaedo* will pronounce "It is because of the acquisition of money that all wars arise, and we are forced to acquire money because of the body, enslaved as we are to its care" (Ramelli, 2016, p. 38). Judaism insisted on a year of jubilee every seventh year and the donation of a portion of one's harvest to the poor. In the words of the Preacher, "He who loves money will not be satisfied with money, nor he who loves wealth with his income; this also is vanity" (Ecclesiastes 5:10), echoed some centuries later by Paul's claim in his letter to Timothy that "The love of money is the root of many evils" (1 Timothy 6:10).

There is certainly a robust correlation between the emergence of the new economy based on money and the Axial Age. That the "spiritual revolution" of the latter occurs smack dab in the middle of an extraordinary expanding of trade along the Afroeurasian belt between 1000 BCE and 500 CE, a "commercial revolution" (Manning, 2005), is undeniable. The claim this is the cause or explains the Axial Age seems to me overstated. The fact of the robust correlation of the Axial Age, not only with money, coinage, property, and increased affluence, but with a whole host of other factors that are part and parcel of the new scale to civilizational power, seems the right emphasis. After all increased affluence does not only lead to "ascetic wisdom and moralizing tradition," it also leads to increased greed, consumerism, and exploitation as well as promoting nihilism(s) rather than moralism(s), too. The cause—more accurately, the motivation—for the Axial Age breakthroughs is an irreducibly complex constellation of factors rooted in the complex constellation of civilizational conditions in which the spiritual *virtuosi* found themselves. Thomassen's (2010) description of the Axial Age efforts within their context of the new scale to civilizational power, for example, is accurate and insightful without invoking a single cause or single explanation: "as a resistance against rising global empires, as attempts to re-establish meaningful human life vis-à-vis an all-menacing situation, finding measures to 'cool down' human matters in the midst of a spiral of violence and limitless military-economic expansion" (p. 330). I see no reason why this multi-dimensional claim cannot be understood as "explanatory" of the Axial Age alongside—that is, not reducible to—the "thesis that the religions and philosophies of that age, since the eighth century BCE, are precisely a response to the development of the new money-property economy" (Duchrow & Hinkelammert, 2012, p. 2).

Innovation in Literacy

The increase in size, complexity, and power of civilizations also meant a transformation in the uses and functions of literacy. Writing appears, independently, in Mesopotamia and Egypt, India, and China, shortly after the emergence of the first civilizations there (around 3000 BC, 2000 BC, and 1500 BC, respectively), and goes on to serve an indispensable role in helping administer civilization as well as underwrite the later emergence of bureaucracy which accompanies the new rule of civilizational power. Analogous to market pressures that necessitate the development of money as "transcending" the chaos of different economies (scare-quoted here to signify its meaning being in an empirical-expansion sense rather than a spiritual-consciousness sense), the pressures attendant upon administering a large complex society push the consolidation and transformation of literacy as it also "transcends" a diversity of social structures, groupings, regional, and ethnic differences, and multiple contending social and political interpretations. Writing as the preserve of a scribal elite is significantly different from a more pervasive literacy, which increase in pervasiveness is also the outcome of the expansion of civilizational power. While the former could be seen as definitive of "scribal culture," the latter marks "literate culture" (Assmann, 2012, uses the distinction "sectorial literacy" vs. "cultural literacy"). It is possible to read a progression from priests as guardians of ritual performance in a ritual culture to priests as guardians of texts in a scribal culture to priests as guardians of doctrine, or correct interpretation, in a literate culture. Changes and developments in literacy are not only sociological; the development of text has enormous implications for the forms and functions of human consciousness. For example, the development of the alphabet (occurring in the second millennium BCE) is considered by a large group of scholars epochal in the evolution of human consciousness (in Ong's [1982] terms, "writing as the technology that restructures thought"). The Axial Age develops in the context of literate culture (cf. Goody & Watt, 1963: "The first society that can be truly called literate did not evolve until the 6th and 5th centuries BCE in the city-states of Greece and Ionia" [p. 317]).

Egyptologist Jan Assmann, who has developed a careful and thorough-going critique of the Axial Age thesis (2005, 2011, 2012), argues that literacy, and within literacy, the process of canonization of texts, is what should be considered in trying to account for the Axial Age:

> What Jaspers sees as the birth of an intellectual world, taking place almost simultaneously in different places on the Earth that we still inhabit today, can be pinned down much more precisely. There was a transformation from ritual to textual coherence and continuity that happened quite naturally through the spread of literacy, which reached many different, very loosely connected cultures at around the same time – namely during the first millennium BCE. (Assmann, 2011, p. 265)

Assmann sees in the widespread distribution and advances of literacy along the E-W axis the key condition underlying and enabling the breakthroughs in consciousness. Beyond that, he sees in the subsequent canonization of texts and the intense exegesis that surrounds them in the following centuries the key condition underlying and enabling the *continuity* of that consciousness from the Axial Age until today. There is not some magical threshold in consciousness crossed at a particular historical juncture that is irreversible, but a social institution organized around selected texts engaged in particular interpretive practices that creates the cultural memory that keeps those texts intelligible and relevant despite the passage of time:

> This period witnessed the birth not only of the foundational texts, but also of the cultural institutions that kept the normative and formative impetus of these texts alive through all the changes in language, social systems, political orders, and other constructs of reality; thus, the framework of conditions was created that made a dialogue with predecessors from thousands of years ago possible. (Assmann, 2011, pp. 265–266)

According to Assmann and as a critical elaboration of Jaspers' claim that during the Axial Age "Man [sic], as we know him today, came into being" (1953, p. 1), this period proves as consequential as it does because of these processes of fixing, not being and consciousness, but fixing texts that enable certain kinds of conscious response and interaction. For Assmann, this is the decisive difference:

> There were presumably always great individuals with "transcendental visions." Decisive is the step to turn these visions into "cultural texts," to select these texts into a canon and to frame the transmission of this canon by institutions of exegesis ensuring its availability, readability, and authority over 3,000 years. (Assmann, 2012, p. 399)

Shifting the focus in this way also has the consequence that the dating of the Axial Age shifts to 200 BCE to 200 AD, as these are the centuries when the various canons (of Judaism, Buddhism, Hinduism, Confucianism, of Greek thought) are formed.

Of course, in doing so Assmann—a thorough-going critic of the Axial Age thesis, who presents a critical alternative thesis of his own—is also shifting some of the basic tenets of the thesis. For Jaspers, the canonizing of what was living experience is precisely the end of the Axial Age; "when the Age lost its creativeness, a process of dogmatic fixation and levelling-down took place" (1953, p. 5). In different words of Jaspers, the "Axial Period too ended in failure" (1953, p. 20): If it had succeeded, presumably in the form of a plurality of lineages of practice within small communities alongside ongoing proliferation of experimental questioning and formation of other practices within other small communities, such that a universal ethics was preached as well as practiced to ever-growing numbers of persons counter to the antispiritual and inhuman power of civilization, then the development of canonical texts would not have been necessary. The creativity, questioning, and deep spiritual tension experienced by the Axial Age philosophers, prophets, sages, and holy men are crucial on Jaspers' existential conception. To the degree that this is passed on to constitute a perennial tension within the post-Axial civilizations, to that extent those civilizations would carry an Axial heritage. In the absence of lineages of practice carried on by practitioners, however, then in order to sustain such a tension, or to periodically return to and renew such a tension, there does need to be some material embodiment of the ideas. The canonizing of the Axial Age visions marks both its failure and an inadequate but service-able way for its ideas to survive. In this respect, Assmann's emphasis on texts, literacy, and canonization, is surely right, as is his criticism of Jaspers as "strangely blind," "having completely ignored the role of writing" (Assmann, 2011, p. 266). The post-Axial civilizations need the canonical texts, derived from the Axial Age, for its members to struggle with and struggle against in order to re-create their own living, experiential version of the Axial tension. Post-Axial religions need the canonical texts to provide the doctrinal center to their institutions for its members—but these may be running in parallel to, in oblivious ignorance of, or in polemical debate against an authentic Axial response to and interpretation of those texts. The latter is about the elements Jaspers presented: questioning and critique, an openness to mystery, a profound inner tension and struggle, the desire for reform. The use of the religious text to prevent, deny, overcome, or somehow resolves these existential experiences of tension—for example, in favor of a dogmatic certainty, an unquestioning faith, or to conserve the integrity of the religious institutions—would be, on the Axial interpretation, mis-use and ab-use of the texts.

Innovation in Ideology

The final innovation correlated to the new scale of power implemented by civilization is ideology. The development of literacy underwrites not only scribal elites and processes of canonization, but also the development and spread of ideologies. The scholar I'm drawing upon for an understanding of ideology, Michael Mann, is well-known and reputable for his extraordinary analysis of power and its historical development contained in his 2 volumes *The Sources of Social Power* (2012). Given the argument that the Axial Age is motivated by, above all, the rise in civilizational power that coalesces into a distinctive form in the first millennium BCE, his account of the history of power is especially relevant to examine. That Mann makes no mention of the Axial Age in his work is surprising, but also useful in the sense that, like scholars like Taagepera, Carneiro, or Wilkinson used above, he provides an independent perspective that largely corroborates and converges on the Axial Age thesis. For example, Mann (2012) begins his concluding summary on ideological power:

> Over several chapters, I have discussed a number of belief systems that all became prominent in the period from about 600 B.C. to about A.D. 700.: Zoroastrianism, Greek humanistic philosophy, Hinduism, Buddhism, Confucianism, Judaism, Christianity, and Islam. They became prominent because of one crucial shared characteristic: a translocal sense of personal and social identity that permitted extensive and intensive mobilization on a scale sufficient to enter the historical record. ...[They] offered a more extensive and universal membership than had any prior social power organization. This was the first great reorganizing achievement of ideological power movements in this period. (p. 363)

I assume the reader finds this quote entirely commonplace, given our discussion of the Axial Age so far. What has been added is the overt emphasis on "belief systems" and "ideological power." The latter is key to Mann's overall presentation based on his analysis of "social power" as deriving from four sources: economic, military, political, and ideological. As discussed above, the new scale of civilizational power manifested a great increase in the first three sources. According to Mann, it also manifests ideology on an unprecedented scale.

Mann, as I do, emphasizes the importance of identity, and the increasingly transcendent possibilities made available for identity with the rise of civilizational power. (In fact, he reserves a special place for transcendence as being the crucial defining feature of ideology: He defines ideology as transcendent power (cf. Mann, 2012, pp. 23, 126–127, 310–340). Unlike economic, military, or political power, ideology gains its power precisely in cutting across and rising above existing powers as these have been institutionalized and networked within civilizations.) Thus, in contrast to the economic, military, and political sources of power, ideology is the most overtly "conscious" and "idealized," invoking beliefs and identity and the claim that these transcend both the economic, military, and political domains and the traditional claims on identity made by family, class, region, ethnicity, etc. However, recalling Assmann's criticism of Jaspers, conscious stuff like beliefs, ideals, and ideology still needs some "material" basis. Mann argues ideology requires two "preconditions and causes."

The first is "*interstitial networks* of social interaction, communicating in the interstices of the empires and (to a lesser extent) across their frontiers" (2012, pp. 363–364, italics his). The great buildup of economic, military, and political power within civilizations and empires had as a side effect increasing power accruing to particular sectors of the "masses" than they had possessed before. In their attempts to exercise their increased power—more precisely increased possibilities of power—however, these newly emerging groups encountered resistance and obstruction from existing institutions and traditional structures which did not, or not yet, recognize their efforts as legitimate. These unofficial groups find common cause and link up in networks in between and around the official networks of the official groups; hence, Mann's emphasizing their interstitial character. (The notion of "interstitial" echoes and elaborates the emphasis above on the anomalous, exceptional, marginal, sociological position of the Axial Age breakthroughs.) Mann's second precondition for ideological power manifesting as it does in these centuries is thoroughly intertwined with these networks: "These interstitial groups relied upon, and in their turn fostered, something that tended to become a specifically ideological infrastructure, *literacy*" (2012, p. 364, italics his). Mann perceives the role of literacy in supporting ideology in somewhat different terms than those discussed above by Assmann.

Mann emphasizes what he calls the "two-step infrastructure of literacy." Although literacy decisively increases in these centuries, it nevertheless remains significantly the minority position by comparison with exclusively oral means of communication. As a communication technology, however, the written text is greatly superior to oral communication, particularly for preserving the integrity of the original message. Combining these two otherwise countervailing tendencies creates a two-step infrastructure: The first step is the delivery of the text to a literate person in a community, with the second step the communication from that literate person to the mostly oral community. In this manner, the consequences of literacy exceed its apparent sphere of influence based on a literal reading of the demographics. Through this two-step model of dissemination of text, the unofficial groups seeking but denied power could coalesce into interstitial networks not bound together by kinship, class, region, ethnicity, or local community. Did anything bind these groups together? One thing: a shared sense of potential power experienced as a shared frustration vis-à-vis established power; in Mann's terms (discussing the rise of Christianity in Rome, but generalizing the point to world religions in general), they shared "exclusion from official power" (2012, p. 323). Their response to this one commonalty was also shared: "a popular belief system [that] was indirectly subversive; for it located ultimate knowledge, meaning, and significance outside the traditional sources of economic, political, and military power – in a realm it considered transcendent" (2012, p. 365).

Mann's discussion of ideology stems from his focus on the rise of the world religions, which entails the period "from about 600 B.C. to about A.D. 700"; however, he later qualifies ("further compresses") this period "to about seven hundred years if we regard Buddhism and Hinduism *as attaining their final forms* around 100 B.C." (2012, p. 301, emphasis added). These two periodizations fit pretty well the two periods proposed for the Axial Age, in terms of the Axial Age as foundation of the world religions thesis (800 BCE–700 CE) vs. Jaspers' thesis (800–200 BCE). Mann's "compressed" dating means his proposed beginning of world religions (100 BCE–700 CE) roughly fits Assmann's canonization dates (200 BCE–200 CE). These dates also loosely match Jaspers' 200 BCE dating, albeit in terms of his rationale that such consolidation, or canonization, or "attaining their final forms," marks the *end* of the Axial Age. In Jaspers' terms, "From about 200 BC onwards great political and spiritual unifications and dogmatic configurations held the field" (1953, p. 194). In the terms of world-systems theorists— who notably rarely make any mention of the Axial Age thesis—they also present a converging periodization. Grinin and Korotaev (2014) argue: "if... we consider that by the moment of the Silk Route emergence there were three main independent world-systems (the West Asian, Chinese, and South Asian ones) which later merged into a single (Afroeurasian) world-system, then it appears quite logical to date the emergence of the single Afroeurasian world-system to the late first millennium BCE" (p. 46). Our own proposal within this chapter—to use the notion of a consolidation of the Afroeurasian world-system or the E-W axis, in terms of its becoming wall-to-wall empires by around the first century CE, as a significant marker in the development of civilizational power that began around 3000 BCE—also roughly fits this dating (broadly, within the 200 BCE–200 CE range).

How to reason through this variety of dates and claims, and how to relate all of this to the Axial Age thesis? First, as discussed above, there is a whole new scale to human power that emerges through dynamics internal to civilization, for which evidence converged on the period 700–430 BCE as the most spectacular growth. Second, there is a second convergence, around 100 BCE according to Mann, in which power takes the form of world religions. World religions are on the one hand—the empirical hand—tied to particular civilizations that endorse and "carry" these religions (the Han empire endorses Confucianism; the Mauryan emperor Asoka in India endorses Buddhism while later Indian rulers will endorse Hinduism; Rome endorses Greek thought, and centuries later under the emperor Constantine, Christianity; Arabic civilization endorses Islam). On the other hand—the transcendent ideology hand—these world religions outlast, outgrow, and expand beyond their particular civilizations. Mann describes this founding of world religions as follows:

> I explained the explosion [of transcendental ideology in the shape of world-salvationist religions] less in terms of the fundamental and stable needs of individuals or societies for meaning, norms, cosmology, and so forth…. than in terms of the world-historical development of power techniques. Only now could ideological messages be stabilized over extensive social spaces. Only now emerged a series of fundamental contradictions between official and interstitial power networks of ancient empires. Only now were the latter generating socially transcendent organizations in which a cosmology of a universal divinity and rational, individual salvation appeared plausible. This was, therefore, a single world-historical opportunity. (2012, p. 370)

In short the formation of world religions founded within particular civilizations followed by expanding beyond them is the natural next stage in the unfolding of a dynamic of expanding power. This dynamic began in 3000 BCE with the formation of civilizations and reaches a crux in the years 700–430 BCE. Near the end of the first millennium BCE, a particular "closure," or "well-differentiated zone-ness," of the world-system organized across Afroeurasia, along the E-W axis, manifests as "wall-to-wall empires" which signals new possibilities for civilizational techniques of power and for their intensification. Beginning around 100 BCE networks of newly emerging elites realize the "single world-historical opportunity" presented them through utilizing the existing structures of power organization—infrastructures of ideology, money, literacy—provided to found what we call in retrospect "world religions."

Based on this reasoning my interpretation is: The natural unfolding of the power dynamics initiated within civilization reaches a point of crisis at a certain level of expansion, that none of the particular innovations (divinization of the ruler, centralization, social and economic hierarchicalization, militarization, money, literacy) proves able to adequately resolve for several centuries. To resolve this crisis from an extant ruler point of view would mean a containment of expanding power within civilizational boundaries as well as stopping its expansive dynamic—something that the historical record has revealed as extremely difficult, if not impossible, for rulers to accomplish. World religions resolve this crisis through developing transcendent ideologies—belief systems centered on a transcendent locus of identification—that in claiming universal status enable power to move beyond civilizational boundaries. In doing so they create internal political tensions vis-à-vis "secular" rule, ultimately posing endless possibilities for criticism of rulers for failing to meet transcendent goals. Phrased in this way it should be no wonder that civilizations or their rulers did not adequately resolve this issue created by expansionism, for it would mean undermining their own sovereignty.

Expansionism Re-visited: Power, Consciousness, Critical Consciousness

Key to this interpretation for the development of world religions is the emergence of transcendence and universality as recurring issues raised by the innovations in ruling, money, literacy, and ideology. Partly this is because any expansion of power, in moving above and beyond limits and affording a synoptic overview of one's prior situation is a type of transcendence. The synoptic overview on the past is qualitatively different than that afforded by hindsight alone. The transcending of limits through an expansion of power means one's existential situation—one's horizon of possibilities and of meanings—has changed. In this respect, hindsight would not accurately remember the past situation, as the prior, invisible restriction of horizon due to particular limits is no longer effective and the past becomes puzzling as to how one could have thought and perceived in the way one did. The point here: This is not transcendence in Jaspers' Axial, "otherworldly," "capitalized," spiritual sense as discussed in the previous chapter, but transcendence in a more empirical, literal, "this-worldly," mundane sense. Transcendence in this sense is the expansion of power uncritically raised into consciousness. (In this respect, transcendence as following expansion is, even further back, following evolution itself: The process of evolution is a process of transcendence [see, e.g., Dobzhansky, 1977].)

Phrased like this, however, immediately raises the question: How is this different from what the Axial Age revolutionaries envision, as the claim stemming from Jaspers is precisely focused on the crucial significance of conscious awareness? The answer is that in the Axial Age case the expansion of power is not merely raised into consciousness as an extension of the self-same natural process of the expansion of power, but that it is raised into critical consciousness. Momigliano (1975) is certainly correct in saying of this time "there is a profound tension between political powers and intellectual movements... We are in the age of criticism" (p. 9). Eisenstadt (1986) specifies the criticism one step further: Criticism is above all aimed at the divine kingship notion; the Axial Age is above all about the desacralization of political domination. The luminaries of the Axial Age do not accept the expansion of power as a natural fact or an inevitability. To the natural fact or natural development, they add "criticism," the exercise of deep, moral-ethical, self-responsible consciousness. They criticize and evaluate the expansion of power as a dangerous evil, that magnifies and enhances what is base, violent, selfish, and egocentric in human nature, and propose an alternative, spiritual vision of a human nature transformed toward its highest goodness, which is selfless, non-violent, compassionate, and loving. (The best articulation of criticism in this sense is articulated by Charles Taylor in a number of his writings as "strong evaluation" and plays a central role in Taylor's take on the Axial Age, especially in Taylor [2007]. Within Axial scholarship specifically, it is described in a diversity of ways, as "second-order thinking" [Elkana, 1986], a formulation that Bellah [2011] particularly likes; perhaps most extensively discussed as "critical reflexivity" by Wittrock [2005].)

The expansion of power raised into (uncritical) consciousness expands and inflates the ego itself through the latter's identification with this power. Identification is an act of consciousness, in the psycho-dynamic sense of consciousness as dynamically active and alive, inclu-sive of but extending far beyond ego-consciousness. Identification is an act of consciousness "naturally", that is "unconsciously" or "auto-matically," performed. It is not a self-conscious or a critically conscious act. As mentioned in Chapter 2 in the context of discussing tribalism, for evolutionary reasons of survival that are deep, basic, primitive, and powerful the ego identifies with the collective group—the "tribe"—that nurtures and raises it. From this identification, both individual identity (in all its forms of self-conscious awareness) and group identity (in all its collective forms of consciousness, i.e., culture) develop. Notice that in this deepest, most basic, and most primitive form, the ego's identi-fication goes beyond the individual to the collective: This is an expan-sion of the ego's identity. It is here, psychologically, that tribalism meets expansionism. The ego expands itself without an accompanying con-scious awareness, and certainly without therefore any criticism, of that change to the ego.

Critical consciousness, or sufficient self-consciousness, does perceive the expansion of the ego and how it has inflated itself and evaluates it. Unlike, the natural evolved psychological ability of identification, this critical, self-conscious activity is not a natural ability. It is not what the ego naturally, unconsciously, or automatically does. Critical con-sciousness is a trained, practiced, and disciplined ability. What a crit-ically conscious person perceives is that as their power expands, their self-knowledge does not. In identifying with expanded power, the ego's willful blindness to itself—willfully blind to its weaknesses, vul-nerabilities, shortcomings, and ultimately to its own evils—expands too. The expansion of power introduces a whole new scale into "val-uing"; it distorts one's values in lockstep with the distortions of one's ego. There is nothing new about grandiosity, exaggerated perceptions of one's own invulnerability and desirability, arrogance, greed, avarice, or cruelty. What is new is the scale to which all of these expand, and the scale of their rationalization in self-serving, self-enhancing, willfully self-blind, terms. Insofar as the ego identifies with the power structures that have served the ego's expansion, the rationalization will extend to include these too. Injustice, inequity, oppression, the dehumanizing of the other, and suffering, and much more evil besides, can find justifi-cation and legitimation once the rationalizations develop into a full-fledged ideology.

In trying to unravel some of the complexity between Axial Age foundations and world religions as their elaboration, we've also moved later in historical time to after the Axial Age proper. To understand these consequences for world history, as well as to make better specific sense of the proper diversity of both Axial Age movements and the world religions they found, we need to look in closer detail at the sociology of the particular Axial Age civilizations themselves.

REFERENCES

Assmann, J. (2005). Axial "breakthroughs" and semantic "relocation" in ancient Egypt and Israel. In J. Arnason, S. Eisenstadt, & B. Wittrock (Eds.), *Axial civilizations and world history* (pp. 133–156). Leiden: Brill.

Assmann, J. (2011). *Cultural memory and early civilization: Writing, remembrance, and political imagination*. New York: Cambridge University Press.

Assmann, J. (2012). Cultural memory and the myth of the Axial Age. In R. Bellah & H. Joas (Eds.), *The Axial Age and its consequences* (pp. 366–407). Cambridge and London: Belknap.

Baumard, N., Hyafil, A., Morris, I., & Boyer, P. (2015). Increased affluence explains emergence of ascetic wisdoms and moralizing religions. *Current Biology, 25*(1), 10–15.

Bellah, R. (2011). *Religion in human evolution: From the Paleolithic to the Axial Age*. Harvard, MA: Belknap.

Bellah, R., & Joas, H. (2012). Introduction. In R. Bellah & H. Joas (Eds.), *The Axial Age and its consequences* (pp. 1–6). Cambridge and London: Belknap.

Blenkinsopp, J. (1995). *Sage, priest, prophet: Religious and intellectual leadership in ancient Israel*. Louisville, KY: John Knox Press.

Carneiro, R. (1978). Political expansion as an expression of the principle of competitive exclusion. In R. Cohen & E. Service (Eds.), *Origins of the state: The anthropology of political evolution* (pp. 205–223). Philadelphia: Institute for the Study of Human Issues.

Chase-Dunn, C., & Hall, T. (1997). *Rise and demise: Comparing world-systems*. Boulder, CO: Westview Press.

Christian, D. (2000). Silk roads or steppe roads? The silk roads in world history. *Journal of World History, 11*(1), 1–26.

Cousins, E. (1987). Spirituality in today's world. In F. Whaling (Ed.), *Religion in today's world: The religious situation of the world from 1945 to the present day* (pp. 306–345). Edinburgh: T&T Clark.

Darwin, C. (2001). *On the origin of species*. University Park: Pennsylvania State University.

Diamond, J. (1997). *Guns, germs, and steel: The fate of human societies*. New York: W. W. Norton.

Dobzhansky, T. (1977). *Humankind: A product of evolutionary transcendence.* Johannesburg, South Africa: Witwatersrand University Press for Institute for the Study of Man in Africa.

Duchrow, U., & Hinkelammert, F. (2012). *Transcending greedy money: Interreligious solidarity for just relations.* New York: Palgrave Macmillan.

Elkana, Y. (1986). The emergence of second-order thinking in classical Greece. In S. Eisenstadt (Ed.), *The origins and diversity of Axial Age civilizations* (pp. 40–64). Albany: State University of New York Press.

Eisenstadt, S. (1986). Introduction: The Axial Age breakthroughs—Their characteristics and origins. In S. Eisenstadt (Ed.), *The origins and diversity of Axial Age civilizations* (pp. 1–25). Albany: State University of New York Press.

Fagan, B. (2010). *Cro-Magnon: How the Ice Age gave birth to the first modern humans.* New York: Bloomsbury.

Giddens, A. (1991). *Modernity and identity: Self and society in the late modern age.* Stanford, CA: Stanford University Press.

Goldin, I., Cameron, G., & Balarajan, M. (2011). *Exceptional people: How migration shaped our world and will define our future.* Princeton and Oxford: Princeton University Press.

Goody, J., & Watt, I. (1963). The consequences of literacy. *Comparative Studies in Society and History, 5*(3), 304–345.

Graeber, D. (2011). *Debt: The first 5,000 years.* Brooklyn and London: Melville House.

Grinin, L., & Korotayev, A. (2012). The Afroeurasian world-system: Genesis, transformations, characteristics. In S. Babones & C. Chase-Dunn (Eds.), *Routledge handbook of world-systems analysis* (pp. 30–38). London and New York: Routledge.

Grinin, L., & Korotayev, A. (2014). Origins of globalization in the framework of the Afroeurasian world-system history. *Journal of Globalization Studies, 5*(1), 32–64.

Hodgson, M. (1974). *The venture of Islam: Conscience and history in a world civilization* (Vol. 1). Chicago: University of Chicago Press.

Jaspers, K. (1953). *The origin and goal of history.* New Haven and London: Yale University Press (originally published in 1949).

Johnson, A., & Earle, T. (2000). *The evolution of human societies: From foraging group to agrarian state.* Stanford, CA: Stanford University Press.

Korotayev, A. (2004). *World religions and social evolution of the Old World Oikumene civilizations: A cross-cultural perspective.* Lewiston, Queenston, and Lampeter: Edwin Mellen.

Mann, M. (2012). *The sources of social power* (Vol. 1). New York: Cambridge University Press.

Manning, P. (2005). *Migration in world history.* London: Routledge.

McBrearty, M., & Brooks, A. (2000). The revolution that wasn't: A new interpretation for the origin of modern behavior. *Journal of Human Evolution, 39*(5), 453–563.

McEvilley, T. (2002). *The shape of ancient thought: Comparative studies in Greek and Indian philosophies.* New York: Allworth Press.

McNeill, W. (1963). *The rise of the west: A history of the human community.* Chicago and London: University of Chicago.

McNeill, W. (1986). *Mythistory and other essays.* Chicago and London: University of Chicago.

Momigliano, A. (1975). *Alien wisdom: The limits of hellenization.* Cambridge: Cambridge University Press.

Ober, J. (2015). *The rise and fall of classical Greece.* Princeton and Oxford: Princeton University Press.

Ong, W. (1982). *Orality and literacy: The technologizing of the word.* London and New York: Routledge.

Pettitt, P. (2018). The rise of modern humans. In C. Scarre (Ed.), *The human past: World prehistory & the development of human societies* (pp. 108–148). London: Thames & Hudson.

Ramelli, I. (2016). *Social justice and the legitimacy of slavery: The role of philosophical asceticism from ancient Judaism to late antiquity.* Oxford: Oxford University Press.

Sanderson, S. K. (1995). Expanding world commercialization: The link between world-systems and civilizations. In S. K. Sanderson (Ed.), *Civilizations and world systems: Studying world-historical change* (pp. 261–272). Walnut Creek, London, and New Delhi: Altamira (Sage).

Sanderson, S. K. (2018). *Religious evolution and the Axial Age: From shamans to priests to prophets.* London: Bloomsbury.

Seaford, R. (2004). *Money and the early Greek mind.* Cambridge: Cambridge University Press.

Shaffer, L. (1994). Southernization. *Journal of World History, 5*(1), 1–22.

Solnit, R. (2016). *Hope in the dark: Untold histories, wild possibilities.* Chicago, IL: Haymarket Books.

Stringer, C. (2002). Modern human origins: Progress and prospects. *Philosophical Transactions of the Royal Society B, 357,* 563–579.

Stringer, C. (2016). The origin and evolution of *Homo sapiens. Philosophical Transactions of the Royal Society B, 371.* http://dx.doi.org/10.1098/rstb.2015.0237.

Taagepera, R. (1978). Size and duration of empires: Systematics of size. *Social Science Research, 7,* 108–127.

Taagepera, R. (1979). Size and duration of empires: Growth-decline curves, 600 B.C. to 600 A.D. *Social Science History, 3*(3–4), 115–138.

Taylor, C. (2007). *A secular age*. Cambridge and London: Belknap.

Thomassen, B. (2010). Anthropology, multiple modernities and the Axial Age debate. *Anthropological Theory, 10*(4), 321–344.

Waters, M. (2014). *Ancient Persia: A concise history of the Achaemenid Empire, 550–330 BCE*. New York: Cambridge University Press.

Webb, S. (2015). *If the universe is teeming with aliens ... Where is everybody? Seventy-five solutions to the Fermi paradox and the problem of extraterrestrial life*. Cham, Switzerland: Springer.

Wilkinson, D. (1993). Civilizations, cores, world-economics and Oikumenes. In A. G. Frank & B. Gills (Eds.), *The world system: Five hundred years or five thousand?* (pp. 221–246). London and New York: Routledge.

Wittrock, B. (2005). The meaning of the Axial Age. In J. Arnason, S. Eisenstadt, & B. Wittrock (Eds.), *Axial civilizations and world history* (pp. 51–86). Leiden: Brill.

Wright, R. (2000). *Nonzero: The logic of human destiny*. New York: Random House.

CHAPTER 5

Sociology of the Axial Age Civilizations

When Robert Bellah and Hans Joas (2012) claim that "[t]he notion that in significant parts of Eurasia the middle centuries of the first millennium BCE mark a significant transition in human cultural history, and that this period can be referred to as the Axial Age, has become widely, but not universally, accepted" (p. 1), they are able to do so above all because of the developments in the comparative sociology of the Axial Age civilizations that have come after Jaspers. While our previous chapter looked from a big picture perspective on the civilizational growth and the expansion of power in the first millennium BCE that forms the world-system, world-historical thesis for the Axial Age civilizations, in this chapter we will look in detail at those civilizations themselves.

THE SECOND PHASE OF AXIAL AGE SCHOLARSHIP: SUBSTANTIATING JASPERS' THESIS

The third chapter looked at Karl Jaspers' proposal for the Axial Age in some detail. I argued that Jaspers marked the end of a first phase of about two centuries of scholarly speculations about the Axial Age. This was not only because he coins the phrase of an "Axial Age" that comes into currency. It is also because, for whatever reasons, his "bold idea, briefly sketched" provides enough of a speculative skeleton—enough structure and system—to work with that an explosion of scholarship comes after in the following decades. Jaspers focused on the Axial Age in

© The Author(s) 2019
C. Peet, *Practicing Transcendence*,
https://doi.org/10.1007/978-3-030-14432-6_5

terms of consciousness, spiritualization, transcendence, the idea of universality, "questioning Being," and so on. His focus was philosophical. Insofar as his existential perspective licensed this terminology and way of working, that many of the really significant contributions to the Axial Age thesis after Jaspers are made by sociologists (above all, by Shmuel Eisenstadt and then Robert Bellah) means a shift in emphasis to a more empirical focus. The importance of this shift in focus—from an existential philosophy of world history to a comparative, historical sociology of civilizations—cannot be overstated. Without the empirical corroboration, the speculative theorizing of the Axial Age might well have continued in the same occasional, intermittent way in which it had for centuries, but without ever gaining the legs it needed to cover in detail the ground over which the theory had speculatively flown. Jaspers seems to be the transitional thinker who, despite continuing in the highly speculative vein of the first phase, provided enough structure and system to the thesis to enable the more detailed empirical investigation that characterizes the second phase.

Shifting our perspective away from an existential philosophy of world history that privileges consciousness and which flew at a speculatively high enough altitude that the Axial Age resolved itself into a dividing line within that world history dramatically changes the degree of resolution, and thus the picture that forms, too. In Chapter 4, we took Jaspers' argument one degree of resolution closer, ensuing in a big picture view of civilization and its growth and development. We put this growth into an evolutionary context of human expansion, of a first radiation across the Old World, followed by a second radiation into the New World, before coming to focus on the great expansion of power that is the defining world-historical characteristic of the first millennium BCE, wherein a geographic dividing line along the E-W axis of Eurasia manifested. However, this abstract, minimal image of a line was soon modified, using Darwin's metaphor of the Tree of Life, into a more elaborate "tree of world history" picture: a trunk with larger and smaller branches, twisting, twining, growing under and over and through each other, old bits dying off, new buds emerging.

As we shift our perspective yet nearer to the ground and sharpen our resolution on the historical landscape some degrees further, it will be above all the simplicity and clarity of a "dividing line" within history that will get broken up into a far more uneven cluster of processes and developments at the "mesosociological" level—nearer the ground than our "macrosociological" big picture of civilizations and world-systems of the previous chapter, but still higher up than the "microsociological" level of resolution of the small communities of spiritual practitioners of the next chapter. Indeed, it will become apparent that a clear-cut dividing line in history only obtains from Jaspers' existential philosophy focus on conscious awareness as defining history. Instead, as Baskin and Bondarenko (2014) rightly point out, "the Axial Age is not just a spiritual *event*, but a socio-cultural *process of transformation*" (p. 9, emphases theirs). Historically, this process takes irreducibly individual forms in each of its particular geographic and sociological original settings of China, India, Israel, and Greece. From those "new buds" of their original settings, from these "multiple axialities," the sociocultural process of transformation has continued until the present, and continues today, in the multiply branching form of "multiple modernities" defining the current shape of globalization (Eisenstadt, 2000, 2006). These origin points when viewed comparatively bear sufficient family resemblance that they warrant the common surname "Axial." When examined more closely, they also attest to their own unique Axial take on spirituality and consciousness, transcendence, inwardness, mystery, identity, and the relation of the universal and the individual. The uniqueness of each "axiality" and thus the "fact of difference" across them become more apparent the deeper into their respective contexts one dives.

This second, sociological phase of scholarship slowly, systematically, and empirically puts meat onto the bones of the skeleton, substantiating and fleshing out Jaspers' Axial Age thesis in far greater detail and with far greater care. In claiming that scholarship substantiates the thesis, I don't mean it confirms all of Jaspers' versions. Much of what Jaspers argued proves overstated, unsupported, too self-assured, or too generalized (all criticisms that apply to this book, too, with the self-conscious caveat that this book is a signpost directing the reader to a scholarly landscape wherein careful statement, supported claim, hesitant probing, and specific detail dominate). Much of the substantiating has been to correct, revise, reject, or refine the thesis. We could see some working examples of this in the previous chapter. For example, Jaspers' rationale for the end of the Axial Age was that "From about 200 BC onwards great political and spiritual unifications and dogmatic configurations held the field" (1953, p. 194). Scholarship provided several loosely overlapping rationales—the consolidation of the Eurasian world-system, the canonization of sacred texts, and the initial formation of world religions—that converged on this dating: Jaspers' view was substantiated here in the sense of confirmed and better supported, in a fairly straightforward way.

A different example: Jaspers' claim as to the radical originality of the breakthroughs to transcendence and universality was shown to be false in the sense of overstating the case. I argued that the need for transcendence and universality was overdetermined by the expansion of power at this time. The state, developments in economics like the invention of money, and increasing trade, the increase in literacy, all led to versions of transcendence and universality. Proving Jaspers wrong here didn't overturn the whole thesis, but it did lead to a correction of overstatement and qualification of a part of the thesis: The Axial Age spiritual revolutionaries don't just "raise transcendence into consciousness," they raise it in terms of a critical consciousness that includes a powerful negative evaluation of power alongside an alternative positive vision of transcendence with a primarily moral and ethical content.

A third example: economics scholars like Graeber (2011), or Duchrow and Hinkelammert (2012), or Baumard, Hyafil, Morris, and Boyer (2015), each argue from the robust correlation between the Axial Age and materialism, money, or increased affluence (respectively) to the latter "explaining" the Axial Age. Jaspers ignored the role of economics in describing the Axial Age. The argument from these scholars substantiates Jaspers' thesis by refining and extending it.

The general point to be taken is that Jaspers' Axial Age thesis is neither followed slavishly nor rejected unilaterally, but more so it provokes careful scholarly responses. By comparison with Jaspers' few, brief, suggestive characterizations, the comparative sociology of the Axial civilizations that come after is extensive and substantial. Can we identify a particular cause of the Axial Age? Is there some common element, or matrix of elements, evident within the particular sociological conditions of the Axial Age civilizations that explains, or perhaps more accurately motivates, the sudden, simultaneous, synchronous appearance of the Axial Age visionaries? Above all the light that sociology could shed on this question involves who, sociologically speaking, the spiritual *virtuosi* were and in what circumstances they lived. In that spirit, my proposal in the last chapter was that their visionary response was motivated by (some degree of) critical conscious awareness of the advent of a whole new scale to civilizational power. The proposal specifies the motivation for the Axial Age more concretely than the usual mere noting of the "sudden, simultaneous, parallel" appearance of spiritual revolutionaries in a handful of civilizations—and thus invites falsification (which, in scholarship, is a good invitation!). The proposal also opens inquiry in the direction of world-system theorizing, a step that Axial Age scholarship has not yet, but I think should, take, and which would bring its current phase of sociological theorizing into contact with bigger picture considerations to better flesh out the world-historical importance of the Axial Age. In the next section, I will sketch out some of these latter implications before turning to the comparative sociology of the Axial Age civilizations proper.

THE AXIAL AGE IN WORLD-SYSTEM CONTEXT: ORIGINS AND INTERRELATIONS

The long East-West axis of Afroeurasia as world-system context within which the Axial Age civilizations emerge sets limits and parameters to inquiry very differently than "civilizational" or "imperial" foci; it also presents different criteria—for example, a certain degree of "consolidation" of that world-system, around the centuries 200 BCE–200 CE, marks the end of the Axial Age and invites fresh questions. One unresolved question concerning the Axial Age which no scholar has answered and most scholars ignore or at the most suggest is fruitless speculation: Did it have a single origin? Were all the apparently "parallel and independent" Axial Age breakthroughs in truth one systemic process diffused throughout the world-system? (And if so, did this process have a particular origin? Western scholars would presumably prefer West Asia and invoke some Sumerian-Mesopotamian "cradle of civilization" origin; some contemporary Indian scholars argue for the Indus and Sarasvati rivers as the true "cradle of civilization" going back more than 7000 years [Feuerstein, Kak, & Frawley, 2001].) If, for example, from the undeciphered seals of the Indus Valley Civilization, those showing a seated figure with a horned helm, surrounded by animals, could be definitively established to indeed be a "proto-Shiva" figure, sitting in a yoga pose, we would have a very ancient date for the origin of systematic meditative practice, and a potential "single origin" claim. However, as Samuel (2008, pp. 3–8) clearly shows, scholars have proposed several different, competing, and incompatible ways to interpret the seated figure, all equally plausible depending on their imported assumptions. There is nothing in the evidence itself to compel any particular one, such as the "proto-Shiva" seated in the lotus posture, as correct.

Or, a different focus opened by the world-system considerations: the tantalizing promise to shed some light on the joker in the Axial Age deck, the mysterious Zoroaster, and Zoroastrianism in ancient Persia. The scholarship at Jaspers' time believed Zoroaster to be living around 600 BCE, but later scholarship has discredited this dating and understood Zoroaster to have lived earlier—perhaps 1000 BCE or 1200 BCE, but really there is no consensus. (In one *History of Zoroastrianism* text, Zoroaster's "date of birth... is placed anywhere between 600 B.C. and 6000 B.C."! [Dhalla, 1938, p. 13].) Axial scholarship for the most part leaves out Zoroastrianism from its considerations (for an exception, see Shaked, 2005). Given this great extent of uncertainty, what was Zoroastrianism's role in the Axial Age developments, its relation to the Achaemenid Empire? Placing the origin question together with the Zoroastrian question: perhaps, a suitably ancient Zoroaster is the "one origin" of the Axial Age that diffused throughout the world-system?

A third focus opened by world-system considerations: I find it immensely plausible that not only material items of trade and commerce (technologies, textiles, goods, grains, animals, tools, weapons) as well as germs and illnesses circulated along the Afroeurasian East-West axis—these are the empirical emphases of world-system researchers—but also ideas and philosophies. I am not suggesting that, for example, Gore Vidal's fictional treatment of the Axial Age in his novel *Creation* (1981) be considered empirical evidence, but pointing out that scholarship tends toward the more conservative side in estimating the conscious awareness and imaginative sensitivity of people in Axial Age times. While this is less dramatic than a "one origin" claim (and in my view, also more plausible), an "ancient interactions" suggestion holds out significant interest for Axial Age theorizing. Still unresolved is what role inner Eurasia played, for example. (Sanderson [2018] reviews some theories along these lines under the phrase "mutual influence" [pp. 192–195]; applied to Greece in the context of the Mediterranean, see some of the articles in Halpern and Sacks [2017].) If, alongside commerce and trade, there was also more conversation and discussion, and more interest in philosophical and religious questions, and this was more widespread and more substantial than we at present realize, it is likely there was significantly more influence between India, the Middle East, and Greece—and China?—than scholarship has yet been able to find. Sanderson (2018) cites Rodney Stark as holding a version of this: "He suggests that if technology and other elements of material culture were diffusing, then ideas would have been even more likely to diffuse" (p. 192).

For example: the ancient fame of Pythagoras rested in part on his reputedly having studied with the Magi of the East (Medes, Chaldeans, Zoroastrians), visiting oracles throughout the Near East, being initiated into the mysteries of Egypt, and perhaps even a stint at the temple in Jerusalem (Barker, 2004, pp. 262–280). To maximize the strain on credibility, Pythagoras purportedly traveled to India, too (several centuries before the apostle Thomas who supposedly also did so, in the first century CE) before setting up his own special community in Croton, southern Italy. We have no definite proof of how far Pythagoras did indeed travel, although it certainly gains some plausibility within a world-system understanding. Compare, for example, world-system scholar John McNeill (1963), who claims post-1500 BCE "Middle Eastern, Indian, and Greek civilization constituted a single, loose geographical continuum, with zones of transition between the three principal segments" (pp. 168–169). Rodney Stark certainly considers it plausible, but Sanderson rightly points out that we just don't have evidence. What are some of the links between the "big context" for the Axial Age and the critical conscious awareness that emerges there, and how are they linked?

McEvilley (2002, pp. 1–22) provides an abundance of tantalizing evidence of early links between Greece and India, mediated by Persia and the Achaemenid Empire (see also Seaford, 2016a). In addition to trade of luxury items (such as elephants, or logs of teak, imported from India to Mesopotamia) reviving from the ninth through seventh centuries BCE, McEvilley notes suggestive anecdotes of Indian ascetics encountering Black Sea shamans influencing Diogenes of Sinope, "who seems to have brought Indian-derived ascetic practices into the Athenian philosophical milieu" (p. 10). He also cites a story of "an Indian yogi [who] came to Athens to talk with Socrates" (p. 10). On more solid ground, he points out that "mercenaries" (like Xenophon), "experts such as Scylax" (a Greek reported to have lived in India), "ambassadors, and physicians," "resided in the vicinity of the Persian court where they would have lived side by side with equivalent functionaries from northwest India" (p. 14). Based on the latter McEvilley claims a "period of unimpeded contact through the medium of Persia" "from 545 till 490" BCE (p. 18) (cf. also West, 1971, 1997). If these interactions could be substantively established in terms of ideas and exchange of practices, then the "parallelism" of the Axial Age breakthroughs is a result of interconnections within a single world-system, rather than being "independent" outcomes of similar sociological conditions obtaining within "autonomous," unconnected civilizations.

Another example where interconnections between ancient civilizations have been very explicitly raised and countered that is directly relevant to Axial Age theorizing: Mair (1990) argues on the basis of evidence of trade and commerce between India and China early in the first millennium BCE, combined with earlier dates for the *Upanisads* and later dates for Taoist texts, alongside textual parallels between the spiritual practices and experiences described in each, that Indian yoga directly influenced Taoist meditation. Roth (1999) disagrees sharply, arguing for "parallel developments" instead, and pointing out that "Mair has not been able to show any archaeological evidence that religious practices and ideas were transmitted" (pp. 137–138). Unresolved since the eighteenth century, speculation about the elusive questions of intercivilizational contact within the Eurasian world-system continues.

THE AXIAL AGE CIVILIZATIONS: OPENING CONSIDERATIONS

Even an initial superficial glance across the four Axial Age civilizations reveals some telling distinctive differences between them geographically that will inform their respective sociologies. Geographically, China is the easternmost, with its particular combination of mountain ranges, deserts, the vast expanses of central Asia, and the Pacific Ocean to its east, making it in the millennium before the development of the "Silk Road" the most isolated and self-contained of the four, in both geographic and world-system terms. By 300 BCE, contact with India, both overland and by sea routes around Southeast Asia, becomes increasingly established, while before this date we have tantalizing clues but nothing definitive (Christian, 2000; Tellier, 2009; Thompson, 2005). This self-contained isolation presumably is crucial for two distinctives of China among the four Axial Age civilizations: First, it has an actual history with accompanying legends of prior empires, the Hsia, Shang, and Zhou. Unique among the Axial Age civilizations, it has an accompanying Golden Age mythology of the Zhou as an idealized past order (cf. Schwartz, 1985, pp. 63–67 on the distinctive character of the Chinese mythicizing of a Golden Age). Second, it displays the greatest degree of historical continuity of memory and cultural homogeneity by comparison with the other Axial Age civilizations. Unlike Greece, for instance, at the opposite westernmost tip, "the political tendency is more biased toward unification and decentralization, as opposed to concentration fluctuations within multipolarity evinced in the Mediterranean area" (Thompson, 2005, p. 27).

India's geography is that of a subcontinent, bounded by the Indian Ocean to southeast and southwest, and the massive Himalayan range to its northeast. The one significant access route into the Afroeurasian world-system is to the northwest, which certainly was the route over millennia for the Indo-European-Aryan waves of migrants, and also the route nearer in time to the Axial Age for the eastern reaches of the Achaemenid Empire (whose eastern border lay in northwest India) followed by the incursion of Alexander the Great from 329 to 325 BCE. Thus with India we don't have what we could call isolation from the world-system as is the case with China, but for reasons of the civilized powers to the west of India a geopolitical boundary means some degree of cultural autonomy within the region of India. The question of the inverse, the degree of intercultural contact between India and places west, remains one of the great unanswered questions the Axial Age thesis poses. To date, we have only some tantalizing clues and glimpses. There are isolated evidences of early trade between Tyre in Phoenicia with India through the port of Ophir (Supara) near modern Bombay in 975 BCE (Feuerstein et al., 2001, p. 116; cf. Karttunen, 1989; Ray, 1995), while, as noted above, scholars like McEvilley (2002) and West (1971, 1997) have proffered efforts at more extensive Greece-India relations via the mediating presence of Persia. The early "Indo-European invasion of India" theory as the centerpiece for an answer is now entirely discredited (on this, see esp. McEvilley, 2002, pp. xix–xxxvi). A related great question, equally unanswered, resides in the relation of the Indus Valley Civilization to early Vedic culture (Fairservis 1997; Samuel, 2008, pp. 1–8). China's relative isolation for geographic reasons, and India's relative cultural autonomy due to a combination of geographic and world-system geopolitical reasons, means sociopolitically each were a patchwork diversity of states and polities that coalesce into imperial formations that end their Axial Ages. That China's patchwork had a mythicized memory of a prior empire, the Zhou, whereas India did not, is a significant difference.

Greece and Israel belong to the "ancient Near East" zone at the then westernmost end of the Eurasian world-system. This westernmost positioning is prior to the world-system's further Western expansion, post-Axial Age—by way of the rise of the Roman Empire—bringing the world-system all the way to the Atlantic. (During approximately the same post-Axial Age centuries, China and India are establishing sufficient contacts over both land and sea for the easternmost end of the world-system to reach the Pacific.) There is a commonalty to Greece and Israel which is a significant difference to China and India: each are small entities in the multi-state, multi-civilizational, and multi-tribal setting of the ancient Near East. "Greece" and "Israel" name both a land and a people with a shared culture. "India" and "China" are geographic names for multi-state, multi-civilizational, and multi-tribal areas.

In fact, this geographic difference poses one of the most significant criticisms of the Axial Age thesis: "India" and "China" are more comparable to the "ancient Near East" as a whole than to Greece or Israel specifically. Yet, all four "civilizations" are treated as comparable, whereas having both Greece and Israel as two "independent" Axial Age civilizations within the same geographic orbit of the "ancient Near East" is surely of enormous significance for how to interpret their developments. (Thinking ahead, this difference is surely critical to consider for the emergence of Christianity and then Islam, both within the ancient Near East. The only comparable development in the east would be Mahayana Buddhism, which emerges through contact between Indian Buddhism and China.) "India" and "China" do not name coherent or singular cultural entities, whereas "Greece" and "Israel" do. One clear way in which this significant difference shows up is in how the Axial Age visionaries are marginal: Since Greece and Israel, as small states on the peripheries of larger civilizations, are themselves already "marginal," the Axial Age philosophers and prophets who emerge within them as minorities will have a "doubly marginal" specification, whereas the holy men and sages of "India" and "China" are clearly marginal in an "interstitial" way—inter-state, inter-culture, inter-city.

Israel has the most vexed relations to its neighbors Egypt, Assyria, Babylon, and Persia. This obviously owes a lot to its geopolitical situation. Israel existed at the margins of, in between, and under intermittent regular threat by the surrounding established empires during the centuries of the Axial Age. In this situation, the precarious survival of Israel as a nation—the distinctiveness of its ethnic and religious identity—is the constant and recurring theme, one that follows a historical narrative line from the exodus from Egypt through to the arrival in "the Promised Land," to its becoming a kingdom, then two kingdoms, to the northern kingdom being conquered, then the southern, prior to its being taken into captivity and exile, followed by its return to Judaea and Jerusalem. Certainly among the different Axial Age formulations, the religiosity of ancient Israel is the most fraught with trauma and angst around its own identity and its relation to transcendent meaning.

For Greece, Achaemenid Persia is the great threat in the fifth century BCE, the imperial eastern civilization hoping to annex and conquer them. Their success at fending off the Persian advance is a crucial event in their history and is intertwined with their particular location as a peninsula at the then Western tip of the Eurasian world-system. Surrounded on three sides by water, the naval superiority of Greece over Persia is a key constituent to their preservation despite their smallness. The marginal status of the scattered Greek *poleis* across the Aegean, Black, and Mediterranean seas at the edge of ancient, established empires proved, unlike any of the other Axial cases, an ultimately positive circumstance. (The Greek "diaspora" [cf. Garland, 2014] is one of expanding influence, whereas the Jewish diaspora is one of exile.) On the one hand, through how the Greeks managed their distinctive situation they saw an "efflorescence" of cultural creativity and wealth (Ober, 2015); their marginality was in part fortuitous, i.e., due to affluence and privilege. On the other hand, and thus setting a unique version of the Axial critique-of-civilizational-power premise: the Greeks benefitted from the great expansions of power in the first millennium BCE, but they did so without resorting to centralized authority invested in a divinized king. Thus their marginality was positive in giving them, above all, freedom from monarchical authority. It seems to have afforded the diverse collection of small city-states, for a few centuries, sufficient space of freedom for them to cultivate distinctively Greek innovations such as democracy, *isonomia* (equality before the law), and philosophy. The Axial Ages of both Israel and Greece come to an end for the same historical reasons: first being conquered by Alexander of Macedon to usher in the Hellenistic period, and then becoming provinces of Rome.

Whether a patchwork of states and nations and cities, with or without a mythicized memory of a past Golden Age of empire, or an imperiled small nation or post-exilic community caught in the midst of vastly greater empires, or a distributed collection of independent city-states celebrating glory and freedom with a distinct awareness of ancient civilizations and powerful empires to their east, each are bit players in a far greater world-system which is breaking through into a new scale of power in the first millennium BCE. Each are also unique and distinctive collections of, or single, civilizations of their own, within which each develops and articulates its own response to that advent of power, experienced and expressed in the specific cultural forms of those particular civilizations; above all, within the unique constellation of sociological conditions engendered within those civilizations because of their specific histories. It is to each of these that we now turn.

AXIAL AGE CHINA

China's patchwork was a result of the collapse and disintegration of the earlier Western Zhou (or Chou) Empire (1045–771 BCE), an event remembered—more precisely mythicized and idealized—and given crucial significance later, in particular by Confucius. Confucius (551–479 BCE) lived at the finish of the "Spring and Autumn Period" of China (722–481 BCE). At the beginning of this period, there are upwards of 148 different states, with 15 of these qualifying as "major" states; by the sixth century BCE within these, four have become dominant (Qi, Jin, Chu, and Qin). These four "extinguish" 128 of the other states (Hsu, 1999, p. 567). Much of this process is also one of assimilation and homogenization of multiple ethnic groups from regions previously outside the boundaries of the former Zhou Empire—an expansion of geographic area and cultural diversity into a more comprehensive framework and greater cultural connectedness, but without any corresponding unity or coherence politically, economically, or ideologically. Against this background of war and amalgamation, an idealization of a unified coherent empire makes eminent sense, especially so as a mythical romanticization. To make the comparison even more poignant, conditions by the finish of the Spring and Autumn period had deteriorated into unceasing warfare and set the stage for the "Warring States" period (450–221 BCE). The "Warring States" period sees the dominance of the four states transform into seven major states (Yan, Qi, Wei, Zhao, Han, Qin, and Chu) and seven minor states. This reconfiguration of the multi-state patchwork of Chinese states happens alongside the transformation of the state from being a city-state into a territorial state, with its expanded power contracted into a centralized court with a supreme ruler (Lewis, 1999, pp. 593–597). These changes are accompanied by a dramatic change in military activity, too:

> While the earlier Zhou world had been composed of a multitude of cities and hinterlands linked by kin ties, religious rites, and a continuous, low-intensity warfare, the Warring States period was characterized by a small number of territorial states involved in constant diplomatic maneuvering and intermittent but frequent large-scale military conflagrations. The century and a half from 481 to the middle of the fourth century was the formative period of this pattern of interstate relations, a pattern that was forged in warfare. (Lewis, 1999, p. 616)

Across this time, there are corresponding technological and economic developments: the appearance of minted coins, state protection of merchants and traders, private traders, an improved road system, advances in agriculture and mining, and great, but disproportionately and unequally distributed, increases in wealth. Absolute extremes between conspicuous wealth and terrible poverty abound (Hsu, 1999, p. 582). Throughout these long centuries, China's overt political consciousness is developed primarily by reference to an imagined historical past of the Zhou Empire as an ideal order from which the present had fallen. Perhaps tied into these changes in political circumstances, religiously a significant change also occurring within China's mythologizing was that by fourth century B.C. "external powers" of gods and spirits, and others "like those of the heavens, were becoming depersonalized" (Graham, 1989, p. 101).

Bellah (2011) argues "the continuity between pre-axial and axial culture in China was without parallel in Greece or Israel" (p. 399), and with only a distant parallel in India, where cultural continuity over time involved more dramatic breaks and relocations. In terms of this continuity as well as the positive value accorded to the past (these are presumably related), China is unlike any of the other Axial civilizations. The ascension of the short-lived Qin (or Ch'in) Empire (221–206 BCE) followed by the long-lived Han Empire (206 BCE–280 CE) proves, in retrospect, consolidations of power that end China's Axial Age, and which in so doing rationalize the great discontinuities and diversities that preceded them. The rationalization allows them to present their legitimacy as venerable and time-honored, as a renewal of the revered Zhou Empire.

As noted above, China is also distinctive within the Afroeurasian belt in being the easternmost and the most geographically bounded by mountains, deserts, and the Pacific Ocean, of any of the four civilizations. McNeill (1963) who was quoted above regarding the continuum between Middle Eastern, Indian, and Greek civilizations claims "Chinese civilization stood apart and isolated in the Far East" (pp. 168–169). Presumably, these reasons of continuity and geographic isolation inform Mann's (2012) claim that, by comparison with any of the other civilizations, what culturally stands out is "the relative uniformity of China" (p. 344). Within this geographic situation of isolation and relative cultural uniformity, across centuries of political volatility and social dynamism, the "scholar-warriors" (*shi*) of China will emerge as a new class of men who traveled widely and studied broadly. For many, the new class enabled upward mobility, offering the possibility of escaping prior positions of poverty or labor to instead win a livelihood for themselves, perhaps even wealth or fame. Among these, some are carrying a new message for the politics, religion, and culture of ancient China: "The thinkers of the Axial Age are all in or on the edge of this now fluid class" (Graham, 1989, p. 3).

THE *SHI* OF CHINA

Who were the *shi*? Defined in the Chinese dictionary as both "warrior" and "scholar," Schwartz (1985) proposes the phrase "men of service" (p. 58; also Lewis, 1999, p. 604), Roth (1999) "scholars" (p. 20) whereas Hartnett (2011) cites Talcott Parsons' phrase "specialists in culture" in the context of proposing his own "learned knights" (p. 23) to characterize the *shi*. Warriors, scholars, men of service, culture specialists, learned knights; this range of characterizations conveys some sense of just what the *shi* were and how they functioned in volatile political times. As status and office ceased to be exclusively hereditary across the states of ancient China, possibilities for upward mobility appeared, for low-ranking nobility and even for commoners. Travel throughout the patchwork of states to offer service to kings, courts, and government provided opportunity for men of intelligence and learning, as well as skill and virtue. Those who established themselves sufficiently to gain reputation could become sought after and sell their services to the higher bidder. "[D]istinguished by their writing skills, knowledge of literature, and martial prowess… [t]hey became a powerful, autonomous cultural elite which would play a critical role not only in the development of higher learning as scholars and teachers, but also in the improvement of statecraft as key advisers and diplomats" (Hartnett, 2011, p. 23). It is especially in the last decades of the Spring and Autumn period—the turn of the sixth century BCE—that the *shi* emerge into prominence and retain this significance through the centuries of the Warring States period. Confucius comes from their ranks—and in turn Mo Tzu, Meng Tzu, Chuang Tzu, Yang Tzu, and others.

In referring to the *shi*'s service to the state as advisers and diplomats, we should not picture here staid civil servants or conservative government bureaucrats. Although this becomes the case with the Han Empire through its support for "Confucianism" as official position—and thus a key component to the end of the Axial Age in China—it was not so

during the turbulent centuries of the Axial Age itself. The first generations of learners under Confucius were called *"ru"* (scholars) rather
than Confucians and they were not party-line bureaucrats but incisive
observers and critics of the status quo: "Confucius and his followers
sprang up around 500 BCE in conscious opposition to existing political and religious practices" (Collins, 1998, pp. 138–139). On the one
hand, this opposition is partly owing to, and certainly fits, the wandering social position of the *shi*: They moved about, cosmopolitan rather
than regional, beholden to no one ruler, and potentially loyal to a higher
truth than that embodied in any particular state. On the other hand, the
conscious critique of power is a distinctive dimension of the new stra-
tum of society, for they could have chosen—as I'm sure a great number
presumably did—a more utilitarian, instrumental interpretation of their
role rather than the more ethical, idealist one. Yet the weight of evidence
uncovered by scholarship shows that a significant number did not.

> Another distinctive tradition of these early Chinese intellectuals was the
> practice of criticizing (*piping*) those in power. It was also referred to as
> "discussing" (*yi*) and "exchanging views" (*lun*), which Confucius identi-
> fied as a distinguishing mark of the intellectual. ...In any case "discussing"
> implied criticism and extensive debate. (Hartnett, 2011, p. 28)

The critique of power as premise for their thought and practice is
a crucial Axial motif. Along with this critical stance as premise, come
two equally Axial corollaries: cognitively-intellectually, the idea of
transcendence, while ethically-spiritually, the appeal to a universal
humanity. To the critique of political power had to be added a deep
reflection, in the case of China, on what the implications this had for
"the Mandate of Heaven." It could not straightforwardly be embodied
in the ruler through the unquestionable fact that he was ruler (as had
been the reasoning, pre-Axially). But somehow a more complex relation between ruler and the Mandate of Heaven had to be construed, in
which it could be Heaven's will that the ruler be corrupt and undeserv-
ing, or in Confucius' phrasing, "That which is under heaven [i.e. the
entire civilized world] has lost the *Tao*." This problem—for Sinologist
Benjamin Schwartz, this is the problem that animates the intellectual
reflections of Axial Age China (cf. Schwartz, 1975)—drives their thinking into a version of transcendent idealizing of the Mandate of Heaven
and of the *Tao*:

> At its deepest level, the idea of Heaven's Mandate presents us with a clear apprehension of the gap between the human order as it ought to be and as it actually is. Here we find clear evidence of that religious-ethical transcendence – that critical spirit toward the anterior development of high civilization which seems to be the earmark of the axial age in all the high civilizations. (Schwartz, 1985, p. 53)

This transcendent gap, this loss of the *Tao*, this manifestation of a corruption within the civilized world that tears it away from what Heaven's will truly is, is also the opening for great evil and the cause of suffering for many. The problem with political rule and its corruption and violence, as well as the problem of great economic inequality and terrible poverty, is neither primarily a political problem nor an intellectual one, but a social problem invoking a profound ethical response. (Roetz [1992] argues China's Axial conception of transcendence consists particularly in the ethical—a salient argument to consider in light of traditional perceptions of Chinese thought as lacking transcendent, otherworldly, and in particular regarding Confucianism, religious, connotations [see also van Norden, 2007].) In regard to their ethics, Old Testament scholar H. H. Rowley finds a clear (and perhaps surprising?) comparison between those among the Chinese *shi* who develop Axial perspectives on civilization like a Confucius or a Mo Tzu and the Hebrew prophets in their outrage:

> Between the followers of Confucius on the one hand and Mo-tzu and his followers on the other, there was mutual criticism and opposition, and that there were differences between them is not to be gainsaid. Yet it is possible to recognize truly prophetic qualities on both sides, and to appreciate how much is common in their concern for the condition of society in their day and in their eagerness to change that condition. All deplored the decay of society in their day and the naked selfishness that reigned. All deplored oppressive and unprincipled government, and desired to see the principles of justice and benevolence put into practice. (Rowley, 1956, p. 72)

Confucius and Mo Tzu are explicitly named here, as the first and second *shi* we know who articulate a critical philosophical stance alongside an educational program, and who found schools based on this articulation. As the geopolitical arena of China increasingly fractionates through the Warring States period, the importance of the *shi* increases as does the importance of this model of founder-and-followers: the paradigm for what becomes called within Chinese history the "Hundred Schools." While Confucius' focus was on self-cultivation, aiming for an ideal of sagehood, Mo Tzu's focus was on social reform, aiming for a political ideal of a total transformation of society and the state. By Chinese Axial reasoning, these are two opposite trajectories for attaining the same goal: The spirituality of individual inwardness is merely the other side of the same coin as the "outward" ethos of society. The coin itself is not minted by tradition, but rather situates the locus of identity for truth and sacred reality transcendentally (and therefore, by implication, posits a transcendent locus of identification for believers and followers, too).

If we could dub the Confucian and Mohist foci as "humanist" (with a lot of careful qualification [Schwartz, 1985, pp. 118–126]), then the most significant critical reaction to them is evident in the rise of "naturalist" schools, most well known among these being Taoism. Eno (1990), for example, discusses "early Taoism, 'Yangist' naturalism, 'Sung-Yin' or 'Chi-hsia' [Jixia] naturalism, Tsou Yen's *yin-yang* naturalism, and 'divinistic' or 'shamanistic' naturalism" (p. 139) as follow-ups to early Confucian "Ruism" and to Mohism. Kohn (2012) points out that "historians writing about the Warring States period after the fact, around 100 BCE, distinguished six major philosophical schools": Confucians, Daoists, Mohists, Legalists, Logicians, and the Yin-Yang cosmologists (p. 12). This description amounts to a formalization and rationalized simplification—"tendencies established retrospectively" (Graham, 1989, p. 31)—of what was certainly a more complex historical process during the centuries of the Axial Age. Hartnett (2011) describes that process in terms of a sequence of creative opposition:

> The Confucian school upheld the ancient Zhou model as an antidote to political upheaval and to the recluses who advocated retreating from the world and refusing to take part in the affairs. The Mohists countered the Confucian movement with a moralistic activism legitimated by religious monotheism (*tian*) and a program of educational utility. This dualism would be followed by Yang Zhu, the ascetic opponent of Mozi, which was countered by Mencius and his doctrine of altruism and human goodness. (p. 49)

While a great degree of emphasis for the Axial Age is placed on visionaries as the individuals who experience and articulate the "breakthroughs to transcendence," that these individuals belong within small groups, and found their traditions beginning with a small following of disciples who remember them and, to an unverifiable extent, also their sayings and teachings, who share stories about them, and some of whom write down some of these memories and stories, is of utmost sociological significance. Often the founders themselves either wrote nothing down at all, like Socrates or the Buddha. Or we cannot be sure what are their words or those of students or later adherents of the tradition, like Confucius (who apparently wrote the *Spring and Autumn Annals*, whereas the *Analects* was written by his pupils) or the prophets of Israel (did they write the books named after them?). Or, the writers were anonymous (the authors of the *Upanisads*). This means that naming an individual is actually a shorthand substitute for naming a tradition that is both sociological and textual. We don't have direct access to what they said and even less so, to what they experienced! We know the Axial Age visionaries only through the communities and traditions they founded that upheld them as founders and constructed texts to sustain the tradition. Was Lao Tzu a real person? We don't know. (Roth [1999] states quite categorically: "a purely legendary figure with no solid historical basis" [p. 6].) We do know that in the fourth century BCE a group of scholars collated the text of the *Tao Te Ching* that lays out many of the founding claims for the schools and tradition of Taoism, and that the text is attributed to Lao Tzu. Sociologist Randall Collins (1998) outlines the reasoning supporting this argument clearly in his opening chapter "Coalitions in the Mind" (pp. 19–53), demonstrating how individuals like Confucius or Lao Tzu are invariably "located in typical social patterns: intellectual groups, networks, and rivalries" (p. 3).

In terms of the legacy of the Axial Age, in the case of China—and as we shall see, this holds across all the Axial Age movements in the other civilizations, too—the institutionalization most faithful to the original visionaries is education: broadly in terms of a whole philosophy of life alongside ways to practically cultivate and develop the self, but also specifically in the founding of schools. "Schools" are meant here in a minimal sense of small communities organized around a teacher(s)–students hierarchy, whose members are committed to a particular way of life, practices, disciplines, and set of values, and the study and learning of texts, alongside but not more important than, the choice of a way of life. These are schools one should not picture in our modern, formal, state-backed, "public" sense, but more akin to monasteries or "intentional communities" where learning was as much, if not more, embodied in rules of living (e.g., how one dresses, how one eats, how one treats and interacts with fellow students, how one goes to sleep) as it was in studying the master's precepts and teachings (see Collins, 1998, pp. 64–65; Roth, 1999, pp. 173–185, who discuss different meanings of "school"). As we will examine more closely in the following chapter, it is the monastery or "intentional community" analogue that best captures the nature of the schools that emerge during the Axial Age, and it is the notion of "spiritual practice" rather than "theoretical studies" that stands at the center of these communities. (Perhaps, the best term would be "spiritual community"?) The distinction is not absolute, but one of emphasis: "schools" or small communities of practitioners practiced both spiritual exercises of self-formation and critical philosophical reflection (cf. Hadot, 1995, 2002; Hartnett, 2011).

For example, Hartnett's book-length study of the Jixia Academy in the fourth century BCE shows it to be "singular among Axial Age institutions of higher learning" (2011, p. 89) in the extent to which it is analogous to modern academies: "stable state support and fixed location, continuous interaction and rivalries among members, prestige and status competition, division of labor, rules and regulations, academic freedom, and collegial control and authority" (p. 89). In addition to this claim for its exceptionalism, however, Hartnett also shows it to be in significant other respects an institutionalization faithful to the Axial aspirations of ancient China. Much of Hartnett's analysis compares Jixia Academy to Greek schools of the fourth century BCE and stresses how for both "the pursuit of philosophy" was about "a way of life as opposed to merely a theoretical concentration," and had "a definite ethical and moral purpose, a journey toward knowing oneself and caring for oneself" (2011, p. 101). This faithfulness to its founding Axial ideals stands in marked contrast to the Han dynasty's transformation a couple of centuries later of Confucian "Ruist" scholarship into "Confucianism" as a new class of government bureaucrats, serving the power of the state and rationalizing it ideologically rather than criticizing this power and advocating, on moral, ethical, and spiritual grounds, alternate ways for the people to live (and, for the ruler to rule).

AXIAL AGE INDIA

The Indian patchwork of the first millennium BCE, which Thapar (1995) describes as "one of distinctive cultures" (p. 88), is quite different from China's "relative uniformity." India is also distinctive vis-à-vis all the other civilizations in terms of its comparatively late development of states and empires—"India historically is the land of weak states" (Collins, 1998, p. 178). It is above all the great increase in urbanization from 700 to 300 BCE and accompanying economic transformations (developing ever larger networks of trade, development of coinage, increasing deforestation for agriculture) that seems to have been the key catalyst for India's Axial Age (Kulke, 1986). Indian scholarship has described this period as that of India's "second urbanization," occurring with the development of cities along the Gangetic plain—the "first urbanization" having occurred with the Indus Valley Civilization in the third to second millennia BCE (Allchin, 1995). (One small group of scholars, whom Samuel [2008] dubs "radical revisionist," consider the second urbanization actually the fourth urbanization in India's history, for which they greatly extend the dates—and asserted cultural continuity—back to at least 5000 BCE(!). Cf. Feuerstein et al. [2001], or Rajaram and Frawley [1995].)

What is particularly of note during these centuries of the first millennium BCE is an emerging effort to assert a hegemony of control by the priesthood and by the aristocratic class of nobles and warriors representing the Vedic heritage (the *brahmans* and *ksatriyas*, respectively), issuing from northwest India. They aim to extend into the areas east along the Gangetic plain and south into the Deccan plateau. (Why eastward and southward? Beyond geography [the Hindu Kush and Himalayas to the north and northeast block expansion, as does the Indian ocean to the southwest], I would hazard a "world-system" answer invisible to the local, insider point of view: that the populations and civilizations of central Asia to the west of India, already ancient and powerful then, did not allow for much intrusion. This markedly becomes the case with the consolidation of the Achaemenid Empire—"around 518 BCE [it] had conquered large parts of the Indus valley" [Kulke, 1986, p. 387]—while Alexander's invasion in 329–325 BCE is the exclamation mark at the end of this answer. From northwest India, eastward and southward were the directions in which to expand.) Witzel (1997) argues that at the beginnings of the first millennium BCE the Vedic heritage was mobilized in such a way that "the *Ksatriya* and *Brahmins* form a united 'political' front (*brahma-ksatra*) against 'the people' (*vis*) and, of course, against the *Sudra* and the aboriginal population (*dasa, dasyu*), in order to exploit them, as the texts themselves – composed by *Brahmins* – underline with Marxist analysis before its day" (p. 294). This "united political front" of the ruling and priestly classes was first developed as such in what is today the Punjab, a development accompanying the amalgamation of about fifty tribes or so into the Kuru "super-tribe" (Witzel's phrase, 1997, p. 266). The Kuru assert political dominance over the region and also attempt to extend their influence further. Over some centuries, the Kuru's expansion efforts meet with mixed success; for example, they eventually develop a strong alliance with another emerging "super-tribe," the Pancala—perhaps because they need such an alliance as their strength was waning, or perhaps because it strategically augments their increasing strength. This Kuru-Pancala alliance, and its particular configuration of rulers/priests as defining the ruling orthodoxy, continues to attempt to expand, continuously eastward and southward.

In short, it is absolutely not an invasion from the northwest by Vedic Indo-european Aryans into non-Vedic indigenous non-Aryan territories. It is a much subtler, historically extended, complex process of interactions unevenly distributed in waves and varying degrees of reciprocity between a Kuru-Pancala alliance that is a dominant power in northwest India with a certain form of state-sponsored priesthood, and a diversity of states and kingdoms in the east (along the Gangetic plain) and toward the south. The latter diversity is not unfamiliar with *brahmanical* culture and the Vedas, but these were one part of the landscape, not its dominant part; one strand in the weave, not its overarching motif. Samuel (2008) puts it in the following way: "If the Kuru-Pancala region was dominated in religious terms by the progressive reworking of Vedic material represented by the Brahmanas, the Central Gangetic region and the northern Deccan was by contrast a 'world of female powers, natural transformation, sacred earth and sacred places, blood sacrifices, and ritualists who accept pollution on behalf of their community'" (pp. 50–51). Bronkhorst (2007) devotes a whole book to this latter region, which he calls "Greater Magadha" to denote a cultural orientation from which the political state of Magadha emerges later.

This difference between the Kuru-Pancala region and the Central Gangetic plain is enormously significant for the history of India in the first millennium (and for recent scholarship, which recasts differences formerly understood as chronological and sequential into being regional and political instead). Key to the Vedic-Brahmanical religiosity issuing from the Kuru-Pancala region is the formation of a "distinctive self-conscious group… which saw itself as 'Aryan'" (p. 100). This is not a foreign conception (e.g., owing to some Indo-European invasion from the west as an older scholarship would have it); the very designation "Aryan," derived from the Sanskrit word "*aryas*," refers to ideas and values describing a "noble," cultural way of life (as the term seemed to have been largely used). It was not taken in either a linguistic or racist sense to describe a people and appears to be mostly indigenous to India (cf. Erdosy, 1995a, 1995b). This self-consciousness will be elaborated further through the creation of the *Mahabharata* with the *Bhagavad-Gita* at its center, with in turn the story of the battle of Kurukshetra as central to it for building on this Vedic-Brahmanic-Aryan orthodox construction of a "Hindu" identity—the Kuru in Kurukshetra (located in present-day Haryana) anchoring this long thread of ideological development back in the earlier Kuru-Pancala state. There are significant resistance and challenges to this effort asserted by those cultures there, cultures from which Buddhism, among others, issues. The effort to assert control was itself complicated and likely divided. While the kings and ruling class (the *ksatriya*) aimed for centralization and consolidation, they needed the *brahmans* to legitimate what they did. Numerous *brahmans* on the one hand—the "extension of power" hand—would support such a development, not only for cynical reasons of interest in power but presumably also for pious ones of extending the faith. However, simultaneously numerous *brahmans* would be uneasy about the centralization of power and its collection in urban centers, much of which ran counter to the highly local, rural, and decentralized nature of traditional *brahmanic* practice. This other hand could be seen as the "traditional piety" hand. Regardless of which hand, the *brahmans* who controlled the performance of ritual sacrifice would respond complexly and non-uniformly to the perceived threat posed to traditional ritual by newly emerging cities, the transformation in the economic base, and the uncertainty of how to negotiate new relations to newly centralizing states or "super-tribes."

Referring to "the *brahmans*" in this way might suggest a homogeneity and uniformity among them. This suggestion is false. In fact, to the contrary, they are engaged in intense competition for legitimacy, power, and ascendancy among themselves; "the Brahmanical tradition was not a monolithic entity" (Olivelle, 2011, p. 14). Much of the Vedas are precisely the record of this conflict between numerous different groups of ritual specialists (Witzel, 1997; see also Collins, 1998, pp. 193–200). Collectively across these differences in how the *brahmans* represented and transmitted their Vedic heritage, this effort toward hegemony sits in constant tension with the diversity of local cultures and indigenous differences with which it engages across the Axial Age centuries. Due to the eventual successful achievement of this hegemony by the first centuries CE, by opposition to these local and indigenous differences, a more uniform identity rooted in the Vedas and their *brahmanic* heritage can be proposed and rationalized as a key formative piece in the development of "Hinduism."

Other than (1) urbanization, (2) economic advances, (3) a generally eastward and southward direction to extend power from the northwest, and (4) the fluctuating success, failures, and challenges that mark the effort at assertion of the *brahmanic* hegemony over Indian religious life as four broad generalizations, the word that best seems to characterize processes in the Indian patchwork across the Axial Age centuries and that appropriately qualifies too broad terms like widespread, hegemony, or, well, broad, is uneven. Alongside the formidable problems with dating and establishing reliable chronologies, the unevenness of these processes makes certain interpretation of what was going on difficult and speculative. The formation of states and empires by the third century BCE signals the end of the Axial Age in India—above all marked by Mauryan Emperor Asoka's conversion to Buddhism (in ~ 260 BCE). This time of state-formation across India is paralleled by a fixing of the Vedic canon (Witzel, 1997). This time of state- and canon-formation is followed by the establishment of Vedic orthodoxy alongside an assertion of *brahmanic* control over religious interpretation which achieves this aim by the first centuries CE. This orthodoxy reads and rationalizes India's past in terms of a longevity, continuity, and uniformity—an early Vedism leading to a Brahmanism succeeded by a later Hinduism, with Buddhism and Jainism "heterodox movements" on the fringes—that isn't really the case. The further outcome to this establishing of *brahmanic* hegemony politically is its ascension to "state religion" status under the Gupta Empire, which arose around 300 CE. Culturally, an outcome manifests in a broad cultural program across the Indian subcontinent that has been called variously "aryanization" or "Sanskritization," which inculcates the values and norms and judgments of that *brahmanic* hegemony throughout the general population (which process some centuries later spreads its influence beyond the subcontinent, above all into southeast Asia; a process of "Southernization," Shaffer, 1994). The eventual success of this program, post-Axial Age, means the reading of ancient Indian history through *brahmanic*-colored glasses, too, spreads far and wide and entrenches itself as established. (Bronkhorst [2011] uses the phrase "the brahmanical colonization of the past"!) Careful scholarship has needed to grind new and different lenses to gain an accurate view of the past.

For India, urbanization and newly emerging wealth economies in the mid-first millennium BCE presaged the arrival of homogenizing processes and foreshadowed the eventual emergence of truly large states. These developments motivate Axial responses. Buddhism and Jainism are the best-known examples of these. Earlier scholarship falsely interpreted these responses as heroic revolts against an already established *brahmanic* hegemony. More recently, these responses have been reinterpreted by scholars as occurring simultaneously with, and in a turning of the chronological tables, as significant motivators for, that hegemonic effort. (To simplify: what earlier scholarship understood as differences due to time period that could be reconstructed into a chronological sequence, contemporary scholars are now understanding as regional and contemporaneous differences signaling a struggle for power.)

Less well known is that there were a great variety of other responses to urbanization and the new economies. Some of these are radical movements, such as materialist approaches (called variously *Carvaka* or *Lokayata*), or the "determinist" approach of Ajivika (led by the ascetic master Makkhali Gosala) that were contemporary with Buddhism and Jainism. Further, within the diversity of perspectives collected in the *Upanisads* (dated, with great uncertainty, from the ninth to fourth century BCE and later; the earliest, however, certainly belong within the mid-first millennium) a significant number are clearly rejections and reformations of the *brahmanic* perspective. Again, the later rationalization of these, above all through Advaita Vedanta philosophy, somewhat homogenizes this diversity under the equation that "*atman=brahman*" (what Eliade [1969] characterizes as "the great discovery of the *Upanisads*," "the systematic statement of the identity between the *atman* and the *brahman*," that the individual soul is part of, is, the universal soul [p. 114]) known through the experience of nonduality, and so forth, but many of the stories in the *Upanisads* escape this characterization (see Collins, 1998, pp. 196–197). From an Axial perspective, the extraordinary insights into nonduality so foundational to the Advaita Vedanta reading of the *Upanisads*, as well as the great diversity of other perspectives and articulations described within them that don't fit this reading, all together evidence Axial breakthroughs vis-à-vis extant understandings of the political and the religious. Finally—as if we don't have enough, but this abundance is apace with the rich spiritual heritage of

India—Heesterman (1986), in fact, advances a sophisticated and fascinating reading of an internal transformation within the *brahmanic* performance of Vedic ritual as itself an Axial breakthrough into transcendence. Many of the demands of Vedic ritual are, functionally, ascetic; and thus, the interiorization of the ritual is simultaneously a continuation and deepening of the ascetic demands placed on the *brahman*, and at the same time, a transformation into their meaning such that the renunciatory aspects implicit within that asceticism becomes the new meaning to *brahmanic* activity; these aspects coalesce into a multifaceted ideal of renunciation (in the Sanskrit, *samnyasa*, from which the term *sannyasi*, or renunciate—plural, *sannyasin*—derives).

Much of the diversity of these latter movements is easy to overlook as the *Upanisads* will figure so centrally in the orthodox rationalizing of the formation of "Hinduism," not least in their being considered faithful to the original Vedas. From an Axial Age scholarship perspective, however, this reading is a post-Axial rationalization of an Axial revolution relative to pre-Axial religion that imposes for the sake of tradition, pedigree, and venerableness, being the "oldest" or the "first," etc., a continuity that a more critical reading of the evidence would reject. (The Feuerstein et al. [2001] claim for continuity back to pre-5000 BCE being exemplary of this sort of rationalization.) Heesterman (1997) is unequivocal about this claim to continuity: "In fact it is a pious fiction," preferring to emphasize the "rupture – real but imperfectly understood – between Vedic sacrifice and Hinduism" (p. 45). Arnason (2005) claims "The *discontinuity* between the whole archaic phase and the prelude to the Axial Age is *much more marked* [in India] than elsewhere" (p. 79, emphases added). This interpretation is upheld by Indologists. That this discontinuity hinges on the emergence of ascetic renunciation in the mid-first millennium BCE is clear support for my interpretation of the distinctive marker of Axiality being the development of systematic spiritual practices within small countercultural communities. Samuel (2008), after reviewing and discussing various arguments and evidence for any earlier dating, claims that "Our best evidence to date suggest that such practices developed in the same ascetic circles as the early *shramana* movements (Buddhists, Jainas, and Ajivikas), probably in around the sixth and fifth centuries BCE" (p. 8). This is also the time when we find the *brahman* renunciates, the *sannyasin*, come into the being. Sociologically, the *shramana* of India, like the *shi* in China, emerge as a new class due to the rapidity of social, political, and economic changes, while these sociological conditions also effect a transformation of ritual specialist *brahmans* into renunciates oriented toward the ideal of *samnyasa*. Both *sannyasin* and *shramana* travel widely, study broadly, and from among them certain ascetics and holy men will become the visionaries carrying a new message for the politics, religion, and culture of ancient India. Their visions challenge the effort from certain regions within India to establish a Vedic-based orthodoxy. From their visions will issue Buddhism and Jainism. In the revolutionary transformation of the *brahmanic* role into *sannyasi*, key foundations for the eventual emergence of Hinduism are laid. Combined, the *shramana* and the *sannyasin* define the Axial Age movement of ancient India.

The *Shramana* and *Sannyasin* of India

Like the *shi* of China, the *shramana* of India are a new class borne of the sociopolitical volatility of mid-first millennium BCE: rapid economic change, war and violence between states, a new scale to human power and human suffering, the transitioning from inherited rural traditions into newly founded cities, unprecedented inequalities in wealth, and on the horizon, the emergence of empires the like of which India had never seen before. Unlike the *shi*, they don't emerge against some idealized backdrop of a long ago great empire. A paradigmatic figure whose biography captures in miniature the *shramanic* class as a whole, and who has become well known, is the Buddha. Born a prince to whom his father the king grants his every desire and pleasure, marries, has a child; but then as a grown man he renounces the throne, the kingdom, desire and pleasure, and family, and travels widely, far from cities and civilization in forests, and studies broadly under different spiritual masters, undertaking severe ascetic practices, self-denials and self-tortures, seeking enlightenment, for several years. Some of the masters he meets and studies with were renowned, such as Makkhali Gosala (leader of the Ajivika). He never meets Mahavira (founder of the Jains), who along with Makkhali Gosala will become eventual rivals to the Buddha upon his innovation of the new spiritual movement of Buddhism. All, however, whether *brahmans* originally, or noble-born *ksatriya* as the Buddha was, are *shramana*: wandering ascetics who turn their back on "this world" and seek out a higher truth.

Mahavira, just mentioned, is not nearly so well known; however, his story is similar. He was also of the noble or warrior caste (*ksatriya*), also the son of a king, also married, and also has a child. Then, "on his thir-tieth birthday the gods performed an initiation ceremony for him and he renounced the world to become a mendicant ascetic. For twelve and a half years, Mahavira wandered in the region of the Ganges basin, part of which time he spent with another ascetic called Makkhali Gosala, often enduring physical abuse from men and attacks by animals, fast-ing and meditating all the while, as a result of which heroic mode of life he received the epithet 'Great Hero' (Mahavira) and subsequently, in accordance with the destiny of all fordmakers, he attained enlight-enment" (Dundas, 2002, pp. 21–22). That is, it is not the life of the Buddha that is the paradigm for the *shramana*, but that his life, like Mahavira's, fits the *shramana* paradigm.

What and who were the *shramana* and why do they emerge where, and when, they do? In terms of what they were, Dundas (2002), says "[t]he term *shramana*, 'striver'… points to the physical and speculative exertion which was necessarily entailed in a life devoted to the minimiz-ing of the performance of external action and an accompanying con-trol of inner activity" (p. 16). As we saw in both the examples of the Buddha and Mahavira, many came from royalty or aristocracy; many too were *brahmans*. Few to none came from the lower classes, although much of the later appeal of Buddhism and Jainism would be to work-ers, merchants, traders, and craftspeople. The fourfold caste system (of priests [*brahman*], rulers, nobles, warriors [*ksatriya*], middle class [*vai-sya*], and workers [*sudra*]) was not yet established in the first half of the first millennium BCE—that develops later. However, the origins of that formalizing, canonizing, rationalizing development are rooted here. To generalize, the role of *brahmans* transforms due to the volatility of events across the first millennium BCE: "The Brahmans shifted from a priest class to an educational status group" (Collins, 1998, p. 194). Within this general transformation, a select number transform more dramatically, into "spiritually revolutionary" *brahmans* who become the *sannyasin*, the renunciates.

The Gangetic region is not dominated by this orthodox understand-ing and instead enters into a creative struggle, reaction, adoption, and resistance to its increased power. What manifests here is "the growth of the ascetic orders, among both non-Brahmins (Jains, Buddhists, Ajivikas) and Brahmins" (Samuel, 2008, p. 75). We ought not to reify this differ-ence between the northwest and further east and south of India: Hindu scholar Olivelle (2011) warns that the Vedic/Aryan vs non-Vedic/

non-Aryan indigenous distinction is a "sterile debate and artificial dichotomy... to attempt to isolate these different strands at any given point in Indian history" (p. 13) is a waste of time. This seems scholarly advice we should heed. Instead, northern India (both west and east) shares what Samuel (2008) calls a "general cultural heritage" characterized by common Indo-Aryan languages, the tripartite Indo-European distinction between ruling warriors, priesthood, and wider population, and a number of deities and rituals shared in common (p. 99). Within this commonalty, there is a power play issuing from expansionary initiatives of the Kuru-Pancala state in the context of economic development, technological innovations (in metallurgy, in coinage), and above all urbanization.

Within this context, the response to Kuru-Pancala expansion from the diverse cultures along the Gangetic plain is key to shaping Indian religiosity from then until the present. Within this response, and what constitutes its Axiality, is the *shramana*'s renunciation of power, of "this world": the doctrines of suffering and rebirth this renunciation articulates (*karma* and *samsara*), the forms of ascetic practice aimed toward transformation or "escape" (*moksha*) this renunciation takes, and the institutions (the mendicant, the anchorite, the monk) this renunciation demands. Hamilton (2000) notes that *karma*, *samsara*, and *moksha* "are usually singled out in descriptions of the Indian worldview as the three principal features of its conceptual framework, and indeed they are" (p. 37). Certainly, a consequence is how the figure of the renouncer (*sannyasi*), too, becomes emblematic of Indian religiosity. Renunciation is shaped powerfully through the emergence of the *shramana* class, from whom the Buddha and Mahavira and others come, and which appears to be a Gangetic creation. However, recalling the diversity and non-uniformity of *brahmans*, it is also true that many *brahmans* will renounce the Vedic emphasis on sacrifice and ritual and in a complex parallel to the *shramana*, explore ascetic practices, renunciation of this world, and the gaining of transcendent knowledge. In fact, it might be in understanding what renouncing the Vedic emphasis on ritual would mean to a *brahman* that we can best understand some of the radicality of the Indian conception of renunciation of "this world."

Olivelle (2011) claims "The main features of the Vedic religion... defined the Vedic homo religious legitimizing thereby social structures, roles, and obligations... Society was the central religious institution" (p. 46). Thus, for those *brahmans* renouncing sacrifice, ritual, and the orthodox religion of the Vedas, they are renouncing all of society, too. If this renunciation came entirely from non-Vedic origins, it would be hard to understand what appeal such would have to a *brahman* born and raised within a Vedic conception of ritual, society, and world. Instead, it is within the articulation and understanding of Vedic religiosity itself, that there is a development of understanding of sacrifice and ritual that moves from their external observance and behavioral performance, inward to their conscious meaning, to the intention of the ritual practitioner, to knowledge of that performance. Heesterman (1997) puts it as follows: "The inner logic of Vedic ritualism unavoidably led to interiorization" (p. 59). The outcome of this process of "interiorization" is that sacrifice comes to be ascetic practice, and ritual performance comes to mean spiritual knowledge; the "outer fire" of the Vedic ritual that sacralized a physical place becomes the "inner fire" (*tapas*) of the ascetic renouncer that burns away mental ignorance and egoistic attachments (Bronkhorst, 1998, 2000; Eliade, 1969; Heesterman, 1986, 1997; Seaford, 2016b). In sum, developments internal to the Vedic tradition, above all evident in transforming the role of *brahmans* into *sannyasin* are key to shaping Indian religiosity from then until the present. It appears that the renunciate *sannyasi* is intended to designate exclusively *brahmanic*-Hindu renunciates, in distinction from the *shramana* in general. Shils (1986) points out that *brahman* intellectuals "acknowledged as genuine *shramana* only the *sannyasi* who were Brahmins by caste and who had taken to the monastic life" (p. 442).

Well, which is it? The *shramana* of the Central Gangetic plain from which emerges an ascetic understanding informing the Buddha, Mahavira, and many others, or an internal transformation within Vedic orthodox understanding originally issuing from the Kuru-Pancala region from which emerges an ascetic understanding informing the *sannyasin*? If this was a domain of mutually exclusive logic, where it has to be one or the other, we would have to choose. But the question is falsely posed: asceticism and renunciation, the Axial "breakthrough" within India during the mid-first millennium BCE, is a complex historical process made up of many factors, and both the revolutionary *shramana* and the revolutionary *brahmans* who become the *sannyasin* within this time contribute to it. Is it possible some of those *brahmans* dissatisfied with the orthodox conception of the Vedas at that time, experiencing it as inadequate relative to the great challenges of ever-more powerful states, urbanization, massive political injustice, and great social suffering, were influenced by conceptions of the unorthodox *shramana*, whom they certainly knew about? Or, could *shramana* striking out to wander the forests in the Gangetic plain discover conceptions of renunciation of society articulated by *sannyasin* based on the latter's deep meditations on the meaning of Vedic ritual, which they certainly knew about? I think the answer is plain and is the same to both questions: most likely. For example, listen to Samuel (2008), who writes: "We seem here to be in a pluralist society of ascetic practitioners whose members are quite willing to regard members of the other semi-renunciate and renunciate religious traditions as 'sages' of a standing comparable to their own" (p. 124). The analytic separation of what was then living movements of people of whom we have only limited knowledge today into discrete categories that serve our contemporary efforts to reconstruct the past, should not be superimposed as historic realities. Perhaps someday scholarship will be able to establish some kind of temporal priority and thus to whom to give precedent; at present, we need to acknowledge these are analytic categories through which we view a historical time far more dynamic than our limited reconstructions. Our best answer at present: both (thus Bronkhorst [1998] *The Two Sources of Indian Asceticism*, and [2000] *The Two Traditions of Meditation in Ancient India*). What both *shramana* and *sannyasin* share, by contrast to the numerous diversity of traditions from which they emerge, is resituating the locus of identity of sacred reality away from "this world" to the transcendent "other world."

In this light, to quote Olivelle (2011) again, "Although the historical development of the Vedic religion may explain certain of its aspects, renunciation erupted into the religio-cultural tradition of India as a totally new and unique phenomenon" (p. 70). Emerging from within the internal development of Vedic orthodoxy, as well as gaining many contributions from numerous sources along the Gangetic plain responding to the aggressive effort at expansion of that orthodoxy issuing from the Kuru-Pancala state to the northwest, members of both the *shramana* and *sannyasin* classes define the Axial Age spiritual revolution of mid-first millennium BCE India through the theme of renunciation.

Like the *shi* in China, a central characteristic and lasting legacy of both *shramana* and *samnyasa* renunciate traditions is the founding of schools: Gurus attract disciples, small counter-cultural communities of followers form, different enlightened masters present different claims as to ultimate reality and the way to gain knowledge of it. The *Upanisads* as well as early Buddhist and Jain writings are filled with numerous, incommensurable accounts issuing from *brahmans, shramana, sannya-sin,* kings, women, warriors, householders, and students, arguing, questioning, disagreeing. Eliade (1982) referring to the *Samannaphala Sutta* describes the other four (in addition to Makkhali Gosala and Mahavira) of the "six rival masters" of the Buddha: "Purana Kassapa seems to have preached that the [karmic] act is of no value; Ajita Kesakambali professed a materialism close to that of the Carvakas; Pakudha Kaccayana taught the eternity of the seven 'bodies' ...and Sañjaya probably taught skepticism, for he avoided any discussion" (p. 84). An enormous diversity of viewpoints seems to be alive during these centuries: the many presented in the *Upanisads,* also Buddhist, Jain, Ajivika, Carvaka, Lokayata, and more besides (for a sense of this diversity, see the mere dozens mentioned in Eliade, 1969, pp. 138–142). From this plurality, a series of lineages emerge, tracing their legitimacy back to historical founders. Some, like the Ajivika and Carvaka, only temporarily succeed at this effort and in the longer term become obsolete. Others do succeed. These become the diverse monastic and ascetic and renunciate orders within Buddhism, Hinduism, and Jainism. Developing alongside these orders and legitimating themselves as being faithful to their founding intentions are the world religions of Buddhism, Hinduism, and Jainism themselves, which accommodate and domesticate the challenges renunciation poses. Through a lengthy process of rationalizing, canonizing, and selective appropriation from its foundations which each undergo, they can present ideologies and institutions amenable to supporting large-scale religious organizations and developing their membership. Asoka gives a particular privilege to Buddhism within the history of the Mauryan dynasty; the Gupta Empire centuries later will do something analogous with Hinduism. Jainism never receives this kind of endorsement, but it too finds a way to legitimize and adapt itself. Dundas (2006) in the following lengthy quote presents an extraordinary summary of one thousand years of Jainist history, which is worth citing in full as exemplary of the historical processes of rationalization, canonization, selective appropriation, domestication, relative to a founding vision:

> The various trends involved would have been the abandonment of the ideal of solitary wandering, if indeed this ever had any concrete actuality beyond the scriptural descriptions of Mahavira's pre-enlightenment career, and the emergence of connected ascetic lineages by the fourth century BCE (with some recruits possibly attracted by the reconfiguration of the

warrior ideal characteristic of Jainism's ascetic mode of self-representation, others by the path's elaboration of a brand of "saving knowledge" akin to but different from that of the Buddhists and brahmins); the identity of this ascetic community being formed and steadily reinforced by a growing body of behavioral rules; the extension of the influence of the Jain worldview from the east throughout central and western India and beyond through the agency of some of the aforementioned ascetic lineages, so that Jainism transforms itself from a local to a transregional phenomenon; the gradual emergence of a fully self-conscious lay community, despite Jain teachings advocating the necessity of withdrawal from social action, ensuring that the ascetic community no longer had to rely on random acts of donation; the appearance of a style of devotionalism involving ritual and liturgy, initially centering on ascetic teachers and then becoming image-oriented; the development, stabilization and consequent bifurcation in western India of an elaborate textual culture (some components of which eventually being accepted as lost) enshrining the intellectual, ethical, and imaginative ideals of the community; and finally, the eventual standardization of Jain doctrine (including a developed cosmology), leading to its attainment by the middle of the first millennium CE of the status of *shastra* and component of the broader Indian intellectual world. (pp. 384–385)

AXIAL AGE ISRAEL

Israel, by contrast to "China" and "India," is a small civilization existing on the margins of established empires (or on the "peripheries" or "semi-peripheries" of powerful "centers"). Small here is meant culturally, demographically, geographically, and politically by comparison with the multi-cultural, multi-state, multi-lingual patchworks of India and China. Really, the proper comparison to the latter two is the ancient Near East as a whole, inclusive of Israel (and Greece) as small patches within the patchwork, bit players alongside larger empires.

Israelite identity seems continuously defined contrastively to the civilizations it is not. The mythical Abraham leaves the city of Ur in Mesopotamia to begin a new life in the Promised Land; in the mid-1200s BCE a people (which we could call, somewhat mistakenly, "the Israelite nation") led by the mythical Moses undertakes its exodus from Egypt in order to return to that Promised Land. From these people, led by a series of judges, is developed through the great (and mythical?) figure David, a monarchy uniting the twelve tribes of Israel (really, two major divisions between north and south), strategically established in Jerusalem (at the time of David's capture of the city, it was on "neutral ground... at the boundary between Judah and the northern tribes" [Sweeney, 2000, p. 27]). David brings the ark of the covenant to Jerusalem, cementing its position as center; (the mythical?) Solomon his son builds the temple there.

This brief period of a united monarchy under, first, David, then Solomon, gives way to two kingdoms by about 1000 BCE. The northern kingdom of Israel is conquered by the Assyrians in 722 BCE, after which no trace remains of the kingdom or its people, and the land becomes Samaria (presumably, some Israelites find refuge in Judah and become assimilated within its population, while many Samarians/Samaritans would be descendants of northern Israel). The southern kingdom of Judah avoids this fate; but some century and a half later is conquered by Babylon (in 587 BCE) and a number taken into captivity. Exile ends in 538 BCE owing to the change in hands of imperial power, and corresponding change in imperial policy, from Babylon to Persia. From the latter exilic community, a small group will return to Jerusalem and what was formerly Judah (now the Persian province, Yehud), rejoin those who had not been taken captive, and rebuild the temple. With Alexander's success against Persia, the area will become Judaea. It is during this period that Judaism originates, as well as the designation Jewish. Judaea will in turn become a Roman province in 63 BCE, and the Second Temple will in turn be destroyed by the Romans in 70 CE. The Second Temple period can be periodized in terms of which foreign power dominated: 538–333 BCE, Persian; 332–63 BCE, Hellenistic; 62 BCE–70 CE, Roman (Murphy, 2000). (To deal with the awkwardness of these numerous different designations of pre-monarchical Israel, the northern and southern kingdoms, Judah-cum-Yehud-cum-Judaea, and so on, I will use the term "Israel" in quotation marks as the umbrella term, dropping the scare quotes when it is possible to speak more specifically. This is not entirely anachronistic; post-exile, the small population of Jews in Yehud, presumably entirely from the conquered kingdom of Judah, adopt a role and self-definition as "Israel" in this umbrella sense [Grabbe, 2004, pp. 170–171].) After the destruction of the Second Temple, the Jewish people become a landless diaspora for two millennia. I emphasize landless to distinguish it from the diaspora-with-a-center as it had been for the six centuries following the Babylonian captivity, wherein the situation was that of a significant population dispersed across the Near East with the temple at Jerusalem providing both a symbolic and real center.

"Israelite" monotheism and the uniqueness of how they understood Yahweh's covenant with them as His people stand out as distinctive by comparison with any of their imperial or tribal neighbors (even as it takes centuries to work out just what this uniqueness of monotheism and covenant exactly means, and "exclusive monotheism" itself needs to be teased apart from variations on the theme like henotheism and monolatry; cf. Edelman, 1996; Smith, 2002, esp. pp. 206–207; also Voegelin, 1956). That said, it has to be emphasized that Israelite or Hebrew monotheism is not entirely original. In fourteenth century BCE in Egypt, the idiosyncratic and revolutionary pharaoh Akhenaten had formulated a monotheism, albeit one that did not last; the Israelite "reinvention" of monotheism, then, is not original, although it is distinctive (cf. Landes, 2011, pp. 149–184, who distinguishes Akhenaten's monotheism from that of Israelite in terms of the kinds of millennialist beliefs each held; the former typifying "iconic/imperial millennialism" and the latter "demotic," i.e., involving all the people). In the ancient Near East, a covenant between subject and king was common while the "Israelite" variation made between a human subject (inclusive of kings!) and the single, transcendent deity Yahweh, was unknown (Nissinen, 2016, p. 19; Smith, 2002; Thompson, 1996, p. 113). "Israel" proposes a different and unique take on the god-king-people complex common throughout the ancient Near East. Its originality in Axial terms by comparison with Egypt resides in its radicalization of monotheism (see Assmann, 2005). Yahweh transcending so far above the gods of other nations, as well as being so far beyond human kings and the peoples they ruled, that all of the latter customarily vertical hierarchy instead becomes "horizontalized" to one mundane sphere of this world, in stark dualistic contrast to the only other higher, transcendent sphere of the other world. To this radical transcendence of the "Israelite" conception of God must be conjoined the radical anxiety around its own survival as a distinctive people. Out of this combination is birthed the strangeness of a "chosen people" being given the role to bear witness to the universal God—"to be a light to all nations" (Isaiah 49:6)—and thus the paradox of one ethnicity, and no other, as the particular glove worn by the hand of universal transcendence.

The prophets above all were the voice for that witness—as they were throughout the entire ancient Near East, "intermediating" between the gods (or, The One God) and the people (Nissinen, 2016). But the prophetic role within society was as ubiquitous as it was ambiguous; priests at the temple and the king at the palace, too, were powerful voices, not to mention the diversity of "unofficial" voices of diviners, soothsayers, mediums, oracles, and seers spread throughout. "Israel" was no exception. The sociology of pre-exilic Israel is composed of a series of tensions: on the one hand, the tension between itself and its neighbors; on the other hand, within its own history, the tensions between itself as a kingdom ruled by a king, itself as religious people centered on a temple administered by priests, and itself as a particular ethnicity called by a transcendent God claiming to be for all peoples, for which the prophets were the crucial social group. In the words of Green (1986) describing "the spiritual life of Israel," he describes "a life that often revolved around the priest and his sanctuary, the prophet and his message, and the king and his throne. It is in the tensions between these three, never resolved before the destruction [of the Temple], that the spiritual uniqueness of ancient Israel is most clearly reflected" (p. xxii). It is within these tensions that we must look to better discern the elusive figure of the prophet, at least in its pre-exilic forms. Within post-exilic Yehud/Judaea, the absence of any king combined with the rebuilding of the temple and the re-establishing of the priests administering the temple cult and ritual dramatically change the prophet-priest-king configuration of power. As well, the greatly increased significance of scriptural and theological interpretation based on text (presaging the emergence of the scribe and the sage and eventually the rabbinic teacher as authoritative interpreter of the written word of God) attests to the greatly transformed social context and reconfiguration of tensions within which the figure of the prophet, as well as the role and function of prophecy, will undergo equally significant transformations.

Unlike the *shi* of China or the *shramana* or *sannyasin* of India, the prophets (*nabi* in Hebrew) of Israel are not a newly emerging class, but a sociological commonplace across the ancient Near East (this claim is inclusive of Greece too: oracles). However, they are so within the sociological distinctiveness of ancient Israel, which would seem to consist above all in the specific quality of how "Israel" was marginal vis-à-vis surrounding empires. In the previous chapter, we used descriptors like marginal, exceptional, peripheral, anomalous, and interstitial as an array of synonyms to describe the general condition that seemed to apply to Axial Age civilizations. As we saw in the previous sections, China and India during the Axial Age centuries were less "civilizations" and more patchworks of volatile, changing societies with nascent forms of new, territorial states hatching within them alongside massive urbanization. Within that volatility and change, and the violence and suffering that accompanied it, the newly emerging *shi*, *shramana*, and *sannyasin* classes are marginal in the sense of interstitial; they emerge as a new class growing in the cracks fissures of societies undergoing convulsive change. Many from within these new or transformed classes traveled, and sought patronage, and switched allegiances, and did not belong to lands or states, or to traditional classes or societal structures.

The case of "Israel" lets us elaborate the sociological meaning of "marginality" further in new directions. Firstly, "Israel" itself as a whole was marginal and under threat, and then indeed conquered, taken captive, displaced, and returning. Post-exile, the themes of exile, captivity, persecution, and diaspora can be worked into the characterization of "marginal." Secondly, the *nabi* themselves, within both pre-exilic and post-exilic Israel, occupy a peculiar status. Perhaps comparable to the dramatic metamorphosis of *brahmans*, who went from being keepers of Vedic ritual that sacralized "this world" to becoming ascetic renunciate *sannyasin* aiming to escape "this world" and gain the "other world," the experience of exile and the destruction of the temple dynamically transforms the *nabi*, eventuating in their being the distinctive voice conveying the uniqueness of how "ancient Israel" experienced exile, captivity, persecution and diaspora, and responded with an Axial vision of transcendence. (That, above all, their voice took the form of prophetic books is an emphasis of contemporary scholarship, rather than the earlier scholarly focus on the prophet as a person [Edelman & Ben Zvi, 2009].)

To the complexity of this history and the strong focus on the significance of the pre- and post-exile divide needs to be added a scholarly complication concerning reconstruction of this history. In short, that so much of the founding story of "Israel" for Judaism (and of Christianity, too, in its sharing of that story through the Biblical Old Testament) is presumably about pre-exile Israel, but that all our literary sources are post-exilic, entails that *all* reconstructions of that founding story are suspect of being post-exilic retrojections and rationalizations projected onto that past rather than claims with some historical accuracy and verisimilitude (Floyd, 2006). While we see this scholarly problem recurs in all the efforts at reconstructing the Axial Age civilizations—did Lao Tzu really exist? How much of the origins of "Hinduism" are really to be found in Vedic orthodoxy or is that claim "a pious fiction"?—I have found this problem to be most acute in the case of ancient Israel. Even a casual glimpse through the scholarship should be enough to alert the reader: We may never know the historical reality "behind" the literary text. The complexity of this problem can't be avoided or minimized (as Bellah does, for example [2011, p. 284]). My strategy for addressing this issue: to put the bulk of the complexity of the scholarly complications into the next chapter when we examine the prophets in "microsociological" terms of their belonging to small communities centered on spiritual practices. For this chapter, I will follow the simpler, more straightforward story, which is also representative of the usual Axial Age interpretation of the prophets of Israel, too (for an invaluable article connecting scholarship on Israeli prophecy to that of the Axial Age, see Buss, 2006). I will present the more problematized version in the next chapter.

The *Nabi* of Israel

Who were the *nabi*? What do we mean by prophets and prophecy? Blenkinsopp (1995) notes: "When readers of the Bible use the term *prophecy*, they probably have in mind the fifteen books attributed to prophetic authorship known as the Latter Prophets. But many other prophetic figures are named throughout the Hebrew Bible...", according to a Talmudic saying 'there are "fifty-five, including seven female prophets." (p. 115). In short, there is a much broader range for what and who a prophet is, and what counts as prophecy, than is conventionally understood. Blenkinsopp continues: "Moreover, the earliest of the Latter Prophets, Amos and Hosea, are dated by most scholars to the eighth century B.C.E., and both refer to prophetic predecessors who can be traced back some three centuries. During the entire course of the history, a great number of different types of individuals and roles have been subsumed under the rubric of prophecy, which greatly complicates the task of coming up with an adequate definition of the phenomena" (p. 115). Some examples of the "great number of different types" are evident from the literature: the prophet described as seer, visionary, and man of God are the three most commonly associated types. Within the book of Deuteronomy, a famous section (Chapter 18: 9–22) includes, among other things, a long list of prohibited forms of prophecy: augur, soothsayer, diviner, sorcerer, caster of spells, consulter of ghosts or familiar spirits, or necromancer (see Blenkinsopp, 1995, p. 124; Grabbe, 1995, p. 122; see also Nicholson, 2010; Noll, 2013; Wilson, 1980, pp. 160–166).

Lindblom (1962), who provides an early classic on the prophets, proposes a number of descriptive claims as to the sociology of the prophets in ancient Israel: First, he makes a clear distinction between earlier prophets and the classical ones. Lindblom emphasizes that neither category is homogenous, diversity being more the rule: "there were in ancient times different, but not necessarily mutually exclusive, groups of prophets: coenobitic prophets, court prophets, sanctuary prophets, free prophets, and prophets of a mixed type" (p. 83). There were prophets in an official role as prophets, for example working at the king's court, or in the temple sanctuary. Also, particular roles—like priest vs. prophet—were not necessarily mutually exclusive; Samuel was both a priest and a prophet. Ezekiel was both priest and prophet, and Isaiah and Jeremiah prophets who certainly give every appearance of having close connections to the temple. King David consults both priests (Zadok and Abiathar) and prophets (Nathan the prophet and Gad the seer) in an official capacity (Grabbe, 2016). Many prophets of whom we know would indeed have been so in an official capacity of working for the king or with the temple cult (see esp. Johnson, 1962). There were also "unofficial" or "free" prophets, prophesying outside of any formal relationship.

It should be clear that there is an extraordinary diversity, in "Israel," and in general across the ancient Near East, of those in roles of "divine intermediary," whether as healer or diviner or ecstatic or medium, at any specific historical moment, and across historical change. Of the lattermost, exile will certainly provide the starkest dividing line within the history of ancient Israel. There was not one kind of prophet—but there might well be one particular subcategory from within the diversity that we are particularly interested in that belongs to and resembles the "Axial family category" of the *shi*, the *shramana* and the *sannyasin*, and Greek philosophers. Nissinen's (2016) characterization can help us make some headway through the diversity and variety of prophets and prophetic activities presented. "What makes prophecy distinguishable from other forms of divination in the ancient world is the lack of the use of inductive or technical methodology, such as observing the livers of sacrificial animals, the stars, or the flight of birds. In contrast, prophecy is understood as a non-technical, intuitive, or inspired kind of divination, with the prophet acting as mouthpiece of the deity" (p. 6). So a first distinction is that by comparison with the numerous other kinds of diviners and many types of divination that use an "inductive or technical methodology," prophecy ultimately devolves on the person of the prophet himself or herself. We will say more about this in the next chapter; in our immediate context, the key piece is the second distinction that the prophet acts "as mouthpiece of the deity."

The importance of prophets speaking "the word of God" cannot be overemphasized (for ancient Israel as for Judaism, and this applies for Christianity and Islam, too; all the "Religions of the Book" uphold "the word of God" as the ultimate authority). Alongside the emphasis on monotheism, radical and distinctive in the ancient Near Eastern context wherein polytheism was ubiquitous, enforced by the prohibition of idols and of any images to represent God, that prophets were persons with no further mediating factors who claimed to speak for the one true God was momentous. This prophetic activity, like God's speaking "in the beginning" that creates the cosmic order, recreates God's plan for Israel and gives articulate shape to its history. For Israelite history and scripture, prophecy as predictive of events—"foretelling"—served as evidence of Yahweh's power and divine planning. It was one of their own internal criteria for judging the authenticity of a prophet; accusing prophets of being false was commonplace and widespread (including, and especially, by other prophets). The predictive power of prophecy was a culturally accepted belief across the ancient Near East that, along with the role of the prophets, itself changes over the course of Israelite history in complex ways (van Seters, 2006).

In the premonarchy days of Israel as a disparate group of tribes ruled by judges, prophetic messages provided social cohesion and maintenance; in the time of the monarchy with king and temple at the center, prophecy in its unofficial forms anyway is pushed away from the center to the margins (Wilson, 1980, p. 252). In this development, prophecy becomes "forthtelling" rather than "foretelling" (the term is Wellhausen's, another classic earlier scholar): The prophets speak truth to power and condemn the idolatry, corruption, and waywardness of the king, of priests, of other prophets, or of the whole nation of Israel. In this respect, the prophets are exemplary Axial Age figures, critical of civilizational power in the form it took for them in ancient Israel and in neighboring civilizations and empires, and arguing for a radically alternative, transcendent and countercultural, conception of God and human being that rejected the usual configuration of the god-king-people complex so characteristic of ancient Near Eastern civilizations (and, as Bellah [2011] generalized, of all archaic civilizations).

Post-exile, this role continues, albeit now in the absence of the monarchy and therefore no longer in primary relation to the king, but in relation to the temple and priesthood at Jerusalem as the new ruling elite. Blenkinsopp (1995) resolves the bewildering diversity of prophecy problem he posed, and with which this section on the *nabi* began, through considering this "forthtelling" role to be the distinctive characteristic of prophecy, both pre- and post-exile, setting it apart from all other ancient Near Eastern prophecy in the prophets' roles as "dissident intellectuals": "What this is meant to say is that they collaborated at some level of conscious intent in the emergence of a coherent vision of a moral universe over against current assumptions cherished and propagated by the contemporary state apparatus, including its priestly and prophetic representatives" (p. 144). In reading this description, we should feel ourselves on familiar Axial Age grounds: Their premise is a critique of civilizational power, in a way that shows critical conscious awareness; they proffer a transcendent alternative that is countercultural, above all, moral and ethical. For a considerable span of the twentieth century, consensus among many scholars has been that this "forthtelling," "dissident intellectual" role for ancient Israeli prophets was distinctive to them. Blenkinsopp (1995) provides here a succinct summary of this accepted position:

> It is remarkable that no other ancient Near Eastern society that we know of developed a comparable tradition of dissident intellectualism and social criticism. Prophets and intermediaries of different kinds are attested practically everywhere in the region. ...There is the occasional inoffensive chiding of the ruler – perhaps he had neglected a ritual or overlooked an earlier oracle – but the role of these intermediaries is almost exclusively supportive, and there is no breath of challenge to the political or social status quo. Only in Israel and, to a lesser extent, Greece did a tradition of dissident and social protest develop. (p. 154)

It is this conception of "Israeli prophet" that, it seems to me, has guided Axial scholarly interpretations, from Jaspers to Bellah. From within the category *nabi* in its bewildering diversity of practitioners who look like magicians or shamans or healers, we can also discern "prophets" as a subcategory in the role of "dissident intellectuals" that belong in the Axial family resemblance, comparable to the *shi* in China, to the *shramana* and *sannyasin* of India, and as we will see with Greece, to the philosophers as well.

Weinfeld (1986) adds a further angle on the material of interest. At least in the case of Isaiah, Nahum, and Habakkuk, he discerns a qualitative difference within their prophecies that signal a move away from criticism of another nation or internal criticism of the unfaithfulness of Israel (both commonplace objects of criticism). Instead, Weinfeld argues that they move to a criticism of imperialism itself—not of the emperor, or of the empire, but the entire imperial project of expansion and conquering. In this regard, Weinfeld argues Israel is both original and unique, as the prophetic rationale is not made exclusively in terms of national self-interest as was the usual basis for criticism. Instead: "We might state then that Israel was the first nation in world history to raise its voice against imperialism" (1986, p. 172).

What of the fact of the conquest, captivity, and exile of the kingdom of Judah, and the destruction of the First Temple, that serves as a great dividing line within the history of "Israel," which also divides our consideration of who were the prophets, and what was prophecy, to "Israel"? We should note that Blenkinsopp's characterization of prophets as dissident intellectuals was based on post-exilic prophets (specifically Amos, Hosea, Micah, and Isaiah), and that their dissent was not against the king, but against the post-exile priestly establishment and its hegemony of control over the spirituality of Yehud through its role administrating the Second Temple. Blenkinsopp (1995) emphasizes that their "antireligious polemic" was directed at the "state-sponsored cults as part of an oppressive apparatus of control and their personnel as the exponents of the official state ideology" (p. 152). The "forthtelling" role of the prophets shows continuity in its "dissident" function from pre-exilic times, when they confronted kings, to post-exilic times, when they confronted the priestly establishment centered around the temple.

In addition to their dissident function, there is an accompanying sociological continuity present: their marginalization by official power. In pre-exile times, kings disapproved of the criticism and marginalized those "dissident intellectual" prophets who spoke against them (Wilson, 1980, p. 252). Post-exile, in addition to the priestly establishment and control of the temple, there is also a turn to the scribes and the written texts as increasingly authoritative, and in relation to the latter, the prophets are again an irritant. Nissinen (2006) in assessing the role of prophecy, post-exile, claims "[s]ome forms of traditional prophetic activity, as attested in the Hebrew Bible as well as in the Near Eastern sources, probably continued to exist, but the texts… reveal that they were despised rather than appreciated by the learned circles and were therefore probably driven to the margins of the society" (p. 41).

These continuities of prophecy—in its "dissident function," in its marginalization relative to official power—across exile are significant to note (with the caveat, to repeat, that these interpretations are profoundly problematized by contemporary scholars). Equally significant are discontinuities. The most significant of such discontinuities: While prophecy continues in its "unofficial" form, albeit increasingly marginalized, by comparison with its pre-exilic function it is no longer primarily in the form of ecstatic possession and vision and speaking the word of God (orally). Instead, prophecy continues, but now in a literary form of inspired reading and interpretation of the word of God (as text). While we do not know at all when the Torah became accepted as primary revelation for "Israel," nor when all the surrounding literature of interpretation began to compile around it, we do know for certain that this was (or became) normative during the Second Temple period. Captivity, exile, and diaspora destroy the monarchy and the temple at Jerusalem, and also greatly reconfigure the hitherto culturally normative status of prophecy within "Israel." Prophecy as actively practiced does not disappear post-exile; some of it continues in a similar form but as a subcultural, unofficial, fringe activity. The remainder is dispersed and differentiated into a number of diverse communities of interpretation focused on sacred texts—including the prophetic books as a record of inspiration of old that itself requires the active practice, in the present, of prophetic inspiration, albeit the latter now takes the form of textual interpretation. Historically, sometime within Second Temple Judaism, we come to the end of the Axial Age of "Israel," timing-wise coinciding with the increasing importance of texts, and hence of the interpretations by the scribe, the Pharisee, the Sadducee, the sage, the teacher, all presaging the imminent emergence of "Rabbinic Judaism" in later centuries.

PROPHETIC SCHOOLS OF ISRAEL?

This last point also clarifies, by way of comparison, a significant question by way of difference between the *nabi* and the *shi*, the *shramana*, and the *sannyasin* (and as we will see, the philosophers too): Were there comparable prophetic schools? Lindblom (1962) claims that the earliest prophets (like Elijah and Elisha) were heads of prophetic guilds (*bene hannebi'im*) that lived and ate in common and traveled together.

Wilson (1980) concurs: "The expression 'son of...' or 'sons of....' is frequently used in Semitic to indicate membership in a group or guild, so there is little doubt that 'sons of the prophets' was a designation applied to members of some sort of prophetic group" (p. 141). These groups or guilds are occasionally presented in competitions with each other; famously, for example, the prophets of Yahweh combat the prophets of Baal on Mt. Carmel and emerge victorious. The competition was fierce: accusations of false prophecy and false prophets abound. This accords with what we know of official temple prophets in the ancient Near East more broadly (Nissinen, 2006, 2010, 2016). By the time of the classical prophets, this form seems to have disappeared. However, in a striking difference from China, India, and Greece, we don't have rival arguing schools: There is no "Isaiah-an" school arguing with the "Ezekiel-ite" school, both of whom despise the "Jeremiads," and so on. Post-exile, we get no hint of any such institution as a "prophetic school"—unless, depending on how the latter is defined, the Essenes count, in which case they would be a striking example. What we do have is a new and intense focus on text, and communities of interpretation gathering around these texts—for example, communities that maintain libraries. By the last centuries BCE, interpretation is divided among groups like the Pharisees and the Sadducees (centered on Jerusalem), the Essenes in Qumran, the Therapeutae in Alexandria centered on different readings of sacred text and different practices and means of interpreting. For our understanding of this post-exilic phenomenon, the Dead Sea scrolls and the Qumran community and the presence of groups like the Essenes (that lived together, ate and fasted in common, shared property and possessions, practiced celibacy to some degree, and participated in ritual, prayer, and textual study, together) as well as the Pythagoreans (who were particularly active in Egypt, whether the community of the Therapeutae in Alexandria or the "gymnosophists" along the Nile, with a number of similar practices to the Essenes [Silver, 2017; Taylor, 2004; Taylor, 2012]) contribute an indispensable piece of the picture and afford us ways of understanding the sociological transformation of prophecy across the great dividing line of exile.

There is one line of interpretation within scholarship that holds out a tantalizing way of understanding this transformation and which fills out a piece of question of prophetic "schools." Middlemas (2016) describes how it has become increasingly common to understand "prophetic books as collections of material that reflect the teaching of a prophetic figure as well as the disciples or school that preserved his words, along with editorial activity that placed the book in its present arrangement and collected material to it while doing so" (p. 38). That is, a "prophetic book" like Isaiah (typically divided into at least 3 different authors) is not the verbatim recording of the actual individual prophet Isaiah's words with a narrative around it. Rather, it is the product of a school of disciples who would presumably have some relation, firsthand, second-hand, and intergenerationally connected to a putative actual Isaiah, taking responsibility to record, edit, collate, redact, and in general organize the prophetic message. For example, the book of Ezekiel, which displays a "high degree of homogeneity," "is thought to be the unified composition by one author, or essentially the prophecies of Ezekiel to which accretions have been added by disciples of the prophet, often spoken of as a school" (Middlemas, 2016, p. 48). If we accept this plausible, and indeed relatively modest, proposal, then "Israel" did indeed have schools none of whose members we know but whose collective identity bears the "name" corresponding to the prophetic books—the school of Isaiah, of Ezekiel, of Jeremiah, and so on.

The more radical scholarly interpretation takes the plausibility of this proposal further to a consequence that inverts the premise: We can be certain there was an Ezekiel school that wrote the prophetic book of that name, but as there is no way to establish what was the "essence" composed by a putative original author over against what were the "accretions" of later disciples, then we dispense with concern about the unknowable original author. Perhaps, like Lao Tzu in China, there was no actual Ezekiel in "Israel," but there was certainly an "Ezekiel school." The school itself understands the original author to be Yahweh himself, so what is paramount is retaining the integrity of the message. We should remember too this is twenty-five hundred years ago: Concerns with authorship and identity were certainly very different relative to our highly individualistic cultural assumptions! Regardless of which modest or more radical version of scholarly interpretation one follows in this case, one conclusion is that "guilds" or "schools" did not disappear by the time of the classical prophets; rather they are hidden behind the title of eponymous individuals whose message they transmit and sustain. Fraade (1991) claims this hiding was intentional, "precisely to maintain the impression that the text before us is a collective, traditional one, constituting the 'words of Torah'" (p. 17).

These prophetic schools would be literate and educated groups, of course, but this does not mean we should rush to call them "mere scribes" so as to set them apart from the "real prophets." As we have seen, the privileged status of God's word as divine, whether oral or written, claimed transcendent, sacred power. That God could inspire scribes' editorial activity rather than an earlier prophet's speaking activity is a plausible continuity. In comparative Axial terms, however, we see one significant difference: In distinction from China, India, or Greece, and in distinction from the competing guilds of the earlier prophets of Israel, there are no argumentation, polemic, and disagreement signaling active engagement between the different "schools." I don't mean that all the prophetic books speak in one voice (they don't) and show no differences or contradictions or inconsistencies between them (they do). But unlike the writings of the other Axial Age movements, which present dialogues often involving the disagreements and arguments attributed to other interlocutors (the Buddha's position regularly defined in opposition to Mahavira's, for example, and vice versa; Mo Tzu opposes Confucius, and both are opposed by the Taoists, and representatives of each show up in argument within their respective texts; Plato presenting Socrates in question and answer mode with others, sometimes the heads of other schools, like with Protagoras), or in Collins' (1998) terms the "structural rivalry of the field," the prophetic books do not present this structure. We don't have an account of Jeremiah arguing with Isaiah about what Elijah meant, and so on. The systematicity during Second Temple Judaism would seem to go primarily into the redaction of material into a coherent narrative of a book. Later still, systematization goes into canonization of texts and an extraordinary proliferation of commentary, exegesis, and response (beyond the Torah, there are the Talmud, Mishnah, Midrash, *halakhah*, and more). While this lattermost proliferation certainly includes argumentation and structural rivalry, it belongs to Rabbinic Judaism and not earlier to the Axial Age centuries.

I've found no explanation for this difference, sociologically or otherwise. One clue that presents itself ties back into our opening considerations: Israel, by comparison with China or India (or in fact, Greece for that matter) is far smaller and a mere "bit player" within the broader context of the ancient Near East as a whole. Uffenheimer (1986) concludes his contribution arguing that "biblical monotheism" is "the result of an existential experience of the whole nation rather than an intellectual achievement of a small elitist prophetic opposition" (p. 168). Perhaps, by analogy, the lack of "structural rivalry" internal to the prophetic books (there is ample such rivalry between Israelite prophecy and all other prophets within the ancient Near Eastern "field") is an outcome of this smallness and hence a relatively compact "existential experience of the whole nation" by comparison with the multi-state patchworks of India and China and the interstitial networks of "dissident intellectuals" each created.

Axial Age Greece

Greece, like Israel a small civilization on the margins of the great empires of the ancient Near East, is unlike Israel in most other respects. Classical Greece is typically considered to originate from a Greek "Dark Ages" around 800 BCE. The Homeric epics mythologize this time and Greek victory over Troy to provide an origin story for Greek identity (Troy's fall is presumably a historic event, datable to 1250–1200 BCE). From the eighth century, originating from mainland Greece, southern Italy, and through the Aegean, the Greeks expand their colonies, trade relations, and cultural influence throughout the Mediterranean (reaching Egypt, north Africa, France, and Spain), along the shores of the Black Sea, and into Western Asia. They did not establish colonies in an imperial conquering sense, but "settler colonies" that partially assimilated themselves to the cultural conditions in which they found themselves (cf. McEvilley, 2002, pp. xxv–xxvii). Awareness of and travel to other civilizations like Babylon, Phoenicia, Egypt, and Persia—and perhaps India?—was high; many Greeks traveled extensively (Garland, 2014). Perhaps, if Barker (2004) is correct, the pre-Socratics, in particular Pythagoras, were also deeply influenced by temple practice at Jerusalem, although Dodds (1951) speculates as to shamanic influence from the Black Sea while McEvilley (2002) speculates even further to yogic influence from India (via the Black Sea route). Regardless, beginning from the eighth century over the next centuries, Greek fortunes rise, and Greek influence expands throughout the region.

From 700 to 300 BCE, they show an extraordinary "efflorescence"; by the fourth century BCE, for example, there are about 1100 city-states while population had grown to three million (from around 330,000 in 1000 BCE) (Ober, 2015). Classical Greece was not an empire but rather "an extensive social ecology of many independent city-states with citizen-centered governments" (Ober, 2015, p. xv). These city-states were also mostly small. "The size of the *polis* ranged from 500 to 2000 male citizens" (Hartnett, 2011, p. 60)—with an exception to be made for Athens, whose population of a quarter million "was unusually large" (Bellah, 2011, p. 335; for Greece-wide population figures, see Ober, 2015, ch. 2). These characteristics—small, independent, widely distributed, and governmentally "citizen-centered"—provide a unique setting for the manifesting of classical Greece's distinctive politics and the manner in which its Axial Age is inflected.

A key significant difference from Israel, and certainly distinctive in comparison with any other Axial case, is due to the Greeks successfully fending off attacks from neighboring empires. The Neo-Assyrian Empire (934–610 BCE), which played such a direct role for Israelite history, is more indirectly influential on Greek history. Neo-Assyrian expansion sent the Phoenicians throughout the Mediterranean, both to gain tribute and to escape their control. The Greeks emulate the Phoenicians—most famously, adopting their alphabet—in part to profit from the demands for goods from Neo-Assyria (Bellah, 2011, pp. 337–338). In doing so, they encounter other empires—Egypt and the Carthaginian Empire in northern Africa. Most momentous for Greek history is their interaction with the Persian Empire. The Greeks support rebellion in Ionia against Cyrus, followed by successfully defending themselves against first Darius and then Xerxes, each of whom led invasions against Greece between 499 and 449 BCE. Victories at Marathon (490 BCE) and Salamis (480 BCE), the latter above all due to naval superiority, were key for retaining freedom for Greece (Meier, 1998).

The mention of naval superiority is not merely an interesting anecdote: In terms of the previous chapter's recognition of the singular importance of the long east-west Afroeurasian belt as the central axis to an emerging singular world-system composed of a number of zones that consolidates itself by the first centuries B.C., that Greece occupies the westernmost tip of this belt is highly relevant. This is a greatly different circumstance from the river-based civilizational possibilities of Egypt, Mesopotamia, India, or China, for example. Mainland Greece is a peninsula surrounded by water except to its north, with a mountainous interior that was not easily traversable. In being the European tip of the belt primarily accessible by water, Greece is in crucial aspects of access set apart from the Asian, land-based civilizations to its east. Greece was able to occupy a fortuitously peripheral position of benefiting through trade and contact, from neighboring empires and older civilizations but not at the cost of becoming vassal or tributary to them. "The Greeks overseas could establish close contact with the highly developed Near Eastern cultures, so that a singular combination of touch and untouchability resulted: inspirations, knowledge, patterns of life as well as numerous goods were within reach of the Greeks, without their coming under the influence of the eastern empires" (Meier, 1986, p. 74).

Modern descriptors like "Europe" or "Asia" should not be reified. Geographically, Greece belongs to Europe and has its share of distinctive features that affect its relation to the other civilizations along the Afroeurasian belt. Culturally during these early millennia BCE, it's better considered "Asian" in belonging to that world-system—primarily in terms of Phoenician influence from 1100 to 600 BCE (from where, for example, the Greeks get their alphabet). (According to Ball [2010], this was followed by significant influence from pre-Islamic Arabian civilization over the next centuries.) Greek victories against the Persians such as the Battle of Marathon were decisively significant for their self-identity. (Whereas from a Persian imperial perspective, "it seems that Darius regarded it as a minor event... more of a raid than an invasion" [Grabbe, 2004, p. 269]. For Persia, Greek victories were minimally registered as a minor setback at the edge of a great empire, a little battle within a far broader imperial campaign.) Momigliano (1975) points out that Greece does not look to Europe for influence or interest, but to Egypt, Persia, and Assyria, a claim amply substantiated by Burkert (1992, 2004). Alexander's decision to conquer by going east and not to the north or west is understandable and meaningful in precisely these Asian world-system terms (cf. Gills & Frank, 1993, p. 162).

These geographic factors would seem to have offset Greek disadvantages vis-à-vis the greater empires to its east and south, to such an extent that Bellah (2011) says "If there is a Greek miracle, it is its geographical situation that allowed the Greeks for almost five centuries, from the eighth through most of the fourth, the freedom to carry out their extraordinary experiment without having to pay the price for their political/military vulnerability" (p. 397). At the center of their "extraordinary experiment," and of crucial significance and difference from the other Axial cases is that the *polis* develops democracy as a political form across these centuries in place of a kingdom. As Ober (2015) convincingly shows, Greece was radically distinctive by comparison with other societies of the time—and, indeed, to most societies since!—in not pursuing highly centralized authority to organize itself and command collective co-operation. "In light of the stubborn refusal of the Greek small-state ecology to coalesce into either an empire or a few large states ruled by strong leaders and narrow elite coalitions, the greatness of ancient Hellas becomes more mysterious" (Ober, 2015, p. 11). Politically, Greek citizen-centered government was quite unique as in every other case of ancient civilizations, whether in the Near East, India, or China, they required a king as key within the god-king-people complex to sustain the social order. As Bellah (2011) notes: "it is significant that ancient Greece in the period of the axial transition was the only case where actual kings were absent, though not absent in the cultural imagination" (p. 326). Instead, the Greeks develop democracy.

The description of "democracy" needs some qualification. For one, incidences of monarchs and tyrants ruling were known, and regularly and intermittently recurred. For a second, numerous and many of the remaining Greek *poleis* were oligarchies: ruled by powerful noble families. Nevertheless, these forms co-existed with the emergence of democracy. For a third: democracy is meant here in the classical Greek sense, not our modern one. This means the city-state was ruled by the assembly of free adult Greek male citizens, excluding slaves, children, women, and non-Greeks from having a voice—Ober's (2015) phrase "citizen-centered governments" seems to accurately capture this specific sense. As Eisenstadt (1986) puts it, "The most important common denominator of the political symbolism of city-states was *citizenship*" (p. 34; my emphasis). It is not only politically that the Greeks are distinctive in their emphasis on citizenship; also distinctive to them in the legal sphere was *isonomia* (equality of free, adult, Greek males before the law), an innovation that helped consolidate the power accorded to a Greek citizen and which should be considered alongside democracy as part and parcel of the Greek Axial Age breakthrough (cf. Sagan, 1991; Landes, 2011, pp. 215–229). Sociologically, the importance of citizenship (rather than kingship) has profound implications for understanding the Axiality of the Greek case: In distinction from all the other cases, in Greece alone the critique of civilizational power, at least civilizational power in the form of a centralized authority as was the ancient norm, was a shared political premise. This premise was a key constitutive feature of classical Greek culture as a whole. It was not the exceptional and revolutionary prerogative of a small group of spiritual luminaries, as it is in all the other Axial cases.

That philosophers come from Greek citizenry—i.e., free, adult, Greek males, with legal and political rights denied all others—inserts complications into their marginal status and how we understand their "critique of civilizational power." For one, they were entitled to a certain degree of power, which although neither monolithic nor hierarchical in the same manner as it was in the other Axial cases was a given degree of "civilizational power," nonetheless. For example, slavery was ubiquitous and thus a citizen who owned slaves a "king" of sorts... a situation that becomes a vexed question for Greek philosophy (cf. Ramelli, 2016, pp. 26–76). As Plato would describe in his *Laws*: "But with regards to slaves there is a big difficulty. ...The question of slave ownership is indeed very difficult" (cited in Ramelli, 2016, pp. 26 and 35). Many philosophers (like Plato) had slaves; in Aristotle's famous formulation, having slaves was a "natural" state and afforded the philosopher the leisure he needed to think. There were also many philosophers who did not have slaves (such as Socrates), while some in fact had been slaves themselves, like Diogenes, Epictetus, and Menippus (all of whom, perhaps not coincidentally, were Cynics). There is a corresponding complexity of philosophical positions for and against slavery.

The democratic expansion of opportunities made available for all citizens accounts for much of the reputation for Greek entrepreneurial daring during its classic age. In avoiding the vertical hierarchy of divine kingship, the arena of politics is both greatly expanded and correspondingly flattened out. Therefore, short of becoming a tyrant (an option a number of Greeks pursued through these centuries, some of them famously; Peisistratos of Athens, for one, and following Athens' defeat following the Peloponnesian War, the rule of the "Thirty Tyrants"), one would be limited to small-scale, internecine politicking; agonistic competition with one's fellow citizen; military glory or economic derring-do. Or: "the fact that Greece consisted of innumerable, diverse, independent cities, and that there was relatively little opportunity for greater concentrations of power, certainly was a condition for the development of intelligence in the interstices between power centers and cities" (Meier, 1986, p. 81). The obligation to be political is much less onerous than the duties a subject owes a divinized king, but in a Greek cultural context where there is an assumption of freedom for citizens as well as their possessing "civic," not universal, "rights" (Ober, 2015, pp. 16–18), this obligation could be experienced as burdensome and an infringement upon free thinking. Thus, the critique of civilizational power in the form of divine kingship as a premise all Greek citizens shared is taken one step further and deeper by its thinkers, to a deep reflection on "civilization" itself and ultimately, a rejection of the "citizen-*polis*" configuration, too: Their criticism will apply to their society's assumptions, its conventions, its often unquestioning acceptance of tradition, of myth, of ritual performance. In large enough power centers—like Athens—critical reflection on the nature of the good life motivates radical thinking and its embodiment in countercultural schools of philosophy. The "this worldly" preoccupations that go into political machinations, which likely dominated most of Greek citizens' thought as a matter of necessity, will be countered in the "other worldly" reflections of philosophy. In Meier's phrasing, these complications around power that come to be institutionalized in distinctively Greek ways like democracy and *isonomia* contribute in crucial ways to "the thesis that the emergence of an autonomous intelligence among the Greeks has a decisive connection with the origins of politics" (1986, p. 91).

A final qualification in our picture of Greece must be added before looking at the philosophers. For in emphasizing its "efflorescence," freedom, affluence, and unique political institutions of citizenship, democracy, and *isonomia*, one might mistakenly also assume Greek life to be leisurely, comfortable, and secure; perhaps even easy. This was certainly not the case. The Greeks show an acute awareness of suffering, injustice, tyranny, and the capriciousness of *fortuna*. If on the macroscale of history it was a Golden Age, on the microscale of ordinary human lives, the same age showed itself to be precarious and more often than not, violent. Garland (2014) estimates that "well over 100,000 men, women, and slaves were displaced as a result of the Peloponnesian War"; across the centuries that scholars have described as its "efflorescence," "about seventy-five centuries were destroyed... some more than once"; "in forty-two cases the population was massacred and/or enslaved" (p. 3). Garland's Appendices cataloguing the tens of thousands of deportees, exiles, and the enslaved bear weighty witness to the claims with which he concludes his analysis: "it is hardly any exaggeration to state that the brilliance of Greek civilization was predicated in part upon the shiftlessness of its population. Being Greek meant facing the prospect of being displaced at some point in one's life without any certainty of return" (2014, p. 199).

It is ironic that the Greek Axial Age is ended not by their Persian imperial neighbor to the east, but by their northern Macedonian neighbor Alexander the Great. Dateable to 336 BCE, Alexander's assumption to Hegemon of the Hellenic League, the irony is compounded as the Greek fall "was precipitated, at least in part, by the successful adaptation of Greek innovations by some of the Greeks' neighbors" (Ober, 2015, p. 18). Their Western neighbor, the Roman Republic, will drive the irony home during the Macedonian wars of the second century BCE when all of the Greek world comes under the rule of Rome. Prior to these conquering moves by neighboring empires, the ensemble of geographic, cultural, and political conditions characterizing ancient Greece combine to become the unique creative matrix, wherein freedom, glory, and the appreciation of beauty are upheld equally alongside tragedy, violence, and the unavoidability of suffering. This combination leads to what Elkana (1986) characterizes as "the central revelation of the Greek Enlightenment of the fifth century was that nothing was any longer taken for granted. Experimentation in all areas resulted, and in a new outburst of confidence reason turned a "'searchlight' upon itself" (p. 57). The citizens who became the spokespersons for this revelation and who presented a new vision of truth were the philosophers.

The Philosophers of Greece

In turning to look at the philosophers of classical Greece, and having reached the westernmost of the Axial movements, and the putative foundation of "the West," I am also assuming we are on the most familiar ground. Socrates, Plato, and Aristotle are, I hope, names familiar to all, with others like Pythagoras, Zeno, Protagoras, Heraclitus, Epicurus, and Diogenes also well known. Within the historical efflorescence of classical Greek culture, there is an efflorescence of questioning, thinking, arguing, and philosophizing, too. Figure 5.1 provides an incomplete list of philosopher, corresponding school, and corresponding dates, which is not exhaustive, but a mere sampling of representative figures to help convey the efflorescence, the proliferation, the numerous and intertwining profusion of twigs, buds, and branches.

This is the age of breakthroughs in rational thinking, empirical inquiry, mathematics and geometry, metaphysics, cosmology and the natural sciences, history. Pythagoras will found his spiritual community in Croton, Italy, and spread his mystical-mathematical vision of the soul and the cosmos by way of his followers to every corner of the Greek world. Tragedians like Aeschylus and Euripides will raise pointed moral questions demonstrating the inadequacy of traditional myth. The different

Philosopher	School	Dates BCE
Thales	Milesian school	636–546
Anaximander	Ionian school	611–547
Anaximenes	Milesian school	585–525
Pythagoras	Pythagoreanism	580–520
Xenophanes	Eleatics	570–480
Heraclitus	Ephesian school	535–475
Parmenides of Elea	Eleatics	515–445
Anaxagoras	"pluralist" school	499–428
Empedocles	"pluralist" school	492–432
Zeno of Elea	Eleatics	490–430
Gorgias	Sophists	485–380
Leucippus	Atomist (materialist)	480–420
Protagoras	Sophists	480–411
Socrates	(no school)	469–399
Democritus	Atomist (materialist)	460–370
Antisthenes	Cynicism	445–365
Plato	Platonism	427–347
Diogenes	Cynicism	412–323
Aristotle	Aristotelianism	384–322
Pyrrho	Pyrrhonism (skepticism)	360–270
Epicurus	Epicureanism	341–271
Zeno of Citium	Stoicism	333–264

Fig. 5.1 Greek philosophers, schools, and dates

cosmologists will speculate about the naturalistic rather than mythical origin of the cosmos in water as the first stuff, or perhaps fire, or "the boundless" as the primal element. Religious observance and belief will come under intense questioning. Seaford (2016b) advances a position similar to the *brahmanic* "interiorization of ritual" we discussed above in looking at the emergence of the *sannyasi* in India, arguing that in Greece there is a process of "interiorization of Greek mystic initiation" as practiced in the mystery schools that informs pre-Socratic philosophers like Heraclitus and Parmenides—the interiorization ultimately motivated by the effects of monetization on Greek thinking (cf., Seaford, 2004). Socrates will be tried and executed for impiety. Plato will propose his theory of transcendent forms. Xenophanes famously mocks the anthropomorphism of myth:

> But if horses or oxen or lions had hands or could draw with their hands
> and accomplish such works as men, horses would draw the figures of the
> gods as similar to horses and the oxen as similar to oxen, and they would
> make the bodies of the sort which each of them had. Aithiopians say that
> their gods are snub-nosed and black, Thracians that they are blue-eyed and
> red-haired. (cited in Obryk, 2016, p. 244)

Indeed, "nothing was any longer taken for granted," in Elkana's phrasing; or in Jaspers': "*Logos* replaces *Mythos*."

What was most radical in the Greek questioning was their rejection of societal conventions themselves as false and ignorant, as enslaving the mind to passion, need, want, pride, reputation, fear, jealousy, and anger. Philosophers and schools could and did vary greatly as to how they conceived overcoming this enslavement and therefore how to conceive and practice an emancipated life of reason: "competition was also rife among philosophers, doctors, and historians, developing in some cases into the institutionalization of rival schools" (Humphreys, 1986, p. 93). The Cynics demonstrate this most drastically through overtly spurning custom and morality, by deliberately seeking out dishonor; Epicureans and Stoics disagree as to what is the best route to finding equanimity, particularly as to the role of pleasure, but they concur in wishing to escape suffering to gain equanimity; Plato will assimilate all that is inferior to the body and propose a dualistic solution residing in the transcendence of the mind. Nevertheless, they share in common a critical distancing away from the very premises of Greek social life. The sophists alone would seem to be the exception to this rule, except that in order to use those social conventions to gain power and reputation for themselves in the way that they did, presupposed the critical, reflexive distance from those conventions only available to a suitably rational mind. The derision of a Socrates or a Plato toward the sophists was for moral and ethical reasons, not intellectual ones; in the latter regard, someone like a Protagoras was a subtle and dangerous opponent. Although the sophists chose to use their gifts for profit and gain, in their very use of those gifts they display "systematic, critical thinking about thinking, i.e. second-order thinking" (Elkana, 1986, p. 48), considered a characteristic Axial achievement that "breaks through" the horizon of "first-order thinking."

In all the cases other than the sophists, however, the philosophers used "second-order thinking" to not only critically distance themselves in theory, but also in practice. The "systematicity of thinking" was elaborated into a working constitution, so to speak, of the small community. As inspirational leaders who attracted followers, Greek philosophers established what Schmidt (2010) characterizes as "small utopian communities" (on the utopian theme in the Axial Age, see also Seligman [1989]).

> Each founder's struggle and enlightenment was based on his personal experience with and rejection of contemporary social order. His community was a philosophically and religiously inspired reaction to the problems of the outside world. These enlightened ancient communities sometimes attracted thousands of followers for generations indicating that there was a widespread desire in the Greco-Roman world to reject and, in some cases, transform the world in the spirit of reform. Each individual member of the community, often following the example of its founder, had to reject his social order. The ancient sources emphasize both the communities' and individuals' rejection of the contemporary social scene. (Schmidt, 2010, p. 5)

Hadot (1995) emphasizes that "to be a philosopher implies a rupture with what the skeptics call *bios*, that is, daily life" (p. 56); Socrates, for example, was called "*atopos*," that is, "unclassifiable" (p. 57), or very literally, "no-place." Elkana (1986): "the Academy, the Lyceum and some monastic orders: all these are characterized by equality among the members and authoritarian separatism towards the outside world" (p. 55).

In moving in this way to the margins of the Greek *polis*—itself, as already noted above, a marginal sociopolitical experiment by comparison with the high civilizations and empires of the ancient Near East—the philosophers are not only breaking from convention, they were posing a troubling challenge to basic premises of Greek civilization founded on "civic rights" extended to citizens defined as Greek, free, adult, males, challenging the citizen-polis premise, and inciting anger and contempt from the *polis*. Schmidt (2010) describes the Pythagoreans as follows:

> With their detailed and very extensive set of rules regarding purity, diet, and ritual behavior, the Pythagoreans were sharply distinguished from their contemporary environment, and in their total vegetarianism they cut themselves off from the rest of society. …The Pythagoreans' hope of "salvation" in the beyond was based on both the "purity" of their way of life and their master's advice as to what was observed regarding "moving away from here." …the Pythagoreans were often accused of having contempt for outsiders. Their sectarian attitude was considered oligarchical, anti-democratic and tyrannical in their insistence on retaining the existing constitution. (p. 71)

In the latter accusations—"oligarchical, anti-democratic and tyranni-
cal"—it is evident that the philosophical challenge went to the heart of
Greek civilizational assumptions. Socrates will be put to death, on false
charges, but coupled to very real anger channeled into murderous scapegoating consequences. In basic respects, the philosophers were turning the Greek world on its head. "Epicurus's school was uncommonly
egalitarian in practice, admitting all classes, including women, slaves and
the poor, who could attend through subscriptions from the wealthy"
(Hartnett, 2011, p. 106). Pythagoras, too, accepted women and taught
them. The Cynics, ever the most extreme, eschewed formally institu-
tionalizing themselves as a school and devoted their life to subverting
convention from within; Diogenes, for example, upon being sold into
slavery, "acted as the real master of his owner... he used to indicate
to his owner how he and his children should behave" (Ramelli, 2016,
p. 47). The Cynics also, like Socrates, willfully lived lives of poverty. All
the other schools, however, did institutionalize themselves; these "were
usually established in the desert or a wilderness physically removed from
pre-existing, urban centers as a means of creating distinctions with the
outside world" (Schmidt, 2010, p. 6).

In a winnowing process similar to China's schools, by the third century BCE there are four remaining philosophical schools in Athens: "the
school of Plato, the school of Aristotle and Theophrastus, the school
of Epicurus, and that of Zeno and Chrysippus," alongside "two movements that are primarily spiritual traditions: Skepticism and Cynicism"
(Hadot, 1995, p. 56). Platonism, Aristotelianism, Epicureanism,
Stoicism, Skepticism, and Cynicism, and further throughout the Greek
world, Pythagoreanism, prove in retrospect "new buds" on the thick
Greek branch of the "tree of world history," that will deeply influence
Hellenism, the Roman Empire, and Christianity in turn, bearing fruit for
millennia in becoming central to the categories of thought and belief to
"the West," until the present day.

Women?

One sociological commonalty that should be clear based on the survey
presented in this chapter: The Axial Age visionaries and the great majority of their followers making up their schools are overwhelmingly male.
On the one hand, of course they were: civilizations before and after the
Axial Age are patriarchal organizations, and the Axial Age movements

merely tiny interstitial spasms within them. On the other hand, the very appeal of transcendence and universality, of a countercultural push against civilized power, of an overturning of traditional boundaries of class, ethnicity, status, and so on, ought to include and apply to gender, too, and thus be emancipatory for women as well. And indeed, we do find some astonishing examples, within this otherwise overwhelmingly male-dominated historical time, of women's involvement and inclusion. Pythagoras is famous for his liberal arguments for, and to some degree practices of, women's equality within Pythagorean communities, but like all things Pythagorean, we cannot tell the factual from the fable. Euripides has unusually emancipatory views on women (and on barbarians and slaves). Plato in the *Republic* "repeatedly stated that there is nothing 'against nature' in educating men and women in the same way, as guardians-philosophers, and in having them share the same responsibilities" (Ramelli, 2016, p. 42). Some women appear among the Epicureans, a few more among the Cynics. While the majority of the prophets of Israel are male, and all the prophetic books are about male prophets, a minority of women do make an appearance as prophetesses (seven of the fifty-five total), of which some are noticeable for their significance (Deborah, Miriam, Huldah). Some of the interlocutors in the *Upanisadic* dialogues are women—and not in a subsidiary role, but presented as speaking intelligently, critically, and independently. From early on, Buddhism included nuns as well as monks. (I could find no reference to women in any of the Chinese material.) If we extend into Christianity and Islam, both Jesus and Muhammad are unusually inclusive in their attitudes and treatment of women.

However, even adding all of these up: a few examples constituting a minority does not a substantial case make. Those who hope to find early versions of women's liberation views in the Axial Age visions are overreaching. In addition to the (few) examples to be found that confirm a "progressive" view toward women, one would also need to look at the (numerous) counterexamples that support the opposite, i.e., a male, chauvinist, patriarchal view. These abound, and the latter elements are more representative of Axial viewpoints than any kind of substantial recognition of women. Some initial version of a feminist view of moral and ethical equality, of the implications for women of a transcendent locus for identity, just isn't there. Viewed through a twenty-first century lens, this is just plain odd, as the situating of the locus of one's true identity in a meaning transcendent of "this world," including many of its received categories such as class, ethnicity, status, wealth, regional affiliation, and so on, should seem obviously and immediately applicable to gender, too. It wasn't. That all the world civilizations emerging from the Axial Age are each, invariably, patriarchal, is unfortunately an accurate representation of the gender politics of the Axial visions. It's also continuous with pre-Axial patriarchal dominance, so in regard to extending their universalizing claims to women the Axial Age would seem to have made effectively no difference.

Nevertheless, the Axial Age is relevant to gender thinking, and more broadly the whole sphere of identity politics, for today. Jaspers' claim from page one is that the ways in which we think, the horizon of understanding within which we live, the space of meaning within which our thought moves, were set during the Axial Age. Cognitively-intellectually, the notion of transcendence sets what in certain respects is an insuperable limit for thinking, and thus sets in motion the potential for "boundless criticism" internal to any perspective. (This is different from Jaspers' appeal for "boundless communication," but as it plays off a similar dynamic in terms of the appeal to transcendence, I'm retaining the "boundless" modifier.) Any particular articulation in specific terms or images will necessarily fall short of the universally transcendent and thus can be criticized for being inadequate. In this respect, the critical premise of Axiality, once full-blown into systematic questioning, is not only a solvent for inadequate particular instantiation of the transcendent universal ideal, it is a universal solvent. It seems to me that within the heated identity politics of the twentieth and twenty-first centuries, which have certainly come to a head under the Presidency of Donald Trump, for example, while writing this book, the truly emancipatory, progressive options are ultimately couched in terms that appeal to a transcendent locus of identification to gain their critical force against current practice. This is so for women and also for the disabled, the disenfranchised, the indigenous, the foreigner, the immigrant, the refugee... i.e., truly universally.

In mis-taking the Axial visions and subordinating select elements to serve again the continuing expansion of power, post-Axial civilization also selected the patriarchal elements biased toward male chauvinism and gender inequity over women (patriarchy, after all, is a power structure). Patriarchy continued. Perhaps, patriarchy continued with even greater tools for subordination and chauvinist self-justification than before. Regardless, the question remains as to a proper interpretation of those

Axial visions of transcendence and universality: If the ultimate meaning of human identity can only truly be resolved in a higher reality of certain ideal qualities of love, goodness, justice, compassion, and what ought to be, and not in terms of "this worldly" power or the empirical facts of what is, then does this not provide a potent and far-reaching condemnation of patriarchy as a distortion of human being? I think it does, and that many religious believers among the world religions think this way too. Rather than throwing out their world religion to which they belong and in which their faith has come to be constituted because of its historic failures, I think they would prefer to critically reform that tradition in a way that is both faithful to its founding ideals and supportive of women's equality. Of course the world religions and feminism are compatible. The contemporary challenge the latter poses to the former (and their respective patriarchal legacies) is a crucial piece within the dynamics of how Axial thought and self-criticism today continue to unfold.

COMPARING CIVILIZATIONS: DEGREES OF RESOLUTION

In the previous chapter, we looked from a high aerial perspective down on the first millennium BCE world. Along the long E-W axis of the Afroeurasian belt, a number of civilizations are becoming increasingly networked together, coalescing into a world-system—the axis formed the "trunk" of the "tree of world-history," with a number of big civilizations the corresponding "large branches" (and, at their "tips" or margins, the Axial movements would be the "new buds" that prove sufficiently "vigorous" to "branch out and overtop on all sides many a feebler branch"). Just as the abstract, minimal image of a "dividing line" became instead a "tree" as we examined the evidence more closely, so too the tree metaphor is forced to give way as we increase our degrees of resolution more; I have been using the metaphor of a landscape instead. Broad configurations could be discerned within the world-system landscape around the expansion of power, growth of civilizations and in urbanization, increase in militarization, the sacralization of kingship, the emergence of money, elaboration of literacy, and so on—the prominent "landmarks," if you will. In this chapter, we've dropped down much closer into the world-system, such that new details began to appear within this landscape: Four "forests" could be discerned and said to belong to the same "Axial" category. All of these "forests" grow interstitially, at the peripheries or within the margins of the prominent landmarks. They take root and grow at the edges of empires, from the outside looking in (Greece), or caught up between them, under threat (initially), then conquered (later), and in and out of exile in relation to them (Israel). Or, the forests grow betwixt and between a great diversity of lesser and greater cities and states that form a dynamic, moving patchwork during turbulent times of urbanization and state-formation (India and China). The patchworks themselves eventually form into a single controlling imperial force (the Magadha Maurya in India, the Qin and then Han in China; within the ancient Near East, Greece and Israel are overrun first by Alexander to initiate the period of Hellenistic dominance, followed thereafter by the Roman Empire). As we drop down further to observe the characteristics of these forests more closely, their more specific "family resemblances" show up.

In each area, the broad civilizational conditions that we observed at the world-system level manifests in terms of unprecedented volatility, dynamism, and change; the rise of cities, of territorial states, of massive empires ever-encroaching, of militarization, of massive social inequality, the great suffering and disenfranchisement of the many in direct and inverse proportion to the great power of the few. In each case, these will manifest in regionally and culturally specific ways. In each of the four cases, a consequence is that a particular class emerges, either entirely new (the *shi*, the *shramana*, the philosopher) or a subset of an existing class, dramatically transformed (the renunciate *sannyasin* from the ranks of the orthodox *brahman*, the "dissident intellectual" prophet from the diversity of the *nabi*). We notice something peculiar and frankly inexplicable: Particular individuals from within these new or transformed classes take an entirely unprecedented critical stance against power, whether against the actual empirical power of the king, the priesthood, the ruling classes, or against the more subtle power of convention and tradition to define what reality was supposed to be. Some born into a guarantee of power and rule, turn their back on it entirely. Others show extraordinary courage in speaking out against kings and rulers, admonishing them, rebuking them, criticizing them. Yet others live in poverty and modesty, scorning comfort, clothes, class distinctions, convention, eschewing fame or fortune. All show an unusual propensity to question received belief and defy, ignore, or adapt tradition and custom. Some pursue these countercultural ideas to ascetic extreme—living naked, undertaking systematic self-mutilation, masturbating in public, starving themselves to death—while most pursuits, although still radical, are less extreme, such as celibacy, vegetarianism, property held in common, fasting, simple dress, equality of all sexes and classes, and so on. Based on their inspirational example, groups of followers gather around these individuals to learn from them, write down their lessons, study their teachings, and live in accord with their principles. Schools form around specially selected texts and specifically chosen shared practices, different teachers and rival schools compete intensely over their interpretations, and from these intergroup dynamics, networks form themselves interstitial to the dominant powers in those areas.

Each, in their own distinctive language and dialect, present a spiritual revolution in consciousness, involving transcendence, inwardness, mystery, identity, the relation of the universal to the individual (the stuff of Chapter 3). Judging from their audience, what comes to the fore as perhaps strangest of all but also perhaps the most intriguing component within their teaching: They offer neither a different version of power nor an alternative form of power, but instead an entirely different sort of orientation. (And when even their most devout disciples get honest about it, they don't claim to understand well this different emphasis on an "other world," but conjoined to the deep regard in which they obviously hold the teacher, the clear attitude embodied in the disciple and conveyed to the casual audience member is that the deficiency lies in their own understanding, not in the sage's teaching.) To specify their critical stance against power one degree of resolution sharper: Above all what the Axial Age visionaries embody in how they live, and teach in both practice and theory, is a refusal to identify with civilizational power. Civilization's kings, its gods, its myths and ideologies, its cultural form of life, its affluence, its values, its conventions, none of these are presented as either necessary or the highest embodiment of human potential and of ultimate meaning. Instead of one based on power, they proffer a wholly different, and new, kind of identity to their followers. They propose a radical turning against "this world" defined by power (and hence, violent), and they offer an alternative identification with a different conception of reality, an "other world," wherein human potential and ultimate meaning are more subtle, more mysterious, and higher—nonviolent, better, more noble, more true—than what the dominant systems of power represent. What makes the "other world" other is that human being and human power are not at its center; what is at its center is the greater good, the better justice, the nobler truth, that transcends a human frame of reference and human scales of meaning.

WORLD CIVILIZATIONAL/RELIGIOUS CONSEQUENCES OF THE AXIAL AGE: SHAPING THE PRESENT

Of course, the world religions would seem to agree with the Axial Age position just articulated. But this appearance is deceptive, as the transcendent ground is also made over by those world religions into an ideological infrastructure that rationalizes transcendence to provide an institutional basis for a very powerful social organization aspiring to universality—meaning, aspiring to make itself not merely very powerful, but the most powerful. The universal, the univocal, "one story" slides into an ideology of exclusivism that arrogates truth and salvation, in the worst egotistic fashion, to only the group of believers. In this light, it is entirely understandable how Arnason, Eisenstadt, and Wittrock (2005) claim "the history of ideological politics can be traced back to the Axial Age" (p. 3). In understanding transcendence as ideology, it provides a group identity claiming universal status for its members, acting as a powerful ego-structure that elevates and expands the ego to an equally powerful degree. In accomplishing this, world religions profoundly mis-take their founding Axial Age intentions and practices that aim at countering power and overcoming the ego; they were not intended to accomplish the expanding of both. But this is exactly what happens in world history. In Lewis Mumford's (1956) words: "axial man took on the vices of the civilization he had become so adept at controlling and extending, and in that very triumph forfeited axial culture's chief reason for existence" (p. 78). The ideology-institution-identity triumvirate articulated by later interpreters of founding Axial visions attains "hemispheric-wide diffusion... in the form of world religions" through their alliance with "the emergence of a number of imperial political orders across the Eurasian hemisphere" (Wittrock, 2005, pp. 63–64).

In the first millennium BCE, the expansion of power of civilization took the form of a host of changes: the largest number and largest size of empires ever, the largest number and largest size of cities ever, the elevation of the ruler to the status of a god, the normalization of hierarchy within society with the ruling classes and priesthood on top and a complex division of labor and classes below, the massive increase in militarization, in slavery, and in warfare, the invention of money and private property, new functions and utilizations of literacy, and a new and greatly expanded role for ideology.

Across these changes, one theme emerges as new and crucially important: the need for a locus of identification that transcends these many differences that were manifesting alongside the expansion of power which would provide some unitary, perhaps even universal, category for membership. The new, unprecedented scale of power, the cluster of innovations composing the form in which power was expanding, and the equally unprecedented scale of suffering incurred and violence incited by this new scale of power and the forms it took add up to the fact that the need for transcendence at this time was overdetermined. If the Axial Age visionaries did not provide an understanding of transcendence as foundational for the formation of the world religions, someone else would have. In articulating breakthroughs to transcendence, the Axial Age sages and philosophers and prophets are not original. Jaspers' emphasis on the originality of the breakthroughs to transcendence and his claim that thinking universally for the first time is a characteristic of the Axial Age are both overstated. Political, economic, ideological, and religious versions of transcendence were already circulating that were each aiming to overcome the existing limits to identity. The explosive expansion in power meant the idea of universality was pushing its way into consciousness in a variety of forms. The originality of the *virtuosi* of the Axial Age lies elsewhere: in their deep sensitivity to suffering, in their conscious awareness of the dangers of power, and in the unique spiritual way in which they practiced and understood transcendence, and thus, the unique moral-ethical way in which they understood universality. What is key is the difference between "mere" consciousness-raising unconsciously and automatically occurring by natural processes, over against being raised into critical consciousness through systematic and sustained spiritual practice.

The state as an entity that transcended kinship, ethnicity, and regionality provides transcendent identity to a degree, i.e., "quasi-transcendentally," on the political front; the new economy based on an ever-increasing range of trade and above all on the quasi-transcendent function of money provides this identity from a different angle; similarly, literacy with its utilization of the quasi-transcendent capacities of text does so by way of the scribal elite of the priesthood; and religious ideology does so by providing an identity for the interstitial networks composed of emerging groups denied official power. In each case, the difficulties of a particular sub-section of the society mediating the transcendent claim to universality reside in their tying particular criteria for group membership, or particular content to reality for its participants, to their putatively transcendent, putatively universal claims.

Cognitively, the truly transcendent, truly universal claim was invariably compromised—rendered paradoxical? rendered hypocritical?—through its particularist coloring. This showed up in that the way the universal was idealized or imagined invariably proves tied to particular characteristics of the particular group idealizing that universal. Empirically, this meant that access to the universal, or criteria for membership for admission to universality, was restricted to the particular group that idealized that universal: The transcendent universality proclaimed by the ruling class of the state proved tied to kinship and ethnicity, as the power of that class was jealously guarded and retained through hereditary and/or ethnic links; the economic claim to transcendence or universality was tied to those with wealth or those who produced or traded the products with sufficient success; the transcendent claim to universal membership by way of literacy or ideology is mediated either by the priests as scribes of the state-sponsored religion or by advocates of new world religions claiming an identity beyond the state, and thus was tied to obeying their particular institutions, subscribing to their particular ideology, believing their particular doctrine. In short, the group identity that in part defines those groups, along with their new-found power, combine to corrupt the truth of the transcendence or universality idealized.

Combining the "macrosociological" big picture of civilizational power and world-system focus of the previous chapter together with the "mesosociological" focus on Axial movements of this chapter, the lineaments of sociology's contributions to understanding post-Axial world history become manifest. Michael Mann's (2012) world religions approach demonstrates how the "interstitial networks" that develop from their Axial Age beginnings go on to underpin ideology as a new competing form of power over against traditional forms of power (economic, military, and political) and which wins a place among them. Once established, this new form of ideological power, based on transcendent identity (in both Mann's terms and mine, although our definitions of transcendence vary slightly), or in the terms of the world religions, based on salvation, proves extraordinarily dynamic within the world-historical development of civilizations and of the world-system. Mann (2012) summarizes this dynamic power of "salvationism":

Such was its enhancement of power techniques, of social solidarity, of the possibilities for diffuse communication both vertically and horizontally, that whoever seized its organizations could change their social structure more radically than had probably ever been the case in prior history. A series of true revolutions rolled across Eurasia, led by ideological power techniques and organizations. (pp. 370–371)

Invoking this dynamism ties Mann's argument for how social power manifests as world religions into Axial Age scholarship claiming the consequences of the Axial Age have been central shapers to world history. It also dovetails quite well with Shmuel Eisenstadt's work, both his sociology of modernity and of the Axial Age. Eisenstadt also focuses on the importance these transcendental ideologies have for political dynamism and revolutionary potentials for those civilizations that incorporate them. Eisenstadt (2000) proposes a "multiple modernities" thesis that explains the current geopolitical state of the multi-civilizational globe in terms of elite networks as carriers and institutionalizers of cosmological visions containing a potent political dynamic within all the modernizing civilizations. This dynamic contains a particularly acute revolutionary potential in certain civilizations whose modernizing moments were announced by "Great Revolutions" (Eisenstadt, 2006). Randall Collins (1998) proposes a "global theory of intellectual change" based on these networks forming and sustaining an intellectual field marked by structural rivalry that began in the Axial Age in China, India, and Greece, and have lasted until the present (with Judaism making its "intellectual entrance" later). I have engaged these theorists in particular because I have focused on sociology as taking on, and taking over, the Axial Age thesis post-Jaspers, moving the scholarly focus away from the philosophy of history.

These are not the only scholars who interpret the Axial Age as having world-historical importance for, in my terms, creating "the shape of the present." I've emphasized them as they, like Robert Bellah, are sociologists who exemplify the turn in Axial Age scholarship from Jaspers' existential philosophy of history toward a more empirical, sociological account. There are other scholars, too, who are not sociologist but who also treat the Axial Age as crucial for understanding the present. Already mentioned a few times is Karen Armstrong, a religious studies scholar, whose argument in the aptly named *The Great Transformation* (2006) is akin to mine in construing the Axial Age as an ethical break from the violence of the past and aiming toward a more compassionate future. Another is philosopher Charles Taylor who in his 874 page tome *A Secular Age* (2007) attempts to theorize what secularization and secularism truly means. Crucial on his account is how the Axial Age "disembedded" aspects of human agency from their previously "embedded" status, due to being fixed by tradition, by way of a sustained attempt at "social reform." Political theorist Jonathan Bowman (2015) attempts something very different, providing a genealogy of conceptions of justice rooted in the Axial Age to ground a truly pluralistic—"cosmoipolitan"—basis for contemporary political understandings of justice that refuses any privilege to, for example, secular vs. religious positions. I will not multiply more examples, but merely want to illustrate the plausibility and productivity of the notion of the Axial Age as formative for the shape of the present.

In post-Axial world civilizations and/or religions—meaning those that incorporated Axial understandings within their ideology, and thus the contradictory, dynamic instability of incorporating both a deep critique of the civilizational status quo and a way to expand it further and deeper—the consequences are that they play the central role in defining the shape of world history over the past two millennia. Recalling our opening chapter, wherein it was pointed out that somewhere between 75 and 95% of the current world population belongs to several collective blocs of world civilizations or world religions, that present-day statistic has now been tied historically to sociological circumstances issuing from the Axial Age. Confucianism, Taoism, and later Buddhism shape Chinese thought and identity. Hinduism and Jainism, an absent Buddhism that haunts them like a ghost, and more recently Islam, compose the bulk of India's thought and identity. Beyond China and India, Buddhism has been crucially significant for Tibet, Mongolia, Korea, Japan, as well as Sri Lanka and much of Southeast Asia. Christianity, along with, building on, and in dynamic tension with, both Judaism and Greek thought, has defined European history (both East and West) and spread via European imperialism into the Americas, Africa, Australia, and parts of Asia. Islam too spread rapidly since its origin, dominating much of the Afroeurasian system for over a millennia prior to the more recent ascendance of Christianity and the West, while today it expands further and deeper into Europe, Asia, and Africa.

Reviewing our previous chapter in terms of providing a "map" of world history: In moving from evolutionary prehistory of the spread of human beings across the world to the emergence of civilizations, to the identification of the signal importance of the Afroeurasian world-system, and then to the further specification of the Axial Age movements within that system, we'd traced many of the most important lineaments of that map. In following the span of about 2500 years from the Axial Age until the present, outlined in this chapter in terms of the specific sociologies of the differing Axial Age movements, followed by the consequences of those movements in the development of world civilizations and world religions that become the multi-civilizational composition of the globe today, completes the map of world history in terms of those post-Axial civilizational dynamics that give the present its shape.

Reviewed critically from an Axial perspective, in every case the claim to transcendence made by the world civilization/world religion would be rejected. Rather than being a true transcendent, which stands over and above every (particular) one, or a true universal, which applies to all and is accessible to all, these claims to transcendence or universality disguised what they really were: elevations through power of particular identities—political, economic, religious, ideological—to highest overarching status. An individual who was a member of the ruling class, or the economic elite, or the priesthood, or post-Axial Age, of the "universal world religion," participated in the transcendent universal by virtue of being a member of that group. The ego identified with the larger group which in turn identified with being a transcendent identity, a universal self—the most high, lord of lords, king of kings. This is a powerful and power-fuelled fantasy, an entirely apposite psychological development that mirrors, on the individual level of the ego, the new scale of power developed on the collective level of the civilization. And it is the fantasy that has structured world history ever since the Axial Age, right until the present where that fantasy has, in apocalyptic fashion, revealed its "end" and its "meaning": as threatening the destruction of the world. But as we have seen in this chapter, in each of the Axial movements, there was a spiritually revolutionary response to this natural development that pierced through the illusions of the ego and the veil it casts over all of reality to force "this world" to fit its fantasy. The Axial Age teachers in each case reject "this world" and offer a transcendent vision of an "other world," irreducible to social convention, civilizational power, or the human ego. How they do so is through sustained, systematic, spiritual practice, the focus of our next chapter.

REFERENCES

Allchin, F. (Ed.). (1995). *The archaeology of early historic South Asia: The emergence of cities and states.* Cambridge: Cambridge University Press.

Armstrong, K. (2006). *The great transformation: The beginning of our religious traditions.* New York and Toronto: Alfred A. Knopf.

Arnason, J. (2005). The axial conundrum: Between historical sociology and the philosophy of history. In E. Ben-Rafael & Y. Sternberg (Eds.), *Comparing modernities: Pluralism versus homogeneity* (pp. 57–82). Leiden and Boston: Brill.

Arnason, J., Eisenstadt, S., & Wittrock, B. (2005). General introduction. In J. Arnason, S. Eisenstadt, & B. Wittrock (Eds.), *Axial civilizations and world history* (pp. 1–12). Leiden: Brill.

Assmann, J. (2005). Axial "breakthroughs" and semantic "relocation" in ancient Egypt and Israel. In J. Arnason, S. Eisenstadt, & B. Wittrock (Eds.), *Axial civilizations and world history* (pp. 133–156). Leiden: Brill.

Ball, W. (2010). *Out of Arabia: Phoenicians, Arabs and the discovery of Europe.* Northampton, MA: Olive Branch Press.

Barker, M. (2004). *The great high priest: The temple roots of Christian liturgy.* New York and London: T&T Clark.

Baskin, K., & Bondarenko, D. (2014). *The Axial Ages of world history: Lessons for the 21st century.* Litchfield Park, AZ: Emergent Publishing.

Baumard, N., Hyafil, A., Morris, I., & Boyer, P. (2015). Increased affluence explains emergence of ascetic wisdoms and moralizing religions. *Current Biology, 25*(1), 10–15.

Bellah, R. (2011). *Religion in human evolution: From the Paleolithic to the Axial Age.* Belknap: Harvard, MA.

Bellah, R., & Joas, H. (2012). Introduction. In R. Bellah & H. Joas (Eds.), *The Axial Age and its consequences* (pp. 1–6). Cambridge and London: Belknap.

Blenkinsopp, J. (1995). *Sage, priest, prophet: Religious and intellectual leadership in ancient Israel.* Louisville, KY: John Knox Press.

Bowman, J. (2015). *Cosmoipolitan justice: The Axial Age, multiple modernities, and the postsecular turn.* Cham: Springer.

Bronkhorst, J. (1998). *The two sources of Indian asceticism.* New Delhi: Motilal Banarsidass.

Bronkhorst, J. (2000). *The two traditions of meditation in ancient India.* New Delhi: Motilal Banarsidass.

Bronkhorst, J. (2007). *Greater Magadha: Studies in the culture of early India.* Leiden: Brill.

Bronkhorst, J. (2011). *Buddhism in the shadow of Brahmanism.* Leiden: Brill.

Burkert, W. (1992). *The orientalizing revolution: Near Eastern influence on Greek culture in the early archaic age* (M. E. Pinder & W. Burkert, Trans.). Cambridge, MA: Harvard University Press.

Burkert, W. (2004). *Babylon, Memphis, Persepolis: Eastern contexts of Greek culture*. Cambridge, MA: Harvard University Press.

Buss, M. (2006). The place of Israelite prophecy in human history. In B. Kelle & M. Moore (Eds.), *Israel's prophets and Israel's past* (pp. 325–341). New York and London: T&T Clark.

Christian, D. (2000). Silk roads or steppe roads? The silk roads in world history. *Journal of World History, 11*(1), 1–26.

Collins, R. (1998). *The sociology of philosophies: A global theory of intellectual change*. Cambridge and London: Belknap Harvard.

Dhalla, M. (1938). *History of Zoroastrianism*. New York: Oxford University Press.

Dodds, E. R. (1951). *The Greeks and the irrational*. Berkeley and Los Angeles: University of California.

Duchrow, U., & Hinkelammert, F. (2012). *Transcending greedy money: Interreligious solidarity for just relations*. New York: Palgrave Macmillan.

Dundas, P. (2002). *The Jains*. London and New York: Routledge.

Dundas, P. (2006). A non-imperial religion? Jainism in its "Dark Age". In P. Olivelle (Ed.), *Between the empires: Society in India 300 BCE to 400 CE* (pp. 383–414). Oxford and New York: Oxford University Press.

Edelman, D. (Ed.). (1996). *The triumph of Elohim: From Yahwisms to Judaisms*. Grand Rapids, MI: Eerdmans.

Edelman, D., & Ben Zvi, E. (Eds.). (2009). *The production of prophecy: Constructing prophecy and prophets in Yehud*. London and Oakville: Equinox.

Eisenstadt, S. (2000). Multiple modernities. *Daedalus, 129*(1), 1–29.

Eisenstadt, S. (2006). *The great revolutions and the civilizations of modernity*. Leiden: Brill.

Eliade, M. (1969). *Yoga: Immortality and freedom* (W. Trask, Trans.). Princeton: Bollingen.

Eliade, M. (1982). *A history of religious ideas: Vol. 2, from Gautama Buddha to the triumph of Christianity* (W. Trask, Trans.). Chicago: University of Chicago Press.

Elkana, Y. (1986). The emergence of second-order thinking in classical Greece. In S. Eisenstadt (Ed.), *The origins and diversity of Axial Age civilizations* (pp. 40–64). Albany: State University of New York Press.

Eno, R. (1990). *The Confucian creation of heaven: Philosophy and the defense of ritual mastery*. Albany, NY: SUNY Press.

Erdosy, G. (1995a). The prelude to urbanization: Ethnicity and the rise of Late Vedic chiefdoms. In F. Allchin (Ed.), *The archaeology of early historic South*

Asia: The emergence of cities and states (pp. 75–98). Cambridge: Cambridge University Press.

Erdosy, G. (1995b). City states of North India and Pakistan at the time of the Buddha. In F. Allchin (Ed.), *The archaeology of early historic South Asia: The emergence of cities and states* (pp. 99–122). Cambridge: Cambridge University Press.

Fairservis, W. (1997). The Harappan civilization and the Rgveda. In M. Witzel (Ed.), *Inside the texts, beyond the texts: New approaches to the study of the Vedas* (pp. 61–68). Cambridge: Harvard University Press.

Feuerstein, G., Kak, S., & Frawley D. (2001). *In search of the cradle of civilization: New light on ancient India*. Wheaton, IL: Quest.

Floyd, M. (2006). Introduction. In M. Floyd & R. Haak (Eds.), *Prophets, prophecy, and prophetic texts in second temple Judaism* (pp. 1–25). New York and London: T&T Clark.

Fraade, S. (1991). *From tradition to commentary: Torah and its interpretation in the Midrash Sifre to Deuteronomy*. Albany: State University of New York Press.

Frank, A. G., & Gills, B. (Eds.). (1993). *The world system: Five hundred years or five thousand?* London and New York: Routledge.

Garland, R. (2014). *Wandering Greeks: The ancient Greek diaspora from the age of Homer to the death of Alexander the Great*. Princeton and Oxford: Princeton University Press.

Grabbe, L. (1995). *Priests, prophets, diviners, sages: A socio-historical study of religious specialists in ancient Israel*. Valley Forge, PA: Trinity Press International.

Grabbe, L. (2004). *A history of the Jews and Judaism in the Second Temple period. Vol. I: Yehud: A history of the Persian province of Judah*. London and New York: T&T Clark.

Grabbe, L. (2016). Prophecy and priesthood. In C. Sharp (Ed.), *The Oxford handbook of the prophets* (pp. 23–36). Oxford: Oxford University Press.

Graeber, D. (2011). *Debt: The first 5,000 years*. Brooklyn and London: Melville House.

Graham, A. (1989). *Disputers of the Tao: Philosophical argument in ancient China*. La Salle, IL: Open Court.

Green, A. (1986). Introduction. In A. Green (Ed.), *Jewish spirituality: From the Bible through the Middle Ages* (pp. xiii–xxv). New York: Crossroad.

Hadot, P. (1995). *Philosophy as a way of life: Spiritual exercises from Socrates to Foucault* (A. Davidson, Ed.). Oxford and Cambridge: Blackwell.

Hadot, P. (2002). *What is ancient philosophy?* (M. Chase, Trans.). Cambridge and London: Belknap (originally published in 1995).

Halpern, B., & Sacks, K. (Eds.). (2017). *Cultural contact and appropriation in the Axial-Age Mediterranean world: A periplos*. Leiden and Boston: Brill.

Hamilton, S. (2000). *Early Buddhism: A new approach: The I of the beholder.* Richmond, Surrey: Curzon.

Hartnett, R. (2011). *The Jixia Academy and the birth of higher learning in China: A comparison of fourth-century B.C. Chinese education with ancient Greece.* London: Mellen.

Heesterman, J. (1986). Ritual, revelation, and Axial Age. In S. Eisenstadt (Ed.), *The origins and diversity of Axial Age civilizations* (pp. 393–406). Albany: State University of New York Press.

Heesterman, J. (1997). Vedism and Hinduism. In G. Oberhammer (Ed.), *Studies in Hinduism: Vedism and Hinduism* (pp. 43–68). Vienna: Österreichische Akademie der Wissenschaften.

Hsu, C. (1999). The Spring and Autumn period. In M. Loewe & E. Shuaughnessy (Eds.), *The Cambridge history of ancient China: From the origins of civilization to 221 B.C.* (pp. 545–586). Cambridge and New York: Cambridge University Press.

Humphreys, S. (1986). Dynamics of the Greek breakthrough: The dialogue between philosophy and religion. In S. Eisenstadt (Ed.), *The origins and diversity of Axial Age civilizations* (pp. 92–110). Albany: State University of New York Press.

Jaspers, K. (1953). *The origin and goal of history.* New Haven and London: Yale University Press (originally published in 1949).

Johnson, A. (1962). *The cultic prophet in ancient Israel.* Cardiff: University of Wales Press.

Karttunen, K. (1989). *India in early Greek literature.* Helsinki: Finnish Oriental Society.

Kohn, L. (2012). *Daoism and Chinese culture.* Dunedin, FL: Three Pines Press.

Kulke, H. (1986). The historical background of India's Axial Age. In S. Eisenstadt (Ed.), *The origins and diversity of Axial Age Civilizations* (pp. 374–392). Albany: State University of New York Press.

Landes, R. (2011). *Heaven on earth: The varieties of the millennial experience.* Oxford: Oxford University Press.

Lewis, M. (1999). Warring states: Political history. In M. Loewe & E. Shuaughnessy (Eds.), *The Cambridge history of ancient China: From the origins of civilization to 221 B.C.* (pp. 587–650). Cambridge and New York: Cambridge University Press.

Lindblom, J. (1962). *Prophecy in ancient Israel.* Philadelphia: Fortress Press.

Mair, V. (1990). Afterword, Part III: Parallels between Taoism and yoga. In *Tao te ching: The classic book of integrity and the way: Lao Tzu* (pp. 140–148 & Appendix, pp. 155–161). New York: Quality.

Mann, M. (2012). *The sources of social power* (Vol. 1). New York: Cambridge University Press.

McEvilley, T. (2002). *The shape of ancient thought: Comparative studies in Greek and Indian philosophies.* New York: Allworth Press.

McNeill, W. (1963). *The rise of the west: A history of the human community.* Chicago and London: University of Chicago.

Meier, C. (1986). The emergence of an autonomous intelligence among the Greeks. In S. Eisenstadt (Ed.), *The origins and diversity of Axial Age civilizations* (pp. 64–91). Albany: State University of New York Press.

Meier, C. (1998). *Athens: A portrait of the city in its golden age* (Robert & R. Kimber, Trans.). New York: Metropolitan Books, H. Holt & Co.

Middlemas, J. (2016). Prophecy and diaspora. In C. Sharp (Ed.), *The Oxford handbook of the prophets* (pp. 37–54). Oxford: Oxford University Press.

Momigliano, A. (1975). *Alien wisdom: The limits of hellenization.* Cambridge: Cambridge University Press.

Mumford, L. (1956). *The transformations of man.* Gloucester, MA: Peter Smith.

Murphy, F. (2000). Second Temple Judaism. In J. Neusner & A. Avery-Peck (Eds.), *The Blackwell companion to Judaism* (pp. 58–77). Oxford: Blackwell.

Nicholson, E. (2010). Deuteronomy 18.9-22, the prophets and scripture. In J. Day (Ed.), *Prophecy and the prophets in ancient Israel* (pp. 151–171). New York and London: T&T Clark.

Nissinen, M. (2006). The dubious image of prophecy. In M. Floyd & R. Haak (Eds.), *Prophets, prophecy, and prophetic texts in second temple Judaism* (pp. 26–41). New York and London: T&T Clark.

Nissinen, M. (2010). Prophetic madness: Prophecy and ecstasy in the ancient Near East and in Greece. In K. Noll & B. Schramm (Eds.), *Raising up a faithful exegete: Essays in honor of Richard D. Nelson* (pp. 3–29). Winona Lake, IN: Eisenbrauns.

Nissinen, M. (2016). Prophetic intermediation in the ancient Near East. In C. Sharp (Ed.), *The Oxford handbook of the prophets* (pp. 5–22). Oxford: Oxford University Press.

Noll, K. (2013). Presumptuous prophets in a Deuteronomic debate. In M. Boda & L. Beal (Eds.), *Prophets, prophecy, and ancient Israelite historiography* (pp. 125–142). Winona Lake, IN: Eisenbrauns.

Ober, J. (2015). *The rise and fall of classical Greece.* Princeton and Oxford: Princeton University Press.

Obryk, M. (2016). On affirmation, rejection and accommodation of the world in Greek and Indian religion. In R. Seaford (Ed.), *Universe and inner self in early Indian and early Greek thought* (pp. 235–250). Edinburgh: Edinburgh University Press.

Olivelle, P. (2011). *Ascetics and Brahmins: Studies in ideologies and institutions.* London, New York, and New Delhi: Anthem Press.

Rajaram, N. S., & Frawley, D. (1995). *Vedic 'Aryans' and the origins of civilization: A literary and scientific perspective.* Quebec City: WH Press.

Ramelli, I. (2016). *Social justice and the legitimacy of slavery: The role of philosophical asceticism from ancient Judaism to late antiquity.* Oxford: Oxford University Press.

Ray, H. P. (1995). Trade and contacts. In R. Thapar (Ed.), *Recent perspectives on Indian history* (pp. 142–175). Bombay: Popular Prakashan.

Roetz, H. (1992). *Confucian ethics of the Axial Age: A reconstruction under the aspect of the breakthrough toward postconventional thinking.* Albany, NY: SUNY Press.

Roth, H. (1999). *Original Tao: Inward training (nei-yeh) and the foundations of Taoist mysticism.* New York: Columbia University.

Rowley, H. H. (1956). *Prophecy and religion in ancient China and Israel.* London: University of London, Athlone Press.

Sagan, E. (1991). *The honey and the hemlock: Democracy and paranoia in ancient Athens and modern America.* New York: Basic Books.

Samuel, G. (2008). *The origins of yoga and tantra: Indic religions to the thirteenth century.* Cambridge: Cambridge University Press.

Sanderson, S. K. (2018). *Religious evolution and the Axial Age: From shamans to priests to prophets.* London: Bloomsbury.

Schmidt, B. (2010). *Utopian communities of the ancient world: Idealistic experiments of Pythagoras, the Essenes, Pachomius, and Proclus.* Lewiston, NY: Edwin Mellen.

Schwartz, B. (Ed.). (1975). Wisdom, revelation, and doubt: Perspectives on the first millennium B.C. *Special Issue of Daedalus, 104*(2), 1–7.

Schwartz, B. (1985). *The world of thought in ancient China.* Belknap: Cambridge, MA.

Seaford, R. (2004). *Money and the early Greek mind.* Cambridge: Cambridge University Press.

Seaford, R. (Ed.). (2016a). *Universe and inner self in early Indian and early Greek thought.* Edinburgh: Edinburgh University Press.

Seaford, R. (2016b). Introduction. In R. Seaford (Ed.), *Universe and inner self in early Indian and early Greek thought* (pp. 1–12). Edinburgh: Edinburgh University Press.

Seligman, A. (Ed.). (1989). *Order and transcendence: The role of utopias and the dynamics of civilizations.* Leiden: Brill.

Shaffer, L. (1994). Southernization. *Journal of World History, 5*(1), 1–22.

Shaked, S. (2005). Zoroastrian origins: Indian and Iranian connections. In J. Arnason, S. Eisenstadt, & B. Wittrock (Eds.), *Axial civilizations and world history* (pp. 183–200). Leiden: Brill.

Shils, E. (1986). Some observations on the place of intellectuals in Max Weber's sociology, with special reference to Hinduism. In S. Eisenstadt (Ed.), *The origins and diversity of Axial Age civilizations* (pp. 427–452). Albany: State University of New York Press.

Silver, K. (2017). *Alexandria and Qumran: Back to the beginning.* Oxford: Archaeopress.

Smith, M. (2002). *The early history of God: Yahweh and the other deities in ancient Israel.* Dearborn, MI: Eerdmans.

Sweeney, M. (2000). The religious world of ancient Israel to 586 BCE. In J. Neusner & A. Avery-Peck (Eds.), *The Blackwell companion to Judaism* (pp. 20–36). Oxford: Blackwell.

Taylor, C. (2007). *A secular age.* Belknap: Cambridge and London.

Taylor, J. (2004). *Pythagoreans and Essenes: Structural parallels.* Paris and Louvain: Peeters.

Taylor, J. (2012). *The Essenes, the scrolls, and the Dead Sea.* Oxford: Oxford University Press.

Tellier, L. (2009). *Urban world history: An economic and geographical perspective.* Québec City: Presses de l'Université du Québec.

Thapar, R. (1995). The first millennium B.C. in northern India. In R. Thapar (Ed.), *Recent perspectives on Indian history* (pp. 80–141). Bombay: Popular Prakashan.

Thompson, T. (1996). The intellectual matrix of early Biblical narrative: Inclusive monotheism in Persian period Palestine. In D. V. Edelmann (Ed.), *The triumph of Elohim: From Yahwisms to Judaisms* (pp. 107–124). Grand Rapids, MI: Eerdmans.

Thompson, W. (2005). Eurasian C-wave crises in the first millennium B.C. In C. Chase-Dunn & E. N. Anderson (Eds.), *The historical evolution of world-systems* (pp. 20–51). New York: Palgrave Macmillan.

Uffenheimer, B. (1986). Myth and reality in ancient Israel. In S. Eisenstadt (Ed.), *The origins and diversity of Axial Age civilizations* (pp. 135–168). Albany: State University of New York Press.

van Norden, B. (2007). *Virtue ethics and consequentialism in early Chinese philosophy.* New York: Cambridge University Press.

van Seters, J. (2006). Prophecy as prediction in Biblical historiography. In M. Floyd & R. Haak (Eds.), *Prophets, prophecy, and prophetic texts in second temple Judaism* (pp. 93–103). New York and London: T&T Clark.

Vidal, G. (1981). *Creation.* London: Heinemann.

Voegelin, E. (1956). *Order and History, Vol. I: Israel and revelation.* Baton Rouge: Louisiana State University Press.

Weinfeld, M. (1986). The protest against imperialism in ancient Israelite prophecy. In S. Eisenstadt (Ed.), *The origins and diversity of Axial Age civilizations* (pp. 169–182). Albany: State University of New York Press.

West, M. (1971). *Early Greek philosophy and the Orient.* Oxford: Clarendon Press.

West, M. (1997). *The east face of Helicon: West Asiatic elements in Greek poetry and myth.* Oxford: Clarendon Press.

Wilson, R. (1980). *Prophecy and society in ancient Israel.* Philadelphia: Fortress Press.

Wittrock, B. (2005). The meaning of the Axial Age. In J. Arnason, S. Eisenstadt, & B. Wittrock (Eds.), *Axial civilizations and world history* (pp. 51–86). Leiden: Brill.

Witzel, M. (1997). The Vedic canon and its political milieu. In M. Witzel (Ed.), *Inside the texts, beyond the texts: New approaches to the study of the Vedas* (pp. 257–346). Cambridge: Harvard University Press.

CHAPTER 6

The Axial Road Not Taken: Spiritual Practices of Transcendence

Practicing Transcendence

In this chapter, I present my own take on what is truly distinctive about the Axial Age. Rather than focus on the consequences the Axial Age had on subsequent history as a way of judging what it was about (as virtually all scholarship has done), I focus on what the Axial Age spiritual *virtuosi* were doing and saying, practicing and preaching, within the horizon of their own historical moment. My interpretation is that the Axial Age's distinctive contribution to world history is sustained, systematic, spiritual practice. As spiritual, this practice is aimed at transforming the self: the sustained systematic disciplining of conscious attentional focus to be inward, such that consciousness is focused on consciousness itself, rather than outwardly on things of "this world." The initial outcome of such practice was (and is) experienced as "breaking through" the horizon of ordinary consciousness and meaning. (The new horizon of meaning "broken into" is therefore experienced as transcendent). As I hope this chapter will make clear, such sustained, systematic, disciplined practice has the further effect of stabilizing this transcendent consciousness for the practitioner, who in precisely this experiential, practical, sense, is now living in an "other world." In Jaspers' terms, a "spiritualization" of consciousness.

Initially, the inward focus of such spiritual practice means a focus on the self. But this focus on the self is not for the sake of the self, it is rather because the self is the problem that has to be overcome.

© The Author(s) 2019
C. Peet, *Practicing Transcendence*,
https://doi.org/10.1007/978-3-030-14432-6_6

Ultimately, the focus of the practice on transcendence—i.e., on the spiritual practitioner realizing transcendence experientially and consciously, a realization that is only possible from a "position" within consciousness beyond the self and its egocentrism. However, to get there, the practice has to go "through" the self; the self is the primary obstacle to transcendence and therefore, until it is overcome, it is the means to transcendence. The egocentric self is also the reason for the deep and pervasive misunderstanding of what transcendence really is and means. Egocentrically misunderstood, for example, the point of the practice would seem to be that the ego gains something, improves itself, betters itself, attains some new status and standing, some greater power or insight. Put most simply, the egocentric misunderstanding of the point of the practice is that the ego gains a new, better identity.

Described negatively, I understand the primary intent of the various Axial Age teachers not to have been to provide the world with ideas, philosophy, metaphysics, dogma, theology, or any kind of intellectual contribution. They do that, but it's a side effect of the practice. Nor do I see their aim being to emancipate and extract the individual from an immersive identification within their particular group, tribe, state, or whatever expanded collective identity the ego can achieve through enlisting the transformations effected through practice back into its service. They accomplish this too, but this is also a side effect of the practice. Their ultimate aim is not intellectual or religious, not to provide ideas or an ideology or beliefs, not to found some new institutions, nor to create some new group identity to which the practitioner belongs. Their primary intent is apparently much smaller and more modest, an intent of practical spirituality. They aim to teach others how to "practice transcendence," which in practical terms simply means conscious experience of reality without the ego at the center of that experience.

In this practical sense, transcendence is nothing mysterious, grand, or mystical. It is certainly not anything supernatural; as Ken Wilber (1998) puts it, "in fact there is nothing special about it all" (p. 239). However, because in ordinary consciousness reality is experienced egocentrically, the claims about transcendence that issue from experienced practitioners are rendered enigmatic, paradoxical, if not incomprehensible. Much of this is due to egocentric misunderstanding of the fullness of reality which reduces the latter to nothing but "this world" centered on the ego. Over the course of life, this egocentrist reduction of the fullness of reality becomes entrenched as ordinary, normal, habitual, conventional, taken for granted, a "realistic" perspective perhaps; as after all what else could there be? Over against this establishment of an egocentrically defined version of "this world" as all there is to reality, through sufficient sustained, systematic, disciplined practice the practitioner increasingly stabilizes a "transcendent consciousness" of "transcendent reality" and becomes increasingly "other worldly." For the practitioner, this transformation in the identity of the world is what they are after; their ego and their self is what prevents the fullness of reality. He or she is not focused on the ego or the self or changing his or her own identity—although it happens, that change, too, is merely a side effect of practice; after all, if the identity of the world transforms because you have overcome your own blindness to it, of course you will "see" yourself differently, as you are part of the world, too.

The Failure of the Axial Age

One piece prompting my interpretation of the Axial Age being above all about spiritual practices is a different remarkable claim made by Jaspers: "the Axial Period, too, ended in failure" (1953, p. 20). I've cited it a few times already in previous chapters. Jaspers is interested in the Axial Age because, presumably, of its "success": i.e., it has substantially impacted world history for the last 2500 years; demographically, 75–95% of the world today thinks or believes in its terms; Jaspers describes in numerous different ways how "the world history of humanity derives its structure from this period" (1953, pp. 262–263), and so on. That he also claims it "ended in failure," when set against this backdrop of its presumably world-historical significance, is remarkable in the extreme! Perhaps most remarkable, it poses a huge question mark directed at the other influential interpretation of the Axial Age—that its meaning or distinctive contribution is the major world religions are founded by it. If the latter interpretation is correct, then it did not fail, but succeeded admirably. According to Jaspers' failure claim, however, there would have to be some significant disjunct between world religions as "post-Axial developments" and the Axial Age proper. This has informed my own interpretation that what is truly distinctive about the Axial Age was its discovery or innovation of systematic practices of transcendence.

In advancing this proposal, the claim is that world religions differ from the Axial Age precisely around the role and significance of these practices. For world religions, my argument is that the ideology-institution-identity triumvirate is what is central: The religious believer makes a particular identification, tied to membership in the group, articulated in terms of particular ideologies and belief systems themselves upheld by and maintained through particular institutions, all of which together make up a particular "big power structure." For the Axial Age visionaries, none of this is central to what they were about, if anything a type of betrayal of their criticism of big power which was their very premise and motivation for small, practical spirituality. Instead, they aim for systematic spiritual practice, which socially requires a small community, and which personally turns the practitioner inward so as to effect a thorough-going transformation of his or her person.

This practice conception is very different from transcendence understood as an idea. The latter leads to an ideology or belief system and becomes elaborated cognitively and intellectually: as metaphysics, philosophy, theology, ontology, theory, doctrine, etc. There is no doubting that every one of the post-Axial elaborations of the original Axial visions—Confucianism, Taoism; Hinduism, Buddhism, Jainism; Judaism; whatever strand of Greek philosophy you choose, but most famously Platonism and Aristotelianism; later Christianity, and later still Islam—are in each case extraordinary theoretical systems of thought. But here is the rub: If *theoria*, on the original Greek conception (from which the English word theory derives), is meant as a practice, as the systematic transformation of one's spirit through rigorous exercises and disciplines, then all of the "cognitive-intellectual elaborations" just enumerated, no matter how sophisticated, are literally "beside" the point. (If they claim to be the truth, they are also "missing" the point, and since they do claim to be the truth, and claim to be the ultimate exclusive truth, the consequences have been, and are, momentous.) Pierre Hadot (1995) makes the point in the following way regarding ancient Greek philosophical texts: "Above all, the work, even if it is apparently theoretical and systematic, is written not so much to inform the reader of a doctrinal content but to form him, to make him traverse a certain itinerary in the course of which he will make spiritual progress. …One must always approach a philosophical work of antiquity with this idea of spiritual progress in mind" (p. 64). Hadot's point, extended to apply critically as a corrective to all the post-Axial elaborations of Axial Age movements in ideological, theoretical terms rather than those rooted in practice, summarizes my own argument in a nutshell.

It was based on practices of transcendence developed during the Axial Age that the claim was made that there was a higher and better truth in which human being participated universally and not tribally; that this higher, transcendent reality was the true source of fulfillment and identity, and carried with it moral and ethical qualities of goodness, love, compassion, and justice that we are called on to realize as the way to participate in transcendence. From this basis, the spiritual *virtuosi* of the Axial Age offer a spiritual evaluation of power at their time that we can apply beyond to the historical record (and today, apply to the evolutionary record too), which accords value in history neither to the sequence of brute events nor to the empirical facts of what happened but to the qualities of meaning that animated these facts or to the degree of consciousness through which the events were experienced, a degree always measured relative to some higher ideal.

To gain such a spiritual perspective, however, we have to turn against ourselves, against our naturally evolved and historically reinforced tribalism, against the natural tendency to expansion and its historically amplified human form of expansionism. Nietzsche (2007) describes the unprecedented nature of this inward turn with a suitable and typically Nietzschean sense of drama: "Let us immediately add that, on the other hand, the prospect of an animal soul turning against itself, taking a part against itself, was something so new, profound, unheard-of, puzzling, contradictory and *momentous* on earth that the whole character of the world changed in an essential way" (p. 57). Nietzsche perceives this "turning against ourselves" claim to amount to "the whole character of the world" being "changed in an essential way." This change is so *momentous* (his emphasis) because Nietzsche perceives (correctly, I think) that the ascetic, self-denying quality involved in "turning against oneself" is radically antithetical to our nature as developed through our evolutionary heritage of self-assertion, egocentrism, tribalism, and expansionism. To turn within consciousness, inwardly toward ourselves, and further against our selves, is truly "momentous" vis-à-vis both our natural evolution and our human history. Evolution and history evidences that we "naturally" turn our attention outward: Our tribe consumes resources within its territory and then moves on; we define our tribe over against other tribes, often violently; and we expand our tribe out into new territory, and fight for it, and consume it. The natural evolution of organisms on earth, developing into the natural history of human beings developing a tribal form of life that expands across the earth, culminating in the last three millennia into unprecedented expansions of human power, has eventuated in our present moment: the whole world in crisis. The inward turn inverts that entire outward expansion, and its violent, consumptive, orientation. Violence and consumption, turned inward against oneself, is an ascetic orientation. The ascetic orientation leads to a position of transcendence, which exercises a deep, moral-ethical, self-responsible consciousness that criticizes and evaluates in spiritual terms the expansion of power as a dangerous evil, that magnifies and enhances what is base, violent, selfish, and egocentric in human nature, and proposes an alternative, spiritual vision of a human nature transformed toward its highest goodness, which is selfless, nonviolent, compassionate, and loving.

For Jaspers, the outcome of this ascetic orientation, of this reflexive turning back and in upon oneself, was the positing of a transcendent universal in which humanity could attain a meaningful unity; this transcendent universal animates the facts of history and brings its events into consciousness in a whole new light, now within an overarching horizon of a "world history" (even if we do not know its "origin" nor can foresee its "goal"). In providing this claim, the sages and visionaries of the Axial Age offered a choice for how to proceed, to continue on the civilizational "road more travelled" of expanding power, or to alter course and take their countercultural "road less travelled" of an ascetic spiritual path. That world religions and world civilizations invariably choose the former means that the Axial Age "ended in failure." "Success," then, would have been if a sufficient critical mass of followers embarked on the road less travelled. In this speculative alternative scenario, world history would have taken a vastly different route, and perhaps sufficient critical conscious awareness would have diverted us from an expansion of power that threatens the world as a whole.

That has not happened, of course, and this book is about the present world in crisis that we have created, trying to face that crisis and take responsibility for it. Axial Age spiritual practices are not some magical solution to our crisis nor will they "save the world" in some supernatural way. My interpretation of Axial spiritualities is far more empirical, small-scale, and practical than that; when it comes to practicing transcendence, "in fact, there is nothing special about it all." In fact, counterintuitively to the ego's assumptions, it is precisely in their empirical, small-scale, and practical terms that I think they have such a vital role to play and contribution to make. Trying to describe more precisely this role and contribution returns us to the issue of understanding Axiality as a family resemblance (a view of the Axial Age which is not entirely distinctive, e.g., see John Hick [1989, pp. 3–5] or Jan Assmann [2012, p. 400]). On a family resemblance basis, to argue for systematic spiritual practice rather than ideas, or an intellectual class, or ideology, or an institutionalization, as the distinctive contribution of the Axial Age isn't an interpretation in terms of which one is right or wrong (nor to argue for which one is the "essence" of Axiality) but to argue for a shift of emphasis in how the whole ensemble of factors that collectively make up "Axiality" was configured and balanced. That is how I'm proceeding. The emphasis on ideas, elites, ideologies, identities, or institutions is only "wrong" to the extent that it ignores or underemphasizes systematic spiritual practice and therefore presents a lopsided, imbalanced picture of the whole ensemble of factors. Recalling Chapter 3, what the Axial Age visionaries accomplish isn't creating something from scratch, but a transformation in meaning of the whole ensemble of myth, ritual, religion. Previously, there were ascetic practices, moments, glimpses, insights, as well as shamans, healers, ritual specialists, magicians, and diviners; after, they have become systematically unified into a new Gestalt of meaning and practice. There is a new and more pronounced degree of systematization of ascetic elements into a coherent whole of spiritual practice that is new. As I tried to show in the previous chapter, each Axial Age movement in each particular civilization was rich, complex, multi-levelled, and multi-dimensional. This should not be misunderstood in anti-intellectual fashion that each movement is therefore whatever you want them to be; definite limits and boundaries should be drawn; and articulations should be made tight enough for scholarship to criticize, reject, and improve generalizations and comparative claims about the Axial Age.

In the case of sustained, systematic, disciplined spiritual practices, this has assumed exemplary and well-known form in Buddhism and Hinduism. I presume it requires no argument to make the case for asceticism as basic to Indian religiosity—images of meditating Buddhas or of yoga postures have become ubiquitous. Rather, the spiritual practice of Indian religions as exemplary and well known provides a starting point from which to build up a family resemblance as we examine the other Axial cases. Unlike the previous chapter where I followed geography and presented each Axial case going from east to west, the sequence we will follow in this chapter proceeds by going from the easiest case to the hardest case. Starting with India we will then look at each progressively harder case to demonstrate systematic spiritual practices in each movement: Thus, we will next look at China, then Greece, and finally Israel.

AXIAL AGE PRACTICES OF TRANSCENDENCE: ASCETIC RENUNCIATION IN INDIA

Olivelle (2011) begins his discussion of asceticism in India with two striking descriptions taken from the *Gautama Dharmasūtra*. The first describes rules for a *brahman* who has chosen to live as an anchorite:

> An anchorite shall live in the forest, living on roots and fruits and given to austerities. He kindles the sacred fire according to the procedure for recluses and refrains from eating what is grown in a village. He may also avail himself of the flesh of animals killed by predators. He should not step on plowed land or enter a village. He shall wear matted hair and clothes of bark or skin and never eat anything that has been stored for more than a year. (p. 12)

This choice of anchorite life is distinct from choosing to be a mendicant, which the *Sūtra* describes as follows:

> A mendicant shall live without any possessions, be chaste, and remain in one place during the rainy season. Let him enter a village only to obtain alms food and go on his begging round late in the evening, without visiting the same house twice and without pronouncing blessings. He shall control his speech, sight, and actions; and wear a garment to cover his private parts, using, according to some, a discarded piece of cloth after washing it. Outside the rainy season, he should not spend two nights in the same village. He shall be shaven-headed or wear a topknot; refrain from injuring seeds; treat all creatures alike, whether they cause him harm or treat him with kindness; and not undertake ritual activities. (p. 12)

In both cases, we see a lengthy set of restrictions, applied to possessions, clothing, food, and shelter. The anchorite is restricted from any kind of contact with anything produced by human culture, except for "kindling the sacred fire," the most basic and ubiquitous ritual overseen by *brahmans*. The mendicant has far more cultural contact; however, this contact is strictly circumscribed—no possessions, no sexual relations, no staying two nights or visiting the same house for alms twice; he must control speech, sight, action, and dress; his relations to both seeds and "all creatures alike" are to be marked by nonviolence (*ahimsa*). Unlike the anchorite, he does not undertake ritual activities nor can he pronounce blessings on houses (i.e., he can contribute nothing to laypeople for which they might owe him, thank him, or expect from him). Olivelle (2011) points out that the anchorite is above all withdrawing "physically" from society, whereas the mendicant's withdrawal is "ideological" (p. 12).

Both roles share, despite several differences that distinguish them from each other as separate approaches, preliminary requirements toward manifesting in full the ideal of renunciation (*samnyasa*). These requirements—evident in the number of restrictions and withdrawals and self-control—are, by societal standards, extreme: Anyone who follows them would not be living a "normal" life nor be pursuing "ordinary" ambitions. By ascetic standards aiming toward renunciation, these requirements are however just preliminary: They merely frame the outer, behavioral conduct of the *sannyasi's* life. The real object of renunciation lies within this frame, wherein the restrictions, withdrawals, and self-control are intensified and internalized through being applied to her own person: her own body, breath, senses, desires, thought-processes, and focus of attention. The descriptions of anchorite and mendicant, respectively, cited above describe how each is to establish a particular "setting" for themselves, their "way of life." They don't describe, beyond the quick phrase "perform austerities," what the *sannyasi* will do within that setting. Just what does the anchorite or mendicant, after following the rules and restrictions outlined above, proceed to then do for the bulk of his or her day? The ancient answer for this was *tapas*, literally meaning "heat" but usually translated as "asceticism"; the developed, elaborated answer that India provides based on the breakthroughs of the Axial Age, is yoga.

Yoga is now a commonplace reference in the Western world—as a new English word, as a regimen of physical exercises, as numerous popular images of iconic yoga postures, and as an Eastern spirituality. In the context of Axial Age India, the meaning of the term is both much broader and much narrower than contemporary reference. It is much broader in terms of the range of spiritual disciplines it encompasses (contra, e.g., a prevalent contemporary Western view of yoga as primarily physical exercises of a series of bodily postures [*asanas*], which are more precisely either only "one limb" of the Eight Limbs of "classical yoga," or a subset of *hatha yoga*, itself one of many possible branches of yoga). It is also much narrower in that these disciplines gained their meaning within the spiritual-religious understanding of ancient India as the range of ascetic practices *par excellence* for gaining liberation from "this world"—not an exotic curiosity, not a stress-reduction approach, and not a way of staying in shape. The great religious studies scholar Mircea Eliade (1969) states: "The word *yoga* serves, in general, to designate any *ascetic technique* and any *method of meditation*. ... there is a 'classic' Yoga, a 'system of philosophy' expounded by Patanjali in his celebrated *Yoga-sūtras*... there are countless forms of 'popular,' nonsystematic yoga; there are also non-Brahmanic yogas (Buddhist, Jainist); above all, there are yogas whose structures are 'magical,' 'mystical,' and so on" (p. 4; emphases his).

Eliade's brief reference to Buddhist meditation as a "non-Brahmanic yoga" is worth noting. Equally prevalent and iconic to images of yoga as representative of "Eastern religiosity" are pictures and sculptures of the Buddha in seated meditation, hands resting on folded legs, calm and reposed. The notion of mindfulness is a direct import from Buddhism into Western culture and terminology; in the last decades, its visibility has moved from the fringes of New Age explorations into mainstream culture. Within scholarly research, there has been a similar change; for example, "there has been explosive growth in the rate of published mindfulness research, expanding from less than a dozen articles a year prior to 1998 to almost 500 per year by 2012" (Waelde & Thompson, 2016, p. 119). Within this research, by far the two most common types of mindfulness practice that dominate the literature are *vipassana* meditation ("insight" meditation, characteristic of Theravada Buddhism) and "TM," or transcendental meditation (taught by the Maharishi Mahesh Yogi, the Hindu guru made famous in the West through the Beatles).

Whether yoga or meditation, certain popular images have entered Western mainstream understanding. These images are not necessarily false; they could, however, become distortive of our understanding if they are made too representative. The historical fact, as Eliade's description of yoga was meant to show, is that a huge spectrum of ascetic practices which could be grouped under the umbrella term yoga, manifest in India. Earlier scholarship (including Eliade) understood this manifestation to occur much earlier and to have a much longer pedigree; as discussed in the previous chapter, scholarship in the last decades (like Bronkhorst, Heesterman, Olivelle, Samuel) has moved the dating for the emergence of these practices to the mid-first millennium BCE. India has some arguable evidence of ascetic persons and ascetic practices that date earlier. The Rig Veda references *munis*, the Atharva Veda discusses *vratyas*; they provide descriptions of them that clearly support ascription, to some extent, of their undertaking ascetic practices—"they remain standing for a year," "are familiar with the discipline of the breaths," etc. (Eliade, 1969, pp. 101–105; 1982, pp. 235–238). A first issue is whether the Atharva Veda really belongs to pre-Axial times or is contemporaneous. A second issue: These practices were always mere elements within a broader non-ascetic ensemble; within a ritual ensemble, a purification ensemble, or a sacrificial ensemble; as part of a priest's ceremonial duties, as part of preparation for a change in life stages, and so on. A third issue: Eliade (1969, 1982) also points out the resemblances between these apparent ascetics and shamans, and in general the resemblance of their practices to those for inducing ecstasy (note similar resemblances obtain between shamanism and ancient Israelite, Chinese, and Greek practice too; see Dodds, 1951; Lindblom, 1962; Paper, 1995, respectively). The latter are far-flung and commonplace; thus, we find ascetic elements within a healing ensemble or a rite of passage ensemble, as part of the ceremony preceding communication with spirits, and so on. The difference marking the Axial Age off from earlier times is not the presence or absence of particular ascetic practices and understandings. Rather, the difference is that during the Axial Age these ascetic elements are taken up for the first time into an ascetic ensemble, that is intentionally assembled into a whole aimed at achieving explicitly ascetic ends; a systematic, methodical group of practices organized together as a thorough-going effort at controlling the body and the mind.

Yoga and Meditation

Eliade rightly mentioned the *Yoga-sutras* as a "classic"; it does indeed present the first formal systematization in text of (a number of) yoga practices. The text is dated to the first centuries CE; at the earliest, it is from the first century BCE. It is centuries too late to serve as representative of Axial Age practice, and given the span of historical time, it is reasonable to assume it is also too systematic to serve as representative of the presumably lesser degree of systematicity attained during the Axial Age. In this excess, however, it serves as the perfect bookend to offset against the other end of several scattered ascetic elements taken up into non-ascetic ensembles that characterized pre-Axial India. Between this earlier set of circumstances, wherein spiritual practice had not yet become coherently organized into an intentional ascetic system, and the later Yoga-Sutras as a highly sophisticated systematization of yoga, falls the Axial Age: both in terms of time frame and in terms of degree of systematization. It is across the Axial Age centuries that yoga, the Indian term for ascetic practice or spiritual discipline, gains the role and form for which it has become famous, and fills in the active, performed content framed by the rules for how a renunciate was to live. Those rules emphasized the renunciate controlling his behavior in order to effect a variety of restrictions and withdrawals relative to the normal practices prescribed by societal convention.

The *Yoga-Sutras* continue this emphasis on self-control, restriction, and withdrawal, and systematically extend this emphasis in "filling in" the framework. The first two of the "eight limbs" of yoga are still relatively "external" forms of self-control: *yama*, "restraints," such as not to kill, not to lie, not to steal; *niyama*, "disciplines," such as cleanliness, serenity, studious intention. These basically moral and ethical precepts are presumably observed as "generic religious practice," too, with the yoga practitioner being asked to intensify her conscious awareness in intentionally observing these restraints and disciplines. Eliade (1969) concurs, emphasizing these are general and preliminary and "have no yogic structure," and that it is only with *asana*, bodily posture, "that yogic technique, properly speaking, begins" (pp. 49–53). With the invoking of proper yogic technique, the meaning is that the techniques of self-control are now turned more inward to the person or self of the practitioner, beginning with the body. Learning conscious, trained control of the anatomical body through the assuming of a systematic series of postures, the practitioner renounces the unlearned, unconscious, untrained, uncontrolled body. As this level of attainment becomes stabilized, the control becomes effortless—gradually and eventually as the result of practice—and the practitioner's consciousness relative to the anatomical body becomes free. (Eliade [1969] draws repeated attention to the *Yoga-Sutras* emphasis on "effortlessness.")

Pranayama, the fourth limb, is conscious control applied to the breathing body. Breathing is something we all do in an unlearned, unconscious, untrained, uncontrolled way; and hence, "unrhythmically." Through deep controlled rhythmic breathing (the "measured rhythm" of *pranayama* is to breath as the "prescribed posture" of *asana* is to body), the practitioner's consciousness becomes effortless and free, relative to her breathing. The fifth limb, *pratyahara*, is applied to the bodily senses: The practitioner's unlearned, unconscious, untrained, uncontrolled way of seeing and smelling, etc., is freed up. Instead of being dominated by the object seen, smelt, etc., and the act of seeing, smelling, etc., therefore a merely passive response to environmental stimuli, the practitioner comes to discern any act of sensing as above all conscious activity that issues from a conscious source "upriver" from the sense objects and from any particular act of sensing. Achieving effortlessness in *pratyahara*, she becomes free in her conscious life from being controlled by sense objects specifically and the body more generally and, "Patanjali tells us… becomes capable of concentration" (Eliade, 1969, p. 68). The practitioner will now turn to concentration itself as the object of yoga technique. The third, fourth, and fifth limbs of yoga are the technique "in the proper sense" being applied to "natural" functions of the body: posture, breath, and the senses. Gaining conscious control of these leads into what is "behind" these functions, the mind or consciousness, starting with concentration.

This is the sixth limb, *dharana*, in which consciousness aims to control the mental act of concentration, and transform it from unlearned, unconscious, untrained, uncontrolled, concentration into a disciplined control. Mastery of concentration, intensified, enables practice of the seventh limb, *dhyana*, or meditation. In being able to control her ability to concentrate, the practitioner can now turn that concentration reflexively onto the mind itself that is doing the concentrating as her focal object. The stage is set for the final, eighth limb, *samadhi*, which is a much deeper state of absorbed meditation—as I understand it, wherein the radical reflexivity exhibited in *dhyana* gives way to a yet higher realization of nonduality or unity-in-consciousness that dissolves, or overcomes, the separation implicit in the notion of "reflexivity" (which presupposes at least two moments in a conscious action). According to Patanjali, attainment of *samadhi* means the practitioner is now able to meet her "true self" (Assuming she successfully navigates the many degrees of complexity and nuance still remaining within the state of *samadhi* itself: *samadhi* "with support" can be subdivided into four stages, while its transition to a higher stage of *samadhi* "without support" itself comprises two levels! [cf. Eliade, 1969, pp. 79–84, 91–95]).

We've only scratched the merest surface of Patanjali's *Yoga-sutras*, which itself is only one of the numerous writings outlining a system of disciplined spiritual practice. We could just as well have picked a Buddhist account outlining meditation with similar systematicity, or a Jain text describing its approach to ascetic renunciation. A commonplace to these systematic accounts, of which we caught a glimpse, are lengthy enumerations classifying reality into its constituent parts—an understandable effort in light of the belief that reality is "consciousness dependent," and thus reality can be broken down into the different experiential states of consciousness elicited at different stages of spiritual practice or according to different techniques. For example in describing Mahavira's teaching, "it speaks of three kinds of consciousness and five kinds of right knowledge, of seven principles or categories, of five kinds of bodies, of six shades or colors that mark the soul's merit and demerit, of eight kinds of 'karmic matter,' of fourteen stages of spiritual qualifications, etc" (Eliade, 1982, p. 87). Buddhism, too, has numerous enumerations of states of mind, classification of its different aspects, degrees of enlightened consciousness (e.g., the Fourfold Noble Truth, Eightfold Noble Path, five constituents of human being), and so on (Hamilton, 2001). These systems are not easily comparable; the "Eightfold Noble Path" of Buddhism, for example, is not equivalent to the "eight limbs" of yoga (although there is some overlap). All attest to a high degree of formal systematization of ascetic practices that occurs following the centuries of the Axial Age. In this respect, they serve as a post-Axial bookend: They are capable of such a high degree of formal systematization because they are coming after, reflecting on, and building upon, some lesser degree of systematization of ascetic practices that preceded them. Presumably, the historical process of systematization was neither straightforwardly linear, but waxed and waned relative to external pushes and pulls, nor was it homogeneous across Buddhism, Jainism, and the nascent forms of Hinduism, but varied considerably, nor was it homogeneous within any of these world-religions-in-formation, as each is marked by considerable internal diversity.

For one example, Buddhism would have certainly been considerably impacted by Asoka's conversion and endorsement. While very early on, perhaps contemporary with the first generation of disciples after the Buddha's death, Buddhism developed monasticism—itself a systematization—such an institution could not but be profoundly transformed by the royal patronage of a conquering emperor who favored it. For a second example from Jainism, Dundas (2002) points out: "Jain literature is full of statements asserting the necessity of meditation (*dhyana*) as a weapon or armour in the battle with the passions" (p. 166). One could surmise a similar pattern to Buddhism—but Dundas immediately follows up with this surprising observation: "Yet Jainism, unlike Theravada Buddhism, has never fully developed a culture of true meditative contemplation... In other words, the Jains can be said to have lost contact with a substantial part of their ancient meditative structure at an early date" (pp. 166–167). Today, therefore, Jainism unlike Buddhism does not have an extensive monastic/ascetic infrastructure as part-and-parcel of its religion. Rather, "[s]trict and precisely defined vegetarianism is the most tangible social expression of adherence to the doctrine of non-violence and the most significant marker of Jain identity" (p. 177).

For a third example, perhaps the most representative version of yoga for modern Hinduism is found in the *Bhagavad Gita*. The *Gita* is one book within the much longer *Mahabharata*, wherein yoga is consistent and dominant theme (the terms yoga and yogins occur almost 900 times in the *Mahabharata* [Brockington, 2003]). Within the larger and longer *Mahabharata*, yoga is presented in similarly systematic terms to the detailed systematization of its "eight limbs" that we've summarized above: "Yoga practice comprises four main aspects of general preparations through moral conduct; diet, posture and surroundings; breath control; and withdrawal of the senses, concentration and meditation" (Brockington, 2003, p. 19). Also like the *Yoga-sutras*, the *Mahabharata* including the *Bhagavad-Gita* is a post-Axial text and presents a highly systematized version of renunciation. The *Gita*, however, is unlike those sutras in that it radicalizes ascetic practice in a wholly different direction—arguably in a "counter-ascetic" direction. For in the *Gita* Krishna advises Arjuna, not on how to renounce action, withdraw from the world, or restrict his behavior—he is advising him to join the battle and kill members of his own extended family, after all!—but advises him on how to renounce the world in the very performance of worldly action. "The *Gita* – in response to the radical renunciation of its day – opposes all flight from socio-cultural involvement. ...Although they must be ever active in the world... the *Gita* frees humans from any concern regarding the fruits or consequences of such action" (Kaelber, 1998, p. 327). As a highly systematized advocacy of what Max Weber calls "this-worldly asceticism" (referring to Protestantism's radical transposition of medieval asceticism's "other-worldly" orientation), the *Gita's* account of a "this-worldly" yoga must build on earlier existing developments within the Indian subcontinent that were opposing "the radical renunciation of its day," even as they utilize the theme of renunciation to develop a system oriented in the opposite direction.

PRACTICING TRANSCENDENCE: PERSONAL
TRANSFORMATION AND CIVILIZATIONAL CRITIQUE

I will assume these examples suffice to convey what some of the diversity and unevenness of the historical process of systematizing ascetic practices looked like within Axial Age India. Emphasizing the diversity and unevenness is crucial so as to block any misinterpretation of India's distinctive contribution of systematic ascetic practice as being reducible to a "singular essence" or a "monolithic homogeneity." Granting that point, let's summarize in idealized and simplified terms the gist of the ascetic system based on our above description. A first step is to control oneself vis-à-vis normal social conventions, such as we saw with the rules for the mendicant or anchorite. (Buddhism and Jainism will propose similar rules for their ascetic practitioners.) The ascetic follows particular prohibitions and restrictions that set her apart from normal society. A second step is to ethically restrain one's person in interpersonal situations and to morally discipline one's personal conduct. While this second step is still preparatory and doesn't look much different than normal rules of morality and ethics, in the context of ascetic preparations these take on a heightened consciousness and corresponding intensification of intention. The third step is to begin applying ascetic technique proper, wherein the focus of control shifts to one's own conscious experience of one's body (in the *Yoga-sutras*, this followed the sequence of posture, then breathing, then use of the senses). Gradually and progressively, the practitioner attaining sufficient conscious control of the body shifts the focus of control yet again, this time to consciousness itself (in the *Yoga-sutras*, this followed the sequence of concentration, to absorbed meditation, then to deeper, more absorbed, meditation).

Buddhism and Jainism do not observe, exactly, this same sequence. But all deal with these aspects—Buddhism doesn't lay out a full range of *asanas* for the meditator to follow, but simplifies dramatically to just sitting. Nevertheless, in just sitting, the Buddhist meditator is controlling posture, and breathing, and the senses; and of course, diving ever deeper into the practitioner's inner world. The process is one of progressively deepening the self-controls inwardly.

With the mastering of each stage of training, the deeper attainments of particular conscious stages or levels are stabilized within the practitioner such that in turn the focus of the practitioner can deepen further, shifting to discern increasingly subtle inner states and qualities of consciousness. At a certain point in this progressive deepening, the very effort of "self-control" itself will come into focus and the realization will develop that the consciousness exerting control over "the self" is not "the self." (What is the relationship of the practitioner to this consciousness? Is the practitioner "tapping into," or "enlisting," this consciousness? Or is the practitioner "participating in" a conscious capacity that has been there all along and unnoticed?) More precisely, the realization develops that "the self" is not what the practitioner conventionally—habitually, unthinkingly, uncritically—has understood "her self" to be; and increasingly, the realization that her manner of acting, behaving, and thinking—untrained, undisciplined, uncontrolled—which she has hitherto identified with her self as "the I" (i.e., the ego), is not her true self. There is something more, something other, a consciousness at work beyond her ego-self. This consciousness would be, on the one hand, the thinking hand, mysterious; on the other hand, the practice hand, she—and it ought not to be clear who the word "she" names or refers to!—has been participating in, or enlisting, that consciousness over the course of practice (presumably, at this point, for years now), and thus in a non-cognitive, nondiscursive, practical sense, she has become very familiar with that consciousness. (It seems the best word to describe this "more," "other," "beyond," "mysterious" aspect of consciousness is that it is transcendent. In terms of the Axial Age defined as a "breakthrough to transcendence," then, I am in full agreement with the scholarship: except that I perceive the "breakthrough" as above all attained through sustained systematic spiritual practice, and thus is an experiential realization transformative of the self, and not primarily a cognitive or intellectual achievement which gives us "new ideas.")

Put differently: Based on this progressive deepening through practice, the realization unfolds that the truth, or perhaps her true self, exists "somewhere beyond" (or "somehow other than") her ego-self. The truth exists where that consciousness issues from, that controls her ego-self's actions and thoughts. Among other consequences of this deepening, a potent psychological one is a dynamic transformation in the locus of identification for the self. While the prohibitions prescribed to be a mendicant or anchorite appear radical relative to normal societal practice, the true radicality of renunciation reveals itself through lengthy practice as the practitioner uncovers layers upon layers of normal ego consciousness en route to discovering the roots to that consciousness ("radical" derives from the Latin for "root"). In discovering these roots, they are in the self-same "action" of consciousness, uprooted; initially, presumably, in unsettlingly sensational, or tantalizingly tempting, glimpses, while through sustained practice, the "uprooting" becomes stabilized as the now-attained ground from which the practitioner is conscious. That is, to gain conscious control through the practice of a previously untrained, undisciplined, uncontrolled aspect of one's self is to free oneself from that aspect. After enough practice, the only "aspect" of the self that remains is "the self" itself.

The promise of a developed system of practice is to free oneself toward whatever it is that transcends the self: Often conceived as one's higher truer self (*atman*, or *purusa*), or as the ultimate reality that is God, such as *Brahman*, or *Isvara* (the Lord of yoga in the *Yoga-sutras*), or that these are in truth identical (*atman = Brahman*), or as a realization of an ultimate truth that the self or god are illusory (as with Buddhism, in which case the ultimate reality is *sunyata* or "emptiness," lacking essence or identity, with its corollary the interdependence of all things, *pratitya-samutpada* or "interdependent causality"), or materialist or atheist versions (as with Ajivika, Carvaka, or Samkhya). To quote the *Yoga Darshana Upanishad*, 10.1: "When there appears within you/the true knowledge of the unity/of your *atman* with the cosmic *atman*,/that is called *samadhi*,/for the *atman* is in truth/identical with *brahman*, the omnipresent,/the perpetual, the One without second" (Varenne, 1976, p. 221).

Alongside this idealized, simplified, generalized sketch, we can also speculate an uneven, centuries-long, historical process within India that goes something like this: The ascetic practices that embody the ideal of renunciation start to become systematized, to varying degrees, in varying forms, by a great diversity of small groups of practitioners. Exemplary individuals within those groups become teachers, and some of these become famous. Alongside genuine teachers, we can imagine charlatans, along with well-meaning but misguided leaders, as well as charismatic manipulators. There is great sharing and cross-fertilization and mutual influence, collaboration and argument, experimentation, hypothesizing, refutation, and confirmation, all taking place alongside equally bitter rivalry and disagreement and acrimonious discord and at times fierce competition between and within these groups. As the teachings and practices get passed on to the next generation, lineages develop. Particular approaches become refined further, some become signature for particular schools, while others are rejected entirely; different teachers and schools will endorse some and condemn others. There will be great breakthroughs in terms of practice-based insights, as well as in the practices and techniques themselves, and rumors of the same; there will be spectacular failures and dead-end explorations and endless rabbit-holes, with hearsay and gossip circulating about all of these, too.

As we know from the previous chapter, a philosophical outcome is the postulating of an ideal of renunciation, while two sociological outcomes of this speculated historical process are the emergence of whole new classes, the *shramana* and the *sannyasin*. We know the textual outcomes: The *Upanisads* will be composed, as well as the earliest scriptures of Buddhism and Jainism. But, and here is a crucial piece: Before anything is set down into text, this entire speculation of a historical process is conceivable in strictly oral terms. The cultivation of ascetic practice, its study and elaboration and dissemination, the formation of schools of discipline around it, do not require text. And one of the crucial constitutive consequences of "textuality"—the sustained systematic development of criticism—is plausibly present within this whole speculated situation, insofar as sustained, rigorous, disciplined spiritual practice has numerous mental and psychological outcomes (on attention, retention, motivation, cognition, intuition, the imagination, the emotions) that underlie and enable sustained critical thinking.

In fact, we can take the function of criticism relative to systematic ascetic practice further and deeper. The dynamic transformation of self-consciousness and in the locus of identification for the self could be understood as a deepening criticism of all immature because undisciplined self-identities. Further than this is the extension of criticism beyond the self to society and civilization and power. Recalling that the premise for Axial Age visionaries is a critique of civilizational power, one could misunderstand that the ascetic practices that follow from this premise then proceed to leave the critique behind in order to get on with their real interest in meditation. After all, "critique" is an intellectual, theoretical activity, that's about exposing ideology and analyzing false claims to truth and abuse of power and so on, whereas ascetics are engaged in a very different activity of deep contemplative reflection. This interpretation is contemporary, however, and misses the holistic aim of spiritual practices which include the intellectual and theoretical but don't overly privilege them. This interpretation also misses out on something that the Axial Age teachers perceived clearly: That each of us as individuals are constituted by society through-and-through (it is only after transcendence as an idea becomes commonplace, courtesy of the Axial Age, that one can glibly assume that "I" am not defined by my society, but can stand apart from it, against it, outside it, on my own, etc.). Critique of civilizational power as premise is something that is never left behind, but it is systematically built upon and deepened, a process that can also be understood as stabilizing a new, post-critical, alternative "transcendent" consciousness.

Every step of the ascetic process could be redescribed in terms of critique: critique of societal values, which means one must live differently; critique of inherited and taken-for-granted moral and ethical rules followed unthinkingly, which means one must perform these self-consciously and intentionally; critique of our untrained bodily comportment, which means one must train it; critique of our undisciplined mind, which means one must discipline it; and critique of our very self, which means one must transcend it. Renunciation as conceived in India during the mid-first millennium BCE was indeed radical in that it "represented an anti-structure to the society of that time, *a total rejection and the reversal of the value system of the world*" (Olivelle, 2011, p. 70; my emphasis). If your entire self, and selfhood, and values and beliefs and mind, were structured through-and-through by society, then renunciation was indeed a "critique" of society, but critique understood as systematically embodied through practices of self-control and self-denial. The outcome of this "self-critical" process was the birth of something new. Viewed through the old lenses (that in actuality, the pursuit of practice would have outgrown), one could say it was the birth of a "new self." But the undertaking of the practice, which develops new lenses through which to see the world, leads the practitioner away from a focus on the self to instead the wholly new vista unfolding: that of an "other world," entirely transcendent of the old world, old self, and old way of seeing, which relative to the transcendent other world has become "this world." In fact, all of the Axial Age approaches seem to equally privilege new versions of cosmology as much as they promote a new understanding of psychological inwardness—practically and experientially, both come together as the outcome of sustained spiritual practice, while critically, both emerge in rejecting and countering the accepted civilizational understanding of cosmos and person.

Of course, phrasing the outcome of practice in terms of "this world" vs the "other world" possibly reopens all our metaphysical and religious and doctrinaire and philosophical notions and connotations about this world vs the other world. In the immediate context of our examination of systematic ascetic practice, we should not allow all of that baggage to come flooding back in, and instead, the meaning we should retain focus on is that of a radically new experience, based on sustained practices that gradually and progressively criticized one's self—criticized here meant practically in the sense of focused on, prior to gaining control over—eventuating in a deep and pervasive transformation in consciousness and the very structure of one's selfhood. At the most basic, practically speaking, a duality must be assumed: between undisciplined and unpracticed over against disciplined and practiced. Although it often has been, this duality need not be inflated into a dualism (see Whicher [1998] for a sustained defense of the anti-dualist interpretation of classical yoga, interpreting Patanjali as instead arguing for "responsible engagement" that integrates, both practically and theoretically, spirit [*purusa*] and matter [*prakrti*], resulting, Whicher summarizes elsewhere [2003], "in a highly developed, transformed, and participatory human nature and identity, an integrated and embodied state of liberated selfhood" [p. 51]).

One of the most sophisticated and careful contemporary analyses of meditation practice traditions based on a comparative study of the Hindu *Yoga-sutras*, the Theravadin Buddhist *Visuddhimaga*, and the Mahayana Buddhist *Mahamudra*, by Daniel Brown (1986), provides the following summary description based on the study:

> Despite the apparent differences across traditions of meditation, there is strong evidence for a single underlying invariant sequence of stages. These stages represent a predictable progression of changes in psychological structure and are experienced subjectively as a systematic unfolding of distinct states of consciousness. This underlying path is best conceptualized as *a systematic deconstruction of the structures of ordinary waking consciousness.* (p. 263; emphasis mine)

Describing what happens gradually and progressively in the inner life of the practitioner due to sustained practice as "systematic deconstruction" concisely captures how the notion of critique, as embodied in practice, operates. Bussanich (2016) uses the phrase "the deconstruction of the empirical person" (p. 87). But while the operating and enacting of "the structures of ordinary waking consciousness" are above all located in the "empirical person," the content and orientations of these structures are not; they are given by the culture to which the person belongs and in which they have grown and developed. On this reading, transcendence is to be understood in experiential terms of the psychological effects of practice, not in absolute terms. Transcendence as an "other world" is a mysterious and powerful experience through which one has been transformed that gains its meaningfulness by way of contrast to all that which has been transcended—all of which becomes "immanent," "this-worldly," stuff, and the criticism of "this world" that was the premise for practice, is confirmed and fulfilled in being given experiential content for the practitioner.

PRACTICING TRANSCENDENCE IN CHINA: TAOIST INNER CULTIVATION

Given the extremism some forms of Indian asceticism takes, and the extent to which their ideal of renunciation of "this world" can lead into release or escape (*moksha*) through attaining the transcendence of the "other world," it is perhaps surprising to turn to China next. Of all the Axial Age cases, China is considered the least radical, or most conservative, in its conception of transcendence. Benjamin Schwartz, a scholar of China, accommodated for this in his treatment of the Axial Age by giving transcendence a modest scope: that of "standing back and looking beyond – a kind of critical, reflexive questioning of the actual and a new vision of what lies beyond" (1975, p. 3). A decade later, Schwartz (1985) substantiates and elaborates this view considerably in his masterful *The world of thought in ancient China*, the most thorough treatment of China as a comparative Axial case. There he makes the case for transcendence as most evident in religious ethics, within the tension between the idealization of "the mandate of Heaven" as what ought to be over against the actuality of what is. Yü (2003) too is cognizant of the complexity of making the Axial case for China, doing so through an appeal to "inward transcendence." Schwartz also locates the tension "inwardly": The mandate of Heaven is no longer the sole prerogative of the ruler to mediate, but is now potentially universal in all persons, although only in the sage can we truly see this manifest. This also applies to the *Tao*, as "the way" of heaven. Confucius, Mo Tzu, the Taoists, will all argue from this same point albeit in markedly different ways. What enables it to manifest, what distinguishes the sage from other people, and thus why it depends on an inward orientation are all three tied up in the notion of "cultivation."

As the title of his book makes clear, Schwartz is approaching the Axiality of China philosophically—as a breakthrough in thought. Thus, one part of his answer as to what "cultivation" consists in is learning and education; as well, what explains the capacity of sages to achieve transcendence "seems to lie in their superior intelligence" (1985, p. 159). In discussing the Taoists, he downplays their "mystical" interpretation, preferring, for example, how they describe their "vision of reality." He repeats, several times, that although the Taoist texts occasionally present examples of persons having mystical experiences, the texts lack description of mystical techniques, particularly in comparison with "certain varieties of Indian mystical literature providing elaborate accounts of yogic and meditative techniques" (Schwartz, 1985, p. 199) such as we just examined in the above sections. And finally: "Without denying the role of the 'mystical' experience in any of them, I am nevertheless struck by the degree to which what might be called strenuous intellectual effort enters into all of them" (Schwartz, 1985, p. 199). These emphases—on learning, education, superior intelligence, vision of reality, strenuous intellectual effort—are all in keeping with the cognitive-intellectual orientation of most Axial Age scholarship. If we turn to the same material with an emphasis on practical spirituality as the distinctive marker of the Axial Age, however, a fairly different picture, like a Gestalt switch wherein an identical image gains an entirely different perception—a duck in place of a hare, for example—because the perspective on the image has changed, readily emerges.

Harold Roth's careful presentation of the early Taoist text, *Inward Training* (1999a), quickly effects this perspectival switch. (To be fair to Schwartz, he based his assessment of Taoism on the two foundational texts of the *Lao Tzu* [or *Tao Te Ching*] and the *Chuang Tzu*; he would not have appeared to have access to *Inward Training* at that time.) Roth says:

> *Inward Training* is a series of poetic verses devoted to the practice of guided breathing meditation and to the ideas about the nature of human beings and the cosmos that are directly derived from this practice. It is a mystical text because its authors followed this practice to depths not normally attained by daily practitioners of breathing for health and longevity, with whom they shared aspects of technical terminology and world view. (p. 4)

The focus on practice and meditation is forefront; there is an emphasis on breathing as basic to the meditative practice; and that it is primarily mystical rather than intellectual or philosophical is also clear. Roth in introducing this Taoist text is also pointing out that the Taoist pursuit of meditative practice was not original to them, but "shared aspects of technical terminology and world view" with others, who in fact preceded them. Following Donald Harper, Roth describes these latter as "macrobiotic hygiene practitioners," who practiced "dietetics, breath cultivation, exercise, and sexual cultivation" (1999a, p. 2). However, they pursued these practices primarily for health and longevity reasons, and consequently, the "early Taoist authors... took care to distinguish themselves from these macrobiotic health practitioners, whom they said cultivated the physical but not the numinous" (p. 4). Similarly to the presence of ascetic elements combined into a non-ascetic ensemble as we observed in India, what is distinctive is their assembly into an intentionally ascetic ensemble. Another difference is the greater "depths not normally attained," which is evidence for a greater degree of systematization of this set of practices: "Simply put, while both groups practiced guided breathing meditation, the early Taoists applied this practice much more assiduously" (p. 5). They also did so with an alternative focus: on the inner life, the "numinous," rather than the outer life of health and long life (the "physical"). Roth uses the term "inner cultivation" as best capturing what the early Taoists had in mind. These three differences are distinctly Axial changes to practice and understanding.

In addition, Roth convincingly demonstrates on a number of grounds that of the three foundational Taoist texts, *Inward Training* is in fact the earliest (and hence the book's title, *Original Tao*). Roth (1999a) claims:

> The common thread that ties together these three philosophical orientations of early Taoism and that differentiates them from other early intellectual lineages is their shared vocabulary of cosmology and mystical self-transformation. ...Furthermore, this shared vocabulary, this common thread, derives from a common meditative practice first enunciated in *Inward Training*, which I call "inner cultivation". ...they were part of a common tradition based on inner cultivation ...these texts were produced by master-disciple groups who all shared this practice. (p. 8)

We have many of the features already discussed in the previous chapter—the importance of texts, master-disciple groups ("schools"), lineages, intellectual philosophy—but in addition we also have meditative practices of mystical self-transformation explicitly named as the central binding factor holding all of these Axial features together. In basing his analysis of the other founding texts on this premise, Roth is able to read them quite differently (i.e., a "Gestalt switch") than did Schwartz. The *Chuang Tzu* has some discussion of practical technique too, and significantly more description of mystical experiences arising from these techniques by comparison with *Inward Training*, whereas the *Lao Tzu* has very little description of technique, more description of mystical experience, and significantly more prescription of social and political reform than either (needless to say, these prescriptions are based on the "vision of reality" emerging from sustained practice of these techniques of inner cultivation).

To simplify greatly, the basic message of *Inward Training* is that the customary or normal human way of being in the world disorders us as persons—posture-wise, emotions-wise, senses-wise, breathing-wise, thinking-wise—such that the natural potency of one's "vital energy" does not flow and thus one is cut off from one's "inner power." Properly "aligning" one's posture, emotions, senses, breathing, and thinking so that they are "well-ordered," one will become reconnected with that "inner power" and through this connection, tranquility comes, wisdom emerges and one becomes a sage, i.e., lives in harmony with the Tao. Instruction in "aligning the body," or also "aligning the four limbs," in tandem with keeping the body "calm and unmoving," describes a meditative posture (Roth speculates the position described is of two knees on the floor forming half of a square completed by the two shoulder points, with the spine and back kept straight [1999a, p. 110]). This aligning is of a piece with proper—"vital"—breathing, as well as control of one's physiology and senses. In Verse XIX: "When the four limbs are aligned/ and the blood and vital breath are tranquil/Unify your awareness, concentrate your mind/Then your eyes and ears will not be overstimulated" (p. 111). This practice extends to the emotions and desires, too; verse III says "If you are able to cast off sorrow, happiness, joy, anger, desire, and profit-seeking/Your mind will revert to equanimity," while verse XXIV claims "You will see profit and not be enticed by it/You will see harm and not be frightened by it" (pp. 111, 113). Throughout, a Taoist version of the Golden Mean seems to be at work, for example, "overfilling yourself with food will impair your vital energy/and cause your body to deteriorate./Overrestricting your consumption will cause the bones to wither/And the blood to congeal./The mean between overfilling and overrestricting:/This is called 'harmonious completion'" (p. 122), while similarly sensory "overstimulation" is also understood as disordering, as is excessive thinking—"when you think about something and don't let go of it,/Internally you will be distressed, externally you will be weak" (p. 114). One of the most powerful images used to describe the point of these practices aimed at countering our customary state of disorder is "cleaning out the lodging place of the numinous." (The parallels to Indian yoga are clear and many. Mair [1990] considers the aspects of Taoist meditation to derive from India—"it appears as if they were taken over directly" [p. 145]—speculating an unproven influence of ideas and techniques by inferring from proven, earlier, commercial and trade contacts between China and India. He suggests that "there are so many correspondences between Yoga and Taoism… that we might almost think of them as two variants of a single religious and philosophical system" [p. 146]. Roth [1999a] acknowledges the parallels but disagrees with Mair's reasoning and conclusion [cf. pp. 137–138].)

When the "lodging place of the numinous" has been adequately "cleaned out," the Taoist practitioner attends to the importance of concentration, to the progressive deepening in awareness, especially discernment of increasingly subtle states of consciousness, and to the cognitive and overall holistic effects of sustained systematic practice. "The passages on inner cultivation practice discussed above all touch upon the establishment of a certain quality of mind that is the basis for experiencing the Way" (Roth, 1999a, p. 112). In one of the most celebrated passages of the *Chuang Tzu*, wherein Confucius gets schooled by his pupil Yan Hui (presumably, this is Taoist polemic against Confucians), it is precisely in this practice and establishment which is called simply "sitting and forgetting" (see Roth, 1999a, p. 154).

In *Inward Training*, the quality of mind established is called variously the "cultivated mind"; "excellent mind"; "concentrated mind"; "well-ordered mind"; and "aligned mind," although the most fascinating description goes as follows: "Within the mind there is yet another mind./That mind within the mind: it is an awareness that precedes words./Only after there is awareness does it take shape;/Only after it takes shape is there a word./Only after there is a word is it implemented;/Only after it is implemented is there order" (pp. 107–108). Roth (1999a) describes the meaning of this other "mind within the mind" as being "a direct, nondual, awareness of the Way" (p. 108), and it is presumably through their cultivation of this awareness that the various authors of the early Taoist texts provide their enigmatic and paradoxical descriptions of the Way (see, e.g., Csikszentmihalyi & Ivanhoe, 1999; Roth, 1999b; Schwartz, 1985, pp. 186–254). That the early Taoists agree on this importance is not to say they provide a uniform interpretation of what it means or its importance; there are several and diverse ways presented of understanding "inner cultivation" (see the Comparative Table in Roth, 1999b, pp. 86–87). As for the development of later Taoism, there is no doubt that for its development meditative practice and "inner cultivation" are absolutely central (Kohn, 1992, 2000, 2010; Kohn & Sakade, 1989; Robinet, 1993).

I understand the argument for Taoism as being crucially constituted through meditative practices of "inner cultivation" to be solid and well-evidenced. That their very premise is one of "counter-cultural" critique of civilization in favor of returning to, or retrieving, a simpler nature, is equally well-established (and far better known as representative of Taoism than are meditative practices). "It is... quite correct to call the *Lao-tzu* a "primitivist" tract – an attack on the entire project of civilization" (Schwartz, 1985, p. 207). *Chuang Tzu*, Ch. XIX: "[T]here is nothing better than abandoning the world" (Roth, 1999a, p. 171). Of course, there is complexity and nuance within the Taoist critique; Ivanhoe (2010), for example, qualifies how "Zhuangzhi's way is not so much a rejection of civilization as a way to live uncorrupted within it" (p. 195). But in the final analysis there is no doubting that the premise for, and guiding thread throughout, Taoist practice is that the way we live is disordered and out of alignment, and that to restore harmony in our life with The Way, we must undertake a sustained practice of "systematic deconstruction" of the disorder of our bodies, breathing, senses, emotions, desires, energy, and minds.

PRACTICING TRANSCENDENCE IN CHINA: CONFUCIAN SELF-CULTIVATION

Unlike India wherein Hinduism, Buddhism, and Jainism all share in a clear commitment to some formulation of systematic ascetic practice, the same cannot be said of the different Axial Age movements of China. The claim that systematic meditative discipline is integral to Taoism cannot be generalized to Mohism or, most significantly as the most influential Axial Age "school" to impact Chinese civilization, Confucianism.

I have found no evidence anywhere of such practice within Mohism. There is no doubt the latter has numerous systematic elements: Graham (1989) claims "rational debate" begins in China with Mo Tzu's reaction against Confucius, and formed a "highly organized community" in the fourth and third centuries BCE (pp. 33, 35). Bellah (2011, pp. 426–435) presents a picture of them as systematic to the point of "relentless" and "ruthless" in their logic, argumentation, utilitarianism, and activism. With some irony, this application was relative to the Mohist ideal of "universal love (*jian ai*)," that Graham prefers to translate as "Concern for Everyone" and David Nivison as "impartial caring" (Bellah, 2011, p. 430). While in part this was polemical against Confucius' emphasis on filial love, it is also a distinctive Axial motif in being proclaimed as "universal"—that Mohism argued for "implementing" such concern indiscriminately according to a kind of utilitarian calculation of costs and benefits tied to an authoritarian conception of obedience holds its share of irony.

As far as evidence in the *Mo Tzu* text itself for the systematic practical pursuit of "inner cultivation" goes, the closest is present in "metaphors of craft-building, constructing, and fashioning" (Michael Puett, cited in Bellah, 2011, p. 427). However, this orientation is not applied inwardly as with the Taoists, rather it becomes applied to "the defence of cities," and the text concludes with sections "full of highly technical information about military engineering" (Graham, 1989, p. 34). Thus for the Mohist, the notion of "cultivation" would be seen somewhat mechanistically, rather than inwardly, as a kind of social or behavioral engineering. The clichéd Western distinction between action and contemplation seems to apply perfectly in this instance, with Mohism decisively belonging to the former: a "school" of systematic action, whether in its utilitarian logic, social and political activism, practical applications, or rhetorically: "notoriously graceless... ponderous, humourless, repetitive" (Graham, 1989, p. 34). In a manner that would find acceptance among twentieth-century behaviorists but few others, there is no attention paid to the inner life here.

The same cannot be said of Confucius. Although, if we attend to what seem to be his foremost concerns—obedience to tradition, the restoration of a Zhou-like imperial rule, attending to the proper observance of ritual (*li*)—and combine this with the historical stereotype of Confucianism as a staid bureaucratic social philosophy, we do not have a promising start. This is quickly dispelled if we lay appropriate emphasis on Confucius' innovations rather than his conservative view, above all in the transposition of "Heaven" from being a mythological power "out there" to instead residing within the heart and to its being capable of embodiment within the figure of the sage. Alongside this transposition, we need to remember what was emphasized in the previous chapter, that the character of "heaven" (*t'ien*, or *tian*) was also transformed by Confucius, into an ethico-religious demand for what ought to be, placed on what is, that Benjamin Schwartz argues qualifies as composing the moderate Chinese version of Axial transcendence. To complete this about-face in our estimation of Confucius, we must attend to his notion of *jen* (or *ren*).

Following Yen Hui in the *Analects*, we can ask: "What is *jen*?" Confucius replies with a sentence that has received differing translations. One is, "Curb your ego and submit to *li*." One is Waley's "He who can submit himself to ritual is good". Fingarette opts for "self-disciplined and ever turning to *li*" (Schwartz, 1985, p. 77). Each of these translations asserts the importance of self-work: Curb your ego, submit yourself, discipline yourself. Within each is the Axial turn to inwardness. This turn takes place alongside the conservative harkening to the pre-Axial importance of *li*, as ritual, the meaning of which connotes much more than a patterned performance on formal occasions. At the macrolevel, it extends to the whole normative ordering of both society, as for example the political order, and the cosmos, as for example the cycle of the seasons. At the microlevel, it is far more prosaic; "rituals involved in daily interchanges and rites of passage intended to smooth and elevate human relations" (Tucker, 2003, p. 5). *Li* is frequently translated as "civility," *jen* as "humaneness." It is in Confucius' sustained reflections on the right way to perform *li*, in his seeking the "basis of rites" (Yü, 2003, p. 68), that he makes the Axial turn toward *jen*—an inner transformation of the meaning of ritual performance toward spiritual interiority that we've already seen a version of among the *brahmans* of India, whose intensive pursuit of Vedic ritual purity aimed at sacralizing the world is turned inside out toward the ideal of renunciation of "this world." Schwartz (1985) emphasizes: "Above all, however, the most strikingly novel aspect of *jen* is that it does not refer to moral power which is simply latently present in men. It is an existential goal which Confucius attempts to achieve for himself through his own self-cultivation. It is the result of a self-effort which he believes can be taught to others" (p. 77). In all of these changes in meaning of traditional concepts that Confucius outlines, he makes the Axial case for a "breakthrough," a "spiritual revolution." In a way, the answer to the question of the "loss of the Tao" that animates Confucius' lifelong quest and the issue of the collapse of Zhou and of a good, just, political order that hovers in the background of his thought, is found where *jen* and *li* meet. This meeting place is not given, but must be achieved, and it must be achieved inwardly. Thus, Tu Weiming claims "the Confucian commitment to ultimate self-transformation necessarily involves a transcendent dimension" (1985, p. 137). However, in terms of my own claim regarding the distinctiveness of the Axial Age being its innovation of systematic, sustained spiritual practice, does Confucius' conception of "self-cultivation" entail a type of ascetic ensemble or a method of "systematic deconstruction" of ordinary consciousness?

Unlike the Taoists, who endorse a state of nature that society has disordered, and therefore their "inner cultivation" was to deconstruct societal constructs and to unlearn civilizational norms, Confucius and his followers do not make a similar "primitivist" appeal. Confucius' appeal to *li* is an appeal to ritual which is not primitive but the opposite, a learned, refined, "high culture" product. Confucius perceived society as disordered, debased, and unjust, and desperately in need of reform, but in arguing for the solution to be cultivation as a refinement of cultural practice toward its ideal performance, the argument is quite opposite to the Taoist notion of cultivation as a retrieving and restoring of our nature which culture has overrun and distorted. In this sense of refinement toward its ideal performance—that Confucians often use archery and music as preferred examples is apropos—Confucius is most certainly critical of "ordinary consciousness," although his "deconstruction" of it is more along the lines of raising into awareness how badly and poorly we've been trained in the rituals of cultural practice alongside advocating a far deeper, more rigorous, more conscientious training in those "ritual forms." Confucianism in terms of degree of asceticism is certainly much more modest than extreme forms of Indian practice and "otherworldliness"; Confucian ethics "does not demand that we sacrifice the more familiar goods of everyday human existence" (Ivanhoe, 2013, p. 81). Ching (2003) observes that "Confucian asceticism... is a discipline of moderation... The Confucian teaching was to control one's passions, not to live as if one were without them" (p. 87). That said, Confucius was extremely critical of the society and conventions and passions of his time and advocated what can accurately be called "austerities" of practice vis-à-vis the easy, lazy, immature, superficial conduct of life. Just as

Indian yoga is founded on an opposition to the untrained, undisciplined, uncontrolled aspects of one's self, so too is Confucianism, and in this respect can be called "ascetic," self-denying practice.

Lest the reader becomes suspicious that I am shoehorning Confucianism into a distorted form to fit my thesis, let's listen to Confucian scholar Philip Ivanhoe (2013):

> [Confucians'] goal is to cultivate a greater awareness, attentiveness, and care for our thoughts and feelings, our actions, speech, comportment, and demeanor, the clothes we wear, the music we play and listen to, and how we conduct ourselves in our interactions with fellow human beings, other creatures, and the greater natural world. ...Such an attitude can and is intended to transform a mundane and uninspired view of everyday life into a challenging and fulfilling task, a form of "spiritual practice" (*gongfu*). (pp. 76–77)

In this quote, we see clearly the non-radical "this-worldly" preoccupation of Confucian thought, but raised and intensified to an "austere" level of demand imposed upon the performer who is to conduct herself with a far greater than ordinary degree of seriousness and intention.

> Many of the most distinctive and important contributions the Confucian tradition makes to our understanding of the human good arise from its characteristic concern with the cultivation of the self and in particular with its advocacy of greater awareness and reflection as foundations for and central constituents of such effort. Such concerns constitute *a kind of engaged, more kinetic form of meditative practice* (Ivanhoe, 2013, p. 78; emphasis added).

Ivanhoe's choice of description of Confucian aims of "greater awareness and reflection" as meditative practice attests to the importance of sustained and systematic training for developing these capacities. He quickly qualifies in just what sense he means "meditative practice: "What I have in mind is only distantly related to more familiar Daoist and Buddhist forms of meditation or the formal regimen known as 'quiet sitting' (*jingzuo*) followed by later Confucians. It is more closely akin to the practices of early Confucians who do not seem to have followed anything as precise and formal as the Daoist, Buddhist, or neo-Confucian regimens" (p. 78). (Elsewhere, Ivanhoe [2010] compares the Confucian practice regimen as akin to Indian yoga [p. 190].) That is, in the development of Confucianism, especially with its renaissance through neo-Confucianism in the eleventh and twelfth centuries CE, its meditative practices of self-cultivation become increasingly formalized (cf. Tucker, 2003, pp. 10–11). Interestingly, Schwartz points out that a key aspect of the neo-Confucian revival included a canonizing of texts that had been neglected and minimized over centuries of a Han version of imperial-bureaucratic Confucianism. Why were these seized upon? Schwartz (1985) says: "I would suggest that it is precisely support for the focus on inner cultivation… In this view, the entire unhappy history of Confucianism after Mencius had been obscured by the long neglect of the vital core" (p. 405). There is no doubt that since the neo-Confucian revival, concepts like Confucian meditation or Confucian spirituality and, indeed, Confucian asceticism become acceptable (see Ching, 2003; more broadly, the recent two volumes on "Confucian Spirituality"; Weiming & Tucker 2003a, 2003b).

Ivanhoe in describing Confucianism as an "engaged, more kinetic form of meditative practice," however, is not only describing a later or neo-Confucian modification. This characterization holds true of Confucius himself and his first disciples, too. Hartnett (2011) in describing early Confucianism as a kind of philosophy says it "originated as a way of life within an organized community or academy, not as a pure articulation of theory transmitted in philosophical discourse" (p. 55), while Eno (1990) points out in reference to the first Confucians that they "viewed their distinguishing trait as a commitment to a particular set of ideas *and* well-defined practices, with no sharp division possible between the two" (p. 6, emphasis his). In their respective emphases on "way of life" and "well-defined practices," Hartnett and Eno underscore the argument for Confucianism as a sustained, systematic set of practices focused inwardly, aiming toward a transformation of the self toward the goal of realizing sagehood, who would be an exemplar of "transcendence." Eno's summary of the four components of sagehood according to Mencius—(1) focus of concentration; (2) integration of phenomena; (3) a sense of total control; and (4) feelings of freedom and joy (1990, p. 175)—further shores up the argument, as the marks of the sage are clearly due to a practical mastery of his own self, based on extensive training, and not an accumulation of knowledge or expertise in some subject matter. To drive the point home, Hartnett (2011) in his discussion of early Confucians at Jixia Academy compares them to the Pythagoreans according to the following parallel:

In both systems, rites and purification ceremonies were not only indispensable pathways to the divine, but were techniques for cultivating the self and living rightly. In this view, the purpose was not so much to produce a set of general doctrines about the world but rather to show the way to live the good life. Practicing this way of life required living in community or a formal learning institution in which the master could train his disciples to renounce the so-called ordinary world and learn the art of living through spiritual exercises, as with Confucius who centered his community on the aesthetic and ethical rituals (*li*) for practicing the spiritual exercises of benevolence, self-restraint, propriety, etc. (p. 53).

Hartnett's comparing of Confucius to Pythagoras in terms of how each taught their disciples "to renounce the so-called ordinary world" and pursue an education based on "spiritual exercises" (rather than, say, "academic study" or "book learning") is also our cue for moving our focus from China to Greece. That some degree of systematization of ascetic practice occurred in Axial Age India didn't need to be established; it was and is obviously central to Indian religiosity and in providing an overabundance of evidence enabled an exemplary model to be proposed. In moving our focus onto China, this claim did need to be established, not through attending to its philosophical ideas, intellectual claims, or metaphysics, but by focusing on the practical techniques propounded by China's Axial Age "schools." I used the metaphor of a Gestalt switch, as it amounts to a change of perception on an image without an actual change of the image itself. This proved relatively easy to do in the case of Taoism, in fact yielding surprisingly strong parallels to Indian yoga in how it developed methods of "systematic deconstruction" of ordinary consciousness and a hierarchy of increasing self-control from the body to the mind to the "mind within the mind." The same proved impossible to do in the case of Mohism, which was indeed systematic but not in the domain of spiritual practices. The true test case for China was Confucianism, as the most influential Axial Age movement for China and, I presume, not an approach typically associated with "spiritual practice," meditation, or asceticism. On the one hand, this could be due to the common association of Confucians with staid state bureaucrats. Over against this image, Eno's (1990) book-long argument is to produce an alternative "portrait" of the early Confucians, "dressed in colorful robes, playing zithers or beating drums, chanting, dancing, and living their lives through an eccentric form of ritual playacting suggestive, perhaps, of nothing as much as Peking Opera" (p. 1)! My Gestalt switch was not so dramatic and ambitious, but I hope to have succeeded in demonstrating that for Confucianism, too, its Axial basis is in sustained, systematic, spiritual practices that accomplish self-transformation.

On the other hand, the non-obviousness of this claim about Confucianism might be due to its associations with philosophy. If Confucius and his followers aren't dull, conservative civil servants, instead they are rational thinkers, ethical humanists who philosophize, teach, read, write, and study. This too was a concern of Eno's, because "the style of this philosophy is fundamentally different from that we have grown to expect from the analytic schools of Western tradition. It was not analytic, and it made no categorical distinction between the spheres of theory and practice" (1990, p. 2). A significant part of Eno's argument throughout is building up an understanding of early Confucian philosophy as "synthetic" or "nonanalytic," demonstrating that "its central methodology involves the careful design of a syllabus of practice rather than in rigor of rational argument" (p. 9).

Insofar as Eno is making an argument for a correct understanding of Confucian philosophy as practice-based, there is neither issue nor difficulty. Insofar as he is making the point by contrast to Western philosophy as analytic, discursive, based on rational argument, and assuming "the essential core of philosophies such as Platonism, Thomism, Rationalism, Idealism, and so forth, lies in the theoretical architectures articulated by the followers of each school" (1990, p. 6), however, does raise issues and difficulties in terms of appreciating ancient Greek philosophy. My argument for the correct "image" of ancient Greek philosophy (including Platonism) by comparison with the modern Western conception of philosophy is that the former is indeed based on "spiritual practices" as foundational, and that we have misunderstood it in an analytic, discursive, rational, cognitive-theoretical way that distorts it—much as Eno argued for Confucianism. I don't mean that the philosophers of Greece strummed the zither and playacted Peking Opera style. But, that they might be wearing robes, engaged in chanting or praying, undertaking fasting or practicing specific diets, and that these activities would not be incidental but an essential aspect of "doing philosophy," is entirely plausible. Pythagoras, for example, "may have worn linen, let his hair grow long, cultivated wisdom, and practiced a vegetarian, silent, sober, purposeful and ascetic life" (Schmidt, 2010, p. 47). Of course, to make this argument will require a much more dramatic Gestalt switch than we undertook with Axial Age China to be performed on our image of the philosophy of ancient Greece.

Philosophy as Spiritual Exercises: Askesis in Greece

I assume that understanding ancient Greek philosophy as a form of systematic spiritual practice rather than as rational theoretical argument is a dramatic shift in perception. It is for the same reason that Greece is a harder Axial case than China and certainly India: The very phrase Greek philosophy evokes all manner of connotations, from the origin of "the West" and of Europe, the birthplace of democracy, the putative beginnings of science and of rationality, famous philosophers like Socrates, Plato, and Aristotle, to twenty-five hundred years of footnotes. In other words, we have greater or lesser degrees of "common knowledge" of Greek philosophy, inflected through our particular historical era's myriad unconscious assumptions and prejudices, such that a particular picture has become firmly established in our minds. A moment's reflection should be enough to realize a couple of things; first, that the picture is almost certainly inaccurate and far less "knowledge" than it is hearsay, stereotype, and oversimplification, and second, that due to its being firmly established, even a fulsome acknowledging of the first point will do little to nothing to change whatever picture you've formed. More than likely, however, Eno is right about what is central to that picture: The image of philosophy you hold, from ancient Greece until today, is very much a heady, abstract, theoretical enterprise. Starting from that simple baseline, let's listen carefully to what classics scholar Pierre Hadot has to say about Greek philosophy, and let's be willing to let our image be changed accordingly. In pursuing this aim, we are aligning ourselves with what is Hadot's own avowed intention. In his aptly named *What is Ancient Philosophy?* (2002), he opens:

> In this book I intend to show that a profound difference exists between the representations which the ancients made of *philosophia* and the representation which is usually made of philosophy today – at least in the case of the image of it which is presented to students... They get the impression that all the philosophers they study strove in turn to invent, each in an original way, a new construction, systematic and abstract, intended somehow or other to explain the universe... (p. 2)

In the remainder of the book, as well as in a separate collection of essays, Hadot (1995) aims to demonstrate instead that philosophy was above all "a way of life" (the name of that essay collection), i.e., practical and embodied, and focused concretely on transforming ourselves in line with an alternative, transcendent vision of the world. It was indeed intellectual and rational; it did produce theoretical discourse. But a key part of the Gestalt switch in our picture of philosophy that Hadot is trying to achieve includes a switch in the very meaning of these words—intellectual, rational, theory, discourse—as part of, contributing to, and justified in, a different way of life. Greek philosophers were theoretical: But for them, theoretical did not primarily mean an abstract and disembodied edifice of ideas. "'[T]heoretical' can be applied to a philosophy which is *practiced, lived, and active*, and which brings happiness" (2002, p. 81; my emphasis).

The word Hadot settles on as most appropriate to get at the heart of this switch in emphasis to philosophy and theory as "practiced, lived, and active" is the Greek word *askesis*, which he translates as "spiritual exercises." (It is the root word from which the word "asceticism" derives, although owing to the extremism connoted by asceticism, Hadot emphasizes that *askesis* is not asceticism.) In referring to "exercises," it is making a direct analogy to physical exercises and athletic practice; as for the adjective "spiritual," Hadot (1995) chooses it over other contenders such as "psychic," "moral," "ethical," "intellectual," "of thought," or "of the soul." While he lingers on "ethical" as the next best choice, he settles on "spiritual" because "these exercises in fact correspond to a transformation of our vision of the world, and to a metamorphosis of our personality" (p. 82). While Ignatius' *Spiritual Exercises* of the sixteenth century are the famous medieval Christian version of this aim, and the original source for the English phrase, Hadot's appropriation of it to define *askesis* is not anachronistic but an intentional effort to reclaim the true, original, root meaning of the phrase as it was embodied in ancient Greek philosophy (which Christianity inherits, appropriates, and adapts, in developing its contemplative tradition; on this point, see Hadot, 1995, pp. 126–144).

Hadot expands this emphasis on *askesis* as "spiritual exercises" as capturing what ancient philosophy was really about in numerous ways. Most basic is that *philosophia* as "love of wisdom" was, prior to any theorizing in a cognitive sense, an existential choice of a way of life that was opposed to ordinary life—i.e., the premise of philosophy is a countercultural critique of "normal society." Inextricable from this choice was that the philosophical way of life was embodied in particular small communities; "schools" (like Plato's Academy, or Epicurus' Garden) or "spiritual communities" (such as that of the Pythagoreans, the Skeptics, or the

Cynics). In Axial Age terms already described in the previous chapter, the "spiritual revolution" or "breakthrough to transcendence" sociologically manifests in a proliferation of such schools. Although each school had its own distinctive take on spirit and transcendence, there is a family resemblance across their differences, too. Hadot (1995) describes their commonalty as follows and in so doing also summarizes the key features of his alternative, corrected image of ancient Greek philosophy:

> Beneath this apparent diversity, however, there is a profound unity, both in the means employed and in the ends pursued. The means employed are the rhetorical and dialectical techniques of persuasion, the attempts at mastering one's inner dialogue, and mental concentration. In all philosophical schools, the goal pursued in these exercises is self-realization and improvement. All schools agree that man, before his philosophical conversion, is in a state of unhappy disquiet. Consumed by worries, torn by passions, he does not live a genuine life, nor is he truly himself. All schools also agree that man can be delivered from this state. He can accede to genuine life, improve himself, transform himself, and attain a state of perfection. It is precisely for this that spiritual exercises are intended. Their goal is a kind of self-formation, or *paideia*, which is to teach us to live, not in conformity with human prejudices and social conventions – for social life is itself a product of the passions – but in conformity with the nature of man, which is none other than reason. ...Underlying this conviction is the parallelism between physical and spiritual exercises: just as, by dint of repeated physical exercises, athletes give new form and strength to their bodies, so the philosopher develops his strength of soul, modifies his inner climate, transforms his vision of the world, and, finally, his entire being. (pp. 101–102)

Phrased negatively, philosophy starts from a critique of social life and social conventions, which ultimately are reducible to uncontrolled passions. As the "critique" is not exclusively intellectual, but embodied in a way of life and in practices of self-control, it will gradually and progressively deepen in its application to the person's inner life, i.e., it can be understood as a "systematic deconstruction" of our undisciplined self. Since "social life is itself a product of the passions," the critique here needs to be understood as both of society and of one's self. Phrased positively, philosophy is a training of "the soul," which through being taught "exercises"—Hadot notes the parallel to physical training—transforms itself toward an ideal "state of perfection," ultimately in the Greek articulation, reason (the *logos*).

We see here the classic Greek distinction of reason vs. passion, with the difference that in its being articulated practically as the result of "spiritual exercises," the duality shifts away from any kind of cognitive reification into ontology or metaphysics and becomes instead a psychological dissonance between the "unhappy disquiet" of a worried, passion-dominated life and the promise of release through pursuit of a "genuine life" wherein reason is in control. "In the view of all philosophical schools, mankind's principal cause of suffering, disorder, and unconsciousness were the passions: that is, unregulated desires and exaggerated fears. People are prevented from truly living, it was taught because they are dominated by worries" (1995, p. 83). In a reversal with which we should becoming familiar, the claim is that "normal" life disorders human being because our untrained, undisciplined selves—"unregulated," "exaggerated"—mislead us as to what is true and truly important, whereas the "abnormal" trained, disciplined self is free from suffering and worry. "Philosophy thus appears, in the first place, as a therapeutic of the passions... Each school had its own therapeutic method, but all of them linked their therapeutics to a profound transformation of the individual's mode of seeing and being. The object of spiritual exercises is precisely to bring about this transformation" (1995, p. 83).

Hopefully, the hold of the established image of philosophy as abstract disembodied theorizing is giving way to an acknowledging of philosophy as a far more holistic, practical, embodied way of life. Hopefully, we are beginning to appreciate a claim such as Bussanich (2016) makes, that "the prominent intellectualism of the Platonic dialogues and of Plato scholars has obscured the existential centrality of the practice of inwardness and tranquillity for philosophers" (p. 87). Acknowledging the hold of that intellectualist image over against the family resemblance of Axial systematic ascetic practice that this chapter is building up, one question that can be directed at Hadot: How far does the "spiritual" component of "spiritual exercises" resemble those of India and China? While those too have rational components, intellectual effort, and instigate philosophical systems in the cognitive sense, it was clear that their notion of spiritual practice had a more inward, non-cognitive object within self-consciousness. Hadot (1995) answers: "every school practices exercises designed to ensure spiritual progress toward the ideal state of wisdom, exercises of reason that will be, for the soul, analogous to the athlete's training or to the application of a medical cure. Generally, they consist, above all, *of self-control and meditation*" (p. 59; my emphasis).

Socrates provides some examples of the latter; Bellah (2011) points out: "If we look at the Socrates described by Alcibiades in *The Symposium*, we will find a man who could lose himself in standing meditation for 24 hours, who could walk barefoot comfortably on ice whereas his fellow soldiers had difficulty walking in boots, who was immune to alcohol, and who did not need sleep" (p. 372). Even supposing this to be glorified hero-worship rather than accurate description, the point obtains: The philosophical ideal is one of radical self-control of body and mind. Bussanich (2016) interprets the Socratic standing meditation claim at face value: "In light of his spiritual experiences – his dreams and daimonic interventions – it is more likely that Socrates was absorbed in a meditative trance of complete detachment from normal sensory awareness and his normal conscious, interactive self" (p. 102). Hartnett (2011) provides the following list in describing the Pythagoreans:

> Life in the Pythagorean community had its own rituals and spiritual exercises and was governed by strict rules ranging from diet to purification rites. The old system of the care of the self that preceded Plato's paradigm was the Pythagorean model with its rites of purification which were necessary to have access to the divine; its techniques for concentrating the soul and keeping it undisturbed, as in preventing the dispersal of the breath, the *pneuma*, and exposure to external danger; withdrawal, disengagement from the world, visible absence; and endurance, to be able to bear ordeals or resist temptation. (p. 53)

Hartnett also points out that in Plato's Academy (the model for which was provided by Plato's experiences with Pythagoreanism alongside the inspiration of Socrates [Hadot, 2002, pp. 57–58]), "[a]s they prepared each evening for sleep, the Academy students practiced meditation to calm their desires; they were cautioned not to sleep too long; to practice calm in the face of misfortune, and to see the study of philosophy as a preparation for death" (p. 101). Bussanich (2016) points out how "Parmenides' practice of stillness, a widespread Pythagorean mental discipline, can be taken as meditative preparation for making the mind changeless and timeless like being" (p. 98). Given this range of examples, it should be evident that Plato's ideal "guardians" of *The Republic* are not so much a piece of imaginative fiction as they are an idealization drawn from practical experience: They "are a kind of monastic order, taking the vow of poverty (significantly, the guardians have no slaves, nor does anyone else in the good city), obedience (to the philosopher king), and, if not the vow of chastity ...at least being saddled with the most profound consequences of the vow of chastity, namely the lack of a spouse or children of one's own" (Bellah, 2011, p. 388). These examples assist in suitably stretching the notion of "school" away from book-learning to being more cultish and monastic. Yet another example, the Cynics, which Hadot (2002) designates as a "spiritual tradition" rather than a "school," provides us with an example of a group whose "philosophy was entirely exercise (*askesis*) and effort":

> There are many typically Cynic philosophical concepts, but they are not used in logical argumentation. Instead, they serve to designate concrete attitudes which correspond to the choice of life: *askesis, ataraxia* (lack of worry), *autarkeia* (independence), effort, adaptation to circumstances, impassiveness, simplicity or the absence of vanity (*atuphia*), lack of modesty (p. 110).

In sum, *askesis* in Greece is indeed comparably "spiritual" in its content and orientation to the Chinese and Indian cases. As we will see below, it is similarly comparable in terms of systematicity in articulating degrees or levels of attainment. However, there are significant differences, too. In terms of the use of the term "meditation," for example, there are two significant differences. The first involves the lack of attention—or in some cases, such as Platonism, the intentional overlooking—paid to the body: "Unlike the Buddhist meditation practices of the Far East, Greco-Roman philosophical meditation *is not linked to a corporeal attitude* but is a purely rational, imaginative, or intuitive exercise that can take extremely varied forms" (1995, p. 59; emphasis added). Not only unlike Buddhist meditation practices, we could further add that this is distinct from Indian yoga, Taoism, and Confucianism as well, insofar as all of the above, to varying degrees, include bodily awareness, control, posture, etc., as a key piece in the development of systematic spiritual practice. Of course, the disparagement of the body in some of the traditions, like Plato's, is not necessarily in order to ignore it, but because the aim of *askesis* is to overcome it. Bussanich (2016), for example, claims "the practice of purification Socrates presents in the *Phaedo* withdraws consciousness from sense-objects through introspective concentration" (p. 98).

Another possibility: Due to the culturally normal existence of physical *askesis* undertaken in the gymnasium during young adulthood, it was assumed as existing and preparatory to spiritual *askesis* but not needing a focus in its own right. Regardless, it is a significantly noticeable difference from the Eastern practices. Although Hadot presents a great variety of different types of *askesis* across different schools and thinkers of ancient Greece, one commonalty is their lack of attention to bodily posture or breathing or to the physiological; all are working at "mental" levels of the will, imagination, intuition, attention, and concentration.

> Some, like Plutarch's *ethismoi*, designed to curb curiosity, anger, or gossip, were only practices intended to ensure good moral habits. Others, particularly the meditations of the Platonic tradition, demanded a high degree of mental concentration. Some, like the contemplation of nature as practiced in all philosophical schools, turned the soul toward the cosmos, while still others – rare and exceptional – led to a transfiguration of the personality, as in the experiences of Plotinus. (1995, p. 101)

A second significant difference from India consists in the meaning of the term meditation. The preferred term for the highest level of philosophical meditation in ancient Greece, *theoria*, will be translated into the Latin as *contemplatio* (and will be taken up by Christianity in that form). This becomes taken up into the basic distinction between *meditatio*, as intense sustained discursive reflection, over against *contemplatio*, as a higher or deeper level, practice of nondiscursive awareness. In terms of comparison, Western contemplation is therefore most directly parallel with Eastern meditation, whereas meditation in the West is, when translated into Eastern terminology, a more cognitively oriented concentration operating at a lower degree of practical attainment—for example, the yogic stage of *dhyana* might be translated into Western meditation, whereas the higher stage of *samadhi* would be translated contemplation.

The latter point begs a further question: Was Greek *askesis* also systematized into different levels and degrees of spiritual attainment? Bussanich answers yes: "The Platonic practice of stillness and concentration, in conjunction with the cultivation of intellectual virtue, leads to the transformation of a person's substance by the removal of hindrances and defilements, as in the yogic traditions. The effects of pains, pleasures and unjust actions on the soul are likened to scars and stamps, rivets, and incrustations attached to the soul" (2016, p. 101). Hadot answers yes, and in fact, he makes the point of "systematicity" even stronger: Greek philosophical texts can only be considered systematic from the practical point of view of a practitioner's spiritual development. Hadot points out that Greek philosophical texts lack the systematicity of pure logic or theory, and interpreters who approach them from that angle have often expressed surprise, consternation, and judgment on these texts for lacking the degree of intellectual rigor that the exegete is (mistakenly) expecting from them. Instead, Hadot (2002) claims "In philosophical works such as these, thought cannot be expressed according to the pure, absolute necessity of a systematic order. Rather, it must take into account the level of the interlocutor, and the concrete tempo of the *logos* in which it is expressed" (p. 105). Hadot occasionally describes the teacher of a philosophical school as a "spiritual director," much of whose work is assessing the level of attainment of a student, and hence the needs of that student relative to that level; they were "genuine directors of conscience who cared for their students' spiritual problems" (2002, p. 156).

> This idea of spiritual progress meant that disciples could not undertake the study of a work until they had reached the intellectual and spiritual level which allowed them to profit from it. Certain works were reserved for beginners; others for those making progress. Thus, the complex questions reserved for students making progress were not raised in works intended for beginners. (2002, p. 154)

Hadot further argues that decontextualizing the theoretical texts of philosophy from their living context of addressing concretely the spiritual progress of the student has contributed greatly to their being misunderstood as abstract systems, and to the false picture of philosophy as heady disembodied reasoning. Instead, he says that texts were subordinate to the practical work of spiritual exercises and the oral communications around that work, and served a heuristic purpose relative to those spiritual goals.

> Unlike their modern counterparts, none of these philosophical productions, even the systematic works, is addressed to everyone, to a general audience, but they are intended first of all for the group formed by the members of the school; often they echo problems raised by the oral teaching. ...Above all, the work, even if it is apparently theoretical and systematic, is written not so much to inform the reader of a doctrinal content but to form him, to make him traverse a certain itinerary in the course of which he will make spiritual progress. ...One must always approach a philosophical work of antiquity with this idea of spiritual progress in mind. (1995, p. 64)

One outcome of systematizing of spiritual practice applied to this "idea of spiritual progress": the emergence in Hellenistic times of the influential notion of the "ascent" of the soul. Already prefigured in Pythagoras and Plato's conceptions, evident in someone like Philo and probably best embodied in the Neoplatonist tradition (think of Plotinus [203–270 CE], briefly mentioned in the above quote by Hadot), the notion is that the soul ascends into the spiritual by a series of stages of attainment of greater degrees of contemplative achievement. Thus, many of the avowedly "mystical" texts by persons like Philo or Plotinus are partly descriptions of this "itinerary" of "ascent." Given the dramatic shift in perception Hadot is attempting to accomplish through his work, we should perceive that the appellation "philosophical" to Axial Age Greek texts over against the later appellation "mystical" to texts of antiquity, is somewhat false.

It is also my hope that the reader will be willing to say something similar regarding the working image of Greek philosophy based on "common knowledge" prior to reading this section: somewhat false. Not entirely, but ideally some degree of a Gestalt switch in perception has occurred relative to philosophy as heady rational theorizing that was abstract and intellectual, becoming instead a systematic practice of spiritual exercises aimed at deep and radical transformation of the personality (to which aim intellectual theory and abstract heady stuff is certainly subordinate). In fact, Bussanich (2016) criticizes Hadot for not going far enough: "It should be noted that Hadot's rich account of philosophy as a way of life, drawing as it does mostly on Hellenistic philosophy and on the Socrates of the early dialogues, largely ignores the other-worldly dimension of the later dialogues. Thus, his picture of Platonic spiritual exercises, which reflect the equivalence of psychology and cosmology, is incomplete" (p. 97). To put a finishing touch on this switch of perception: it is well known—"common knowledge"—that the most avowed enemy to Socrates and Plato were the Sophists. On Hadot's (2002) account, they were the enemy to all philosophy:

> They constantly attacked those who... seek to be admired for their skill at syllogistic arguing but contradict themselves in the conduct of their lives. ...Traditionally, people who developed an apparently philosophical discourse without trying to live their lives in accordance with their discourse, and without their discourse emanating from their lived experience, were called "Sophists." (p. 174)

Like the Mohists discussed last chapter and this chapter in the context of China, insofar as the Sophists displayed "systematic rationalism" and "second-order thinking" in their philosophizing, they too can be considered Axial. By my argument as to the distinctiveness of the Axial contribution being their systematization of spiritual practice, however, the Sophists like the Mohists would be excluded from consideration. As for the irony of this quote vis-à-vis our modern picture of the philosophers and in light of this section's examination of philosophy as above all spiritual exercises, it deserves a wry chuckle and requires, I assume, no elaboration.

SCHOLARLY COMPLICATIONS OF AXIAL AGE ISRAEL

Turning to search for evidence of the development of systematic ascetic practice in ancient Israel, we also encounter the hardest case. To put it bluntly, this is because by comparison with all the other cases, we have no evidence. Recalling the previous chapter's discussion of Israel, which made note of the scholarly complications to our picture of ancient Israel, the heart of the issue is that we may never know the historical reality of pre-exilic, pre-sixth century BCE Israel "behind" the literary texts written, post-exile, in the sixth century and later. Our only access to the former is the latter, and why should the latter be considered historically or empirically accurate? Over the past couple of generations of scholars—going through a particular sea change in the 1980s, and apparently going through another again in the past two decades—the ahistorical, unhistorical, and antihistorical possibilities have been explored as increasingly plausible owing to the fact that almost the entirety of the substance of the feast that is "ancient Israelite history" is text written, edited, revised, redacted, and collated centuries after those putative historical events (Davies, 2000; Holt, 2016). Thus, the interpretation offered in the previous chapter which accords with the usual way of presenting Axial Age scholarship on ancient Israel is open to critical revision insofar as it unproblematically assumes a fair degree of historical accuracy to the texts.

To cite one dramatic version of the critical scholarly thesis, for example: Perhaps the "Davidic/Solomonic states did not exist at all"! Rather, their existence was "carefully constructed" by "a Judaean diasporic community, or a quasi-political minority under Persian hegemony" (Smith-Christopher, 2002, p. 26; see, e.g., Davies, 1992). Yes, some archeological crumbs help to counter some of the problems around ascribing empirical certainty to any of the claims from the texts: A thirteenth century BCE inscription from Egypt mentions the Israelites (Sweeney, 2000, p. 24); we have "an inscribed potsherd from Lachish, written shortly before the fall of Jerusalem in 587 B.C.E" (Blenkinsopp, 1995, p. 119). How far this (minimal) archeological evidence can take us should not, however, be overvalued. The reliability of the prophetic texts to speak to historical fact is a wide-open and unresolved question.

If the point of these writings was not historical accuracy but "an exercise in self-definition, in a conscious attempt to invent an 'Israel' that had an ancient history, a constitution, a land, and a wisdom ethic" (Davies, 2000, p. 45), such that, for example, the representation of "a prophet in the Former Prophets is similar to actual ancient noninductive diviners as a television cop is similar to actual police investigators," then verisimilitude is off the table (quote from Noll, 2013, p. 126). Obviously, this questionability impacts substantially understanding the Axial Age of Israel. Nevertheless, it should be emphasized up front that this more recent, more critical, reading of ancient Israel does not in itself contradict the Axial Age hypothesis—the dates for exile to Babylon (587 BCE) and the return to Jerusalem (538 BCE) are sixth century BCE, after all—but it would considerably qualify how the Axiality of "Israel" could and should be interpreted.

If we follow the later, more critical scholarly view of the literature on prophecy as developed, post-exile, alongside the development of Second Temple Judaism, with prophets and prophecy constructed to meet needs contemporary to their times, the Axial thesis holds but with considerable qualification. Scribal accounts from the sixth century BCE in the context of a conquered, captured, exiled, and returned people (Smith-Christopher, 2002), proposing descriptions of those earlier centuries when Israel or Judah were independent nations with their own kings, priesthood, temple, prophets, etc. are obviously to a much greater degree less historically accurate stories regarding pre-exilic times. In view of this changing interpretive landscape, scholarly strategy—from earlier efforts to winnow from the mythical chaff the empirical kernels of actual history, actual persons, and actual events, to current efforts to provide textual- and literary-critical interpretations that go at best only modestly beyond the texts, if at all—has changed accordingly. And, of course, a third option is available that is a compromise between the previous two. Yes, as the later critical scholarly view emphasizes, the texts are a post-exilic construction of pre-exilic times and prophecy. But they are not "pure fantasy" nor constructed primarily for "entertainment"—the comparison to a television cop show, while insightful to an extent, is also anachronistic and misleading, too—and they might well be basing their constructions on existing practice and examples of living extant prophets of the sixth century BCE. The difference here is the "historical kernels" are not derived from seventh or eighth or tenth century BCE originals, but derived from sixth-century examples contemporaneous with the authors, projected into the past and claimed to be ancient. (It would not be the first time an "ancient" tradition was "invented" [Hobsbawn & Ranger, 1983].)

Later scholarship presents a very different premise to dissident intellectuals who courageously "spoke truth to power" against corrupt kings and rulers, temples and priests, and against the whole project of "imperialism," from a premise of "ethical monotheism." Instead, it presents traumatized exiles creating literary constructions of prophetic personas as dramatic figures populating a mythical story to supply identity for a diasporic community. This "literary construction" approach of later scholarship could well be based on "small kernels of truth" based on the persons and practices of prophets and prophetic groups active at the time of that writing. That is, they are not historically accurate in terms of a past Israel of the twelfth or tenth or ninth century BCE; but they can provide us some historical access to their present moment of the sixth or fifth century BCE.

For example: "Elijah apparently fasted during the forty days and nights required to reach the sacred mountain" (Wilson, 1980, p. 197). Let's assume this is entirely false, and the author is recreating an "Elijah" based on Moses as paradigmatic prophet; "Elijah" is not real, as there is no real Elijah he didn't really fast, the forty days and nights is clearly a symbolic number that recalls Israel's wandering for forty years in the desert, reaching the sacred mountain merely replays Moses ascent to Sinai. (Of course, the myth-making, fictional construction claim goes deeper, too; Moses and the Exodus from Egypt and Israel's wandering in desert may well all be "entirely false"!) If we take this example as "purely symbolic," presenting in literary stereotypical form a prophetic vision-quest to a mountaintop including a period of time for purification along with fasting as part of the symbolic form, where did the stereotypes and symbols come from? That some form of actual prophetic practice of mountain vision-questing, with a preparatory period, and with accompanying purificatory practices like fasting, existed, on which the literary idealization was based, seems incontrovertible. (That it was what was practiced, and how it was practiced, four centuries earlier; very controvertible!) Thus, for example, Lindblom's (1962) *Prophecy in Ancient Israel*, which claims to reconstruct the historical aspects and developments of pre-exilic prophecy from early to classical to later prophets across centuries, could be recast as a projection from post-exilic prophecy as practiced in the sixth century, or more complexly, how it would have been typified and re-imagined by sixth-century writers—for instance, to address the trauma of exile and return.

In short, the current state of specialist scholarship on ancient Israel provides Axial Age scholarship with some options to choose from and considerable critical work to be done. Whether we choose option two or three, it is far beyond the scope of my aims in this book, let alone in this chapter, to explore the implications of this specialized scholarship for the Axial Age thesis. To repeat: owing to the problem of dating, this does not negate the Axial Age thesis for "Israel," as both pre- and post-exilic dates for "Israel" fall within the time-span of the Axial Age. In fact, the contemporary, more critical scholarly claim of a traumatized post-exilic literary construction for a diasporic identity confirms and deepens the Axial Age hypothesis in a fascinating way—but it also dramatically qualifies earlier versions of the Axial Age thesis.

Prophecy in Pre-exile Israel: Ecstasy, Guilds, and Training?

Lindblom (1962), who belongs to the earlier phase of scholarship, presents a fascinating picture of the prophets of ancient Israel that, if we were to endorse his premise (i.e., the first option), is a "historically accurate" picture for pre-exile. If we endorse the second option, it has little worth as its premise is false. If we endorse the third option it has some worth, not for knowing what pre-exilic philosophy was like, but in being derived to some extent from post-exilic prophecy with which the authors of the prophetic books had some degree of familiarity.

Lindblom (1962) points out that "[s]ometimes [the earlier prophets] appeared in groups or bands, accompanied by music and raving in ecstasy" (p. 69). This latter point is crucial for Lindblom's reconstruction: Ecstasy is the central concept undergirding his conception of prophecy. Rowley (1956), another early scholar, asserts "there can be no doubt whatever that Israelite prophets were often ecstatic" (p. 14). We are reminded of Nissinen's (2016) distinguishing characteristic for prophets among the great diversity of divine intermediaries mentioned the last chapter: "the lack of the use of inductive or technical methodology"; "in contrast, prophecy is understood as a non-technical, intuitive, or inspired kind of divination, with the prophet acting as mouthpiece of the deity" (p. 6). By comparison with the numerous other kinds of diviners and many types of divination that use an "inductive or technical methodology," prophecy ultimately devolves on the person of the prophet himself or herself. The notion is that the deity does not work via some other medium that the diviner interprets, but more directly, the "person" of the prophet himself or herself is the medium for the message of the god. In this sense, prophecy is "non-technical, intuitive, or inspired kind of divination." The connection to the deity is direct and personal (the prophet, unlike other diviners, cannot blame his or her "tools"). It also stands in strong contrast to the temple cult and to the priests who administered the ritual, as the prophet's source of knowledge was "due to direct personal contact with Yahweh" (Johnson, 1962, p. 57). That it devolves on the person rather than any other tool or technique, presumably means it would manifest in or through that person in some way. The common phrasing in the Hebrew Bible texts is that "the hand of God came upon" the prophet, usually understood to mean the appearance of an altered state of consciousness, most specifically an ecstatic state. While Nissinen (2016) finds "no specific set of skills required" according to the sources, he does go on to add that "the ability to reach an altered state of consciousness and to combine it with a convincing public behavior and performance was probably a general expectation" (p. 6). This "ability to reach an altered state of consciousness" that prophets possessed suggests the possibility of precisely skilfull training in that ability. This was the evidence Lindblom found using contemporary analogies, and that he claims to find among the early prophetic groups or guilds: Each of these groups was under the direction of a leader who "had to train the members of the guild in ecstatic exercises and ecstatic practice and also instruct them in matters belonging to true Yahwistic religion and cult" (1962, p. 69). "The main business of those early 'bene hannebi'im' seems to have been exercises in the art of ecstasy and oracle-giving" (p. 161). "The ecstasy of the professional prophets of early times was induced. Under the guidance of the teacher the members of the prophetic guilds trained themselves in ecstatic exercises until the desired psychical state was experienced" (p. 181). By comparison with the rest of the ancient Near East, that prophets could "self-induce" states of ecstasy seems solidly evidenced; however, by the same token, prophecy as culturally normative, widespread, enormously variable in its expression, and largely "unpoliced," it was also recognized that the mere existence of an ecstatic state did not qualify to make the corresponding vision or message authentic (Nissinen, 2010, 2016).

These claims of Lindblom's are premised on his assumption that the Hebrew Bible texts contain enough historical accuracy to reconstruct the pre-exilic past of Israel. Based on this premise, he goes on to discern a significant change within Israelite prophecy by the time of the classical prophets. One key part of the difference: The role of ecstasy and training for it has been either greatly minimized or disappeared altogether. A second key difference: Rather than large groups or "guilds" of prophets gathered together, we encounter either small circles of disciples gathered around a lead prophet, who communally sustain that prophet's message through shared story and through writing it down; or the classical prophets were individuals without a following (Lindblom, 1962, pp. 161, 181). If we adopt the premise of the second or third option based on later critical scholarship, I don't know what would be made of this distinction for which Lindblom argues. Perhaps, for example, the basis of this distinction for the post-exilic authors of the texts was that the "earlier prophets" were based on oral histories and legends inherited from before exile, while the "classical prophets" were drawn from living memories or existing practices? Perhaps the authors had no first-hand experience of prophets or prophetic groups, and we have a solely literary imagining that in some respects is therefore entirely unrealistic? Questions like this remain for specialized scholarship to answer. Unfortunately for my thesis, there is no "Prophet Sutra" comparable to the *Yoga Sutra*, no *Ecstatic Training* text comparable to the Taoist *Inward Training* text, and no scholars arguing for some kind of "prophetic *askesis*." The lack of specification opens up differing scholarly interpretations.

A very different interpretation of the lack of specification of skills or training is provided by Fishbane (1986). He agrees with some version of the importance of an "ecstatic" state of consciousness, in the sense of the prophets being "persons who believed themselves to be transmitters of divine words that obsessed and possessed them" (p. 70). Their experience of God's calling to them to become prophets he describes in appropriately dramatic language; its "tremendous power," the consequences of a "striking state of self-surrender"; "the singular self shudderingly succumbs to the force of a divine presence that finds thereby both a 'mouth' and a means of earthly expression" (p. 66). Thus, for Fishbane the solitary aspect of this happening to an individual is a crucial feature, rather than any social solidarity; like Abraham in Kierkegaard's (2006) *Fear and Trembling*, the prophet must bear the ordeal of God's command alone. Further, the spontaneous, unprompted, "unexpected eruption" of God's revelation into the prophet's life is also a crucial feature. In fact, Fishbane emphatically insists, discussing Isaiah, Ezekiel and Amos, that "the suddenness and transforming character of these experiences suggests that *they were not the climax of spiritual or contemplative exercises, or the inheritance of some spiritual lineage*" (p. 64; my emphasis). (He uses this distinction to set classical prophecy apart from later apocalyptic writing; the visions of the prophets are "far removed from the contemplative ecstasies of later Jewish mystics" [p. 64].) "The overriding criterion of a true prophecy lay in its subjective impact on the prophet himself" (p. 72).

Of course, a first problem with Fishbane's interpretation is that he, like Lindblom, assumes the first option of earlier scholarship. If we don't take these accounts as historically accurate it takes much of the power of his account of prophecy away (relocating that power within theology instead). The claim that the criterion for the truth of prophecy resides in its "subjective impact" is multiply problematic, most basically in the logical contradiction between the relativistic implications of the claim undermining the very rationale for having a criterion. It is also problematic if the text is primarily a literary construction rather than empirically descriptive, as there would no longer be any "subjective impact" but rather rhetorical effectiveness and literary technique in conveying a story or belief.

Of most interest for this chapter is the claim that the "sudden and transforming character of these experiences" is an argument against "spiritual and contemplative exercises." To accept this, we need to concede two points. First, we have to concede the plausibility of the argument for a whole series of individuals appearing to become prophets, regularly across centuries, again and again, because of the transformative power of those experiences which are ultimately unpredictable and in every case occurring to an unprepared individual "by accident," i.e., due to God's will. This is of course what the overt narrative of the texts claim, based on the theological belief of the authors of the Hebrew Bible in the truth of prophetic experience as being revelatory of God's will; that is, a powerful God intervenes into those individuals' lives causing those experiences. Obviously, my own argument, based on a historical effort to empirically investigate the conditions of the Axial Age comparatively, proceeds quite differently. If we start from the first option of earlier scholarship on ancient Israel that the textual descriptions have some kernels of historical truth (as Fishbane does), then I find much more plausible that the regular appearance of comparable visionary experiences across centuries is due to a comparable systematicity in how those individuals were members of certain groups or communities that were trained in particular techniques aimed at inducing ecstatic states and visionary experiences, and that those few who succeeded at achieving such powerful experiences become remembered along with the visions they presented (as Lindblom argues, also based on assuming the first option).

The second concession we'd have to make to Fishbane's argument is his assumption that sustained spiritual exercises would gradually and expectably transform the person, over against the "sudden" and "transformative" prophetic call, which is unexpected, immediate, and impactful. As far as I can tell, this misunderstands sustained spiritual practice. Yes, such practice aims for a transformation of self but this does not mean that if such a transformative moment occurs it is *not* experienced as sudden or unexpected or impactful. In fact, by all accounts, the contrary. Whether the moment occurs is not guaranteed, and in instances where it does, the moment of insight or enlightenment and the breakthrough in the practitioner's understanding are invariably described as sudden, unexpected, and impactful. There is a hugely significant difference between maximizing the potential for something to occur (as spiritual practice aims to do) and guaranteeing that it will (an ego-driven demand for certainty that misunderstands the truth of the "other world" of spirit and hence the true import and aim of spiritual exercises). The mysterious "otherness" of non-egocentric consciousness, which is inconceivable to egocentric consciousness, can and does "erupt" spontaneously and surprisingly into a practitioner's inner life. Ironically, most of the literature on spiritual practices warn practitioners away from attending to spectacular experiences; these are mere side effects.

The point here is not to decide. The point is we have no definitive evidence for systematic training in ecstatic practices undertaken by the Israeli prophets, and Lindblom's strong argument for the latter proves ultimately based more on his contemporary analogies which he reads into the Hebrew Biblical material, than it is on textual evidence proper.

We can at best only speculate, through the complexly indirect evidence afforded us by post-exilic texts, as to the sociology of pre-exile Israel prophets centered on ecstatic states of consciousness in which they orally proclaimed the word of Yahweh, that they accomplished this through sustained systematic practice aimed inwardly. We can with far greater certainty point to the emergence of written text as the post-exilic center for the authoritative word of Yahweh. Both share the notion of inspiration and both share claim to access the word of Yahweh (although they differ in how they understand the nature of that access). That prophecy takes the form of prophetic books that add to the growing textual corpus that will become the basis for the Torah and for Rabbinic Judaism (a distinctively Judaic development, found nowhere else in the ancient Near East [Middlemas, 2016])—i.e., scripture as "the Law *and* the Prophets"—clearly signals a sea change from ecstatic visions as evidence of Yahweh's "direct contact" with a person, the prophet, who speaks the word, to a deep engagement in interpretation of God's word as text as the center for inspiration.

THE "ENDS" OF PROPHECY POST-EXILE: SAGES, APOCALYPSES, MYSTICS, ESSENES, AND ASCETIC JUDAISM

Captivity, exile, and diaspora, destroys the monarchy and the temple at Jerusalem and in so doing reconfigures the unofficial and unpoliced, culturally normative status of prophecy. Prophecy does not disappear; some of it continues in nominally a similar form but as a subcultural, fringe activity. The remainder is dispersed and differentiated into a number of diverse communities of interpretation organized around text (legal texts, prophetic texts, wisdom texts, apocalyptic/mystical texts, etc.). A note of caution regarding this last claim: We should not impose the later development of Judaism, based on its transformation by the rabbinic elite in the context and aftermath of the destruction of the Second Temple, nor the pre-eminent emphasis on the Torah for the meaning of texts, back onto these centuries. As Neusner (1986) puts it: "Surveying the landscape of ancient Judaism from the perspective of the Maccabean times, ca. 150 B.C.E., we search in vain for the rabbi as model and authority, Torah as the principal and organizing symbol, study of Torah as the capital religious deed, the life of religious discipline as the prime expression of what it means to be Israel, the Jewish people" (p. 171).

Post-exile, in the absence of a monarchy but in the presence of the Second Temple and with a greater emphasis on scriptural text, prophecy becomes contested quite differently than within the power trio of prophet-priest-king. From a later perspective, claims would be made that make this contestation clear: "Prophecy, [the Sages] claimed, had ceased after the construction of the Second Temple: [quoting a Qumran text] 'After the later prophets Haggai, Zechariah and Malachi had died, the Holy Spirit abandoned Israel'" (Elior, 2005, p. 214). Elior (2005) cites one rabbinic tradition as claiming that before Alexander the Great, but not after, "prophets would prophesy in the Holy Spirit"; she quotes another that "puts the disappearance of prophecy even earlier, dating it to the destruction of the First Temple" (p. 214). Clearly, from the later rabbinic perspective, the intention is to delegitimate prophecy (in line with, albeit even more radically than, the Deuteronomist). Influential as these views were, they were not the entirety of reality, and prophecy did continue. To jump ahead some centuries to the turn of the millennium and the beginnings of Christianity (as presumably more familiar to most readers than mid-first millennium BCE Judaism), both John the Baptist and Jesus attest to "prophetic activity" continuing to happen, even if only on the fringes of official religion; centuries later still, the prophet Mani (third century CE), and the prophet Muhammad, founding Manicheism and Islam respectively, further attest that prophecy did not end in the sense of disappear.

After a careful review of the evidence, Nissinen (2006) provides this summary conclusion:

> ...it appears that prophecy did not cease altogether. However, it is very difficult to draw a trustworthy image of the prophets of the period that covers some three centuries. ...It is evident, however, that *the bloom of literary prophecy, triggered by the continuation of prophecy on the literary level as a kind of scribal divination*, eclipsed the traditional, more or less ecstatic manifestations of prophecy. ...Some forms of traditional prophetic activity, as attested in the Hebrew Bible as well as in the Near Eastern sources, probably continued to exist, but the texts discussed in this article reveal that they were despised rather than appreciated by the learned circles and were therefore probably driven to the margins of the society." (p. 41; emphases mine. cf. also Brooke, 2006)

Note that in terms of the continuation of traditional ecstatic prophecy being "driven to the margins of the society," insofar as the little post-exilic province of Yehud/Judaea was itself marginal in ancient Near Eastern civilizational terms, the prophet in this context would be "doubly marginal."

Central to what Nissinen identifies as the key transformation wrought on prophecy, however, is that as inspiration and as voicepiece for the word of Yahweh, in the post-exilic context prophecy continues but no longer primarily in the form of ecstatic possession and vision and speaking the word of God (orally), but in a literary form of inspired reading and interpretation of the word of God (as text). The prophetic message of God to the Israelites doesn't have a due date or become past tense, but if it is continuous and ongoing in the life of Israel (as believers believed), then its meaning in the present would require effort and renewal in the work of interpretation. And ultimately what would guarantee this effort and renewal would have to be God's guiding hand, inspiring the interpreter to the proper interpretation. In a complex sense well-captured by the ambiguity and polysemy in the word "end"—as finished, but also as purpose, completion, or fulfillment—this transformation into the ongoing interpretation of text is one "end" of pre-exilic prophecy.

To this dramatic post-exilic transformation of prophecy (from ecstatic orality to inspired text), a further piece must be added that further complicates our historical picture of the Axial Age Israeli *nabi*: the emergence of the new genre(s) of apocalyptic/mystical literature that displaces— or extends?—prophetic literature. The Persian period ends abruptly with the conquests of Alexander the Great and ushers in the Hellenistic period starting from 333 BCE. While there is much speculation about to what degree the Persian religion of state-sponsored Zoroastrianism influenced Israelite religion, particularly in terms of introducing eschatological and apocalyptic motifs, none has been substantiated (cf. Grabbe, 2004, pp. 361–364). On the other hand, that Hellenistic thought has influenced apocalypticism within Judaism is not contested. While Grabbe (2003a) disputes that, as some scholars argue, the apocalyptic is the *product* of Hellenization, he does claim "there is no doubt that the Hellenistic period provided a congenial context for the apocalyptic" (p. 34). A motivation for finding non-Judaic influences is due to the shifts that occur from the prophetic texts to the apocalyptic texts, a shift first discernible in texts from third century BCE (Himmelfarb, 1986).

Prophetic messages are usually clearly defined in a specific historical and social setting, speaking to a definite ruler or audience, with a critical message including relatively immediate circumstances, whereas the apocalyptic stories are more fantastical, mystical, or visionary in tone, often veiled, elusive, or esoteric in their references, without a definite audience or with a mystical one (e.g., angels), and set in a more mythical, often eschatological ("end-of-time"), context, rather than a historical one. Some of these shifts seem very understandable given the dramatic change effected by conquest and captivity; pre-exile, whether Israel or Judah, the people have a monarch and land of their own and the temple at Jerusalem, whereas post-exile, many are living in a diaspora across the Near East. The prophetic and apocalyptic modes address the needs of identity and religious belonging that have become very different. Certainly, the meaning of "nationalistic self-consciousness," which both modes assume and presuppose, was not problematic to invoke pre-exile, whereas post-exile it is far more problematic. Analogously, an eschatological claim dramatically transforms, too; pre-exile, it would clearly speak to the nation of Israel or Judah coming to an end. Post-exile, the text could no longer mean that, and the imagined end-time becomes less immediate and concrete, more fantastical and mythicized. On the basis of these kinds of differences, "[m]any scholars have seen a gradual shift from prophetic to apocalyptic literature, via 'late' or 'post-exilic' prophetic books" (Grabbe, 2003b, p. 194). The apocalyptic texts can be seen as another "end" of prophecy, akin to but different than ongoing "official" interpretation, framed by an eschatological reordering of history.

Also emerging during the Second Temple period in the last centuries BCE and into the first centuries CE are a number of Jewish mystical texts. A number are the same as, or overlap significantly with, the apocalyptic texts. The key difference is how they found the later "mystical traditions" of the *Merkavah* ("chariot") or *Heikhalot* ("heavenly palace") (Dan, 1986; Gruenwald, 1980). Elior (2005) provides a fascinating account based on the Qumran scrolls of the emergence of Jewish mysticism rooted specifically in the politics of access to the Second Temple of competing priestly traditions in the first centuries BCE. It is also rooted, in a more general way, in a shared anxiety across Judaism over the meaning of access to Yahweh in light of the undeniable fact that the temple could be destroyed. The replacement of the literal, physical visit to the temple with a more spiritualized mystical "ascent" of the soul of the believer to heaven, as first articulated in the famous vision of Ezekiel and subsequently elaborated in a great variety of ways in numerous mystical/

apocalyptic texts, shows a potent transformation of the prophetic (see McGinn, 1991, pp. 12–18). Himmelfarb (1986) points out that Enoch "is able to stand before [Yahweh's] throne! In doing so he continues the tradition of the prophets who stand in the heavenly council" (p. 162). The apocalyptic/mystical text retains the ecstatic, visionary, experiential aspect of earlier prophecy on the one hand adumbrated with distinctly Hellenist and particularly Neoplatonist themes of the soul's ascent from the earth into the heavens, and/or from the physical into the spiritual, but grounds it in the increasingly important basis of textual authority on the other. Himmelfarb (1986) is cautious about to what extent something like the *Book of the Watchers* or *1 Enoch* could be interpreted as describing actual mystical experiences, but she notes as a generalization based on Gershom Scholem's work that "the *hekhalot* texts… are generally regarded as reflecting actual ascents, in part because some describe the procedure for achieving assent" (p. 153). McGinn (1991) similarly argues "Although direct proof is lacking, there seems to be good arguments for claiming that the visionary accounts found in the other-worldly-journey apocalypses are based, at least in part, on the practices and experiences of individuals and groups in the Judaism of the time" (p. 17). Fraade (1986) points to a slightly different reading of the books of the *Apocrypha* and *Pseudepigrapha* (several of which are the same apocalyptic/mystical texts to which Himmelfarb refers) and observes that they "repeatedly" refer to a host of ascetic practices, and that these are undertaken to obtain a variety of goals.

> These practices are employed for such purposes as: (a) preparing to receive a revelation or vision; (b) accompanying supplication to God, whether for revelation, wisdom, divine protection, or healing; (c) repenting for intentional or unintentional sins; (d) curbing the appetites and passions and guarding against sin. The specific practices mentioned include the following, often in combination: (a) fasting; (b) other forms of voluntary diet restriction (e.g., no wine or meat); (c) abstaining from washing or anointing; (d) sexual continence (temporary or permanent); (e) simple, coarse dress; and (f) flight to an uninhabited "wilderness." (pp. 261–262)

The list is fairly extensive, of both practices as well as their purposes. However, it is a list, which amounts to an impressive collection, but in both respects there is a lack of coherent systematization of how these would be organized. As such they lack the degree of intentional asceticism that would set them apart from the asceticism of religious-practice-in-general. This orientation toward apocalyptic and mystical themes, with some degree of ascetic practices, and a strong emphasis on mystical visionary experience, is a significantly different, yet still related, development of post-exilic prophecy than that of "literary prophecy as scribal divination." Transformation into mystical accounts of spiritual experience could be seen as yet another "end" of prophecy.

It is also significant, to return to Elior's account (2005), that this kind of mystical experiential text might issue from a priestly lineage deprived of Temple access and rights (Zadokite priests, traditionally in charge of the temple, having been removed from that role during the Hasmonean dynasty and a rival group appointed). This is a significantly different innovation for prophecy than, for example, a priest like Ezekiel also being a prophet; now an entire community over time, committed to priestly rites of purity and rituals of purification normally performed in the temple, write prophetic books in which their visionary experiences attest to the presence of Yahweh, in lieu of his presence at the temple. Following the discovery of the Dead Sea scrolls and the excitement over solving the mysterious identity of the Qumran community, the initial solution was that these were Essenes (following second-century BCE Jewish historian Flavius Josephus). An abundance of scholarship and criticism later, the identity of the Qumran community as well as just who the Essenes were has been more carefully delineated (Taylor, 2012). No consensus has developed.

As we've just briefly summarized, Elior argues they were Zadokite priests dispossessed by Hasmonean-appointed priests. Without the same type of in-depth detail as Elior, Neusner (1986) agrees with the "dispossessed priestly lineage" argument, emphasizing that what was crucial for them was that the community itself had become the replacement of the Temple (pp. 186–188). Joan Taylor (2012), just mentioned, argues they were Essenes supported by Herod and that Qumran was a "scroll-burying center." Silver (2017) contends the community was indeed Essene, but that this means they were Pythagoreans; he argues that the Qumran-Essenes were a branch developed in parallel alongside the Jewish Therapeutae from Alexandria, and that the community "may well have been an elitist, aristocratic escape retreat" (p. 507). Justin Taylor (2004) argues something of a compromise position, that they were Essenes who were heavily influenced by Pythagoreanism, by way of Alexandria, which distinguished them from most other Jewish groups who tended to look east to Babylon rather than west to Egypt (pp. 106–107). Talmon (1993) argues that this "community of the renewed covenant" (*yahad*) arose during the Second Temple period from the prophetic-apocalyptic orientation in parallel with, and in direct contrast and competition to, a "rationalist stream" (p. 22) that become the rabbis and sages, above all the within the ranks of the Pharisees, of Rabbinic Judaism.

Fortunately, we do not need to resolve this argument relative to our purposes of understanding the transformations of post-exilic prophecy. Talmon (1993) in concluding his argument provides a useful consideration regarding the diverse scholarly theories: "Analogies or similarities of the *yahad's* ritual laws with Sadducean *halakhah*, of its communal structure with that of the Essenes, of their hyper-nomistic outlook with that of the Samaritans, or of a religious vocabulary which at times overlaps with the creedal terminology of nascent Christianity, spring from common traditions rooted in the Hebrew Bible, in which all configurations of Judaism at the turn of the era had a share" (1993, p. 24). Nowhere do we see, however, a "configuration" claiming to be prophets such as presumably existed in pre-exilic Israel. What we do see as crucial is these "configurations of Judaism" being "rooted in the Hebrew Bible."

The Essenes are worthy of further attention. Leaving aside the unresolved issues of the specific nature of their identification with the Qumran community, we do know a number of features of Essene organization. Most basically, they set themselves apart from the rest of Jewish society of the times. Their reason for doing so was to maintain a high degree of ritual purity, around possessions, clothing and appearance, sexual relations, food; in separating themselves from the rest of society and in setting themselves numerous restrictions and prohibitions, they evidence clearly ascetic themes that we have already observed in our other Axial Age cases.

Of course, in doing so they excite a lot of hearsay and rumor, too. Joan Taylor (2012) provides a book-length exploration of the Essenes; one conclusion she provides: "Supposed characteristics of the Essenes such as a rejection of the Temple, vegetarianism, extreme insularity, adoption of small children, or pacifism have no basis in the ancient texts and result from faulty readings" (p. 195). Justin Taylor (2004), who conducts a thorough comparison of Pythagoreans and Essenes (including much more comparative material beyond, looking throughout the ancient Near East, Graeco-Roman voluntary associations, and a comparison to India, too), also presents us with a careful scholarly assessment of the Essenes. Altogether, they numbered about 4000 ("second numerically only to the Pharisees (about 6,000 men)" [Taylor, 2012, p. 196]) and were spread throughout Israel. They lived communally with colleagues, holding land in common and eating together and working the land together, engaging in a range of mostly simple labor so as to enable economic self-sufficiency. In terms of sexuality, they practiced a full spectrum from celibacy to marriage, with the main rule for the collective communities primarily being that women did not live with the men. "We may suppose that their wives may then have lived in separate women's communities, also following Essene purity regulations" (Taylor, 2012, p. 197). The men could be and many were ordained as priests in the Temple; they shared clothing, which was simple and intentionally rough and plain; they were not allowed to touch perfumed oil, and if they came in contact with it, were to rub it off; they rejected slavery. Initiation into the community was a long process (usually, one year) and carefully vetted; part of this initiation involved aggregation of the individual's private goods into the community's store; members could be expelled for a range of offences. Their day-to-day lives were marked by numerous rituals of purification and by regular prayer; they awoke at sunrise and said prayers to the sun, and purified their bodies in late morning as well as before dinner, and practiced the Sabbath assiduously. In addition to all of this, their central privileged activity was studying; they displayed a keen interest in studying and collecting texts, especially "ancient" texts.

In short, we gain a picture of the Essenes as an ascetic movement with a number of fascinating precepts they endorsed in order to maintain the "purity" of the community apart from general society. Within this picture, what stands out as most relevant to our question regarding the development of systematic spiritual practice aimed inwardly, are their emphases on ritual purification as built into their daily life, prayer, and study of texts. If we had a better sense of what these were or how they were conducted, perhaps we could begin to answer our question; but we have very little. Further, we have a positive reason for this lack: "What is significant is the degree to which the ascetic aspects of Essene practice and ideology are communalistic in focus. They distinguished less the practicing individual from his or her society than the unity of the sanctified community (*yahad*) from the outside world" (Fraade, 1986, p. 268). This certainly seems to accord with all the accounts of the Essenes, and while on the one hand it perfectly fits with an Axial Age description of "small communities organized around spiritual practices," due to the communal spiritual purpose of the community as a whole—rather than a community that forms to safeguard its members from "this world" and enable them to pursue, both collectively and individually, the "other world" through spiritual practices—its "inwardness" would not be that of individuals. Rather it would be, in more "cultish" or "sect-like" fashion, that of contributing and co-operating with community life. In this sense, Taylor's (2012) clarification that the Essenes were not "a Greek philosophical school," but a "Jewish legal school" (p. 196) is a significant point insofar as the piety of an Essene would be in matters of obedience to communal law, not a systematic deconstruction of their own structures of consciousness. However, insofar as the whole community aimed to set itself apart "from the outside world," that the Essene community as a whole meant to embody a "systematic deconstruction of ordinary, i.e., "this-worldly," structures of waking consciousness," could still apply.

Fraade writing elsewhere does provide us with a further tantalizing tidbit. He cites a Qumran scroll's description: "They shall separate themselves from the settlement of men of iniquity and shall go into the wilderness to prepare there the true way... *This refers to the study of Torah*" (1991, p. 175, n17, my emphasis). This suggests very directly that the community members may well have engaged in all manner of corresponding ascetic practices (of purification, sanctification, and so on) as part of the preparation for, and indeed practice of, interpretation. How did they study and read texts? We know from Hadot's revision of Greek philosophical texts that to understand them as disembodied theory mistakes their true usage, which was secondary to spiritual exercises of self-control and meditation. How much more so would some kind of analogous revision apply to the reading of Jewish scriptural texts, whose readers after all fervently believe them to be the revealed word of God... but without more potent evidence, we just don't know. The question of how were the texts read by these communities does suggest one last avenue to explore: asceticism within "orthodox" Judaism itself, in the study of the Torah.

This last emphasis is very much the domain of Rabbinic Judaism, within the practices of rabbinic study. Of course, in dallying thus far afield from the Axial Age proper, are we becoming unhelpfully desperate? The careful reader will have noted that none of the examples we've presented thus far—whether apocalyptic texts, mystical experiential texts, or the Essenes—fit well into the Second Temple Judaism time period.

All are temporally bookends to the Axial Age proper, as the *Yoga Sutras* were for the Indian Axial Age. However, in the case of India the *Yoga Sutras* as presumably more systematic than anything earlier were in terms of content also a convenient bookend for dealing with an overabundance of evidence for systematic ascetic practice. This is not the case for Israel. Instead, we have a huge gap where we wish evidence would be. However in gleaning what evidence we can from multiple bookends, we can inform our best guess as to what content might fill the gap.

By and large, there has been a large bias against perceiving asceticism within Judaism. There are numerous reasons for this bias. Fortunately, Fraade (1986) and Diamond (2004) summarize these reasons well and offer a convincing counter-argument in their work. Fraade (1986) offers some relevant observations regarding the Pharisees:

> What seems clear is the Pharisees dedicated their lives to the careful study and strict practice of Torah precepts received from earlier generations of pietists. They organized themselves separately but not in isolation from the larger Israelite society... The Pharisees are noted for having been scrupulous in the practice of ritual purity, especially at meals ...They are also reported to have been particularly careful concerning Sabbath observance and tithing and were known for their fasting, simple living, and close-knit communities. (p. 270)

One point to note is the strong parallels to the Essenes, with one major difference that the Pharisees "organized themselves separately but not in isolation." However, what is more important are the numerous strong parallels, that in combination is clear evidence of a systematic organization of a number of ascetic elements aimed at self-control, renunciation of "normal" societal rules, restrictions and prohibitions around food, possessions, and interpersonal relations. Fraade (1986) also notes that the Pharisees' name derives from the Hebrew *perishut*, or *perushim*, which denoted an ideal of holy, sanctified, separate, abstinent (p. 270). He goes on to point out two different meanings attached to *perushim*: One is that it is "a stage in the attaining of spiritual perfection" (p. 270); the other is a typology of seven types of *perushim*, the first six based on degrees of those who perform abstinences and asceticisms in order to gain merit or to appear pious, i.e., for egocentric reasons, while "the seventh and highest level of abstinence is that of one who is abstinent out of love of God" (p. 271). In reading these descriptions—of an ideal of abstinence, various practices oriented toward that ideal, claims of spiritual perfection, the distinction of graded stages—we should feel ourselves comfortably back on Axial comparative ground. Fraade (1986) concludes: "rabbinic writings express concern for the spiritual perfection of the individual and the ascetic means to that end primarily within the context of a communal, institutionalized discipline" (p. 277). Diamond (2004) has a book-length argument to provide an answer in the affirmative, contra "the Jewish predilection to see itself as nonascetic," to the question "whether one can find enough points of contact between rabbinic and Christian asceticism to conclude that they are conceptually similar and therefore capable of illuminating each other" (p. 20).

It is time to summarize this lengthy excursion into ancient Israel as the hardest case for my claim that the distinctive contribution of the Axial Age lies, not in the idea of transcendence or its institutionalization or the development of elites that "carry" those ideas and institutions, but in the innovation of sustained, systematic practices turned inwardly so as to transform the person, away from egocentric consciousness, toward the realization of transcendence. Unlike any of the other cases, we have no definitive evidence. Also unlike any other cases, this issue devolves on scholarly complications of interpretation around the textual evidence available for "ancient Israel," with recent changes and critical revisions within the field of specialized scholarship pushing further and further away any kinds of confidence in historical claim or empirical accuracy. Nevertheless, we have a suggestive possibility.

Pre-exile, in monarchic Israel and Judah, we have an argument for early prophetic guilds who "trained for ecstasy" prior to the advent of classical prophets who are presented as radically individual sites for visionary, prophetic proclamation, but whom outside these prophesying moments belonged to small groups, disciples who gathered around them. The conquering of Israel, then the conquering of Judah and destruction of the First Temple, its exile, and then return to rebuild a Second Temple is a massive, traumatic interruption in Israelite prophecy. Classical prophecy as a phenomenon largely centers around exile, putatively before, certainly during and presumably after, above all in the form of "dissident intellectuals." Then, a few centuries after exile, we have a number of developments: One, which seems no longer incisively relevant for the self-understanding of "Israel," is the diminishing continuation of traditional prophecy, increasingly marginalized, with a corresponding de-emphasis on the importance of ecstasy. The dominate theme at the center of the other developments is the increasing importance and authority of text. Two other developments are found in the creation of apocalyptic and mystical texts attesting to some degree of a systematization of the gaining of mystical experience, in large part presumably due to the traumatic meaning of exile and the temple destruction, and perhaps to replace the absence of ecstatic visionary prophets with mystical visionary experience. Throughout these texts, significant references to ascetic practices can be found, but it is unclear as to how systematically these were organized. A fourth development is the Essenes, and the particular importance of the Qumran community, which attests to a group who undertook extensive ascetic practices aimed at purification, much of it cohering around engagement with textual production and interpretation. Moving a couple centuries later, our fifth development is emergence of rabbinic Judaism "proper" (i.e., dating from 70 CE and later), wherein versions of the systematic ascetic practice similar to the Essenes come into view as characteristic and commonplace among the rabbis and the studious: What Diamond (2004) dubs "the ascetic study of the Torah." (Therefore, *in toto*, by the onset of Rabbinic Judaism we have clear evidence of systematic ascetic practices.)

Before all these latter developments, but after earlier forms of ancient Israelite prophecy, we have the emergence of "prophetic books." How did these emerge? My speculation, which in the absence of definitive evidence remains speculation, runs as follows: There were scribal schools responsible for the production of these books. These schools were not the prophetic guilds of old (about which we're not sure of), nor are they the Essenes or the Pharisees or the Jewish mystical schools of centuries later. Further, the words "scribal" and "production" hide an accurate picture of what their interpretive practices of reading, writing, editing, collating, redacting, looked like. To continue my speculation: In the transformation of focus from ecstasy to interpretation as the site of prophetic revelation, these "scribal schools" take over the prophetic function, including engaging in systematic spiritual practices aimed at self-discipline and purification, preparing them for encountering the word of Yahweh (in the form of reading, writing, editing, etc.) in the correct spirit. Our notion of "interpretation" is much too banal to capture the sacred seriousness with which the prophets-scribes-spiritual practitioners-ascetics(?) approached their task of interpreting God's revelation, the criterion for which would be "inspiration." I suggest this speculative picture of schools aiming at "inspired interpretation" would provide a transitional form between the ecstatic prophetic utterance of pre-exile (which plausibly stemmed from systematic training for ecstasy within prophetic guilds) and the established prophetic texts that become Jewish scripture, post-exile, during the period of Second Temple Judaism (and which were certainly read, studied, and obeyed, through sustained systematic practices developed by the first centuries CE and the advent of Rabbinic Judaism).

If this above sequence of speculation of "scribal schools" producing "prophetic books" were accepted, then we could triumphantly say "yes" to establishing ancient Israel, too, as belonging to the "Axial family" as far as my thesis concerning the Axial Age's distinctive contribution being the innovation of systematic spiritual practices is concerned. But we should not go so far. The argument in the end remains speculation, and thus we should admit that despite our efforts the case has not been definitively made. However, I hope that the speculative line of argument is plausible, and that although Israel is sufficiently unlike India, China, and Greece, where we can certainly check off each of their "spiritual practices?" box with a "yes," I would like to think that I've succeeded in preventing placing a definite "no" beside the Israel box, and that we place a question mark there instead. To move from a question mark to a yes or a no, we need better evidence than we've been able to find.

Axial Age Spiritualities

As we saw in Chapter 4, the overriding factor that defined the horizon of meaning of civilization through which the Axial Age visionaries broke was developed through an "axial achievement" of its own. The latter was not a breakthrough in terms of consciousness, but an "unconscious" development into a new scale of power unprecedented throughout 195,000+ years of sapient evolution. As "unconscious," this development is "natural": To revert to Darwin's metaphor of a tree, the expansions of power within the Afroeurasian world-system along the E-W axis became a solid trunk from which many civilizational branches grew. As we saw in Chapter 5, at the tips of those branches new buds preaching "universality" and "transcendence" prove most world-historically "vigorous," to become the thickest, strongest branches of world civilizations/world religions which overgrow and supplant the others, and eventually branch out far beyond that axis throughout the geography of the whole world, to cover more and more of it.

That expansion of power has not ceased. What we are witnessing today—and undergoing ourselves, and contributing to—is that expansion of power reaching global limits far beyond those of the E-W axis of Afroeurasia. The Afroeurasian world-system, at its westernmost tip, i.e., Western Europe, expanded into the other world-systems—of the Americas, of Australasia, of Oceania, of the remainder of Africa—and assimilated and colonized and annexed those world-systems. Following that expansion, the now-singular global world-system is intensifying its expansion into the earth-system, and in doing so exceeding ecological limits, bypassing natural thresholds, overflowing environmental capacities, and changing the climate, all on a global scale. And beyond, as our contemporary space programs explore the solar system: expansionism indeed!

What we examined in this chapter was how in the first millennium BCE, the Axial Age teachers respond critically to the new scale of power to civilization, to the forms it took, as well as to the versions of transcendence and universality offered. They propose a spiritual vision of universality, tied to particular disciplined practices that effect a transformation of personal consciousness aimed at overcoming the ego. The successful outcome of such a transformational process was a realization of a transcendent reality, transcendent here meaning above and beyond the ego. Unlike the "quasi-transcendent" claims of the state, the market, the state religion, or (later) the world religion, all of which are powerful groups with which the ego identifies and thus becomes elevated beyond its individual limits—expanded ego-structures, for short—the realization of spiritual transcendence proposed by the Axial Age *virtuosi* is only available to those who overcome their egos. Transcendence is not an expanded ego-structure, but the structure that remains "in" or "to" consciousness after the ego has been systematically deconstructed—the structure that the Axial Age visionaries called reality and truth.

In short, and this is crucial for distinguishing the Axial Age teachings proper from the world religions they found: To "identify" with transcendence in the Axial Age sense cannot be performed by the ego. The ego cannot desire transcendence in the Axial Age sense. To "attain" transcendence is not possible through the ego's doing, but the opposite: Transcendence is realized in and through the ego's undoing. As an "identification" of consciousness with ultimate reality, it entails a radical surrender and total divestment of power. Often the first literal steps on this path of personal transformation toward transcendence were the divestment of the expanded ego-structures of power provided by group identities. In the particular world-historical moment of the first millennium BC, defined by the new and unprecedented scale of power attained, group identification had reached its greatest size in the form of the biggest and most powerful civilizations ever. That the Axial Age spiritual masters give up position, status, money, influence, distinction—and in a number of cases, their lives—is striking and impressive; that they do so in this context seems almost unbelievable, until we remember that they and the movements they inspire are not found at the centers of these powerful civilizations, but at their margins.

Often, they literally give up civilization: They leave the city, or the palace, or the temple, and go into the wilderness, travel, go to "new land." Abraham being called to leave the civilized city of Ur and to go west into an unknown land and future is a paradigmatic moment for all three religions of the book. The Jewish people undertake an exodus out from the great civilization of Egypt; the royal prince Buddha leaves the palace, his family, and imminent kingship to seek enlightenment; Socrates doesn't literally leave Athens, but in his poverty, endless questioning for truth, and willing acceptance of an unjust sentence of execution, he embodies how the city has no hold on him. The Taoists, like the Cynics, the Jains, several Hebrew prophets, or the Essenes, scorn convention, status, and the "trappings" of civilization for simplicity, nature, the wilderness. They are tempted by power but spurn it for what is good. Or to use more religious terminology, they despise "this world" (meaning the world experienced and interpreted through the ego, ego-structures and group identities, civilization, and all of its associated powers) and advocate an "other world" (meaning this very same world just described, but transformed and re-visioned without the ego at its center: without the greed and grandiosity, the violence, the injustices and hatreds, but rather with selflessness—nonviolence, love, compassion, equity, justice—at its center). In Buddhism, the selflessness is explicitly named as such; while Christ will command "Give up all you have and follow me." The ultimate symbolization of such divestment of power (to give up the power of "this world"), or the last possible literal step (to invest, against and beyond the ego, in an "other world"), is self-sacrifice.

While the need for transcendence was overdetermined due to the dynamics of the expansion of power, and while transcendence itself was often articulated in such a way that it disguised the expansion of power as essence of the transcendence, the formation of the world religions—which take the Axial Age ideas of transcendence as their cornerstone rather than the "quasi-transcendence" options—shows another outcome for transcendence. The world religions mis-take these ideas as a locus of identification for their members, around which the religions build a corresponding transcendent ideology as the doctrinaire, institutionalized basis for themselves as a new form of organizational power. In so doing, the meaning of transcendence, as well as of "this world" vs the "other world," is shifted away from their Axial Age sense.

To mis-take transcendence as a locus of identification for the believer's ego, reinserts the hiding of the ego within the expansion of power embodied in the group identity of the world religion. (The ego believes it will be saved! The spiritual fact is that the ego must be sacrificed in order for the believer to be saved.) Analogously, world religions themselves reinsert power, as a necessity for their (big) organization, while disguising it behind a transcendent ideology. The danger, of course, is that in demanding the surrender of the ego to transcendence, the believer gives himself or herself over to the authority of a human organization in the same stroke as the religion consolidates itself as a more efficient system of control. Stated as baldly as this oversimplifies a far more complex scenario and biases interpretation toward the more cynical pole of what should be a broad spectrum: It overlooks, above all, the true believer within the religion who could be fully aware of, and on guard against, the possibility of the scenario just sketched. By the same token, there is no reason to exonerate world religions that, in the name of universal love or compassion, have perpetuated incredible hatred, violence, torture, genocide, racism, sexism, misogyny, and so on. The idealist is right that we should not perform blanket condemnations on something as sprawling and complex as a world religion, but the cynic is also right that the historical record of the hypocrisy of world religions judged on their own terms demands an accounting. World religions in taking Axial ideas of transcendence as foundational both expand their power dramatically in generating the possibility of universal membership that transcends any possible limitations and insert an equally extensive possibility for the critique of power, including especially their own because the critique is leveled in their very own terms, because true transcendence demands an utter divestment of power. At base the issue is, just as it was when it first emerges in the first millennium BCE, the relation of this-worldly power to ("otherworldly") ideals of transcendence.

For the spiritual *virtuosi* of the Axial Age, the ego and not this relation is the basic issue. Both this-worldly power and ideals of transcendence presuppose identifications from the ego. Instead, the Axial Age visionaries understand transcendence as the locus of sacred reality (or, of ultimate truth, of God). In order to understand, experience, access, gain a glimpse, touch, participate in, the transcendent—whatever locution for indwelling this mystery is adequate—one had to overcome the ego. One did so through spiritual practice. Strictly speaking, the ego cannot identify with the transcendent, because the latter is an oblivion or a nothingness to the ego, a nonsense to its thinking, a "dark night" for the soul; it is the ego's death, and hence frightening, awful/awe-full, fascinating, numinous. It is in part so mysterious because it is egoless; to those who have experienced it, it is blissful, joyful, loving, compassionate, a "peak experience" (to use Abraham Maslow's term). The kingdom of heaven that is within you is the selfless truth of how you participate in a reality both greater than you and that includes you. This is a truth that the ego is unable to see. And, as the common denominator of mystical descriptions of ultimate reality attest, it is an ineffable truth; language is unable to adequately evoke it. The only reality the ego can imagine is one with itself at the center. In moments of selflessness (like love or compassion, but also justice, forgiveness, mercy, and in fact the entire spectrum of morality and ethics), the ego is momentarily transcended and the simple, unmysterious truth that the ego is not central to reality manifests. Beyond these moments and extended to suffuse throughout all of reality, it is true that transcendence is not simple and is mysterious, but it is not a supernatural, superhuman, metaphysical mystery. For that matter neither is the "other world" a supernatural, superhuman, or metaphysical reality. All of these interpretations are ego-based interpolations, and all therefore are egocentric misunderstandings. The ego asks what transcendence is; the experienced practitioner responds, but not by "giving an answer"… smiles in compassionate but inscrutable silence like the Buddha, sincerely confesses ignorance and endlessly questions around it like a Socrates, provides the ultimate paradox in commanding love like the prophetic witness to YHWH, offers an aphorism that seems to miss the obvious point but in so doing points enigmatically deeper like a Confucius or a Chuang Tzu, and tells an accessible parable that is impenetrable in its ultimate meaning like a Jesus. The response that addresses the question without giving an answer would be: pray more; meditate again; just sit, watch your breath. What the teacher as expert practitioner wants to convey to the neophyte is to practice until you mature beyond your (ego's) demand to know the (egoless) outcome.

What the Axial Age movements—their critical responses, alternative visions, formation of small, counter-cultural communities, undertaking of spiritual practices—have in common along with the world religions eventually founded upon them is a critical response to the new scale of power manifesting in the civilizations of their time. Where they significantly differ is in how they understand the transcendent ground for that response: For the Axial Age teachers, the transcendent ground is only accessed through sustained systematic spiritual practice that transforms the person such that they overcome the ego.

References

Assmann, J. (2012). Cultural memory and the myth of the Axial Age. In R. Bellah & H. Joas (Eds.), *The Axial Age and its consequences* (pp. 366–407). Belknap: Cambridge and London.

Bellah, R. (2011). *Religion in human evolution: From the Paleolithic to the Axial Age*. Belknap: Harvard, MA.

Blenkinsopp, J. (1995). *Sage, priest, prophet: Religious and intellectual leadership in ancient Israel*. Louisville, KY: John Knox Press.

Brockington, J. (2003). Yoga in the Mahabharata. In I. Whicher & D. Carpenter (Eds.), *Yoga: The Indian tradition* (pp. 13–24). London: Routledge Curzon.

Brooke, G. (2006). Prophecy and prophets in the Dead Sea scrolls: Looking backwards and forwards. In M. Floyd & R. Haak (Eds.), *Prophets, prophecy, and prophetic texts in second temple Judaism* (pp. 151–165). New York and London: T&T Clark.

Brown, D. (1986). The stages of meditation in cross-cultural perspective. In K. Wilber, J. Engler, & D. Brown (Eds.), *Transformations of consciousness: Conventional and contemplative perspectives on development* (pp. 193–271). Boston and London: Shambhala.

Bussanich, J. (2016). Plato and yoga. In R. Seaford (Ed.), *Universe and inner self in early Indian and early Greek thought* (pp. 87–103). Edinburgh: Edinburgh University Press.

Ching, J. (2003). What is Confucian spirituality? In T. Weiming & M. Tucker (Eds.), *Confucian spirituality* (Vol. 1, pp. 81–95). New York: Crossroad.

Csikszentmihalyi, M., & Ivanhoe, P. (Eds.). (1999). *Religious and philosophical aspects of the Laozi*. Albany, NY: SUNY Press.

Dan, J. (1986). The religious experience of the *Merkavah*. In A. Green (Ed.), *Jewish spirituality: From the Bible through the Middle Ages* (pp. 289–307). New York: Crossroad.

Davies, P. (1992). *In search of ancient Israel*. Sheffield: JSOT Press.

Davies, P. (2000). Judaism and the Hebrew scriptures. In J. Neusner & A. Avery-Peck (Eds.), *The Blackwell companion to Judaism* (pp. 37–57). Oxford: Blackwell.

Diamond, E. (2004). *Holy men and hunger artists: Fasting and asceticism in Rabbinic culture*. Oxford and New York: Oxford University Press.

Dodds, E. R. (1951). *The Greeks and the irrational*. Berkeley and Los Angeles: University of California.

Dundas, P. (2002). *The Jains*. London and New York: Routledge.

Eliade, M. (1969). *Yoga: Immortality and freedom* (W. Trask, Trans.). Princeton: Bollingen.

Eliade, M. (1982). *A history of religious ideas: Vol. 2, from Gautama Buddha to the triumph of Christianity* (W. Trask, Trans.). Chicago: University of Chicago Press.

Elior, R. (2005). *The three temples: On the emergence of Jewish mysticism* (D. Louvish, Trans.). Oxford and Portland: Littman Library of Jewish Civilization.

Eno, R. (1990). *The Confucian creation of heaven: Philosophy and the defense of ritual mastery*. Albany, NY: SUNY Press.

Fishbane, M. (1986). Biblical prophecy as a religious phenomenon. In A. Green (Ed.), *Jewish spirituality: From the Bible through the Middle Ages* (pp. 62–81). New York: Crossroad.

Fraade, S. (1986). Ascetical aspects of ancient Judaism. In A. Green (Ed.), *Jewish spirituality: From the Bible through the Middle Ages* (pp. 253–288). New York: Crossroad.

Fraade, S. (1991). *From tradition to commentary: Torah and its interpretation in the Midrash Sifre to Deuteronomy*. Albany: State University of New York Press.

Grabbe, L. (2003a). Introduction and overview. In L. Grabbe & R. Haak (Eds.), *Knowing the end from the beginning: The prophetic, the apocalyptic, and their relationships* (pp. 2–43). London and New York: T&T Clark.

Grabbe, L. (2003b). Poets, scribes, or preachers? The reality of prophecy in the Second Temple period. In L. Grabbe & R. Haak (Eds.), *Knowing the end from the beginning: The prophetic, the apocalyptic, and their relationships* (pp. 192–215). London and New York: T&T Clark.

Grabbe, L. (2004). *A history of the Jews and Judaism in the Second Temple period. Vol. I: Yehud: A history of the Persian province of Judah*. London and New York: T&T Clark.

Graham, A. (1989). *Disputers of the Tao: Philosophical argument in ancient China*. La Salle, IL: Open Court.

Gruenwald, I. (1980). *Apocalyptic and Merkavah mysticism*. Leiden: Brill.

Hadot, P. (1995). *Philosophy as a way of life: Spiritual exercises from Socrates to Foucault* (A. Davidson, Ed.). Oxford and Cambridge: Blackwell.

Hadot, P. (2002). *What is ancient philosophy?* (M. Chase, Trans.). Cambridge and London: Belknap (originally published in 1995).

Hamilton, S. (2001). *Identity and experience: The constitution of the human being according to early Buddhism.* London: Luzac.

Hartnett, R. (2011). *The Jixia Academy and the birth of higher learning in China: A comparison of fourth-century B.C. Chinese education with ancient Greece.* London: Mellen.

Hick, J. (1989). *An interpretation of religion: Human responses to the transcendent.* New Haven, CT: Yale University Press.

Himmelfarb, M. (1986). From prophecy to apocalypse: *The book of the watchers* and tours of heaven. In A. Green (Ed.), *Jewish spirituality: From the Bible through the Middle Ages* (pp. 145–165). New York: Crossroad.

Hobsbawm, E., & Ranger, T. (1983). *The invention of tradition.* Cambridge: Cambridge University Press.

Holt, E. (2016). The prophet as persona. In C. Sharp (Ed.), *The Oxford handbook of the prophets* (pp. 299–318). Oxford: Oxford University Press.

Ivanhoe, P. (2010). The values of spontaneity. In K. Yu, J. Tao, & P. Ivanhoe (Eds.), *Taking Confucian ethics seriously: Contemporary theories and applications* (pp. 183–207). Albany, NY: SUNY Press.

Ivanhoe, P. (2013). *Confucian reflections: Ancient wisdom for modern times.* New York and London: Routledge.

Jaspers, K. (1953). *The origin and goal of history.* New Haven and London: Yale University Press (originally published in 1949).

Johnson, A. (1962). *The cultic prophet in ancient Israel.* Cardiff: University of Wales Press.

Kaelber, W. (1998). Understanding asceticism—Testing a typology. In V. Wimbush & R. Valantasis (Eds.), *Asceticism* (pp. 320–328). New York: Oxford University Press.

Kierkegaard, S. (2006). *Fear and trembling* (S. Walsh, Trans.). Cambridge and New York: Cambridge University Press.

Kohn, L. (1992). *Early Chinese mysticism: Philosophy and soteriology in the Taoist tradition.* Princeton: Princeton University Press.

Kohn, L. (Ed.). (2000). *Daoism handbook.* Leiden and Boston: Brill.

Kohn, L. (2010). *Sitting in oblivion: The heart of Daoist meditation.* Dunedin, FL: Three Pines Press.

Kohn, L., & Sakade, Y. (Eds.). (1989). *Taoist meditation and longevity techniques.* Ann Arbor: Center for Chinese Studies, University of Michigan.

Lindblom, J. (1962). *Prophecy in ancient Israel.* Philadelphia: Fortress Press.

Mair, V. (1990). Afterword, Part III: Parallels between Taoism and yoga. In *Tao teaching: The classic book of integrity and the way: Lao Tzu* (pp. 140–148 and Appendix, pp. 155–161). New York: Quality.

McGinn, B. (1991). *The foundations of mysticism: Origins to the fifth century.* New York: Crossroad.

Middlemas, J. (2016). Prophecy and diaspora. In C. Sharp (Ed.), *The Oxford handbook of the prophets* (pp. 37–54). Oxford: Oxford University Press.

Neusner, J. (1986). Varieties of Judaism in the formative age. In A. Green (Ed.), *Jewish spirituality: From the Bible through the Middle Ages* (pp. 171–197). New York: Crossroad.

Nietzsche, F. (2007). *On the genealogy of morality* (K. Ansell-Pearson, Ed. and C. Diethe, Trans.). Cambridge: Cambridge University Press.

Nissinen, M. (2006). The dubious image of prophecy. In M. Floyd & R. Haak (Eds.), *Prophets, prophecy, and prophetic texts in second temple Judaism* (pp. 26–41). New York and London: T&T Clark.

Nissinen, M. (2010). Prophetic madness: Prophecy and ecstasy in the ancient Near East and in Greece. In K. Noll & B. Schramm (Eds.), *Raising up a faithful exegete: Essays in honor of Richard D. Nelson* (pp. 3–29). Winona Lake, IN: Eisenbrauns.

Nissinen, M. (2016). Prophetic intermediation in the ancient Near East. In C. Sharp (Ed.), *The Oxford handbook of the prophets* (pp. 5–22). Oxford: Oxford University Press.

Noll, K. (2013). Presumptuous prophets in a Deuteronomic debate. In M. Boda & L. Beal (Eds.), *Prophets, prophecy, and ancient Israelite historiography* (pp. 125–142). Winona Lake, IN: Eisenbrauns.

Olivelle, P. (2011). *Ascetics and Brahmins: Studies in ideologies and institutions.* London, New York, and New Delhi: Anthem Press.

Paper, J. (1995). *The spirits are drunk: Comparative approaches to Chinese religion.* Albany: State University of New York Press.

Robinet, I. (1993). *Taoist meditation: The Mao-shan tradition of great purity.* Albany, NY: State University of New York Press.

Roth, H. (1999a). *Original Tao: Inward training (nei-yeh) and the foundations of Taoist mysticism.* New York: Columbia University.

Roth, H. (1999b). The Laozi in the context of early Taoist mystical praxis. In M. Csikszentmihalyi & P. Ivanhoe (Eds.), *Religious and philosophical aspects of the Laozi* (pp. 59–96). Albany, NY: SUNY Press.

Rowley, H. H. (1956). *Prophecy and religion in ancient China and Israel.* London: University of London, Athlone Press.

Schmidt, B. (2010). *Utopian communities of the ancient world: Idealistic experiments of Pythagoras, the Essenes, Pachomius, and Proclus.* Lewiston, NY: Edwin Mellen.

Schwartz, B. (Ed.). (1975). Wisdom, revelation, and doubt: Perspectives on the first millennium B.C. *Special Issue of Daedalus, 104*(2), 1–7.

Schwartz, B. (1985). *The world of thought in ancient China.* Belknap: Cambridge, MA.

Silver, K. (2017). *Alexandria and Qumran: Back to the beginning.* Oxford: Archaeopress.

Smith-Christopher, D. (2002). *A biblical theology of exile.* Minneapolis: Fortress Press.

Sweeney, M. (2000). The religious world of ancient Israel to 586 BCE. In J. Neusner & A. Avery-Peck (Eds.), *The Blackwell companion to Judaism* (pp. 20–36). Oxford: Blackwell.

Talmon, S. (1993). The community of the renewed covenant: Between Judaism and Christianity. In E. Ulrich & J. Vanderkam (Eds.), *The community of the renewed covenant* (pp. 3–24). Notre Dame, IN: University of Notre Dame.

Taylor, J. (2004). *Pythagoreans and Essenes: Structural parallels.* Paris and Louvain: Peeters.

Taylor, J. (2012). *The Essenes, the scrolls, and the Dead Sea.* Oxford: Oxford University Press.

Tucker, M. (2003). Introduction. In T. Weiming & M. Tucker (Eds.), *Confucian spirituality* (Vol. I, pp. 1–35). New York: Crossroad.

Varenne, J. (1976). *Yoga and the Hindu tradition* (D. Coltman, Trans.). Chicago and London: Universty of Chicago.

Waelde, L., & Thompson, J. (2016). Traditional and secular views of psycho-therapeutic applications of mindfulness and meditation. In M. West (Ed.), *The psychology of meditation: Research and practice* (pp. 119–152). Oxford: Oxford University Press.

Weiming, T., & Tucker, M. (Eds.). (2003a). *Confucian spirituality:* (Vol. I). New York: Crossroad.

Weiming, T., & Tucker, M. (Eds.). (2003b). *Confucian spirituality:* (Vol. II). New York: Crossroad.

Whicher, I. (1998). *The integrity of the yoga darsana: A reconsideration of classical yoga.* Albany: State University of New York Press.

Whicher, I. (2003). The integration of spirit (*purusa*) and matter (*prakrti*) in the Yoga Sutra. In I. Whicher & D. Carpenter (Eds.), *Yoga: The Indian tradition* (pp. 51–69). London: Routledge Curzon.

Wilber, K. (1998). *The eye of spirit: An integral vision for a world gone slightly mad.* Boston & London: Shambhala.

Wilson, R. (1980). *Prophecy and society in ancient Israel.* Philadelphia: Fortress Press.

Yü, Y. (2003). Between the heavenly and the human. In T. Weiming & M. Tucker (Eds.), *Confucian spirituality* (Vol. I, pp. 62–80). New York: Crossroad.

CHAPTER 7

Concluding Reflections

TAKING STOCK: INVOKING PRECEDENTS TO CONFRONT OUR WORLD IN CRISIS

Our present-day world, taken as a holistic moment spanning the entire globe, is unprecedented. Particular aspects analytically isolated from the moment as a whole, however, have historical precedents. Thus, we can learn lessons from these precedents that would helpfully inform our understanding of our unprecedented moment, even as we should acknowledge they will fall short of a full understanding. A key aspect within the unprecedentedness of our present moment is the fact that our world is in crisis. The best of our prognoses and predictions are dire for the near future. Human activity is causing a massive extinction of species. It is also causing global climate change which threatens our own civilizations with collapse. We don't want these things to happen, we don't want them to happen! Even a child could tell you that.

In echoing Olivia's cry, we also need to realize that it is not a merely human perspective on things nor a "merely subjective" response. Our world in crisis is not exclusively an issue of human self-interest, for example, in survival. As Theodore Roszak (1979) puts it: "We must come to see that what we experience in ourselves as the emerging need of the person is the Earth's urgent cry for rescue. Our proper response to that cry is to scale down the structures and institutions which endanger the living variety of the planet: to name their evil, to resist it, to expunge it" (p. 320). The issue, emerging from a long history rooted in an even longer

C. Peet, *Practicing Transcendence*,
https://doi.org/10.1007/978-3-030-14432-6_7

evolutionary process, that is, an issue of scale rooted in nature, is how natural tendencies to expand into the space around us and to form ourselves into ever-larger groups ("tribes"), have now manifested in destructive potentials threatening the whole world, both human and natural.

We have to take responsibility for this crisis. We need to bring to bear all the possible knowledge we can to aid us in addressing our present predicament, anticipating that insofar as our situation is unprecedented, this knowledge alone will not be enough—we will need creativity and ingenuity and courage too—but that it will help to guide us.

The potential for a collapse of the global world-system of economics and power has precedents in the collapse of civilizations and societies. These have invariably been relative to consumption practices exceeding resources; societies needed to dramatically change, above all to scale back, their consumption, or collapse. Most collapsed rather than change. It is in these societies that political choice forces itself upon the people due to the consequences of their ecological choices. Jared Diamond's (2005) study of the question "how societies choose to fail or succeed" when faced with the imminence of their collapse due to unsustainable consumption practices is exemplary. He takes a comparative approach, comparing across examples of societies that have collapsed (like Easter Island or the Greenland Vikings) and also those that haven't (such as the Iceland Vikings or the Greenland Inuit). In cases where resource consumption (including waste production) exceeded resource provision (inclusive of resource renewal), the ensuing ecological damage evident in resource depletion signaled the society's imminent demise unless it could change its way of life. Of the utmost significance in the cases of failure is the extent to which the excessive resource consumption was due to particular established practices that the society was unwilling to change in the face of imminent collapse. The Greenland Vikings, for example, persisted in the pasturing of cows and sheep for food rather than adapt to a diet of the far more abundant indigenous animals like fish, whale, and ringed seals (which was a staple for the Greenland Inuit). That they persisted despite the increasing untenability of doing so is worth remarking; quoting Diamond (2005), "The [Greenland] Norse starved in the presence of abundant unutilized food resources" (Diamond, 2005, p. 274).

Of all the cases Diamond presents, the most apt parallel to our contemporary globalizing world is Easter Island. A remote island in the vastness of the Pacific ocean, it had neither the threat of external enemies to justify its consumption practices or to overcome internal competition for limited resources, nor did it have external trade partners to rely on to assist it, nor was pulling up stakes and moving an option. The archaeology of Easter Island reveals a long history of increasing extinction of numerous plant and animal species as well as increasing deforestation, the latter being a direct consequence of timber over-utilization for the building, transporting, and erecting of the huge stone heads that cover the island. While the monumental heads clearly served cultural and religious aims tied to political ends around prestige, status, and competition, these were at cross-purposes to basic survival. For whatever unknown rationale, the Easter Islanders did not give up this pattern of conspicuous consumption, wasteful to the point of self-destructive; "the collapse of Easter society followed swiftly upon the society's reaching its peak of population, monument construction, and environmental impact" (2005, p. 110).

The Earth is not a remote island in the Pacific, but the analogy to our unsustainable global world-system is I presume clear: Relative to the global natural resources available, modern lifestyle patterns of affluence with high levels of consumption and waste are unsustainable. We, like the Easter Islanders, living in our contemporary "global village," a remote planet in the vastness of space, with no external (extraterrestrial) enemies to blame for our issues nor unite against to bring us together, no external (extraterrestrial) trade partners to rely upon, and no feasible place to move for at least the next few centuries (such as the moon or Mars), are thrown back upon our own resources. And lest we exonerate ourselves by blaming religion for the demise of Easter Island (as the giant stone heads, by scholarly best guess, served a primarily religious function), Diamond (2005) points out "The modern world provides us with abundant secular examples of admirable values to which we cling under conditions where those values no longer make sense" (p. 432). Religious or secular, we are on this earth and in this world in crisis together.

Unlike Easter Island's fate, which entailed the collapse of a geographically isolated (island) society, the fact of technology's effecting a globalizing world-system means it is a complexly interconnected globalizing world (which is in "cosmic" terms "isolated" in being a planet), that is at risk. Diamond concludes his study summarizing twelve sets of problems that involve non-sustainable practices which are confronting the world, pointing out that any one set of the dozen problems is inextricable from the others, insofar as the world-system has become global in its interconnectedness, pervasiveness, and impact. Diamond summarizes:

Our world society is presently on a non-sustainable course, and any of our 12 problems of non-sustainability that we have just summarized would suffice to limit our lifestyle within the next several decades. They are like time bombs with fuses of less than fifty years. ...they all interact with each other. If we solved 11 of the problems, but not the 12th, we would still be in trouble, whichever was the problem that remained unsolved. We have to solve them all. ...The only question is whether they become resolved in pleasant ways of our own choice, or in unpleasant ways not of our choice, such as warfare, genocide, starvation, disease epidemics, and collapses of societies. (2005, p. 498)

The scale of consumption built into our affluent ways of life is unsustainably high and ecologically destructive. We must scale back consumption. The challenges of our world in crisis are challenges for the next decades and the remainder of this century and cannot be put off. Too many of our political practices do not counter this scale of consumption or its non-sustainability but protect it and rationalize this approach in tribalist terms it considers ultimate: our freedom, our values, our tradition, and our way of life. In the face of global ecological and political crisis, we cannot continue these practices and rationalizations.

Another consequence of our actions is that we are causing a mass extinction of species. While this too has many precedents in Earth's evolutionary history, unlike any previous mass extinction event our own is in the final analysis not reducible to being a natural outcome but has to be evaluated as a consequence of human conscious choice. As the event of the Sixth Extinction enters increasingly into critical conscious awareness, we should responsibly choose biodiversity as a deep, pervasive, and precious good, and do everything we can to mitigate mass extinction. To do so requires turning against the natural evolutionary impulse of any organism to expand into "available space," requires turning against our naturally evolved human capacity to adapt (i.e., to "develop" and "consume") our environments, and requires turning against our whole human history of expansionism.

Of course, appealing to "us" as a universal humanity, or appealing to "our whole human history," is also working against another naturally evolved human capacity, our tribalism. Tribalism holds the frightening potential for a global war with a corresponding worldwide scale of death, destruction, and suffering. The latter has one clear precedent, World War II, when a local conflict implicated networks of world nations and superpowers and escalated into global proportions. The key difference then and now is not great: an increase in scale. Perhaps, positively, this increase in scale means an increased potential for peace and nonviolence as countries and economic systems have become more interdependent and democracy has become more widespread (cf. Pinker, 2012). Negatively, the same increase has also meant terrorism and unprecedented numbers of displaced peoples, emigration, and refugees. (Global climate change contributes significantly to these negatives as well.) It has also increased potential for mass destructiveness through the greater number of weapons (including weapons of mass destruction); these have a further reaching distribution across more nation-states and are based on more advanced technology than was the case with World War II. Regardless of what shape a World War III would take, the potential scale of death, destruction, and suffering is terrifying to imagine—if indeed we can truly imagine it at all. We must confront this potential for violence and counter its deep evolutionary roots in tribalism. We must do whatever we can to prevent its manifestation worldwide; we must be prepared to scale down rather than scale up (escalate) violent conflict whenever it occurs.

Expansionism combined with tribalism, which first came together in pronounced form during the "axial time" of the first millennium BCE which witnessed an unprecedented expansion in human civilizational power, has manifested in an ever-increasing scale to human collective identities and to human violence, including the violent amalgamation of the smaller or weaker (or unlucky) tribe, and an ever-increasing scale to our consumption of the earth's resources and its natural habitats. We must scale back and turn against both expansionism and tribalism and recognize the earth's biodiversity along with human ethnodiversity as deep and profound goods, as well as spiritual resources, that we need to preserve, and draw upon to assist us in confronting, our world in crisis.

That our world is in crisis incites intense anxiety, despair, and fear that the "world is going to end." Such fears are also not new. There are significant and many precedents for end-of-the-world anxieties. The key significant differences between those and today are two. First, there is a strong component of irrational hyperbole in such anxieties in the past relative to "the world" in truly global terms as such anxiety in the past conflated a local or regional change, destruction, or collapse, with "the world." Today, the anxiety about "the end of the world" is indeed rationally correct about its scale of concern, it is the world as a whole. The interconnectedness of the world-system technologically means that no "human world" is autonomous or independent, a fact that mirrors

the environmental interconnectedness of the Earth as a complex ecological system. Second, such anxiety in the past was usually mediated
through an apocalyptic lens provided by religious warrant. Today our
end-of-the-world anxieties are provided scientific warrant with an abundance of reasoning and evidence to support them. In an ironic inver-
sion of history, it is hopeful scenarios for world survival that are more
likely candidates for irrationality! One response to such anxiety, which
plays to expansionism, is the promise of science and technology to save
us by developing new energy resources from within the Earth or beyond
(such as the moon), to colonize Mars, to fix our pollution problems, etc.
Another response to such anxiety, which plays to tribalism, is to put our
hope in populist leaders—political "strong-men"—who promise "us"
(i.e., our tribe, or nation or state or ethnicity or whatever "in-group"
is their audience) safety, security, and prosperity. Or perhaps they promise us the moon. Both responses are as understandable as they are inadequate, regressive, and dangerous. We must admit, face, and overcome
our anxiety in order to act responsibly.

Can we?

Further Precedents: The Axial Time of Power and Axial Age Spiritualities

A fifth precedent, which has been the focus of this book, is that the significant precedent to the scale of power today which has now reached global
proportions taking an interconnected form of a global world-system,
occurred during the massive increase in scale in civilizational power in the
middle of the first millennium BCE across the E-W axis of the Afroeurasian
world-system. The outcome of this advent to a new scale of power was a
consolidation of that world-system as "wall to wall empires" reaching
from the Atlantic to the Pacific, which happens at roughly year zero CE,
i.e., this consolidation marks the beginning of the "Common Era." Out
of that consolidated world-system emerge the major world religions and
world civilizations that go on to dominate the geopolitics of world history
over the last two millennia, and which extended consolidation today has
become the global world-system. Within the first millennium BCE "axial
time of power" that is a precedent to our own time and to which direct
parallels can be made, in a handful of spiritual-intellectual movements
occurring at the margins and interstices of civilizational power, visionaries at the center of small communities respond with what at that time

was unprecedented in both evolutionary and historical terms: They reject power and advocate moral, ethical, and spiritual ideals as the true universals to which human being, as a being capable of critical conscious awareness and hence capable of self-responsible action, needs to orient itself. It has been my argument that in order to scale back our degree of consumption and change our consumption practices, in order to scale back the potential for violence, to turn against some of our deepest evolutionary instincts of expansionism and tribalism, to protect the threatened goods of biodiversity and ethnodiversity, and to uphold ideals and practices of sustainability and nonviolence, all of which are needed in our world in crisis of today, we need to examine and retrieve the distinctive contribution of the Axial Age, which lies in their spiritualities: sustained, systematic, spiritual practices, undertaken in small communities, aiming at overcoming the ego and transforming oneself.

The new scale to civilizational power in the first millennium BCE was certainly exhilarating to those few near its center or at its top—kings imagining themselves gods—as they rode a wave of history greater than any that had been witnessed before. To those numerous others whose lives, families, communities, livelihoods, values, ways of life, lands, freedom, and so on, were at best at the mercy of the power of the few, at worst under threat to be crushed by this tidal wave of power; however, it was not exhilarating but terrifying. (For some graphic depictions of Neo-Babylonian, Assyrian, and Persian conquest and corresponding imperial "policies" see Smith-Christopher, 2002, pp. 49–54.) The unknown Old Testament writers of the story of the tower of Babel which "reached into heaven," for instance—presumably based on the temple-ziggurats of the city-states of Mesopotamia to the east—were far removed from such a center of power or from such kings, and yet despite their distant, marginal, location, they vividly imagine its power as excessive, to the point of overstepping proper human bounds and being god-like: "Look now, what they have begun to do; *and now nothing will be impossible for them, that they imagine to do*" (Gen. 11, emphasis added). To these many who suffered as a consequence of the expansion of power, as well as for those who empathized with those who suffered, they experienced these events as if the world had come out of all proper proportion, as if it might be coming to an end, unless something extraordinary or miraculous were to happen to save it.... Without belaboring the parallels to contemporary experience, my argument is this overarching generalization plausibly describes, for the majority of the people in the Afroeurasian civilizational belt, their experience of the dramatic increase in power. Of course, there were children like Olivia then, too, verging on a panic attack, crying to adults about what they did not want to happen.

Within this experience, four civilizations display a subset of responses with communities at their margins that stands out as unusual by comparison with the rest: a diverse proliferation of responses that share, to varying degrees, a critical rejection of this power. These rejections have in common sustained systematic spiritual practices that involve a conscious turning against consciousness itself and against "this world," leading to an overcoming of the ego and a transformation of the self such that their accomplished practitioners perceive an "other world" which transcends—subtly, mysteriously—"this world." The meaning and reality of the world become radically other than that which the ego or power sees, understands, or makes available.

Thus, the breakthrough to transcendence is not a mere natural extension of the reach of power or its workings, nor is it an unconsciously being swept along by the tidal forces of history. Power had reached an unprecedented scale during the Axial Age centuries, but in doing so this was a natural (and unconscious) development or logical next step in the dynamics of the expansion of civilization. The refusal to identify with this power is unprecedented, too, but in a quite different, truly extraordinary sense of the word: It is an effort of consciousness and spirit that runs counter to the natural course of human history. Chapter 4 followed the evolutionary expansion of human being out of Africa into the continents of the world, which intensified along the long east-west Afroeurasian belt into agrarian civilization and then in turn into ever-larger civilizations, setting the expansionist trajectory that world history has followed ever since. Across this history, the other natural evolved capacity upon which all human beings rely was their collective identification always in terms of the group, i.e., tribalism. Thus, the Axial Age effort of consciousness and spirit that refuses to expand and which refuses to identify with the tribe runs counter to the natural course of evolution. Rather than merely a response to force—which after all any natural thing also does—or a conscious response to the perception of force—which any animal also does—it is a critically conscious response, composed of both high degrees of self-responsibility and high degrees of ethical responsibility for others, a response that critically evaluates the meaning of power and its unprecedented expansion in moral, ethical, and spiritual terms.

The Axial Age achieves the raising into critical consciousness of the meaning of civilizational power and a plurality of efforts to consciously realize another meaning to reality than that of that civilizational power: A spiritual meaning that immediately manifests in terms of a universal humanity that we are called upon to love, and that further manifests in a fullness of meaning that transcends beyond humanity—perhaps what we could call awkwardly "the love of the world" or "the love of the cosmos," or more precisely, the love that is the world or cosmos, or most precisely, the love that is the true spiritual meaning of the world or cosmos.

One of Karl Jaspers' points is that over two millennia before the earth through technology, industry, and science became in fact an interconnected, singular, "universal" world, the visionaries of the Axial Age lived this singularity, this universality, in practice—and strove to think the moral, ethical, and spiritual meaning of this practice in how they lived and to articulate its radical implications for those who followed this practice. The consequence of globalization and technological and scientific advance means that the phrase "the world" means both the earth and all the peoples on it as a complexly interrelated whole. Twenty-five hundred years after the Axial Age, technology has enabled the world as a whole now to catch up to what several small communities first practiced and thought then, and what a great diversity of fringe, marginal, minority communities based on that Axial Age inspiration have practiced and thought from then until now.

TRANSCENDENCE, AGAIN

Transcendence is the term most associated with the Axial Age, but is also a term so heavily loaded with all kinds of religious, philosophical, and metaphysical baggage, misunderstandings both popular and scholarly, and a host of negative associations and controversial meanings, that many readers may have been at best suspicious of, at worst rejecting in advance, any serious considerations of the thesis. Something I hope this book achieves for the reader is a more nuanced, refined, better historically grounded, and above all a more *practical* understanding of transcendence (rather than a cognitive, intellectual, metaphysical, or theoretical one). To really accomplish this I think we need to develop a better appreciation for what the Axial Age visionaries and *virtuosi*, in contradistinction to the world religions, really mean by transcendence.

The Axial conception of transcendence was a visionary response to the crisis of their civilizational moment. Their experience of transcendence was grounded in practice; their exhortations to disciples and followers were above all to practice; their elliptical, paradoxical, enigmatic, indirect, cryptic, aphoristic, parabolist, elusive circumlocutions around what transcendence is—their reticence about describing its content, or outright silence—all point and redirect their interlocutors back to practice. Transcendence is not an idea to be thought (as happens in the post-Axial appropriation of transcendence by philosophers, political thinkers, or by "world civilizations" in general) nor a belief system to be believed (as happens in the post-Axial appropriation of transcendence by exegetes, interpreters, theologians, or by "world religions" in general). Ideology as a blanket term that encompasses the post-Axial philosophical, political, and religious appropriations of transcendence is the best word here: The idea of transcendence systematically built up into a complex, sophisticated, whole of an "ology." I've been arguing for a practice conception of transcendence over against an ideological one.

I emphasize the practice of transcendence rather than the idea as being true to what the *virtuosi* of the Axial Age really meant because I think this is the truth. And because of how I perceive its potential contemporary relevance: Insofar as the civilizational crisis for the Axial Age visionaries, like our world crisis, devolves on an unprecedented and frightening scale of collective human power conjoined to underdeveloped, self-centered, individual human egos, their response might well be the correct one to our crisis, too. Insofar as it is nonviolent and ascetically self—denying-that is, anti-consumption—it seems both correct, and hopeful, too. But to appreciate this fully, on the interpretation of the Axial Age that I'm offering here in this book, their conception of transcendence needs to be rescued and disentangled from its post-Axial appropriations, above all its elaborations by the world religions that trace their origins to Axial Age founders.

One route the ideology of transcendence can be taken, and often has been, is that of an exclusivist universality: Our version of ultimate truth is the right one, and everyone else's is wrong (and everyone else is also therefore excluded and inferior, too). Another route, well-known today, is fundamentalism: The truths of the world religion I believe in are reducible to certain core beliefs that are timeless and unchanging which must be professed, and this profession gains you admission for membership (and saves you, and condemns all others). (Notice that both of these routes betray the universalist intent of the Axial Age message by reinserting the tribalism that Axial universality was meant to overcome;

my tribe's universal is right and therefore yours is wrong; my tribe is saved, yours is damned.) A third route, specific to the post-Axial development of "the West," is the elaboration of transcendence into modern science: The transcendence of the YHWH of Israel, the *Logos* of Greece, the God of Christianity, becomes radically re-organized and transposed into a transcendent human subjectivity (free, rational, conscious, immaterial, with the power to exploit the world) over against a transcendent natural objectivity (universally lawful, mathematically describable, mysteriously given as causal mechanism, and thus "neutrally" available to be exploited). In Robert Bellah's (2011) terms, a particular understanding of transcendence enables "theoretic culture" (this is his version of what is characteristic about the Axial Age). This becomes taken yet further in the post-Axial elaboration of transcendence in the West until "disengaged theory" emerges with modernity in the seventeenth century. Contra the holistic spiritual visions of the Axial *virtuosi*, which aimed at transforming our egocentric engagement in "this world" (and thus the uses to which our cognitive and intellectual abilities were put) into a moral, ethical, and spiritual engagement, its modern elaboration achieved a disengagement of the cognitive and intellectual mode from moral and ethical and spiritual concerns. The rescue effort of this book by appealing to transcendence as practice is meant to undercut these differing ideological appropriations of transcendence, whether religious or technoscientific, as dangerous appropriations and exposes them as the roads taken by history mistaken relative to their founding intentions.

The emphasis on transcendence as practice immediately implicates the meanings of the "this world"/"other world" distinction or duality, too. The ideological interpretation of transcendence by world civilizational philosophies and world religions leads to metaphysics and supernaturalism and "superhumanism" to make sense of what is meant by the "other world." A practice-based interpretation of transcendence as above all a moral, ethical, spiritual transvaluation of "this world" through an overcoming of the ego leads to a very different consequence. Perhaps, "transfiguration" is the most appropriate word to use here to describe how the "figures" of self and world become transformed through overcoming the ego. In this-worldly terms of power and force and effectiveness and space-time, transcendence makes no difference, whereas in other-worldly terms of love and justice and forgiveness and grace, it makes all the difference. This is an apparent paradox unless one remembers that the practical change transcendence marks are a change in consciousness, a change in the quality of meaning, a change in the locus of identity of ultimate reality: A change wherein nothing is any different than before and yet everything is different.

At the heart of the baggage and negativity that leads to the suspicion, if not rejection, of any proposal concerning transcendence today, is the otherworldly religious interpretation of transcendence as a despising or most dramatically a *rejection* of this world. The suspicion has a venerable pedigree: From the European Enlightenment through the entire period now called modern, "rational men" [sic!] put their faith in science and debunked religion, myth, and metaphysics, all of these being fairy tales about transcendence that ought to be, as David Hume puts it, consigned to the flames. More recently, in the period called postmodern, this positivistically inspired rejection of religion and affirmation of progress was itself exposed as something of an irrational myth founded on its own hidden metaphysics and a Western secular variant of faith. But the postmodern criticism was not intended to rehabilitate or welcome back religion: Transcendence presents itself as the best kind of stuff of what Grand Narratives are made. Instead, both modernity's view of science and traditional views of religion come under criticism for espousing "Grand Narratives," toward which we ought to cultivate "incredulity" (Lyotard, 1984). At its intellectual best, the postmodern critique has done us an indispensable service at clarifying the all too human roots of transcendence and exposing how so many of our supposed high ideals prove to be nothing but sophisticated disguises for the workings of power. Postmodern critical thought doubles down on the modern suspicion of religion and tradition, with transcendence or any appeals to it at the receiving end of both formidable attacks.

Acknowledging this considerable background and moving into the present, the issue appears that it would seem impossible to square anxieties and fears about our world in crisis, and therefore, our hopes and wishes for some kind of, well, salvation for this world of ours, with an otherworldly focus that despises and rejects this world and longs for salvation from it. Part of my ambition has been to afford a different way of framing this issue. Historically, world religions have opted for an ideological conception of transcendence that makes of otherworldly faith a metaphysics and a supernaturalism due to an inadequate recognition of their own complicity in power at too large a scale. The effects of this scale of power are to distort religion out of proper proportion and thus out of proper apportioning of the relation of human beings to this world; what we are to envision and what we are to hope for are thrown out of true. Given this legacy, that modernity followed by postmodernity respond by throwing out the practical baby along with the ideological bathwater is rather understandable. But while the Axial critique of power was indeed intellectual, it was also much else, and ultimately, the appeal to transcendence of Axial Age visionaries was an affirmation of an alternative, holistic, counter-civilizational way of life inclusive of, but irreducible to, the intellectual. In these respects, the postmodern critique risks reproducing a counterpoint remaining at the level of what Bellah (2011) described as "disengaged theory," amounting to a hollow victory insofar as it misses the point of transcendence as a reorientation, not of the mind or of theory, but of one's whole person and the fullness of life (from which a reorientation of mind and theory will follow).

Critically clarifying the difference between Axial Age visions of transcendence and the world religions mis-taking of transcendence even as the religions insist (as they must) on their being faithful to their founding visions, should open a more nuanced appreciation of world religions and the role they have played in world history. Insofar as world religions are trans-cultural social organizations that directly inherit, and then embody within themselves, a whole new scale of power, their claims to transcendence and universality devolve on dogmatic-ideological claims for membership. However, this whole dogmatic-ideological power-centered orientation sits in a tension as dynamic as it is unresolvable, with the founding visions of transcendence: The latter are premised on a critique of power inseparable from the expansion in the scale of power, and advocated transcendence not as ideal, idea, belief, or ideology but as an experiential reality accessible to all. This critical reading could also work for adherents of world religions themselves as a critical reflection that informs their own ongoing work of self-criticism and self-reform—work that shows a faithful adherence to one-half of their Axial heritage—in two ways.

One way: It suggests a way forward for spiritual renewal within religions on their own terms (or, on their own foundations). This project of renewal could take place alongside the second way: Interreligious dialogue and engagement between religions, with a key component of this dialogue and engagement that these are not based exclusively in dogmatic terms internal to the religious traditions but they include world-historical terms deriving from the Axial Age. In contrast to the meaning of internally referential terms, the latter provide stronger potential for comparison, commonalty, and mutual understanding.

World religions have been key contributors to our current world in crisis, both ecologically and politically, and both a way forward for spiritual renewal as well as dialogue and engagement between themselves beyond dogmatic grounds, are necessary to enable the internal transformation of world religions to meet that crisis. Conversely, world religions are one of our most potent spiritual resources upon which to draw for dealing with our world in crisis, and renewed attention to the Axial Age and its spiritual practices might well draw the Golden Mean, or act as a Middle Way, between a critical reform of world religions and appropriating them as spiritual resource.

OLIVIA, AGAIN

In the end, though, let us remember Olivia. Her cries and tears have been the guideline to this book from beginning to end, expressing clearly and directly what I have only ever expressed inadequately and indirectly by thinking about it during lonely peregrinations through woods and wild places, in mute despairing communion with animals and wild things. How does the Axial Age hold out hope for children, for wild things, for all of us today?

First, the scholarly answer: The precedent for perceiving that the world is in crisis, that this crisis is rooted in human nature, and that this crisis needs to be faced and overcome, and that it can be, is the Axial Age. It was during the Axial Age that for the first time, the phrase "the world" was conceived as applying universally to everyone, rather than to one's own tribe, one's own bounded local ethnic group or civilization, one's own ego-centered self-interest. It was during the Axial Age that sages and prophets and philosophers thought beyond the crisis of their particular civilization and thought into the more sweeping claim that all of our human ways of living, believing, and thinking were understood to lead to a state of crisis and to be inadequate. Over against "this world" of suffering, ignorance, injustice, desire, violence, and tribalism all ultimately centered on and reducible to egotism, they claimed an "other world" of a transcendent reality existed that gave this world its ultimate meaning that applied universally to everyone.

This claim was foundational for, and inseparable from, their preaching of salvation from this world and its crisis. Insofar as the great world religions took the idea of transcendence and made it the dogmatic basis for their doctrines and institutions, the primary interest of their adherents is in this promise of salvation. In this book, I don't advance the same claim—on my reading the Axial Age is the ideal resource for the criticism and reform of the world religions. If, however, the key contribution of the Axial Age is the road not taken (of spiritual practice in small communities aimed at personal transformation toward realizing transcendence, not as an idea, but as spiritual reality) the question becomes: To what extent does the Axial Age salvation-solution to its crisis apply to our world in crisis today? Put bluntly, if we practiced what the spiritual masters of the Axial Age practiced, would we "save the world"?

To understand universality in Axial Age terms they articulated an "other world" of spirit, where neither the ego nor power were central, but one where human consciousness transcended its own limitations to connect to a higher form of consciousness whose concerns went beyond ego and power. Contrary to the power of civilization and the size of empires of their time, which precipitated a spiritual crisis as deeply felt then by those sensitive souls of the Axial Age as Olivia's anxious response today to the potential of cities flooding due to global warming, they advocate a very different way of life and values. The Axial Age presents us with the example of a small set of exceptional individuals establishing countercultural communities based on a critical rejection of civilizational power and its accompanying values, explicitly emphasizing self-denial, and consciously choosing spiritual practices. It thus proposes a more relevant, practicable, and applicable model for us to consider for the world's crisis and humanity's future than our current way of life and its values, which have brought our world to a crisis point.

Relative to our ecological crisis, the connection between sustained systematic spiritual practices and developing an ecological awareness or sustainable practices is not direct. I am not arguing the Axial Age visionaries were deep ecologists. However, the connection is neither distant nor strained, either. If the practices serve to raise into critical conscious awareness the spiritual meaning of our ordinary consciousness, of our civilizational norms, of the effects and consequences of its power—which prior to such practice was unconsciously performed as if "natural" and "automatic," but through such practice becomes "systematically deconstructed"—then I offer that if undertaken today "practicing transcendence" will raise into critical conscious awareness the unsustainable scale of our consumption, the deep realization of its consequences upon the natural world in global climate change and a mass extinction of species, and the realization of the irreplaceable, fragile good of biodiversity.

As scholarly answers go, I think the above is a pretty good one. However, what it retains throughout is a focus on egocentric concerns, rather than on how the wise teachers, philosophers, sages, and holy men of the Axial Age themselves would answer. Their response was to critically distance themselves from "this world," i.e., from the allure and appeal of the power of civilization, through establishing small communities on the margins of society, focused on spiritual practices that transform the self. What this response does, however, among other things, is rescale the problem into what they considered the proper proportion: a spiritual response to world problems radically alters the basic categories for thinking the problems. Psychologically speaking, there is more than a little genius in this response. The Axial Age response resituates the force of the imperative of "thinking the world" away from an overwhelming, frightening, and perhaps insurmountably complex object ("the world") to focus instead on the thinking. More basically yet, it resituates the focus onto one's self as the thinker. The task of thinking the world seems dauntingly impossible, an impossibility rendered even more so when the world one is trying to think is in crisis, and one's thinking clouded by end-of-the-world anxieties. The task of focusing on one's own thinking and self seems quite humbly achievable. The spiritual-practical Axial Age response to crisis: practice the self that thinks, such that the self is transformed from thinking egocentrically into being able to think universally. In Lao Tzu's justly famous words from the *Tao Te Ching*, a journey of a thousand miles (like saving the world from its crisis) begins small, with a single step (like spiritual practice on one's self). That this journey leads along the way to compassion for all things (in Buddhist terms), or love for all of God's creation and of one's neighbor (in Jewish and Christian terms), is not irrelevant. No doubt, the story of this imperiled jewel Earth as staging ground to an immense evolutionary journey, surmounted at its current end by a long history of sapient tribal beings who have expanded so enormously in power and violence that we now threaten to shatter this jewel and destroy what should be our beloved home, needs a compassionate reading.

So if we try to think the Axial Age, spiritual answer to Olivia's tears, or to our own adult, end-of-the-world anxieties, in their compassionate terms rather than our own egocentric ones, we should admit that our untrained, undisciplined minds are reinserting the ego onto center stage at every point. Without that training and discipline, the ego naturally identifies with power at the biggest scale that it can, power which based on both our evolved capacities and our history working together we have expanded to global proportions, and it is at that large scale that we are committing evil. The response of the Axial Age teachers is to resituate that identification and rescale that overriding concern and thus our overwhelming anxieties, to their proper proportion. Their response is humble and humbling, practical and spiritual, compassionate and hopeful, into which they pour their wisdom so as to resituate our locus of identification and rescale our anxieties, in the form of two simple questions. Together, these compose the single small step that begins each of our individual journeys to save the world, together:

What is your small community?

What is your spiritual practice?

REFERENCES

Bellah, R. (2011). *Religion in human evolution: From the Paleolithic to the Axial Age*. Harvard, MA: Belknap.

Diamond, J. (2005). *Collapse: How societies choose to fail or succeed*. New York: Viking.

Lyotard, J. (1984). *The postmodern condition: A report on knowledge* (G. Bennington & B. Massumi, Trans.). Minneapolis: University of Minnesota Press.

Pinker, S. (2012). *The better angels of our nature: Why violence has declined*. New York: Penguin.

Roszak, T. (1979). *Person/planet: The creative disintegration of industrial society*. New York: Doubleday.

Smith-Christopher, D. (2002). *A biblical theology of exile*. Minneapolis: Fortress Press.

Further Reading

Chapter 1

p. 2: There is a small but growing literature linking psychological concerns, such as anxiety, fear, grief, loss, mourning, and denial, to global climate change. An incomplete list, but a place to start: Angus (2016), Cunsolo and Landman (2017), Dodds (2011), Gow (2009), Hamilton (2010), Hertsgaard (2011), Kiehl (2016), Lertzman (2015), Mann (2016), Nemeth, Hamilton, and Kuriansky (2012), Orange (2017), and Weintrobe (2013).

This literature is distinct from scholarly literature on "apocalypticism" proper, which is much older; the famous psychological analysis is Festinger, Riecken, and Schachter's *When Prophecy Fails* (1956). A famous historical series is Norman Cohn's *Pursuit of the* millennium (1957, 1969; cf. also 1993). Landes (2011) is particularly useful for both analysis and overview, as are Bull (1995a), Griffin (2007), and Ruthven (2015). Oreskes and Conway (2013) provide a particularly imaginative and insightful approach. Some others: Amanat and Bernardsson (2002), Boyer (1992), Bull (1995b), Carroll (1979), Himmelfarb (2010), Tonning, Feldman, and Addyman (2015), and Veldman (2012).

p. 5: Obviously much of the book's bibliography bears on the Axial Age! Jaspers (1953) is the centerpiece book, outlining the main thesis on pp. 1–21, Bellah (2011) the most recent full-length treatment. Jaspers also provides a brief accessible summary in *Way to Wisdom* (1951, pp. 96–109). The two most publicly accessible book-length

C. Peet, *Practicing Transcendence*,
https://doi.org/10.1007/978-3-030-14432-6

summaries are Armstrong (2006) and Baskin and Bondarenko (2014); also accessible and recent is Torpey (2017). The best short introductions are: Armstrong (2006, pp. xv–xxiii), Arnason, Eisenstadt, and Wittrock (2005, pp. 1–12), Bellah (2005), Bellah (2011, pp. 265–282), Eisenstadt (1982; 1986, pp. 1–25), Schwartz (1975, pp. 1–7). Lewis Mumford (1956) provides a brilliant interpretation and summary. Most of the major texts are edited anthologies; in chronological order: Schwartz (1975), Eisenstadt (1986), Seligman (1989), Arnason, Eisenstadt, and Wittrock (2005), Bellah and Joas (2012). Muesse (2013) gives an excellent account largely congruent with my own emphases, however focused only on the eastern religions. Halton (2014) provides a critical correction to the "Jaspers-centric" Axial literature in discussing Stuart-Glennie (1873); in the process Halton also points out overlooked contributions from Mumford and D. H. Lawrence. The most extensive bibliography to both primary and secondary literature is provided in Bellah and Joas (2012, pp. 471–537). Thomassen (2010), Boy and Torpey (2013), and Mullins et al. (2018) provide excellent critical overviews of Axial Age thesis and scholarship.

p. 13: Horizon and space of meaning: space is simply too short to discuss the existential and phenomenological movements to which Jaspers belonged, and which develop a whole vocabulary and "thought-style" centered on notions like horizon and space of meaning, beginning with Husserl, developed extensively by Heidegger (who derisively labeled Jaspers' "that transcendent philosopher") and numerous others.

p. 21: Asceticism connotes overly sensational versions: like transcendence, positive arguments for asceticism will encounter deep resistance in our contemporary climate, as postmodernism has doubled down on the modernist reaction against religious "otherworldly" claims, anything hinting at dualisms or Grand Narratives (as I argue in Chapter 7). I think this is profoundly unfortunate at a time when the need for self-denial and self-sacrifice to be built into overly-consumptive ways of life has become paramount. Rejecting the pathologies and extremes to which asceticism can be carried can go hand-in-hand with affirming and upholding the wisdom and goodness of its more prudent, moderate exercise. Fraade (1986, esp. pp. 253–260) and Diamond (2004) in the context of arguing for ascetic elements within Judaism—which has been stereotyped as non- or anti-ascetic—provide excellent brief discussions of asceticism more generally; see Wimbush and Valantasis (1998a). Nietzsche (2007) of course offers a brilliant and penetrating critique of (Western) asceticism.

p. 25: Fringe possibilities: Cousins (1994) argues for monasticism as a distinctive contribution of the Axial Age. In a loose sense I agree, but see monasticism, like the world religions, as emerging some centuries later and thus only indirectly an institutionalized legacy that domesticates much of the Axial practices of, and interpretations of, transcendence. How monasticism within Buddhism, Hinduism, and Christianity relates to organized world religion and orthodoxy on the one hand, and mysticism and fringe spiritual experience, on the other, lies beyond the scope of this book but clearly bears in intriguing ways upon questions of Axial influence.

Chapter 2

p. 37: Multiple modernities. To my knowledge Eisenstadt first introduces the notion in Eisenstadt (2000). Sachsenmaier (2002) gives an excellent discussion in the edited anthology devoted to the topic Sachsenmaier, Reidel, and Eisenstadt (2002). See also Eisenstadt (2006), and an excellent discussion of the relationship of the concept to the Axial Age in Thomassen (2010).

p. 42: Clash of civilizations: Huntington (1993) is the article (1996), the full-length book. The "clash of civilizations" phrase and basic thesis was in fact first developed by the Western historian of Islam, Bernard Lewis, in 1990 to characterize his "Islam vs. the West" views in an article called "The Roots of Muslim Rage". Said (1997) provides the trenchant critique, of both Lewis and Huntington.

p. 47: Ethnodiversity: my source, and to my knowledge this phrase originates here, is Wade Davis' *The Wayfinders* (2009).

p. 47: Mass extinctions: The literature I consulted on mass extinction events and the Sixth Extinction: Brannen (2017), Ceballos, Ehrlich, and Dirzo (2017), Eldredege (1991, 1995), Hallam and Wignall (1997), Kolbert (2014), Leakey and Lewin (1995), Raup and Sepkoski (1982, 1984), Tennesen (2015), Ward (2007), and Ward and Kirschvinsk (2015).

p. 50: Darwin was right... Darwin was wrong. I have found Steven Jay Gould's *The structure of evolutionary theory* (2002) authoritative and comprehensive on Darwinian "gradualism" vs. the newer "punctuated equilibrium" revision.

p. 57: Violence as basic to our nature: Halton (2014, pp. 64–65) provides a provocative counter-argument to this claim that is more radically "anti-civilizational" than my own "counter-civilizational" approach. Pinker (2012) provides an optimistic Enlightenment argument of humans progressing away from violence via civilization and democracy.

p. 58: Culture… symbolic reference. The work of Merlin Donald (1991, 2001) has been hugely influential on Axial Age scholarship via Bellah's (2011) account of "religious evolution", especially Donald's arguments regarding the reliance of cognition on "external" symbol systems. Aspects of this influence are discussed throughout Bellah and Joas (2012). Personally I am more taken with Deacon's (1997) version of evolution and "symbolic reference", and find Jung's (2012) effort at "reconciling" the Donald-Deacon differences to advance the Axial Age thesis on transcendence in the direction of semiotic structures the most promising and exciting contemporary avenue of inquiry. Of especial interest is Jung's notion of "paying attention to the temporal lag between the emergence of a new means of signification and its conscious appropriation" (p. 83). On the one hand as Jung notes, because it enables a means to "connect" evolutionary anthropology and historical discourse. On the other hand my argument for sustained systematic spiritual practice as "systematically deconstructing" ordinary consciousness while "stabilizing" emerging levels of consciousness would seem profoundly implicated relative to Jung's postulating of the "temporal lag". I'd like to think my argument poses a "practical spirituality" correlative to Jung's emphasis on semiotic structure, both helping articulate how transcendence depends on an "inescapable embodiedness of meaning" (p. 80).

Chapter 3

p. 64: An explosion of scholarship: The most extensive bibliography to both primary and secondary literature on the Axial Age is provided in Bellah and Joas (2012, pp. 471–537), based on which I derive the numbers for Figure 4. There are forty primary sources noted dating from 1771–1989 (eleven from 1771 to 1900, sixteen from 1900 to 1948). Of the twenty-three from 1948–1989 thirteen are from Karl Jaspers & Eric Voegelin. For secondary sources (encyclopedia entries, monographs & articles) the bibliography identifies a total of 931; Shmuel Eisenstadt, either singly or co-authored, accounts for 121.

p. 67: Voegelin: Eric Voegelin developed his own idiosyncratic, original, and conceptually difficult theory of historical development over a series of five volumes called *Order and History* (1956–1974). He is more sympathetic to the Axial Age thesis initially (1956, 1957), albeit with numerous critical reservations, most especially his restriction of the thesis to "the West" (Israel and Greece). Later in the project he has abandoned the thesis (1974). Glenn Hughes (1993, 2003) provides excellent summary discussions of Voegelin's intricate position, which certainly theorizes transcendence in deep and provocative ways.

p. 77: Transcendence. The concept is the center of gravity to the Axial Age thesis, and has generated no shortage of theory and research. See Dalferth (2012) for an article that takes it on directly as theme in context of Axial Age scholarship. Outside that context, Kerr (1997) provides an anthology of differing views on transcendence, including some summary of Charles Taylor's and Martha Nussbaum's discussion.

p. 80: Inwardness. Also a crucial concept, usually discussed in the scholarly literature in attempts to trace the history of the individual, or of individualism. See Dumont (1986) or Taylor (1989) for different magisterial accounts of the Western historical development of the concept, or see Sue Hamilton (2000, 2001) on Buddhist views.

p. 82: Mystery and mysticism. I find Gabriel Marcel's (1960) existential articulation of "*The Mystery of Being*" compelling and still unsurpassed. Mysticism of course has an enormous literature and includes such famous thinkers as William James, Evelyn Underhill, Aldous Huxley and "the perennial philosophy", Abraham Maslow in terms of "peak experience", and more besides. Probably the best critical series is the four volumes edited by Steven Katz (1978a, 1983, 1992, 2000); Katz (1978b) presents the "contextualist" rebuttal of the perennial philosophy position, classically represented by, e.g. W. T. Stace (1960). See Forman (1990) for a response to Katz and a qualified defense of the perennialist position, and an account with which I am in sympathy vis-à-vis the notion of spiritual practice as "systematic deconstruction", or in Forman's preferred term taken from Meister Eckhart, "forgetting". Much of this treats on the key notion of "ineffability" within mystical experience; see Bagger (2006), Nishitani (1982), and Sells (1994). Although now some decades old, McGinn's (1991) Appendix remains exceptional for a history of different treatments of mysticism.

p. 91: Ken Wilber's "orienting generalizations". See Wilber (1995), Introduction, and Jack Crittenden's Foreword in Wilber (1998).

p. 95: Boundless communication rising to heights of noble emulation. It seems to me that encounters between experienced spiritual practitioners from different traditions has often taken this route; curiosity and interest in the other with neither fear of that difference nor evangelical conversion attempts. See some of the stories in Nataraja (2012); or the notion of "dialogical dialogue" in McEntee and Bucko (2015), or the example of such dialogue in Miles-Yepez (2006).

CHAPTER 4

p. 102: First *homo sapiens sapiens*: For early hominid origins in Africa, see McBrearty and Brooks (2000) and Stringer (2002, 2016). I also consulted Fagan (2005, 2010) and Pettitt (2018). For the migration patterns across the earth, see Goldin, Cameron, and Balarajan (2011) for an excellent summary (up till the fifteenth century CE, pp. 11–38); see Manning (2005) for the long version. "Neolithic Revolution" phrase is attributed to archaeologist V. Gordon Childe. Still the most fun and best synthesis of all of the above, and beyond, is Jared Diamond (1997).

p. 103: Long Afroeurasian belt: Diamond (1997) is the source for this, above all in terms of the argument for the E-W axis of Eurasia. Although as I understand he is not the originator, but rather synthesizer, of earlier theories; esp. McNeill (1963, 1986, 1993, 1998). Diamond's book also provides means for making the transition from evolutionary prehistory considerations to world-system literature.

p. 109: World-system literature. Where to begin? There is so much! In addition to Diamond and McNeill already cited, here's an alphabetic listing, with most (but not all) addressing issues around the Eurasian world-system: Babones and Chase-Dunn (2012), Barfield (1989), Chase-Dunn and Anderson (2005), Christian (1994, 2000), Di Cosmo (1999), Fenelon (2012), Frank and Gills (1993), Grinin and Korotayev (2012, 2014), Korotayev (2004), Mair (2006), Sanderson (1995), Shaffer (1994), Tellier (2009), Wilkinson, Sherratt, and Bennet (2011). Of particular interest within the world-system theory questions is just what causes the emergence of "the state"; cf. Carneiro (1978) as well as Cohen (1978), in Cohen and Service (1978), and Johnson and Earle (2000).

p. 123: Well-documented significant effects: As I note in Chapter 6 in the quote from Waelde and Thompson (2016), published research on mindfulness has increased "from less than a dozen articles a year prior to 1998 to almost 500 per year by 2012" (p. 119). This article itself appears in an edited volume by West (2016), one of dozens of handbooks, anthologies, and collections appearing over the past decade alone putting together psychology, counseling, clinical psychology, psycho-therapy, and mental health (on the one side) with spirituality, religion, meditation, mindfulness, contemplation, and so forth, on the other side. Slightly older work in the field like that of Jon Kabat-Zinn (who creates "mindfulness-based stress reduction", MBSR) or Herbert Benson ("the relaxation response") now have the status of "classics" and appear rel-atively solitary compared to the current deluge. Although claims about meditation and mindfulness and their effects falls on the "softer" side of research and often veers into unsubstantiated claims and "popularizing", nevertheless there is also a rapidly growing body of solid research show-ing the positive effects of sustained spiritual practices of meditation on mental, physical, emotional, and spiritual health.

p. 130: Alphabet as epochal: a whole separate scholarly argument as to the consequences of writing, which I have yet to see connected to the Axial Age thesis. Such an effort would be fascinating, if monumental, and would likely bear out Jung's (2012) claims about "temporal lag"; see Jack Goody and Ian Watt (1963), Eric Havelock (1963), and Walter Ong (1982).

p. 138: Charles Taylor and strong evaluation: a number of Taylor's writings are compiled in his 2 volumes of "Philosophical papers" (1985a, 1985b) that outline his theory of "strong evaluation"; cf 1985a, Chapters 1, 2, 4, 9, and 10; 1985b, Chapters 1–6. It is also crucial theo-retical preface to his historical treatment in Taylor (1989, Chapters 1–4).

Chapters 5 and 6

Owing to the case by case nature of the material covered in these two chapters with accompanying reference and documentation of sources, the best guide to further reading, unlike the initial four chapters, are embedded within these chapters themselves in the authors cited.

p. 150: Unresolved since the eighteenth century: As I hope Chapter 4 made clear, I perceive world-system theorizing to hold out signifi-cant promise for answering many Axial Age questions, especially in the world-system emphases on trade and interconnections. The Silk Roads and the sea-routes between China, India, and the Near East need far greater examination to begin to answer questions about Axial Age "par-allels" and "independence". The other tantalizing factor within all of these many, in addition to Zoroastrianism and Achaemenid Persia, is the role of the far-traveling nomads of inner Eurasia, who also connected all three geographic areas; for the latter, see Barfield (1989), Christian (1994, 2000), and Di Cosmo (1999).

p. 176: Akhenaten. In addition to the scholars cited, there is a small industry centered on the fascinating and enigmatic "monotheistic" Pharaoh. See Dodds (2009, 2014), Hornung (1999), Kemp (2012), Montserrat (2003), and Reeves (2001).

p. 222: A choice for how to proceed: a fascinating triangulation of alternatives to civilizational power are provided if we take two other arguments into account. The first is advanced by Mann (2012), attributed originally to Stuart Piggott: that the "hunter-gatherers" or foragers, among other things, intentionally held onto their way of life in order to prevent the onset of civilizational power as "too big". The second is proposed by Morris Berman (2000) in *Wandering God: A study in nomadic spirituality*, wherein the choice of a nomadic life is a rejection of civilizational power and conscious pursuit of an alternative outside the sedentary and "big power". Interestingly, Berman's argument also challenges the depth and authenticity of Axial spiritualities, too, as ultimately flawed and too deeply beholden to the alienating premises of civilization. My own version of Axial spirituality is that it is a critically conscious attempt from within civilization to transcend the hold of power from within. The three options – prevent power from developing, choose an alternative that remains outside power, or transcend the power from within – sketch out a fascinating set of critiques of civilizational power and countercultural ways of living "on the margins" or "in the interstices" of "big power".

BIBLIOGRAPHY

Allchin, F. (Ed.). (1995). *The archaeology of early historic South Asia: The emergence of cities and states.* Cambridge: Cambridge University Press.

Amanat, A., & Bernardsson, M. (Eds.). (2002). *Imagining the end: Visions of apocalypse from the ancient Middle East to modern America.* London: I.B. Tauris.

Anderson, E. N., & Chase-Dunn, C. (2005). The rise and fall of great powers. In C. Chase-Dunn & E. N. Anderson (Eds.), *The historical evolution of world-systems* (pp. 1–19). New York: Palgrave Macmillan.

Angus, I. (2016). *Facing the anthropocene: Fossil capitalism and the crisis of the earth system.* New York: Monthly Review Press.

Armstrong, K. (2006). *The great transformation: The beginning of our religious traditions.* New York and Toronto: Alfred A. Knopf.

Arnason, J. (2005). The axial conundrum: Between historical sociology and the philosophy of history. In E. Ben-Rafael & Y. Sternberg (Eds.), *Comparing modernities: Pluralism versus homogeneity* (pp. 57–82). Leiden and Boston: Brill.

Arnason, J., Eisenstadt, S., & Wittrock, B. (Eds.). (2005a). *Axial civilizations and world history.* Leiden: Brill.

Arnason, J., Eisenstadt, S., & Wittrock, B. (2005b). General introduction. In J. Arnason, S. Eisenstadt, & B. Wittrock (Eds.), *Axial civilizations and world history* (pp. 1–12). Leiden: Brill.

Ashvaghosa. (2008). *Life of the Buddha* (P. Olivelle, Trans.). New York: New York University Press.

Assmann, J. (2005). Axial "breakthroughs" and semantic "relocation" in ancient Egypt and Israel. In J. Arnason, S. Eisenstadt, & B. Wittrock (Eds.), *Axial civilizations and world history* (pp. 133–156). Leiden: Brill.

© The Editor(s) (if applicable) and The Author(s) 2019
C. Peet, *Practicing Transcendence*,
https://doi.org/10.1007/978-3-030-14432-6

Assmann, J. (2011). *Cultural memory and early civilization: Writing, remembrance, and political imagination.* New York: Cambridge University Press.

Assmann, J. (2012). Cultural memory and the myth of the Axial Age. In R. Bellah & H. Joas (Eds.), *The Axial Age and its consequences* (pp. 366–407). Cambridge and London: Belknap.

Babones, S., & Chase-Dunn, C. (Eds.). (2012). *Routledge handbook of world-systems analysis.* London and New York: Routledge.

Bagger, M. (2007). *The uses of paradox (religion, self-transformation, and the absurd).* New York: Columbia University Press.

Ball, W. (2010). *Out of Arabia: Phoenicians, Arabs and the discovery of Europe.* Northampton, MA: Olive Branch Press.

Barfield, T. J. (1989). *The perilous frontier: Nomadic empires and China, 221 BC to AD 1757.* Cambridge and Oxford: Blackwell.

Barker, M. (2004). *The great high priest: The temple roots of Christian liturgy.* New York and London: T&T Clark.

Basham, A. L. (1951). *History and doctrines of the Ājīvikas: A vanished Indian religion.* London: Luzac.

Baskin, K., & Bondarenko, D. (2014). *The Axial Ages of world history: Lessons for the 21st century.* Litchfield Park, AZ: Emergent Publishing.

Baumard, N., Hyafil, A., Morris, I., & Boyer, P. (2015). Increased affluence explains emergence of ascetic wisdoms and moralizing religions. *Current Biology, 25*(1), 10–15.

Bellah, R. (2005). What is axial about the Axial Age? *European Journal of Sociology, 46*(1), 69–89.

Bellah, R. (2011). *Religion in human evolution: From the Paleolithic to the Axial Age.* Harvard, MA: Belknap.

Bellah, R., & Joas, H. (2012a). Introduction. In R. Bellah & H. Joas (Eds.), *The Axial Age and its consequences* (pp. 1–6). Cambridge and London: Belknap.

Bellah, R., & Joas, H. (Eds.). (2012b). *The Axial Age and its consequences.* Cambridge and London: Belknap.

Ben-Rafael, E., & Sternberg, Y. (Eds.). (2010). *World religions and multiculturalism: A dialectic relation.* Leiden and Boston: Brill.

Berman, M. (2000). *Wandering god: A study in nomadic spirituality.* Albany, NY: SUNY Press.

Berquist, J. (2016). Prophecy in Persian Yehud. In C. Sharp (Ed.), *The Oxford handbook of the prophets* (pp. 55–66). Oxford: Oxford University Press.

Blenkinsopp, J. (1977). *Prophecy and canon: A contribution to the study of Jewish origins.* Notre Dame and London: University of Notre Dame Press.

Blenkinsopp, J. (1995). *Sage, priest, prophet: Religious and intellectual leadership in ancient Israel.* Louisville, KY: John Knox Press.

Blenkinsopp, J. (1996). *A history of prophecy in Israel.* Louisville, KY: John Knox Press.

Bowman, J. (2015). *Cosmoipolitan justice: The Axial Age, multiple modernities, and the postsecular turn*. Cham: Springer.

Boy, J., & Torpey, J. (2013). Inventing the Axial Age: The origins and uses of a historical concept. *Theory and Society, 42*(3), 241–259.

Boyer, P. (1992). *When time shall be no more: Prophesy belief in modern American culture*. Cambridge, MA: Harvard Belknap.

Brannen, P. (2017). *The ends of the world: Volcanic apocalypses, lethal oceans, and our quest to understand Earth's past mass extinctions*. New York: HarperCollins.

Braudel, F. (1980). *On history* (S. Matthews, Trans.). Chicago: University of Chicago.

Braudel, F. (1994). *A history of civilizations* (R. Mayne, Trans.). New York: A. Lane.

Brockington, J. (2003). Yoga in the Mahabharata. In I. Whicher & D. Carpenter (Eds.), *Yoga: The Indian tradition* (pp. 13–24). London: Routledge Curzon.

Bronkhorst, J. (1998). *The two sources of Indian asceticism*. New Delhi: Motilal Banarsidass.

Bronkhorst, J. (2000). *The two traditions of meditation in ancient India*. New Delhi: Motilal Banarsidass.

Bronkhorst, J. (2007). *Greater Magadha: Studies in the culture of early India*. Leiden: Brill.

Bronkhorst, J. (2011). *Buddhism in the shadow of Brahmanism*. Leiden: Brill.

Brooke, G. (2006). Prophecy and prophets in the Dead Sea scrolls: Looking backwards and forwards. In M. Floyd & R. Haak (Eds.), *Prophets, prophecy, and prophetic texts in second temple Judaism* (pp. 151–165). New York and London: T&T Clark.

Brown, D. (1986). The stages of meditation in cross-cultural perspective. In K. Wilber, J. Engler, & D. Brown (Eds.), *Transformations of consciousness: Conventional and contemplative perspectives on development* (pp. 193–271). Boston and London: Shambhala.

Bull, M. (1995a). On making ends meet. In M. Bull (Ed.), *Apocalypse theory and the ends of the world* (pp. 1–17). Oxford and Cambridge: Blackwell.

Bull, M. (Ed.). (1995b). *Apocalypse theory and the ends of the world*. Oxford and Cambridge: Blackwell.

Burkert, W. (1992). *The orientalizing revolution: Near Eastern influence on Greek culture in the early archaic age* (M. E. Pinder & W. Burkert, Trans.). Cambridge, MA: Harvard University Press.

Burkert, W. (2004). *Babylon, Memphis, Persepolis: Eastern contexts of Greek culture*. Cambridge, MA: Harvard University Press.

Buss, M. (2006). The place of Israelite prophecy in human history. In B. Kelle & M. Moore (Eds.), *Israel's prophets and Israel's past* (pp. 325–341). New York and London: T&T Clark.

Bussanich, J. (2016). Plato and yoga. In R. Seaford (Ed.), *Universe and inner self in early Indian and early Greek thought* (pp. 87–103). Edinburgh: Edinburgh University Press.

Calhoun, C., Mendieta, E., & VanAntwerpen, J. (Eds.). (2013). *Habermas and religion*. Cambridge and Malden, MA: Polity Press.

Carneiro, R. (1978). Political expansion as an expression of the principle of competitive exclusion. In R. Cohen & E. Service (Eds.), *Origins of the state: The anthropology of political evolution* (pp. 205–223). Philadelphia: Institute for the Study of Human Issues.

Carpenter, D. (2003). Practice makes perfect: The role of practice (abhyasa) in Patanjali yoga. In I. Whicher & D. Carpenter (Eds.), *Yoga: The Indian tradition* (pp. 25–50). London: Routledge Curzon.

Carroll, R. (1979). *When prophecy failed*. New York: Seabury.

Ceballos, G., Ehrlich, P., & Dirzo, R. (2017, July). Population losses and the sixth mass extinction. *Proceedings of the National Academy of Sciences, 114*(30), E6089–E6096. https://doi.org/10.1073/pnas.1704949114.

Chase-Dunn, C., & Anderson, E. N. (Eds.). (2005). *The historical evolution of world-systems*. New York: Palgrave Macmillan.

Chase-Dunn, C., & Hall, T. (1997). *Rise and demise: Comparing world-systems*. Boulder, CO: Westview Press.

Ching, J. (2003). What is Confucian spirituality? In T. Weiming & M. Tucker (Eds.), *Confucian spirituality* (Vol. 1, pp. 81–95). New York: Crossroad.

Christian, D. (1994). Inner Eurasia as a unit of world history. *Journal of World History, 5*(2), 173–211.

Christian, D. (2000). Silk roads or steppe roads? The silk roads in world history. *Journal of World History, 11*(1), 1–26.

Christian, D. (2005). *Maps of time: An introduction to big history*. Oakland: University of California.

Cohen, R. (1978). State foundations: A controlled comparison. In R. Cohen & E. Service (Eds.), *Origins of the state: The anthropology of political evolution* (pp. 141–160). Philadelphia: Institute for the Study of Human Issues.

Cohen, R., & Service, E. (Eds.). (1978). *Origins of the state: The anthropology of political evolution*. Philadelphia: Institute for the Study of Human Issues.

Cohn, N. (1957). *The pursuit of the millennium: Revolutionary messianism in medieval and Reformation Europe and its bearing on modern totalitarian movements*. New York, NY: Harper.

Cohn, N. (1969). *The pursuit of the millennium: Revolutionary millenarians and mystical anarchists of the Middle Ages*. London: Paladin.

Cohn, N. (1993). *Cosmos, chaos and the world to come: The ancient roots of apocalyptic faith*. London and New Haven: Yale.

Collins, R. (1998). *The sociology of philosophies: A global theory of intellectual change*. Cambridge and London: Belknap Harvard.

Conze, E. (1959). *Buddhist scriptures*. Harmondsworth, Middlesex: Penguin.

Cousins, E. (1987). Spirituality in today's world. In F. Whaling (Ed.), *Religion in today's world: The religious situation of the world from 1945 to the present day* (pp. 306–345). Edinburgh: T&T Clark.

Cousins, E. (1994). *Christ of the 21st century*. London and New York: Bloomsbury Academic.

Credit Suisse Research Institute. (2017). *Credit Suisse Global Wealth Report*. https://www.credit-suisse.com/corporate/en/research/research-institute/global-wealth-report.html.

Csikszentmihalyi, M., & Ivanhoe, P. (Eds.). (1999). *Religious and philosophical aspects of the Laozi*. Albany, NY: SUNY Press.

Cunsolo, A., & Landman, K. (2017). *Mourning nature: Hope at the heart of ecological loss and grief*. Montreal and Kingston: McGill-Queen's University Press.

Dalferth, I. (2012). The idea of transcendence. In R. Bellah & H. Joas (Eds.), *The Axial Age and its consequences* (pp. 146–188). Cambridge and London: Belknap.

Dan, J. (1986). The religious experience of the *Merkavah*. In A. Green (Ed.), *Jewish spirituality: From the Bible through the Middle Ages* (pp. 289–307). New York: Crossroad.

Darwin, C. (2001). *On the origin of species*. University Park: Pennsylvania State University.

Davies, P. (1992). *In search of ancient Israel*. Sheffield: JSOT Press.

Davies, P. (2000). Judaism and the Hebrew scriptures. In J. Neusner & A. Avery-Peck (Eds.), *The Blackwell companion to Judaism* (pp. 37–57). Oxford: Blackwell.

Davis, W. (2009). *The wayfinders: Why ancient wisdom matters in the modern world*. Toronto: Anansi.

Deacon, T. (1997). *The symbolic species*. London and New York: W. W. Norton.

Di Cosmo, N. (1999). State formation and periodization in inner Asian history. *Journal of World History, 10*(1), 1–40.

Dhalla, M. (1938). *History of Zoroastrianism*. New York: Oxford University Press.

Diamond, E. (2004). *Holy men and hunger artists: Fasting and asceticism in Rabbinic culture*. Oxford and New York: Oxford University Press.

Diamond, J. (1997). *Guns, germs, and steel: The fate of human societies*. New York: W. W. Norton.

Diamond, J. (2005). *Collapse: How societies choose to fail or succeed*. New York: Viking.

Dobzhansky, T. (1977). *Humankind: A product of evolutionary transcendence*. Johannesburg, South Africa: Witwatersrand University Press for Institute for the Study of Man in Africa.

Dodds, E. R. (1951). *The Greeks and the irrational*. Berkeley and Los Angeles: University of California.

Dodds, J. (2011). *Psychoanalysis and ecology at the edge of chaos: Complexity theory, Deleuze/Guattari and psychoanalysis for a climate in crisis*. London and New York: Routledge.

Dodson, A. (2009). *Amarna sunset: Nefertiti, Tutankhamun, Ay, Horemheb, and the Egyptian counter-reformation*. Cairo and New York: American University in Cairo Press.

Dodson, A. (2014). *Amarna sunrise: Egypt from golden age to age of heresy*. Cairo and New York: American University in Cairo Press.

Donald, M. (1991). *Origins of the modern mind: Three stages in the evolution of culture and cognition*. Cambridge, MA: Harvard University Press.

Donald, M. (2001). *A mind so rare: The evolution of human consciousness*. New York: W. W. Norton.

Duchrow, U., & Hinkelammert, F. (2012). *Transcending greedy money: Interreligious solidarity for just relations*. New York: Palgrave Macmillan.

Dumont, L. (1986). *Essays on individualism: Modern ideology in anthropological perspective*. Chicago: University of Chicago Press.

Dundas, P. (2002). *The Jains*. London and New York: Routledge.

Dundas, P. (2006). A non-imperial religion? Jainism in its "Dark Age". In P. Olivelle (Ed.), *Between the empires: Society in India 300 BCE to 400 CE* (pp. 383–414). Oxford and New York: Oxford University Press.

Edelman, D. (Ed.). (1996). *The triumph of Elohim: From Yahwisms to Judaisms*. Grand Rapids, MI: Eerdmans.

Edelman, D., & Ben Zvi, E. (Eds.). (2009). *The production of prophecy: Constructing prophecy and prophets in Yehud*. London and Oakville: Equinox.

Eisenstadt, S. (1982). The Axial Age: The emergence of transcendental visions and the rise of clerics. *European Journal of Sociology, 23*(2), 294–314.

Eisenstadt, S. (1986). Introduction: The Axial Age breakthroughs—Their characteristics and origins. In S. Eisenstadt (Ed.), *The origins and diversity of Axial Age civilizations* (pp. 1–25). Albany: State University of New York Press.

Eisenstadt, S. (2000). Multiple modernities. *Daedalus, 129*(1), 1–29.

Eisenstadt, S. (2006). *The great revolutions and the civilizations of modernity*. Leiden: Brill.

Eldredge, N. (1991). *The Miner's Canary: Unraveling the mysteries of extinction*. New York: Prentice Hall.

Eldredge, N. (1995). *Dominion*. Berkeley: University of California.

Eliade, M. (1969). *Yoga: Immortality and freedom* (W. Trask, Trans.). Princeton: Bollingen.

Eliade, M. (1982). *A history of religious ideas: Vol. 2, from Gautama Buddha to the triumph of Christianity* (W. Trask, Trans.). Chicago: University of Chicago Press.

Elior, R. (2005). *The three temples: On the emergence of Jewish mysticism* (D. Louvish, Trans.). Oxford and Portland: Littman Library of Jewish Civilization.

Elkana, Y. (1986). The emergence of second-order thinking in classical Greece. In S. Eisenstadt (Ed.), *The origins and diversity of Axial Age civilizations* (pp. 40–64). Albany: State University of New York Press.

Engleman, R. (2008). *More: Population, nature, and what women want.* Washington, DC: Island Press.

Eno, R. (1990). *The Confucian creation of heaven: Philosophy and the defense of ritual mastery.* Albany, NY: SUNY Press.

Erdosy, G. (1995a). The prelude to urbanization: Ethnicity and the rise of Late Vedic chiefdoms. In F. Allchin (Ed.), *The archaeology of early historic South Asia: The emergence of cities and states* (pp. 75–98). Cambridge: Cambridge University Press.

Erdosy, G. (1995b). City states of North India and Pakistan at the time of the Buddha. In F. Allchin (Ed.), *The archaeology of early historic South Asia: The emergence of cities and states* (pp. 99–122). Cambridge: Cambridge University Press.

Fagan, B. (2005). *World prehistory: A brief introduction.* Upper Saddle River, NJ: Prentice-Hall.

Fagan, B. (2010). *Cro-Magnon: How the Ice Age gave birth to the first modern humans.* New York: Bloomsbury.

Fairservis, W. (1997). The Harappan civilization and the Rgveda. In M. Witzel (Ed.), *Inside the texts, beyond the texts: New approaches to the study of the Vedas* (pp. 61–68). Cambridge: Harvard University Press.

Fenelon, J. (2012). Indigenous peoples, globalization and autonomy in world-systems analysis. In S. Babones & C. Chase-Dunn (Eds.), *Routledge handbook of world-systems analysis* (pp. 304–312). London and New York: Routledge.

Festinger, L., Riecken, H., & Schachter, S. (1956). *When prophecy fails: A social and psychological study of a modern group that predicted the destruction of the world.* New York: Harper & Row.

Feuerstein, G., Kak, S., & Frawley, D. (2001). *In search of the cradle of civilization: New light on ancient India.* Wheaton, IL: Quest.

Fishbane, M. (1986). Biblical prophecy as a religious phenomenon. In A. Green (Ed.), *Jewish spirituality: From the Bible through the Middle Ages* (pp. 62–81). New York: Crossroad.

Floyd, M. (2006). Introduction. In M. Floyd & R. Haak (Eds.), *Prophets, prophecy, and prophetic texts in second temple Judaism* (pp. 1–25). New York and London: T&T Clark.

Forman, R. (1990). Introduction: Mysticism, constructivism, and forgetting. In R. Forman (Ed.), *The problem of pure consciousness: Mysticism and philosophy* (pp. 3–49). New York: Oxford.

Fraade, S. (1986). Ascetical aspects of ancient Judaism. In A. Green (Ed.), *Jewish spirituality: From the Bible through the Middle Ages* (pp. 253–288). New York: Crossroad.

Fraade, S. (1991). *From tradition to commentary: Torah and its interpretation in the Midrash Sifre to Deuteronomy.* Albany: State University of New York Press.

Frank, A. G., & Gills, B. (1993a). The 5,000-year world system. In A. G. Frank & B. Gills (Eds.), *The world system: Five hundred years or five thousand?* (pp. 3–55). London and New York: Routledge.

Frank, A. G., & Gills, B. (Eds.). (1993b). *The world system: Five hundred years or five thousand?* London and New York: Routledge.

Freeland, C. (2012). *Plutocrats: The rise of the new global super-rich and the fall of everyone else.* Toronto: Doubleday.

Gardner, G. (2002). *Invoking the spirit: Religion and spirituality in the quest for a sustainable world.* Washington, DC: Worldwatch Institute.

Garland, R. (2014). *Wandering Greeks: The ancient Greek diaspora from the age of Homer to the death of Alexander the Great.* Princeton and Oxford: Princeton University Press.

Giddens, A. (1991). *Modernity and identity: Self and society in the late modern age.* Stanford, CA: Stanford University Press.

Gills, B., & Frank, A. G. (1993a). The cumulation of accumulation. In A. G. Frank & B. Gills (Eds.), *The world system: Five hundred years or five thousand?* (pp. 81–114). London and New York: Routledge.

Gills, B., & Frank, A. G. (1993b). World system cycles, crises, and hegemonic shifts, 1700 BC to 1700 AD. In A. G. Frank & B. Gills (Eds.), *The world system: Five hundred years or five thousand?* (pp. 143–199). London and New York: Routledge.

Goldin, I., Cameron, G., & Balarajan, M. (2011). *Exceptional people: How migration shaped our world and will define our future.* Princeton and Oxford: Princeton University Press.

Goody, J., & Watt, I. (1963). The consequences of literacy. *Comparative Studies in Society and History, 5*(3), 304–345.

Gould, S. (2002). *The structure of evolutionary theory.* Cambridge, MA: Belknap Harvard.

Gow, K. (Ed.). (2009). *Meltdown: Climate change, natural disasters and other catastrophes—Fears and concerns for the future.* New York: Nova Science Publications.

Grabbe, L. (1995). *Priests, prophets, diviners, sages: A socio-historical study of religious specialists in ancient Israel.* Valley Forge, PA: Trinity Press International.

Grabbe, L. (2003a). Introduction and overview. In L. Grabbe & R. Haak (Eds.), *Knowing the end from the beginning: The prophetic, the apocalyptic, and their relationships* (pp. 2–43). London and New York: T&T Clark.

Grabbe, L. (2003b). Poets, scribes, or preachers? The reality of prophecy in the Second Temple period. In L. Grabbe & R. Haak (Eds.), *Knowing the end from the beginning: The prophetic, the apocalyptic, and their relationships* (pp. 192–215). London and New York: T&T Clark.

Grabbe, L. (2004a). *A history of the Jews and Judaism in the Second Temple period. Vol. I: Yehud: A history of the Persian province of Judah.* London and New York: T&T Clark.

Grabbe, L. (2004b). *A history of the Jews and Judaism in the Second Temple Period. Vol. II: The coming of the Greeks: The early Hellenistic period (335–175 BCE)*. London and New York: T&T Clark.

Grabbe, L. (2016). Prophecy and priesthood. In C. Sharp (Ed.), *The Oxford handbook of the prophets* (pp. 23–36). Oxford: Oxford University Press.

Grabbe, L., & Haak, R. (Eds.). (2003). *Knowing the end from the beginning: The prophetic, the apocalyptic, and their relationships*. London and New York: T&T Clark.

Graeber, D. (2011). *Debt: The first 5,000 years*. Brooklyn and London: Melville House.

Graham, A. (1989). *Disputers of the Tao: Philosophical argument in ancient China*. La Salle, IL: Open Court.

Green, A. (1986a). Introduction. In A. Green (Ed.), *Jewish spirituality: From the Bible through the Middle Ages* (pp. xiii–xxv). New York: Crossroad.

Green, A. (Ed.). (1986b). *Jewish spirituality: From the Bible through the Middle Ages*. New York: Crossroad.

Griffin, R. (2007). *Modernism and Fascism: The sense of a beginning under Mussolini and Hitler*. Basingstoke: Palgrave Macmillan.

Grinin, L., & Korotayev, A. (2012). The Afroeurasian world-system: Genesis, transformations, characteristics. In S. Babones & C. Chase-Dunn (Eds.), *Routledge handbook of world-systems analysis* (pp. 30–38). London and New York: Routledge.

Grinin, L., & Korotayev, A. (2014). Origins of globalization in the framework of the Afroeurasian world-system history. *Journal of Globalization Studies, 5*(1), 32–64.

Gruenwald, I. (1980). *Apocalyptic and Merkavah mysticism*. Leiden: Brill.

Habermas, J. (1983). *Philosophical-political profiles* (F. G. Lawrence, Trans.). Cambridge: MIT Press (originally published in 1981).

Hadot, P. (1995). *Philosophy as a way of life: Spiritual exercises from Socrates to Foucault* (A. Davidson, Ed.). Oxford and Cambridge: Blackwell.

Hadot, P. (2002). *What is ancient philosophy?* (M. Chase, Trans.). Cambridge and London: Belknap (originally published in 1995).

Halal, W., & Marien, M. (2011). Global megacrisis: Four scenarios, two perspectives. *The Futurist, 45*(3), 26–33.

Hallam, A., & Wignall, P. B. (1997). *Mass extinctions and their aftermath*. Oxford: Oxford University Press.

Halpern, B., & Sacks, K. (Eds.). (2017). *Cultural contact and appropriation in the Axial-Age Mediterranean world: A periplos*. Leiden and Boston: Brill.

Halton, E. (2014). *From the Axial Age to the moral revolution*. Basingstoke: Palgrave Macmillan.

Hamilton, C. (2010). *Requiem for a species: Why we resist the truth about climate change*. London and Washington, DC: Earthscan.

Hamilton, S. (2000). *Early Buddhism: A new approach: The I of the beholder.* Richmond, Surrey: Curzon.

Hamilton, S. (2001). *Identity and experience: The constitution of the human being according to early Buddhism.* London: Luzac.

Harrington, D. (1993). Wisdom at Qumran. In E. Ulrich & J. Vanderkam (Eds.), *The community of the renewed covenant* (pp. 137–152). Notre Dame, IN: University of Notre Dame.

Hartnett, R. (2011). *The Jixia Academy and the birth of higher learning in China: A comparison of fourth-century B.C. Chinese education with ancient Greece.* London: Mellen.

Havelock, E. (1963). *Preface to Plato.* Cambridge: Belknap.

Heesterman, J. (1986). Ritual, revelation, and Axial Age. In S. Eisenstadt (Ed.), *The origins and diversity of Axial Age civilizations* (pp. 393–406). Albany: State University of New York Press.

Heesterman, J. (1997). Vedism and Hinduism. In G. Oberhammer (Ed.), *Studies in Hinduism: Vedism and Hinduism* (pp. 43–68). Vienna: Österreichische Akademie der Wissenschaften.

Hertsgaard, M. (2011). *Hot: Living through the next fifty years on earth.* Boston and New York: Houghton Mifflin.

Hick, J. (1989). *An interpretation of religion: Human responses to the transcendent.* New Haven, CT: Yale University Press.

Hick, J. (1998). Foreword. In V. Wimbush & R. Valantasis (Eds.), *Asceticism* (pp. ix–x). New York: Oxford University Press.

Himmelfarb, M. (1986). From prophecy to apocalypse: *The book of the watchers* and tours of heaven. In A. Green (Ed.), *Jewish spirituality: From the Bible through the Middle Ages* (pp. 145–165). New York: Crossroad.

Himmelfarb, M. (2010). *The apocalypse: A brief history.* Chichester: Wiley.

Hobsbawm, E., & Ranger, T. (1983). *The invention of tradition.* Cambridge: Cambridge University Press.

Hodgson, M. (1974). *The venture of Islam: Conscience and history in a world civilization* (Vol. 1). Chicago: University of Chicago Press.

Holt, E. (2016). The prophet as persona. In C. Sharp (Ed.), *The Oxford handbook of the prophets* (pp. 299–318). Oxford: Oxford University Press.

Hornung, E. (1999). *Akhenaten and the religion of light* (D. Lorton, Trans.). Ithaca, NY: Cornell University Press.

Hsu, C. (1999). The Spring and Autumn period. In M. Loewe & E. Shuaughnessy (Eds.), *The Cambridge history of ancient China: From the origins of civilization to 221 B.C.* (pp. 545–586). Cambridge and New York: Cambridge University Press.

Hughes, G. (1993). *Mystery and myth in the philosophy of Eric Voegelin.* Columbia: University of Missouri Press.

Hughes, G. (2003). *Transcendence and history: The search for ultimacy from ancient societies to postmodernity.* Columbia: University of Missouri Press.

Humphreys, S. (1986). Dynamics of the Greek breakthrough: The dialogue between philosophy and religion. In S. Eisenstadt (Ed.), *The origins and diversity of Axial Age civilizations* (pp. 92–110). Albany: State University of New York Press.

Huntington, S. (1993). The clash of civilizations? *Foreign Affairs, 72*(3), 22–49.

Huntington, S. (1996). *The clash of civilizations and the remaking of world order.* New York: Simon & Schuster.

Ivanhoe, P. (2006). *Confucian moral self cultivation* (Rev. 2 ed.). Indianapolis, IN: Hackett Publishing.

Ivanhoe, P. (2010). The values of spontaneity. In K. Yu, J. Tao, & P. Ivanhoe (Eds.), *Taking Confucian ethics seriously: Contemporary theories and applications* (pp. 183–207). Albany, NY: SUNY Press.

Ivanhoe, P. (2013). *Confucian reflections: Ancient wisdom for modern times.* New York and London: Routledge.

Jaspers, K. (1951). *Way to wisdom.* New Haven and London: Yale University Press.

Jaspers, K. (1953). *The origin and goal of history.* New Haven and London: Yale University Press (originally published in 1949).

Jaspers, K. (1962). *Socrates, Buddha, Confucius, Jesus: The paradigmatic individuals.* From *The Great Philosophers* (Vol. 1) (H. Arendt, Ed. and R. Mannheim, Trans.). New York and London: Harcourt Brace Jovanovich (originally published in 1957).

Jaspers, K. (1974). Philosophical autobiography. In P. Schilpp (Ed.), *The philosophy of Karl Jaspers* (pp. 5–94). La Salle, IL: Open Court.

Joas, H. (2012). The Axial Age debate as religious discourse. In R. Bellah & H. Joas (Eds.), *The Axial Age and its consequences* (pp. 9–29). Cambridge and London: Belknap.

Johnson, A. (1962). *The cultic prophet in ancient Israel.* Cardiff: University of Wales Press.

Johnson, A., & Earle, T. (2000). *The evolution of human societies: From foraging group to agrarian state.* Stanford, CA: Stanford University Press.

Jung, M. (2012). Embodiment, transcendence, and contingency: Anthropological features of the Axial Age. In R. Bellah & H. Joas (Eds.), *The Axial Age and its consequences* (pp. 77–101). Cambridge and London: Belknap.

Kaelber, W. (1998). Understanding asceticism—Testing a typology. In V. Wimbush & R. Valantasis (Eds.), *Asceticism* (pp. 320–328). New York: Oxford University Press.

Kakar, S. (2000). *The ascetic of desire: A novel of the Kama Sutra.* New York: Harry Abrams.

Karttunen, K. (1989). *India in early Greek literature.* Helsinki: Finnish Oriental Society.

Katz, S. (Ed.). (1978a). *Mysticism and philosophical analysis.* New York: Oxford University Press.

Katz, S. (1978b). Language, epistemology, and mysticism. In S. Katz (Ed.), *Mysticism and philosophical analysis* (pp. 22–74). New York: Oxford University Press.

Katz, S. (Ed.). (1983). *Mysticism and religious traditions.* New York: Oxford University Press.

Katz, S. (Ed.). (1992). *Mysticism and language.* New York: Oxford University Press.

Katz, S. (Ed.). (2000). *Mysticism and sacred scripture.* New York: Oxford University Press.

Kemp, B. (2012). *The city of Akhenaten and Nefertiti: Amarna and its people.* London: Thames & Hudson.

Kerr, F. (1997). *Immortal longings: Versions of transcending humanity.* Notre Dame, IN: University of Notre Dame Press.

Kiehl, J. (2016). *Facing climate change: An integrated path to the future.* New York: Columbia University Press.

Kierkegaard, S. (2006). *Fear and trembling* (S. Walsh, Trans.). Cambridge and New York: Cambridge University Press.

Klare, M. (2012). *The race for what's left: The global scramble for the world's last resources.* New York: Metropolitan Books.

Kohn, L. (1992). *Early Chinese mysticism: Philosophy and soteriology in the Taoist tradition.* Princeton: Princeton University Press.

Kohn, L. (Ed.). (2000). *Daoism handbook.* Leiden and Boston: Brill.

Kohn, L. (2010). *Sitting in oblivion: The heart of Daoist meditation.* Dunedin, FL: Three Pines Press.

Kohn, L. (2012). *Daoism and Chinese culture.* Dunedin, FL: Three Pines Press.

Kohn, L., & Sakade, Y. (Eds.). (1989). *Taoist meditation and longevity techniques.* Ann Arbor: Center for Chinese Studies, University of Michigan.

Kolbert, E. (2014). *The sixth extinction: An unnatural history.* New York: Henry Holt.

Korotayev, A. (2004). *World religions and social evolution of the Old World Oikumene civilizations: A cross-cultural perspective.* Lewiston, Queenston, and Lampeter: Edwin Mellen.

Kulke, H. (1986). The historical background of India's Axial Age. In S. Eisenstadt (Ed.), *The origins and diversity of Axial Age Civilizations* (pp. 374–392). Albany: State University of New York Press.

LaFargue, M. (1994). *Tao and method: A reasoned approach to the Tao Te Ching.* Albany: SUNY Press.

Landes, R. (2011). *Heaven on earth: The varieties of the millennial experience.* Oxford: Oxford University Press.

Leakey, R., & Lewin, R. (1995). *The sixth extinction: Patterns of life and the future of humankind.* New York: Anchor Books.

Lertzman, R. (2015). *Environmental melancholia: Psychoanalytic dimensions of engagement.* Hove, East Sussex: Routledge.

Levenson, J. (1986). The Jerusalem temple in devotional and visionary experience. In A. Green (Ed.), *Jewish spirituality: From the Bible through the Middle
Ages* (pp. 32–61). New York: Crossroad.

Lewis, M. (1999). Warring states: Political history. In M. Loewe & E.
Shuaughnessy (Eds.), *The Cambridge history of ancient China: From the ori-
gins of civilization to 221 B.C.* (pp. 587–650). Cambridge and New York:
Cambridge University Press.

Lindblom, J. (1962). *Prophecy in ancient Israel.* Philadelphia: Fortress Press.

Lovelock, J. (1979). *Gaia: A new look at life on Earth.* Oxford and New York:
Oxford University Press.

Lovelock, J. (2006). *The revenge of Gaia: Earth's climate crisis and the fate of
humanity.* New York: Basic Books.

Lyotard, J. (1984). *The postmodern condition: A report on knowledge* (G.
Bennington & B. Massumi, Trans.). Minneapolis: University of Minnesota
Press.

Mair, V. (1990). Afterword, Part III: Parallels between Taoism and yoga. In *Tao
te ching: The classic book of integrity and the way: Lao Tzu* (pp. 140–148 &
Appendix, pp. 155–161). New York: Quality.

Mair, V. (Ed.). (2006). *Contact and exchange in the ancient world.* Honolulu:
University of Hawaii.

Mann, M. (2012). *The sources of social power* (Vol. 1). New York: Cambridge
University Press.

Mann, M. (Ed.). (2016). *The madhouse effect: How climate change denial is
threatening our planet, destroying our politics, and driving us crazy.* New York:
Columbia University Press.

Manning, P. (2005). *Migration in world history.* London: Routledge.

Marcel, G. (1960). *The mystery of being* (2 Vols.). Chicago: Gateway Edition.

Masuzawa, T. (2005). *The invention of world religions.* Chicago: University of
Chicago.

McBrearty, M., & Brooks, A. (2000). The revolution that wasn't: A new interpretation for the origin of modern behavior. *Journal of Human Evolution,
39*(5), 453–563.

McEntee, R., & Bucko, A. (2015). *The new monasticism: An interspiritual mani-
festo for contemplative living.* Maryknoll, NY: Orbis Books.

McEvilley, T. (2002). *The shape of ancient thought: Comparative studies in Greek
and Indian philosophies.* New York: Allworth Press.

McGinn, B. (1991). *The foundations of mysticism: Origins to the fifth century.*
New York: Crossroad.

McNeill, W. (1963). *The rise of the west: A history of the human community.*
Chicago and London: University of Chicago.

McNeill, W. (1986). *Mythistory and other essays.* Chicago and London: University
of Chicago.

McNeill, W. (1993). Foreword. In A. G. Frank & B. Gills (Eds.), *The world system: Five hundred years or five thousand?* (pp. vii–xiii). London and New York: Routledge.

McNeill, W. (1998). *Plagues and peoples.* New York: Anchor (originally published 1976).

Meier, C. (1986). The emergence of an autonomous intelligence among the Greeks. In S. Eisenstadt (Ed.), *The origins and diversity of Axial Age civilizations* (pp. 64–91). Albany: State University of New York Press.

Meier, C. (1998). *Athens: A portrait of the city in its golden age* (Robert & R. Kimber, Trans.). New York: Metropolitan Books, H. Holt & Co.

Mendieta, E. (2013). Appendix: Religion in Habermas's work. In C. Calhoun, E. Mendieta, & J. VanAntwerpen (Eds.), *Habermas and religion* (pp. 391–407). Cambridge and Malden, MA: Polity Press.

Middlemas, J. (2016). Prophecy and diaspora. In C. Sharp (Ed.), *The Oxford handbook of the prophets* (pp. 37–54). Oxford: Oxford University Press.

Miles-Yepez, N. (Ed.). (2006). *The common heart: An experience of interreligious dialogue.* New York: Lantern Books.

Momigliano, A. (1975). *Alien wisdom: The limits of hellenization.* Cambridge: Cambridge University Press.

Montserrat, D. (2003). *Akhenaten: History, fantasy, and ancient Egypt.* London and New York: Routledge.

Muesse, M. (2013). *The age of the sages: The Axial Age in Asia and the Near East.* Minneapolis: Fortress Press.

Mullins, D., Hoyer, D., Collins, C., Currie, T., Feeney, K., François, P., … Turchin, P. (2018). A systematic assessment of "Axial Age" proposals using global comparative historical evidence. *American Sociological Review, 1,* 1–31. https://doi.org/10.1177/0003122418772567.

Mumford, L. (1956). *The transformations of man.* Gloucester, MA: Peter Smith.

Murphy, F. (2000). Second Temple Judaism. In J. Neusner & A. Avery-Peck (Eds.), *The Blackwell companion to Judaism* (pp. 58–77). Oxford: Blackwell.

Nataraja, K. (Ed.). (2012). *Journey to the heart: Christian contemplation through the centuries—An illustrated guide.* Maryknoll, NY: Orbis Books.

Nemeth, D., Hamilton, R., & Kuriansky, J. (Eds.). (2012). *Living in an environmentally traumatized world: Healing ourselves and our planet.* Santa Barbara, CA: Praeger.

Neusner, J. (1986). Varieties of Judaism in the formative age. In A. Green (Ed.), *Jewish spirituality: From the Bible through the Middle Ages* (pp. 171–197). New York: Crossroad.

Nicholson, E. (2010). Deuteronomy 18.9-22, the prophets and scripture. In J. Day (Ed.), *Prophecy and the prophets in ancient Israel* (pp. 151–171). New York and London: T&T Clark.

Nicol, D. (2015). *Subtle activism: The inner dimension of social and planetary transformation*. Albany: State University of New York Press.

Nietzsche, F. (2007). *On the genealogy of morality* (K. Ansell-Pearson, Ed. and C. Diethe, Trans.). Cambridge: Cambridge University Press.

Nishitani, K. (1982). *Religion and nothingness* (J. Van Bragt, Trans.). Berkeley: University of California.

Nissinen, M. (2006). The dubious image of prophecy. In M. Floyd & R. Haak (Eds.), *Prophets, prophecy, and prophetic texts in second temple Judaism* (pp. 26–41). New York and London: T&T Clark.

Nissinen, M. (2010). Prophetic madness: Prophecy and ecstasy in the ancient Near East and in Greece. In K. Noll & B. Schramm (Eds.), *Raising up a faithful exegete: Essays in honor of Richard D. Nelson* (pp. 3–29). Winona Lake, IN: Eisenbrauns.

Nissinen, M. (2016). Prophetic intermediation in the ancient Near East. In C. Sharp (Ed.), *The Oxford handbook of the prophets* (pp. 5–22). Oxford: Oxford University Press.

Noll, K. (2013). Presumptuous prophets in a Deuteronomic debate. In M. Boda & L. Beal (Eds.), *Prophets, prophecy, and ancient Israelite historiography* (pp. 125–142). Winona Lake, IN: Eisenbrauns.

Ober, J. (2015). *The rise and fall of classical Greece*. Princeton and Oxford: Princeton University Press.

Obryk, M. (2016). On affirmation, rejection and accommodation of the world in Greek and Indian religion. In R. Seaford (Ed.), *Universe and inner self in early Indian and early Greek thought* (pp. 235–250). Edinburgh: Edinburgh University Press.

Olivelle, P. (1993). *The āśrama system: The history and hermeneutics of a religious institution*. New York: Oxford University Press.

Olivelle, P. (2008). Introduction. In Ashvaghosa (Ed.), *Life of the Buddha* (pp. xvii–lvii) (P. Olivelle, Trans.). New York: New York University Press.

Olivelle, P. (2011). *Ascetics and Brahmins: Studies in ideologies and institutions*. London, New York, and New Delhi: Anthem Press.

Ong, W. (1982). *Orality and literacy: The technologizing of the word*. London and New York: Routledge.

Orange, D. (2017). *Climate crisis, psychoanalysis, and radical ethics*. London and New York: Routledge.

Oreskes, N., & Conway, E. (2013). The collapse of western Civilization: A view from the Future. *Daedalus, 142*(1), 40–59.

Otto, R. (1923). *The idea of the holy: An inquiry into the non-rational factor in the idea of the divine and its relation to the rational* (J. W. Harvey, Trans.). London and New York: Oxford University Press.

Paper, J. (1995). *The spirits are drunk: Comparative approaches to Chinese religion*. Albany: State University of New York Press.

Partridge, C. (2005). *Introduction to world religions.* Minneapolis: Fortress Press.

Pettitt, P. (2018). The rise of modern humans. In C. Scarre (Ed.), *The human past: World prehistory & the development of human societies* (pp. 108–148). London: Thames & Hudson.

Pinker, S. (2012). *The better angels of our nature: Why violence has declined.* New York: Penguin.

Prantzos, N. (2000). *Our cosmic future: Humanity's fate in the universe.* Cambridge: Cambridge University Press.

Rajaram, N. S., & Frawley, D. (1995). *Vedic 'Aryans' and the origins of civilization: A literary and scientific perspective.* Quebec City: WH Press.

Ramelli, I. (2016). *Social justice and the legitimacy of slavery: The role of philosophical asceticism from ancient Judaism to late antiquity.* Oxford: Oxford University Press.

Raup, D., & Sepkoski, J. (1982). Mass extinctions in the marine fossil record. *Science, New Series, 215*(4539), 1501–1503.

Raup, D., & Sepkoski, J. (1984). Periodicity of extinctions in the geologic past. *Proceedings of the National Academy of Science, USA, 81,* 801–805.

Ray, H. P. (1995). Trade and contacts. In R. Thapar (Ed.), *Recent perspectives on Indian history* (pp. 142–175). Bombay: Popular Prakashan.

Ray, R. (1994). *Buddhist saints in India: A study in Buddhist values and orientations.* New York: Oxford.

Rees, W. (1992). Ecological footprints and appropriated carrying capacity: What urban economics leaves out. *Environment and Urbanization, 4*(2), 121–130.

Reeves, N. (2001). *Akhenaten: Egypt's false prophet.* New York: Thames & Hudson.

Reid, J. (Ed.). (2015). *Religion, postcolonialism, and globalization: A sourcebook.* London and New York: Bloomsbury Academic.

Rhys-Davids, T. (1903). *Buddhist India.* New York: Putnam.

Robinet, I. (1993). *Taoist meditation: The Mao-shan tradition of great purity.* Albany, NY: State University of New York Press.

Rockström, J., Steffen, W., Noone, K., Persson, Å., Chapin, III, F. S., Lambin, E., … Foley, J. (2009). Planetary boundaries: Exploring the safe operating space for humanity. *Ecology and Society, 14*(2), 32. https://www.ecologyand-society.org/vol14/iss2/art32/.

Roetz, H. (1992). *Confucian ethics of the Axial Age: A reconstruction under the aspect of the breakthrough toward postconventional thinking.* Albany, NY: SUNY Press.

Roszak, T. (1979). *Person/planet: The creative disintegration of industrial society.* New York: Doubleday.

Roth, H. (1999a). *Original Tao: Inward training (nei-yeh) and the foundations of Taoist mysticism.* New York: Columbia University.

Roth, H. (1999b). The Laozi in the context of early Taoist mystical praxis. In M. Csikszentmihalyi & P. Ivanhoe (Eds.), *Religious and philosophical aspects of the Laozi* (pp. 59–96). Albany, NY: SUNY Press.

Rowley, H. H. (1956). *Prophecy and religion in ancient China and Israel.* London: University of London, Athlone Press.

Runciman, W. (2012). Righteous rebels: When, where, and why? In R. Bellah & H. Joas (Eds.), *The Axial Age and its consequences* (pp. 317–334). Cambridge and London: Belknap.

Ruthven, M. (2015). The apocalyptic social imaginary. In E. Tonning, M. Feldman, & D. Addyman (Eds.), *Modernism, Christianity and apocalypse* (pp. 354–383). Leiden: Brill.

Sachsenmaier, D. (2002). Multiple modernities: The concept and its potential. In D. Sachsenmaier, J. Reidel, & S. Eisenstadt (Eds.), *Reflections on multiple modernities: European, Chinese & other interpretations* (pp. 42–67). Leiden: Brill.

Sachsenmaier, D., Reidel, J., & Eisenstadt, S. (Eds.). (2002). *Reflections on multiple modernities: European, Chinese & other interpretations.* Leiden: Brill.

Sagan, E. (1991). *The honey and the hemlock: Democracy and paranoia in ancient Athens and modern America.* New York: Basic Books.

Said, E. (1997). *Covering Islam: How the media and the experts determine how we see the rest of the world* (Rev. ed.). New York: Vintage.

Samuel, G. (2008). *The origins of yoga and tantra: Indic religions to the thirteenth century.* Cambridge: Cambridge University Press.

Sanderson, S. K. (Ed.). (1995a). *Civilizations and world systems: Studying world-historical change.* Walnut Creek, London, and New Delhi: Altamira (Sage).

Sanderson, S. K. (1995b). Expanding world commercialization: The link between world-systems and civilizations. In S. K. Sanderson (Ed.), *Civilizations and world systems: Studying world-historical change* (pp. 261–272). Walnut Creek, London, and New Delhi: Altamira (Sage).

Sanderson, S. K., & Hall, T. D. (1995). Introduction to Part III: Civilizations and world systems: Dialogue and interplay. In S. K. Sanderson (Ed.), *Civilizations and world systems: Studying world-historical change* (pp. 229–238). Walnut Creek, London, and New Delhi: Altamira (Sage).

Sanderson, S. K. (2018). *Religious evolution and the Axial Age: From shamans to priests to prophets.* London: Bloomsbury.

Schmidt, B. (2010). *Utopian communities of the ancient world: Idealistic experiments of Pythagoras, the Essenes, Pachomius, and Proclus.* Lewiston, NY: Edwin Mellen.

Schwartz, B. (Ed.). (1975). Wisdom, revelation, and doubt: Perspectives on the first millennium B.C. *Special Issue of Daedalus, 104*(2), 1–7.

Schwartz, B. (1985). *The world of thought in ancient China.* Cambridge, MA: Belknap.

Seaford, R. (2004). *Money and the early Greek mind.* Cambridge: Cambridge University Press.

Seaford, R. (Ed.). (2016a). *Universe and inner self in early Indian and early Greek thought.* Edinburgh: Edinburgh University Press.

Seaford, R. (2016b). Introduction. In R. Seaford (Ed.), *Universe and inner self in early Indian and early Greek thought* (pp. 1–12). Edinburgh: Edinburgh University Press.

Seaford, R. (2016c). The interiorisation of ritual in India and Greece. In R. Seaford (Ed.), *Universe and inner self in early Indian and early Greek thought* (pp. 204–219). Edinburgh: Edinburgh University Press.

Seligman, A. (Ed.). (1989). *Order and transcendence: The role of utopias and the dynamics of civilizations.* Leiden: Brill.

Sells, M. (1994). *Mystical languages of unsaying.* Chicago and London: University of Chicago.

Shaffer, L. (1994). Southernization. *Journal of World History, 5*(1), 1–22.

Shaked, S. (2005). Zoroastrian origins: Indian and Iranian connections. In J. Arnason, S. Eisenstadt, & B. Wittrock (Eds.), *Axial civilizations and world history* (pp. 183–200). Leiden: Brill.

Sharp, C. (2016). *The Oxford handbook of the prophets.* Oxford: Oxford University Press.

Sherratt, S., & Sherratt, A. (1993). The growth of the Mediterranean economy in the early first millennium BC. *World Archaeology, 24*(3), 361–378.

Shils, E. (1986). Some observations on the place of intellectuals in Max weber's sociology, with special reference to Hinduism. In S. Eisenstadt (Ed.), *The origins and diversity of Axial Age civilizations* (pp. 427–452). Albany: State University of New York Press.

Silver, K. (2017). *Alexandria and Qumran: Back to the beginning.* Oxford: Archaeopress.

Smith, M. (2002). *The early history of God: Yahweh and the other deities in ancient Israel.* Dearborn, MI: Eerdmans.

Smith-Christopher, D. (2002). *A biblical theology of exile.* Minneapolis: Fortress Press.

Solnit, R. (2016). *Hope in the dark: Untold histories, wild possibilities.* Chicago, IL: Haymarket Books.

Spengler, O. (1926–1928). *The decline of the West* (2 Vols.) (C. Atkinson, Trans.). New York: Alfred A. Knopf (originally published 1918).

Stace, W. (1960). *Mysticism and philosophy.* Los Angeles: Tarcher.

Stringer, C. (2002). Modern human origins: Progress and prospects. *Philosophical Transactions of the Royal Society B, 357,* 563–579.

Stringer, C. (2016). The origin and evolution of *Homo sapiens. Philosophical Transactions of the Royal Society B, 371.* https://doi.org/10.1098/rstb.2015.0237.

Stuart-Glennie, J. (1873). *In the Morningland or The law of the origin and transformation of Christianity, Volume 1: The new philosophy of history, and the origin of the doctrines of Christianity.* London: Longmans.

Swartz, M. (1996). *Scholastic magic: Ritual and revelation in early Jewish mysticism.* Princeton, NJ: Princeton University Press.

Sweeney, M. (2000). The religious world of ancient Israel to 586 BCE. In J. Neusner & A. Avery-Peck (Eds.), *The Blackwell companion to Judaism* (pp. 20–36). Oxford: Blackwell.

Taagepera, R. (1978a). Size and duration of empires: Systematics of size. *Social Science Research, 7,* 108–127.

Taagepera, R. (1978b). Size and duration of empires growth-decline curves, 3000 to 600 B.C. *Social Science Research, 7*(2), 180–196.

Taagepera, R. (1979). Size and duration of empires: Growth-decline curves, 600 B.C. to 600 A.D. *Social Science History, 3*(3–4), 115–138.

Tainter, J. (1988). *The collapse of complex societies.* Cambridge and New York: Cambridge University Press.

Talmon, S. (1993). The community of the renewed covenant: Between Judaism and Christianity. In E. Ulrich & J. Vanderkam (Eds.), *The community of the renewed covenant* (pp. 3–24). Notre Dame, IN: University of Notre Dame.

Taylor, B. (2010). *Dark green religion: Nature spirituality and the planetary future.* Berkeley: University of California.

Taylor, C. (1985a). *Human agency and language: Philosophical papers* (Vol. 1). Cambridge and New York: Cambridge University Press.

Taylor, C. (1985b). *Philosophy and the human sciences: Philosophical papers* (Vol. 2). Cambridge and New York: Cambridge University Press.

Taylor, C. (1989). *Sources of the self: The making of the modern identity.* Cambridge, MA: Harvard University Press.

Taylor, C. (2007). *A secular age.* Cambridge and London: Belknap.

Taylor, J. (2004). *Pythagoreans and Essenes: Structural parallels.* Paris and Louvain: Peeters.

Taylor, J. (2012). *The Essenes, the scrolls, and the Dead Sea.* Oxford: Oxford University Press.

Tellier, L. (2009). *Urban world history: An economic and geographical perspective.* Québec City: Presses de l'Université du Québec.

Tennesen, M. (2015). *The next species: The future of evolution in the aftermath of man.* New York: Simon & Schuster.

Thapar, R. (1995a). The first millennium B.C. in northern India. In R. Thapar (Ed.), *Recent perspectives on Indian history* (pp. 80–141). Bombay: Popular Prakashan.

Thapar, R. (Ed.). (1995b). *Recent perspectives on Indian history.* Bombay: Popular Prakashan.

Thomassen, B. (2010). Anthropology, multiple modernities and the Axial Age debate. *Anthropological Theory, 10*(4), 321–344.

Thompson, T. (1996). The intellectual matrix of early Biblical narrative: Inclusive monotheism in Persian period Palestine. In D. V. Edelmann (Ed.), *The triumph of Elohim: From Yahwisms to Judaisms* (pp. 107–124). Grand Rapids, MI: Eerdmans.

Thompson, W. (2005). Eurasian C-wave crises in the first millennium B.C. In C. Chase-Dunn & E. N. Anderson (Eds.), *The historical evolution of world-systems* (pp. 20–51). New York: Palgrave Macmillan.

Tonning, E., Feldman, M., & Addyman, D. (Eds.). (2015). *Modernism, Christianity and apocalypse*. Leiden: Brill.

Torpey, J. (2017). *The three Axial Ages: Moral, material, mental.* New Brunswick, NJ: Rutgers University Press.

Toynbee, A. (1934–1961). *A study of history* (12 Vols.). London: Oxford University Press.

Tucker, M. (2003). Introduction. In T. Weiming & M. Tucker (Eds.), *Confucian spirituality* (Vol. I, pp. 1–35). New York: Crossroad.

Uffenheimer, B. (1986). Myth and reality in ancient Israel. In S. Eisenstadt (Ed.), *The origins and diversity of Axial Age civilizations* (pp. 135–168). Albany: State University of New York Press.

Ulrich, E., & Vanderkam, J. (Eds.). (1993). *The community of the renewed covenant*. Notre Dame, IN: University of Notre Dame.

van Norden, B. (2007). *Virtue ethics and consequentialism in early Chinese philosophy*. New York: Cambridge University Press.

van Seters, J. (2006). Prophecy as prediction in Biblical historiography. In M. Floyd & R. Haak (Eds.), *Prophets, prophecy, and prophetic texts in second temple Judaism* (pp. 93–103). New York and London: T&T Clark.

Varenne, J. (1976). *Yoga and the Hindu tradition* (D. Coltman, Trans.). Chicago and London: Universty of Chicago.

Veldman, R. (2012). Narrating the environmental apocalypse: How imagining the end facilitates moral reasoning among environmental activists. *Ethics & the Environment, 17*(1), 1–23.

Vidal, G. (1981). *Creation*. London: Heinemann.

Voegelin, E. (1956). *Order and history, Vol. I: Israel and revelation.* Baton Rouge: Louisiana State University Press.

Voegelin, E. (1956–1974). *Order and History: 5 volumes.* Baton Rouge: Louisiana State University Press.

Voegelin, E. (1957). *Order and History, Vol. II: The world of the polis.* Baton Rouge: Louisiana State University Press.

Voegelin, E. (1974). *Order and History, Vol. IV: The ecumenic age.* Baton Rouge: Louisiana State University Press.

Waelde, L., & Thompson, J. (2016). Traditional and secular views of psychotherapeutic applications of mindfulness and meditation. In M. West (Ed.), *The psychology of meditation: Research and practice* (pp. 119–152). Oxford: Oxford University Press.

Ward, P. (2007). *Under a green sky: Global warming, the mass extinctions of the past, and what they can tell us about our future.* New York: HarperCollins.

Ward, P., & Kirschvink, J. (2015). *A new history of life: The radical new discoveries about the origins and evolution of life on earth.* New York and London: Bloomsbury.

Ware, K. (1998). The way of the ascetics: Negative or affirmative? In V. Wimbush & R. Valantasis (Eds.), *Asceticism* (pp. 3–15). New York: Oxford University Press.

Waters, M. (2014). *Ancient Persia: A concise history of the Achaemenid Empire, 550–330 BCE.* New York: Cambridge University Press.

Wattles, J. (1996). *The golden rule.* New York: Oxford University Press.

Webb, S. (2015). *If the universe is teeming with aliens … Where is everybody?: Seventy-five solutions to the Fermi paradox and the problem of extraterrestrial life.* Cham, Switzerland: Springer.

Weiming, T. (1985). *Confucian thought: Selfhood as creative transformation.* Albany, NY: SUNY Press.

Weiming, T., & Tucker, M. (Eds.). (2003a). *Confucian spirituality: Volume I.* New York: Crossroad.

Weiming, T., & Tucker, M. (Eds.). (2003b). *Confucian spirituality: Volume II.* New York: Crossroad.

Weinfeld, M. (1986). The protest against imperialism in ancient Israelite prophecy. In S. Eisenstadt (Ed.), *The origins and diversity of Axial Age civilizations* (pp. 169–182). Albany: State University of New York Press.

Weintrobe, S. (Ed.). (2013). *Engaging with climate change: Psychoanalytic and interdisciplinary perspectives.* Abingdon, Oxon and New York: Routledge.

West, M. (1971). *Early Greek philosophy and the Orient.* Oxford: Clarendon Press.

West, M. (1997). *The east face of Helicon: West Asiatic elements in Greek poetry and myth.* Oxford: Clarendon Press.

West, M. (Ed.). (2016). *The psychology of meditation: Research and practice.* Oxford: Oxford University Press.

Whicher, I. (1998). *The integrity of the yoga darsana: A reconsideration of classical yoga.* Albany: State University of New York Press.

Whicher, I. (2003). The integration of spirit (*purusa*) and matter (*prakrti*) in the Yoga Sutra. In I. Whicher & D. Carpenter (Eds.), *Yoga: The Indian tradition* (pp. 51–69). London: Routledge Curzon.

Whicher, I., & Carpenter, D. (Eds.). (2003). *Yoga: The Indian tradition.* London: Routledge Curzon.

Wilber, K. (1995). *Sex, ecology, spirituality: The spirit of evolution.* Boston: Shambhala.

Wilber, K. (1998). *The eye of spirit: An integral vision for a world gone slightly mad.* Boston and London: Shambhala.

Wilkinson, D. (1993). Civilizations, cores, world-economics and Oikumenes. In A. G. Frank & B. Gills (Eds.), *The world system: Five hundred years or five thousand?* (pp. 221–246). London and New York: Routledge.

Wilkinson, T., Sherratt, S., & Bennet, J. (Eds.). (2011). *Interweaving worlds: Systemic interactions in Eurasia, 7th to the 1st millennia BC.* Oxford: Oxbow.

Wilson, R. (1980). *Prophecy and society in ancient Israel.* Philadelphia: Fortress Press.

Wiltshire, M. (1990). *Ascetic figures before and in early Buddhism: The emergence of Gautama as the Buddha.* Berlin: Mouton de Gruyter.

Wimbush, V., & Valantasis, R. (Eds.). (1998a). *Asceticism.* New York: Oxford University Press.

Wimbush, V., & Valantasis, R. (1998b). Introduction. In V. Wimbush & R. Valantasis (Eds.), *Asceticism* (pp. xix–xxxiii). New York: Oxford University Press.

Wittrock, B. (2005). The meaning of the Axial Age. In J. Arnason, S. Eisenstadt, & B. Wittrock (Eds.), *Axial civilizations and world history* (pp. 51–86). Leiden: Brill.

Witzel, M. (1997). The Vedic canon and its political milieu. In M. Witzel (Ed.), *Inside the texts, beyond the texts: New approaches to the study of the Vedas* (pp. 257–346). Cambridge: Harvard University Press.

Woolf, G. (2017). Empires, diasporas and the emergence of religions. In J. Paget & J. Lieu (Eds.), *Christianity in the second century: Themes and developments* (pp. 25–38). Cambridge: Cambridge University Press.

World Spirituality: An Encyclopedic History of the Religious Quest. (1985–). 25 Vols. (intended). New York: Crossroads.

Wright, Robert. (2000). *Nonzero: The logic of human destiny.* New York: Random House.

Yü, Y. (2003). Between the heavenly and the human. In T. Weiming & M. Tucker (Eds.), *Confucian spirituality* (Vol. I, pp. 62–80). New York: Crossroad.

INDEX

© The Editor(s) (if applicable) and The Author(s) 2019
C. Peet, *Practicing Transcendence*,
https://doi.org/10.1007/978-3-030-14432-6

U

Uffenheimer, Benjamin, 187
Uffenheimer, Benjamin, 189
ultimate, 21–25, 35–37, 39, 40, 47,
    52, 57, 58, 71, 77, 78, 80, 82,
    87, 92, 93, 95, 135, 174, 183,
    203, 205, 222, 224, 238, 285,
    286, 288, 298, 304, 306, 308.
    See also boundless communica-
    tion, ideal of
clash of ultimates, 37, 39–42, 46,
    47, 58, 60, 94, 96
universality, 4, 8, 16, 21, 24, 25, 68,
    70, 71, 73, 77, 83, 84, 93, 95,
    96, 101, 119, 137, 146–148,
    159, 201–203, 206–208, 211,
    284, 285, 303, 304, 307, 309
Upanishads (or *Upanisads*), 6, 66, 74,
    76, 77, 80, 87, 152, 162, 168,
    169, 174, 201, 239
utopian, 199

V

van Norden, Bryan, 160
Van Seters, John, 183
Varenne, Jean, 238
Vedas, 165–167, 169, 173
Vidal, Gore, 150
vipassana, 230
Voegelin, Eric, 7, 11, 22, 67, 78, 80,
    178, 316

W

Ward, Peter, 50
Ware, Kallistos, 29
Warring States period, 123, 156, 158,
    160, 161
Watt, Ian, 130, 319
Wattles, Jeffrey, 26
Weber, Max, 7, 17, 91, 235
Weiming, Tu, 250, 252

Weinfeld, Moshe, 185
West, Martin, 151, 153
Whicher, Ian, 241
Wilber, Ken, 91, 92, 222, 317
Wilkinson, David, 111–113, 115, 133
Wilson, Robert, 181, 187, 266
Wittgenstein, Ludwig, 89–92
Wittrock, Bjorn, 68, 138, 206
women (role in Axial Age), 29, 175,
    193, 195, 200–202
world history, 6, 8, 11, 13, 14, 22, 23,
    25, 27–29, 44, 60, 64, 66, 68,
    71–74, 90, 94, 96, 99–101, 109,
    116, 119, 122, 123, 140, 146,
    185, 206, 208–211, 221, 223,
    226, 300, 302, 307
world population, 9, 10, 38, 41, 55,
    102, 104, 105, 110–112, 210
world religions, 6, 8, 9, 11, 12,
    15–17, 19, 20, 25, 34, 45, 116,
    135–137, 140, 147, 175, 203,
    206–211, 223, 226, 284–287,
    289, 300, 303–308
world spirituality, 34
world system, 35, 36, 39, 106–109,
    111, 112, 115, 116, 125, 135,
    136, 145, 147, 149–153, 155,
    164, 191, 192, 203, 204, 208,
    211, 284, 285, 296, 297, 299,
    300, 318
worldview, 7, 9, 11, 13, 19, 20, 36,
    47, 70, 172, 176
Wright, Robert, 109

X

Xenophanes, 197

Y

Yahweh (or YHWH), 23, 84, 86, 92,
    178, 183, 187, 188, 268, 272,
    274, 275, 277, 283, 288, 305